129479

AF795616

Monsters and Monstrosity

Law & Literature

Edited by
Daniela Carpi and Klaus Stierstorfer

Volume 16

Monsters and Monstrosity

From the Canon to the Anti-Canon:
Literary and Juridical Subversions

Edited by
Daniela Carpi

DE GRUYTER

ISBN 978-3-11-065219-2
e-ISBN (PDF) 978-3-11-065461-5
e-ISBN (EPUB) 978-3-11-065358-8
ISSN 2191-8457

Library of Congress Control Number: 2019933809

Bibliographic information published by the Deutsche Nationalbibliothek
The Deutsche Nationalbibliothek lists this publication in the Deutsche Nationalbibliografie; detailed bibliographic data are available on the Internet at http://dnb.dnb.de

© 2019 Walter de Gruyter GmbH, Berlin/Boston
Typesetting: Integra Software Services Pvt. Ltd.
Printing and binding: CPI books GmbH, Leck

www.degruyter.com

FSC www.fsc.org
MIX
Papier aus verantwortungsvollen Quellen
FSC® C083411

Contents

3 Comic and Grotesque Monstrosity

4 Monstrosity and Migration

Appendix

Daniela Carpi

Introduction: What Is a Monster?

> "There are more things in heaven and earth, Horatio, / Than are dreamt of in your philosophy"
> *William Shakespeare,* Hamlet, *1.5.167–168*

Every culture knows the phenomenon of monsters, terrifying creatures that represent complete alterity and challenge every basic notion of self and identity within a cultural paradigm.[1] In Latin and Greek culture, the monster was created as a marvel, appearing as something which, like transgression itself, did not belong to the assumed natural order of things. Therefore, it could only be created by a divinity responsible for its creation, composition, goals, and stability, but it was triggered by some in- or non-human action performed by humans.

The term "monstrous" stems from old French "monster"; from Latin "monstrum" (portent or monster). The Latin word "monstrum" has to do with the verb "monere," meaning "warning," and "monstrare," meaning "showing." Another derivation is the Greek word "teras," meaning "monster" connected to "marvel," that is a phenomenon the emergence of which does not follow the rules of other repeatable or explainable phenomena. The monster is a liminal creature embodying the very boundaries humans have overreached. The identification of something as monstrous denotes its place outside and beyond social norms and values. Such extraordinary warnings or reminders proceed from divine power to humankind when they have transgressed, or are about to transgress, the limits of what humans are supposed or rather allowed to do. In the Middle-Ages the term "contra naturam" was used for such fatal actions.

The monster-evoking transgression is most often indistinguishable from reactions to the experience of otherness, merging the limits of humanity with the limits of a given culture. In some cultures, supported by the religions they embraced, a transgressive movement may be called mortal sin, as in Christianity; disobedience to the Law based on the Covenant, or Covenants, as in Judaism; sins, ithm, called major, kaba'ir, in Islam; blasphemy, shirk, being the worst; or simply transgressing taboos of various kinds in various cultures underpinned by religion. There is only a short distance between locating the source of such transgressions in human agents to identifying these persons with the monstrous itself.

1 Albrecht Classen, "The Epistemological Functions of Monsters in the Middle Ages," *Lo Sguardo – Rivista di Filosofia* 9.2 (2012) – Spazi del Mostruoso, Luoghi Filosofici della Mostruosità: 13–34.

https://doi.org/10.1515/9783110654615-001

Whatever could be regarded as the culturally foreign could be subsumed in the category of the monstrous which then could be legitimately excluded or destroyed by a blended legalistic and religiously charged justification, with the overall aim of strengthening the domestic identity of the community. In other words, the religious left aside, monstrosity has for ages been a non-analytical cultural tool to assume and secure individual and collective identity in absolute terms. Hence, even when the religiously grounded understanding of the monster vanishes, the cultural function of labelling the foreign in various guises survives, now and then underpinned excessively by spurious religious arguments, as in present day terrorism. Clearly, there is an ambiguity even in the earliest use of the monstrous between the cultural and the religious which, right into the modern secular world, makes it a dangerously flexible tool of emotional criticism that today can move freely from one context to another.

The reasons for this fascination with alterity at large are many, such as the quest to determine one's own identity, to explore the dialectics of good and evil, of self and other, and then to comprehend how to decipher this world, so much filled with endless but often incomprehensible manifestations of God.[2]

By revealing that difference is arbitrary and potentially free-floating, mutable rather than essential, the monster threatens to destroy not just individual members of society, but the very cultural apparatus through which individuality is constituted and allowed.[3] Because it is a body across which difference has been repeatedly written, the monster seeks out its author to demand its *raison d'être*.[4] This is what happens in the novel *Frankenstein* where the Creature asks his creator why he made him and then rejected him. The monster prevents mobility (intellectual, geographic, or sexual) delimiting the social spaces through which the cultural bodies may move. To step outside this official geography is to risk attack by some monstrous border patrol or to become monstrous oneself.[5]

The linking of monstrosity with the forbidden makes the monster all the more appealing as a temporary egress from constraint.[6] We distrust and loathe the monster at the same time as we envy its freedom, and perhaps its sublime

---

2 Richard Kearney, *Strangers, Gods and Monsters: Interpreting Otherness* (London and New York: Routledge, 2003), cfr. 83–110.

3 Jeffrey Jerome Cohen ed., *Monster Theory. Reading Culture* (Minneapolis: University of Minnesota Press, 1996); see also Kirk Combe and Brenda Boyle, *Masculinity and Monstrosity in Contemporary Hollywood Films* (New York: Palgrave Macmillan, 2013).

4 Cohen, *Monster Theory*, 19–20.

5 Cohen, *Monster Theory*, 20.

6 Jeffrey Andrew Weinstock, *The Ashgate Encyclopaedia of Literary and Cinematic Monsters* (London and New York: Routledge, 2014), 3.

despair.[7] The critical examination of monster lore, miracles, marvels, portents, and the like has a long history, especially because the study of the Other, the complete alter, has proven to be fundamental in the analysis of the history of mentality, spirituality, and ideology both in the past and in the present.[8]

The topic entails a large intersection among the cultural domains of law, literature, philosophy, anthropology, and technology. Monstrosity has transcended its status as a metaphor and has indeed become a necessary condition of our existence in the 21st century. Monstrosity serves as a discourse and as a representation of change itself. In the process of analysis there are three theoretical approaches: psychoanalytical, representational, ontological.

The psychoanalytical approach situates the power of horror in its evoking of something familiar that has been repressed: in Freudian terms, the uncanny. The feeling of the uncanny occurs when either infantile complexes or primitive beliefs are revived through the encounter with monsters.

A representational approach to the study of monsters focuses on the process of repression outlined as a cultural and social phenomenon. It focuses on a taxonomy of monsters to study the portrayal and representation of Otherness. Monsters produce meaning that goes beyond any existing category of identification. Monstrosity, according to Foucault, not only refers to exceptionality relative to the species form but also to the disturbance it brings to juridical regularities. Foucault asserts that monstrosity is a double violation of the law: "la loi naturelle" (natural law) because it does not respect categories or genres, and "la loi de la société" (social law) because the monster "provoque une certaine impossibilité à appliquer cette loi civile, religieuse ou divine."[9]

The ontological approach analyzes the monsters' nature in its being or becoming. Following Derrida, a monster can only be that which is not yet familiar or recognized as such. As soon as one starts to deal with the initially monstrous, it is domesticated and transformed into something known and thus no longer appears as the monster. The monster in fact epitomizes difference and separation: once it is accepted it loses its status of monster. But Derrida also intends monstrosity as a different form of writing:

---

7 Cohen, *Monster Theory*, 30.

8 Classen, "The Epistemological Functions of Monsters in the Middle Ages," 13.

9 Michel Foucault, *Les anormaux. Cours au Collège de France (1974–1975)*, Édition numérique réalisée en août 2012 à partir de l'édition CD-ROM, Le Foucault Électronique (ed. 2001), 52: "the monster makes it impossible to apply civil, religious or divine law."

> In the work of Jacques Derrida, the figure of the monster embodies a means of thinking otherwise—a means of passing "beyond man and humanism" and reaching for other posthuman futures—that has traveled under the name of deconstruction. The "event" of the Derridean text, signaling a "rupture" with the discourses in which it gestated, terrifies with its unprecedented deformation of the normal and its threat to the boundaries of conventional thought.[10]

Deconstruction itself is monstrous because it denaturalizes the text. This is another interesting approach that deals with monstrosity in language and in text structure, however, this perspective does not come into this volume's categorizations.

Richard Kearney[11] centres the analysis of monstrosity on the ethical examination of evil, distinguishing the origins of the experience of evil in myth, writing, metaphysics and anthropology.

In myth (first perspective) the origins of evil are set in a cosmogonic view, that is, evil is ingrained in the formation of the cosmos itself. We have to face the ethical sphere where evil is the monstrous. *Unde malum?* Where does evil come from? What is questioned is the human, natural and supernatural origin of evil. To answer this question Kearney has recourse to myth, Holy Scriptures, metaphysics and anthropology. Evil is seen as a form of alienation, as something that is pre-determined by forces beyond our control.

The second perspective, the Biblical one, distinguishes between evil as sufferance from evil as misdeed. The genre of Biblical lamentation transforms sufferance into a personal question: "why me?," thus implying a problem of law and justice. Such a question tries to reproduce justice within an apparently unjust perspective (see "The Book of Job"), deriving moral sense from the monstrosity of evil.

The third perspective consists in a sapiential discourse which paves the way to a speculative discourse, or a discourse of metaphysical theology. Evil is not something ingrained in the universe but a punishment (*poena*) for a sin (*peccatum*): in this case the monstrous is the sinful.

The anthropological perspective (the fourth one) eliminates the mystical view of evil to make it a human responsibility.

The latest contemporary perspective (not present in Kearney's distinction) can be called "teratology of the sublime": it is focused on the monstrous character of evil, connecting it to horror, abjection, nihility and to whatever exceeds

---

10 Colin Nazhone Milburn, "Monsters in Eden: Darwin and Derrida," *Modern Language Notes* 118.3 (2003): 603–621.

11 Kearney, *Strangers, Gods and Monsters.*

language. Evil in this case is the un-representable, it is radical otherness. In its absoluteness it is the other side of the divine. The Holocaust, the extreme limit of evil, represents the subliminal of the good. In this sense we can also mean by monstrous a horrid presence that destroys all criteria of harmony or of ethical conduct.[12]

All these perspectives gradually outline two forms of projected monstrosity which today constitute the primary contexts of monstrosity: technophobia and xenophobia, which will be the main themes of this volume. They are themes that foster the literary formation of identity questions in relation to the limits of humanity. Science fiction of a dystopic bend is a well-known example of technophobic monstrosity. In the case of technological progress, the monstrous does not concern the interface between humans and a divine natural order, but between humans and technology. Here, the monstrous lies in the fact that the maximum of human skill, creativity, talent and control to decide how to move in the world is turned against itself precisely at the point where it manifests itself in the most ingenious way. An object is turned against its own kind or type – human but no longer human. In this case, though, the monster denomination is an arbitrary description of something made by humans to boost their control but which actually confuses them.

The other fundamental theme of this volume, xenophobia, means the responsibility for the demonization of peoples from other cultures. This strategy is also as old as Prometheus. The barbarians were labeled as such in order to construct the identity of the Greeks, that is to say the Athenians, as creators and guardians of civilization, but also to legitimize slavery, killings or oppression of others, thus avoiding the question of the potential for destruction. Is what has been called evil universally human or just located with the Other?

The present time is also bringing to light an anthropological, juridical, linguistic, and literary "superdiversity" which can hardly be traced back to established canons; it underscores that the very idea of the Other (the monster, but also the "different from") has been overtaken by an unsteady socio-economic, political, juridical interplay of variables. Up to the present time, law has codified norms and behaviours according to a principle of belonging, which implies a shared set of values along with common linguistic and cognitive frameworks. However, the contemporary worldwide crisis is showing the effects of the collapse of logical structures and national or supra-national political institutions. After the postmodern coexistence of opposites and the questioning of truth statements, it is "contradiction" that now rules politics, society, reference

12 Joseph Campbell, *The Power of Myth* (New York: Anchor, 1988), 222.

systems, values, and the way the real and the virtual are represented. As a consequence, law itself has become structurally inconsistent, to the point that the possibility to configure a juridical order is deeply undermined. An investigation of this issue is crucial to acquire awareness of this new complexity.

In order to describe and analyze this complexity, the theme of the 'monstrous' has been frequently used as a metaphor not only in literary and cultural theory, but also and most of all in political theory. Monstrosity offers a space where society can safely address and exorcise the anxieties of its time, resulting in a powerful allegory of violence and fear. In this sense this volume will inquire into the subtle relation between the concept of monster and the new legal and political idea of subjectivity in order to disclose both the mutual influences of these concepts and the ideologies that have nourished the discursive narrativization of such kind of articulated connections. In this sense monstrosity becomes a regulatory construct of modernity, which imbricates questions of culture, law and politics. Moreover, in a trans-disciplinary perspective of Law and the Humanities, the issues of monstrosity and monstrous geographies allow the project to argument the connection between spatio-legal transformation and literary resurgent identities. Indeed, zombies and aliens come to stigmatize, with a detectable and recognizable signifier, the not intelligible convolution of the present: they embody the spectral excess encompassing the new world order.

The volume therefore aims at examining the concept of monstrosity from the above- mentioned perspectives: technophobic, xenophobic, superdiversity. Today's globalized world is shaped in the unprecedented phenomenon of international migration. Large numbers of individuals and often entire groups or even nations are on the move for a wide variety of reasons. This transiency creates massive challenges to nation states and civil societies, culturally, economically, politically and in the realm of jurisdiction. The resistance to this phenomenon causes the demonization of the Other, seen as the antagonist and the monster. The monster becomes therefore the ethnic Other, the alien. To reach this new perspective on monstrosity we must start by examining the many facets of monstrosity, also diachronically: from the philological origin of the term to the Roman and classical viewpoint, from the Renaissance medical perspective to the religious background, from the new filmic exploitations in the 20th and 21st centuries to the very recent ethnological and anthropological points of view.

The emerging methodology shares its interests in cross-fertilization between cultural domains stemming out of the by now well-assessed relation between law and literature (or law and humanities, according to the latest evolution). These interdisciplinary fields tend to focus on the ways in which the various cultural practices mutually negotiate with one another and in how far the structural and practical characteristics and mechanisms of one domain also apply to the others. By offering a space in which such reflections may be conducted, literature fulfills an essential function in shaping a general understanding of monstrosity and thus filling "the ethical void in which legal thought and practice [. . .] exist."[13] The examination of the concept of monstrosity literature, as an integrative inter-discourse, becomes a crucial arena.

This function is thus indispensable for our understanding of monstrosity in a globalized world, where different notions of personhood encounter each other and daily affect human beings in sometime grievous circumstances. Ideas multiply through the rapid spread of cultural, political and economic phenomena resulting from post-modern "cosmopolitanism," contacts between cultures, systems, and people. These encounters may create positive and negative experiences, and they remind us of the responsibility we have towards others as well as of the necessity of fundamental ethical grounding. An investigation of these encounters and their ethical implications necessarily depends not only on legal or literary analysis conducted in isolation, but on the perspective that is provided through an interdisciplinary approach informed by the comprehensive study of law and literature as cultural spheres in the wider field of monstrosity.

What are monsters? Let us try to find definitions: the most extreme oppositional figures; monsters must be terrifyingly similar to us, otherwise we would not recognize them as such; psychologically speaking, it is the beast in us; for thinkers and writers in antiquity, monsters were odd creatures, mere results of extraordinary births, portents of future events, while medieval authors generally regarded monsters as inexplicable but inclusive elements of God's creation. We find representations of monsters in many art forms, both in stone sculptures (gargoyles, column capitals, ceiling bosses), wood carvings (misericords), and in book illustrations; these monsters all contributed to the broad discourse on 'the Other,' a deep current regarding foreigners, and foreign worlds; they reify a fear while satisfying a need both intellectual and cultural. St. Augustine identified monsters as integral elements of providential history which reveal God's greatness and expose human ignorance. The monster is, since the Middle Ages, a violation of a "bio-juridical" order; "Monster": an imaginary creature that is typically large, ugly and frightening. A special usage implies an inhumanly cruel or wicked person. The struggle against monsters thus emerges as an

13 Richard Weisberg, *Poethics and Other Strategies of Law and Literature* (New York: Columbia University Press, 1992), 12.

existential endeavor, and each person, so to speak, must find his/her own monster and defeat it to regain his/her own self.[14]

> The interrogation into sacrificial monsters reveals the paradox that the monster is not only a portent of impurity (the root of *Monstrum* in *monere*, to warn) but also an apparition of something utterly other and numinous (from the root *monstrare*, to show). In this double sense the monstrous can fill us both with awe and awfulness.[15]
>
> A *monstrum* is a message that breaks into this world from the realm of the sacred [. . .] the otherness of the monster is considered not only horrifically unnatural but also horrifically supernatural, charged with religious import. Likewise, the experience of horror in relation to the monstrous is often described in terms reminiscent of religious experience.[16]

In contrast to other figures generated within social theory for thinking about outsiders, such as Réné Girard's "scapegoat," Zygmunt Bauman's "stranger" or Carl Schmitt's "enemy," Michel Foucault suggests that the figure of the monster can help us understand how the figure of the outsider is constituted. The monster is the effect of a double breach: of law and nature. For Foucault the monster does not simply refer to a morphological or psychological irregularity, but it must also pose a threat to the categorical structure of law. A challenge to the idea of the "proper" legal subject.[17]

Alex Neville Sharpe argues that the figure of the monster contributes something novel in the contemporary debate over the figure of the outsider. In his turn Bauman[18] asserts that society can only define itself against its strangers (the Nazis defined themselves as pure race against Jews, the outsiders): it needs outsiders to constitute itself. The figure of the monster might prove useful because it addresses not only the question of why outsiders are necessary, that is sociologically and psychologically functional, but also the conditions necessary for their production. Sharpe, speaking of Foucault's concepts, discusses how certain individuals or groups come to receive the label of monsters and why this appellation proves successful in cultural terms (consider the figure of Shakespeare's Shylock). While the legal category of monster no longer has a formal existence in law, contemporary legal regulation of embodied difference bears its legacy. According to Foucault, each epoch has its "privileged monster."

14 Campbell, *The Power of Myth*, 20.

15 Kearney, *Strangers, Gods and Monsters*, 34.

16 Timothy Beal, Introduction, *Religion and its Monsters* (London and New York: Routledge, 2001), 7.

17 Alex Neville Sharpe, *Foucault's Monsters and the Challenge of Law* (New York: Routledge, 2010).

18 Zygmunt Bauman, "Making and Unmaking of Strangers," *Thesis Eleven* 43 (1995): 1–16.

> Within Western philosophy there has been a long tradition of privileging the mind over the body in understanding and constructing humanness. Yet in the context of English law, in the corpus of law dealing with monsters, it is the body that indicates what it means to be human.[19]

Foucault speaks of the abnormal individual,[20] linking him to the monster archetypes, emphasizing the shift from the body to the soul as the object of legal concern. Rather than being written on bodily surfaces, monstrosity, in the context of the abnormal individual, becomes internalized. It is the internalization and therefore the invisibility of monstrosity that constitutes the abnormal individual as a figure of modernity.

This is why we may say that the monster is born at a metaphoric crossroads and reflects the ideology and culture of a given historical moment. The body of the monster becomes the quintessence of fear and desire, a construct and a projection of the unconscious. The monster signifies something other than itself. "It is always a displacement, it always inhabits the gap between the time of upheaval that created it and the moment into which it is received, to be born again."[21] It is the embodiment of Derrida's concept of "différance." Monsters must be examined within the social, cultural, and literary-historical relations that typify the society that has produced them. The monster is the dialectical Other, it is the Outward projection of the Inside, of what exceeds normality: it is the Beyond.

Moving out of this allotted space (metaphorical and real) entails the risk of being attacked by some monstrous essence or becoming monstrous oneself: consider Lucy in *Dracula* who becomes monstrous because she has overstepped the patriarchal space attributed to women; therefore, Dracula's bite becomes symbolic of a rebellious behaviour ingrained in the woman herself. And consider also Doctor Frankenstein who becomes monstrous and is exchanged for his own creature. In the sphere of literary and cultural imagination these subversive beings are endowed with a freedom of speech and action which is denied to normal characters: this is why the monster may reach the status of allegory, extending his influence across centuries.

Paradoxically the physical ugliness of many monsters in the literary and cultural tradition is contrasted to the moral ugliness of seemingly perfect human beings (such as the perpetrators of genocides and mass murders), so

---

19 Sharpe, *Foucault's Monsters*, 9.
20 Foucault, *Les anormaux. Cours au Collège de France.*
21 Cohen, *Monster Theory, Reading Culture*, 12.

that sometimes we feel more empathy toward them than toward their creators and masters.

The intersections of the anthropological, psychoanalytical and representational domains as well as the approach to monstrosity via the fields of law, literature and culture shape the point of entry for this volume. Many literary works have discussed this issue. Therefore, literature becomes a means to reflect on the two main monster generating differences, the technophobic and the xenophobic, and their historical development as an element embedded in our attempt to create our identities. Literature does not create monsters, but it may give them a name, forcing us never to forget the basic question, that is how to live in a world of new differences without turning them into monster engendering transformations.

The essays in this volume aim at examining the concept of monstrosity diachronically from many different perspectives: from the concept of monstrosity connected to *parricidium* and legal violation in Roman times, to monstrosity as a state of exception; from 19th-century fiction, with the analyses of some genetic experiments, to the 20th-century concept of monstrosity dealing with trauma, androgyny, racial and postcolonial perspectives; to digital humanities, dealing with artificial intelligence and the cyborg (the problematization of the concept of legal persona when facing sentient machines). In addition, the volume includes also two appendixes: the first one by François Ost is a narration where the author gives voice to a bear who is going to be hanged on the accusation of witchcraft because it was born with five paws. The story is based on real 16th-century events and on the terrible witch hunting of that bloodstained period. The obsession with witches, also triggered by treatises on the topic, was launched even against beasts, which could be excommunicated as devilish as well as human beings. The monstrosity of the situation is double: first of all, because we are dealing with a beast considered to be monstrous not qua beast but because it is considered to be possessed; secondly, because all witch hunting was a monstrous application of law. The second appendix by Filippo Sgubbi is a note marking how monstrosity has always been a core concept within criminal law. The author remarks how legal monstrosity is often triggered by media that need to identify the presumed guilty person to be thrown to a public, hungry for monsters.

Cristina Costantini in "The Monster's Mystique. Managing a State of Bionormative Liminality and Exception" considers the transposition of the concept of monstrosity from theology to law. Being a subversive concept that marks an unredeemable difference, monstrosity suggests the presence of a liminal zone where law is transgressed, thus calling exception into question. Therefore, the debate takes place between theology and philosophy. Law is made monstrous in itself: this is how Costantini re-reads Derrida's idea of the monstrification of law. Sin, from a theological perspective, is the monster emplotted within law, but that would not exist if the law did not exist: law and sin (the monstrous) are reciprocally connected and derive from each other. "The concept of monster abuses the norm," the author argues, thus laying bare the inconsistency of law and its abjection. Being open to exception, to the sacred, monstrosity becomes a source of wonder and fear in law. The monstrous pushes the force of law to its ontological limit.

Svend Eric Larsen in "Monsters and Human Solitude" asserts that the main characteristic of monsters is not that they are scary or that they are composed of human, animal, and maybe technological fragments, but rather, and more importantly, because they are unique. If they form families or societies we move into the world of proto-humans or aliens or, in other words, into the realm of another species. Real monsters, however, do not belong to a species. Hence, when monsters enter the human world they act as a sign of its limit, and as an invitation (maybe a message from the gods or other non-human essences), an opportunity to reflect on the boundaries of the human vis-à-vis a trans-human sphere. Through a set of literary examples, the paper explores how monsters have been important for the meditation on the limits of humanity, which is shaped differently in different cultural and historical contexts.

Carlo Pelloso in "Sew It Up in the Sack and Merge It into Running Waters! *Parricidium* and Monstrosity in Roman Law" starts with the assessment that the crime of *parricidium* in the Roman world was considered monstrous. He analyzes the various meanings of the term *parricidium:* it can be the murder of a parent, of a relative, or it can also be applied to the betrayal of the fatherland or to the act of conspiracy against the emperor's life. The author reports the assertions of many philosophers of the time for whom the person that committed a parricide was a monster or a portent in human form. But the broad terminology to indicate monstrosity in ancient Rome, such as *ostentum, portentum, prodigium, miraculum,* also implies future forecasts or the supernatural sphere. Therefore, the birth of monstrous or prodigious children also had a religious perspective and suggested a fatal separation from the gods. The crime of parricide represented the climax of such natural subversion and the severity with which it was punished conveyed the idea that the parricide had to be rejected by the earth itself and cancelled from the order of the cosmos even in death. The *poena cullei* represented a ceremony of removal of the monster and the cleansing of the cosmos.

Daniela Carpi in "The Technological 'Monstrum': *Her* by Spike Jontze" considers monstrosity from the technological perspective in the context of the new theories concerning posthumanism. Posthumanism implies a radical onto-existential re-signification of the notion of the human. We are facing new unprecedented situations where experience is powerless and demands a new conception of duties and rights. In the movie *Her* (2013) the disembodied voice can be considered responsible for the character's sense of abandonment, betrayal and loneliness. Technological change has become a core component of contemporary imagination about posthumanity. Here the clash is between responsible subjects and programmed behavioral system. The movement of science has necessarily eroded the foundations from which norms could be derived; it has destroyed the very idea of norm.

Heinz Antor in "Monstrosity and Alterity in H.G. Wells' *The Island of Doctor Moreau*" discusses the subtle line dividing man from beast and the collapse of the taxonomy and categorization that traditionally characterize the monstrous. If the monstrous is generally connected with what is unfamiliar and not immediately intelligible, the novel problematizes these boundaries and the very notion of man. What can be defined as bioethical experiments *ante litteram*, that is the vivisections Doctor Moreau performs on animals on the island, highlights the Victorians' fear of humankind's degeneration after Darwin's discoveries: the human-animal divide becomes problematic. What appears particularly monstrous in the novel is the instability of human identity. Doctor Moreau himself appears to be monstrous because of his absolute lack of ethics. In the novel man becomes monstrous, in fact we witness the gradual devolution of Prendick towards the animal state, and beasts become monstrous because their true nature is subverted: alterity is the debated topic, in a sort of social, racial and anthropological re-negotiation.

Susana Onega in "Patriarchal Law and the Ethics and Aesthetics of Monstrosity in Mary Shelley's *Frankenstein*" centres her analysis on three figures of otherness: the wanderer, the vampire, and the seeker. Otherness implies monstrosity. The common basis for these monstrous figures is the sin of ingratitude, thus connected to rebellion and disobedience. The aspiration to forbidden knowledge brings on the culprit the wrath of God: defying patriarchal law entails a life of solitary errantry. Mary Shelley's denunciation of progress as monstrous is an accusation against the excess of reason that produces monsters. Forbidden knowledge involves incapacity to enjoy the love of family and friends and perverts the perspective of birth and regeneration.

Enrichetta Soccio in "Victorian *Frankenstein*: From Fiction to Science" examines some of the many derivations, also metaphorical, of Mary Shelley's monster, such as Gaskell's idea of the working class as the inhuman monster in Mary Barton or the Victorian fears concerning science. Even Dickens in *The Haunted Man* tries to exorcise the spectre of monstrosity. Therefore, the monster in Victorian fiction is internalized and epitomizes our savage repressed part. The monster takes shape in the reader's mind as the embodiment of cultural fears and ethical anxieties.

Jean-Michel Ganteau in "Exposed: Dispossession and Androgyny in Contemporary British Fiction" tries to define monstrosity by using Margrit Shildrick's terms: the monster introduces "a failure of the proper," a phrase by which she stresses its liminal position: neither completely similar nor completely different, neither outside nor inside, both the same and the other. In other terms, the monster reconfigures the subject, and pushes him or her to re-locate alterity within, thereby striking at the roots of the modern vision of the self as autonomous and sovereign. This provides a vision of the human as essentially open and hybrid, i.e. inherently vulnerable and anthropologically exposed. The "failure of the proper," for which the fictional monster provides a figuration, finds its inspiration in a secular fascination for the teratomorphous. The figure of the androgyne, glorified by Coleridge and Woolf, comes to the fore in many contemporary novels. With the figure of the androgyne – and its darker version, the hermaphrodite – the monster explicitly locates alterity within and presents the reader with a vision of the self as composite. Contemporary British fiction's androgynous figures contribute to an aesthetics and an ethics of vulnerability by cracking the Self open and trading in dispossession. In so doing, they renew the monster's agenda of ostentation by making the reader aware of the norms of visibility that have come to orient and determine our perception.

Paola Carbone and Giuseppe Rossi in "Who Is the Monster? Laughing at Friends and Foes" start with an overview of the legal meaning of "monster," from the Roman sources to, following the Enlightenment, the final setting aside of a legal idea of "monstrosity." Furthermore, the essay tackles the relationship between law and the comic: while law claims its capacity to regulate rationally a coherent world, the comic constantly reminds that irrationality is an unavoidable aspect of life. The authors analyze three examples from literature and comic movies, which show that legal provisions aimed at distinguishing law-abiding citizens from violators ("monsters") can lead to astounding outcomes, as a consequence of unavoidable fallacies in legal drafting and enforcement techniques. Finally, taking hints from Paolo Villaggio's Fantozzi works, the essay proposes a view of "monstrosity" as an inherent part of everyday life that even the law has to cope with. The essay highlights how humour can strike a balance between jurisdiction and justice.

Fernando Armando Ribeiro in "The Monster as a Denial of Difference: a legal approach to Kafka's *The Metamorphosis*" takes Kafka's novel as a guideline for the perception of monstrosity. The story brings to the fore some of the main contradictions in the structural preconceptions of ethical models, which end up making room for the emergence of the idea of monstrosity.

Marc Amfreville in "The Sleep of Reason Brings Forth Monsters: O'Brien's *In the Lake of the Woods*" argues that the very final lines of Tom O'Brien's novel powerfully lead us away from the circumstantial question of the protagonist's guilt to help us measure the full ethical and philosophical scope of a novel wrongly considered as a mere example of "Vietnam War Fiction." The initial interrogation – "Can we believe?" – takes the inhuman nature of a (war) crime bordering on a crime against humanity for granted to ask us readers whether we are willing to acknowledge that monstrosity is intrinsic in our humanity. The novel implies that "human life" itself is the very source of the death drive, and of the destruction instinct. This contemporary novel addresses the question of "monstrosity" through the prism of trauma. Drawing from Freudian knowledge that a given trauma is "always second" (the massacre of innocent victims in Vietnam/the enigmatic suicide of Wade's father when he was a child), Amfreville brings together Tim O'Brien's *In the Lake of the Woods*, Charles Brockden Brown's 1798 ground-breaking American Gothic novel *Wieland or the Transformation: an American Tale* and 1799 *Edgar Huntly; or Memoirs of a Sleepwalker*. A hundred years before the advent of psychoanalysis, the father of American Letters had already perceived and exposed the links between monstrosity, filiation and trauma.

Marita Nadal in "Southern Gothic: The Monster as Freak in the Fiction of Flannery O'Connor" identifies monstrosity with violence and doom. The American South has traditionally served as the nation's "other," becoming the repository of everything from which the nation wants to disassociate itself: racism, classism, irrationality, madness, decay, violence, religious fanaticism, poverty, rural parochialism and sexual deviance. Southern Gothic explores all these subjects, underscoring a fixation with the grotesque and its aberrant creatures: its freaks. Taking these characteristics as the point of reference, the chapter analyses the grotesque and the figure of the freak in Flannery O'Connor's fiction, especially focusing on "A Good Man Is Hard to Find," "Good Country People," and "Wise Blood." The essay highlights the subversive and prophetic potential of O'Connor's freaks, who, despite their seeming marginality and even ludicrous appearance, have transcended their Southern otherness to prefigure the violence and monstrosity that characterize the 21st century.

Annalisa Ciampi in "Kafka's Trial and the EU Dublin Asylum System" focuses her attention on the problem of immigration, particularly on the faults of the Dublin Regulation of the asylum system (2013), establishing the criteria for determining the member state responsible for examining applications for international protection. The Dublin system appears monstrous in that it puts all the burden of acceptance and responsibility on the Mediterranean states, which in this case are geopolitically disadvantaged. Therefore, rather than alleviating the countries geopolitically disadvantaged, such as Italy or Greece, the regulation exacerbates their problems. The monstrosity of the situation lies in the fact that both the nations involved and the immigrants themselves are victimized.

Matteo Nicolini in "Monstrosity 'Overseas'? Civilization, Trade, and Colonial Policy in Conrad's African Tales" considers that colonization is rooted in a perverse aesthetics of domination, in its turn connected to horror, monstrosity and danger. The pretended process of civilization of Africa is a question of trade and commercial globalization. Conrad's novel *Heart of Darkness* gives voice to the sordid saga of European colonial policy with its monstrous exploitation of natural resources. The monstrosity of the so-called civilizing mission is represented by slave trade. Several metaphors have been used to describe the violence operated on the African continent: one of these is considering Africa as a female body that is being violated; imperialism as sexual rape. This monstrous approach is triggered by trade, which is denounced by Kurtz in the novel. Kurtz is the trading agent that has the monopoly of the ivory market. Nicolini examines the term "trade" also from a philological perspective and traces a sort of history of the term "trade" (from the Latin "to walk") connected to monstrosity going as far back as the poem *Beowulf*, where the monster's path is covered with blood. Therefore trade, blood and monstrosity have always been synonyms.

Roberta Zanoni in "Harry Potter and Monstrous Diversity: The Brexit Case" develops a reflection on the concept of monstrosity, filtered through contemporary popular culture. The Harry Potter saga was able to foreshadow ensuing real-life events, thanks to its capacity to register even the slightest details of the culture from which it originated. The Harry Potter books present various delineations of diversity and monstrosity and the condemnation and exclusion of the monster show a sentiment of fear and hatred for what is different and divergent from the norm. The theme of the Other is epitomized by the figure of Voldemort who initially represents the monster, the outcast, and the parasite, but who eventually manages to reverse the rhetoric of exclusion when he becomes the ruler in the last books. The profoundly rooted discourses on the Other, the pursuit of the Greater Good, and various other elements of the books find a striking parallel with the Brexit Leave Campaign propaganda and with its xenophobic aftermath. The latter failed to take into consideration the complexity of the Brexit question, thus reducing it to a mere discourse on exclusion and inclusion stemming from a vague definition of national identity. The essay exhibits literature's profound insight into reality which makes it an instrument through which we can better understand and approach our everyday world.

1 Ontology of the Monstrous

Cristina Costantini

The Monster's Mystique: Managing a State of Bionormative Liminality and Exception

[...] etwas Morsches im Recht.
W. Benjamin, Zur Kritik der Gewalt[1]

We were trapped [...] completely stranded for all practical purposes, in a region of the country, and of the entire world, where all the manifestations of that bleak time of year, or rather its absence of manifestations were so evident in the landscape around us, where everything was absolutely stripped to the bone, and where the pathetic emptiness of forms in their unadorned state was so brutally evident.[2]

1 "There is something rotten in Law"; Walter Benjamin, *Critique of Violence*, in *Reflections: Essays, Aphorisms, Autobiographical Writings*, ed. Edmund Jephcott (New York: Schocken, 1986), 286.
2 Thomas Ligotti, *The Shadow, The Darkness* in Thomas Ligotti, *Teatro Grottesco* (London: Virgin Books, 2008), 243–280, 243–244.

Note: This essay is part of a research project exploring the ontological tensions embedded in the process of secularization and their impact on the Law's *presentification*, that is the way in which Law is worldly communicated. The synthetic title of the project is "Icons of Law. From mondanization to mondialization of Law." In particular, in the following pages the attention is posed on the concepts of monster and monstrosity, as they have been transposed from Theology to Law and Politics. Monster is originally conceived as a critical paradigm of investigation. It is meant as the mark of an irredeemable difference; as the subversive device apt to unveil what exceeds the possibilities of the real; as the sign that disfigures every kind of taxonomy. Monster terrifies Law: living a zone of liminality, it shows the fictionality of order and representation. In this perspective, the essay, making use of the idea of "monster," is proposing an iconic lecture of the relationship between Law and Exception; the Sovereign and the Beast. The monster is a secularized item which allows us to rethink the content of transgression with respect to Law. The arguments discussed are *emplotted* in an interdisciplinary discourse, at the confluence of theological and philosophical domains. The version of exception proposed by Giorgio Agamben and here reinterpreted as the product of the *monstrification* of Law, can be thought as a mondanized form of the sin defined by Paul in his Epistle to the Romans. Here it is said: "What shall we say, then? Is the law sinful? Certainly not! Nevertheless, I would not have known what sin was had it not been for the law. For I would not have known what coveting really was if the law had not said, "You shall not covet." (7.7). Exception is like sin a concrete form of transgression, and, once again, like sin is indispensable to constitute Law as Law. The "monstrous" violence of Exception suspends the force of Law pushing it towards its ontological limit. A special emphasis has been given to the words and terms specifically designed to innovate the lexicon of comparative law theory.

https://doi.org/10.1515/9783110654615-002

> While I was in the throes of my gastrointestinal episode at the hospital where I was treated I descended, so to speak, to that deep abyss of entity where I could feel how this shadow, this darkness was activating my body. I could also hear its movement, not only within my body but in everything around me, because the sound that it made was not the sound of my body – it was the sound of this shadow, this darkness, which is not like any other sound. Likewise I was able to detect the workings of this pervasive and all-moving force through the sense of smell and the sense of taste, as well as the sense of touch with which my body was equipped. Finally I opened my eyes, for throughout much of this agonizing ordeal of my digestive system my eyelids were clenched shut in pain. And when I opened my eyes I found that I could see how everything around me, including my own body, was activated from within by this pervasive shadow, this all-moving darkness. And nothing looked as I had always known it to look.[3]

With these words, Reiner Grossvogel, a second-rate artist turned onto a murky, crepuscolar philosopher after a traumatic physical illness, proposes a journey towards the pervasive shadow, the insubstantial darkness monstrously concealed at the centre of the world's ontology. In a disrupted geography apt to destroy the distinction between the real and the imaginary, in a perverted region where the vigil meets the dream, the primordial Shadow is and persists. In its consistency dark matter is exuding from every apparently substantial and existing thing, it is rising "as if a torrent of black blood had begun roaring through its pale body"[4]; it is resisting in its enigmatic epiphany. This is the metaphysical strategy enacted by the gloom, auratic darkness: finally, it reveals the sense of its phenomenological camouflage. In the absence of light, it keeps its inner, constitutive force, that "moves all the objects of this world, including those objects which we call our bodies."[5] The myth of Plato's cave is under question: the gloomy umbra is not a projected, derivative or, even worse, false entity, but on the contrary the true face of the real. The world is merely a gothic mask, the ontic instrument used to cover it, to disguise and keep secret the *powerful nothing at the origin of the Beginning.*

This fascinating and disturbing novel written by Thomas Ligotti (not by chance entitled *The Shadow, The Darkness*) is deliberately chosen to introduce a philojuridical thought about Law's Monstrosity and Law's secularized ontology. In this perspective, Ligotti's hallucinatory and hypnotic style, intellectually

---

3 Ligotti, *The Shadow, The Darkness*, 259.
4 Ligotti, *The Shadow, The Darkness*, 276.
5 Ligotti, *The Shadow, The Darkness*, 259.

assembled in order to traduce in words the unstable ontologies of derangement, deformation and disease, is one of the most brilliant creations apt to open a speculative window over a *constitutive abyss*, to tell through literature the philosophical story of the *presence of an absence*.[6] Such an evocative and dramatic aesthetics can be recalled to reveal a kind of metaphysical swindle, so to provide Law with a metamorphic healing.

As in the theological domain, the paradigm encrypted into the announced formula of the "Ecce Homo"[7] has disrupted the conventional image of God's nature,[8]

---

6 For a comprehensive view of Thomas Ligotti's style, see Darrell Schweitzer, *The Thomas Ligotti Reader: Essays and Explorations* (Holicong: Wildside Press, 2003).

7 The expression "*ecce homo*" ("behold the man") is the Latin form of the utterance used by Pilate in presenting Jesus to a hostile crowd of Jews before His crucifixion. The Christ, who is proclaiming Himself to be God, is *presentified* in His secular dimension of a "bare man," divested of every attribute of divinity: He is bound, scourged, mocked, crowned with thorns and girded with a purple robe. The passion narrative could be read as an earthly confrontation between two human beings – Pilate and Jesus –, both of them made of flesh and blood, nerve and passion. For a theological perspective, Camille R. La Bossière, *Ecce Homo*, in *A Dictionary of Theological Biblical Tradition*, ed. David L. Jeffrey (Grand Rapids Michigan: W.B. Eerdmans Pub. Company, 1992), 221. The voice is interesting insofar as it proposes intriguing, even if synthetic comments on the literary and iconographic transposition of the biblical expression.

8 The lecture of God's incarnation in terms of "monstrosity" can be found in the Hegelian Christology. According to the German philosopher, reconciliation cannot be direct, but it has first to generate a *monster* [*ungeheure Zusammensetzung*], a momentous combination of human and divine nature. The main passages are the following: God appears in a sensible presence and has no other shape (*Gestalt*) than that of the sensible mode of spirit (moving from the premise that the only *Gestalt* in which God can appear is that of *Geist* and reciprocally there can be no *Geist* without *Gestalt*, insofar as the spirit free from form or shape dissipates into the air); the appearance of God in the flesh constitutes a monstrous reality (*das Ungeheure*); the unity of divine and human nature must appear in just one human being. Hegelian thought has been developed in the *Lectures on the Philosophy of History*; for the integral text, Georg Wilhelm Friedrich Hegel, *Lectures on the Philosophy of History* (Berkeley: University of California Press, 1990), Vol. III, 1824, 214; 1827, 313–314. In a following passage, Hegel emphasizes that Christ, the "God-man," is a monstrous compound which directly contradicts both representation and understanding. At the same time, he points out that "what has thereby been brought into human consciousness and made a certainty for is the unity of divine and human nature, implying that the otherness, or [. . .] the finitude, weakness, and frailty of human nature does not damage this unity, just as otherness does not impair the unity that God is the eternal idea." Georg Wilhelm Friedrich Hegel, *Lectures on the Philosphy of History: One Volume edition – The Lectures of 1827*, ed. Peter C. Hodgson (Berkeley: University of California Press, 1998), 457–458. For the transformation of Hegelian concept of monstrosity into Bonhoeffer's idea of life and death struggle between *Menschenlogos*, the human logos, and *Gegenlogos*, the transcendent counter-logos brought by Christ, see David S. Robinson, *Christ and Revelatory Community in Bonhoeffer's Reception of Hegel* (Tübingen: Mohr Soebeck, 2018), 117 ff.; Brian Gregor, *A Philosophical Anthropology of the Cross: The Cruciform* in a secular perspective it seems to be momentous to claim for an "Ecce monstrum" with respect to the Law.[9]

To cultivate this perspective, it could be intellectually provoking to pose and solve these questions: what is a monster? What constitutes its deeper sacrality? And how can we assess the *monstrification* of Law, or the process through which the Law comes to be confronted with its transformative Other?

The Latin etymology of the word "monster" is at the basis of its meaningful ambiguity. On the one side, it moves from the verb *monstrare*, meaning "to show and display": the monster is inherently demonstrative, it is that which appears, a sign, a signifier.[10] The monster is also that which occurs for the first time and for

Self (Bloomington: Indiana University Press, 2013), 93 ff. Hegel's hermeneutics of the central mystery of Christianism has been commented by Slavoj Žižek in dialogue with John Milbank in the work Slavoj Žižek, John Milbank, *The Monstrosity of Christ: Paradox or Dialectic* (Cambridge: The Mit Press, 2009). In a specific paragraph of the book, Slavoj Žižek further clarifies the Hegelian monstrosity of Christ. Moving from the idea that, through the means of incarnation, God appears as human to itself, Žižek notes that "Christ is God's "partial object," an autonomized organ without a body, as if God picked his eye out of his head and turned it on himself from the outside. We can guess, now, how Hegel insisted on the monstrosity of Christ. It is therefore crucial to note how the Christian modality of "God seeing himself" has nothing whatsoever to do with the harmonious closed loop of "seeing myself again" of an eye seeing itself and enjoying the sight in this perfect self-mirroring: the turn of the eye toward "its" body presupposes the separation of the eye from the body and what I see through my externalized/autonomized eye is a perspectival anamorphically distorted image of myself: Christ is an anamorphosis of God (see Žižek, Milbank, *The Monstrosity of Christ*, 82).

9 Making use of the evocative expression chosen by Jeremy Biles as the title of his work on Bataille's philosophy; Jeremy Biles, *Ecce Monstrum: Georges Bataille and the Sacrifice of Form* (New York: Fordham University Press, 2007).

10 "*Monster – monstrare.*" Lat. *Monstrum; monstrare*, to point out, make a show of. Hence *Demonstrare*, to point out; *Remonstrare*, to show reasons against; Hensleigh Wedgwood, *A Dictionary of English Etimology* (London: Trübner & Co., 1872, 2nd ed.). In the same sense, but moving from the Latin roots, "Monstr-o v. 1. *To show, to point out; to tell* or *to declare*: as, *demonstrate, to show* or *to prove* with the highest degree of certainty; *monster, a prodigy, a being out of the common course of nature; muster*, to collect troops for review, to assemble"; John Oswald, *A Dictionary of Etymology of the English Synonymes and Paronymes* (Edinburgh: Adam & Charles Black, 1866, 12th ed.), 321. For a critical inquiry on the classical thought, Margrit Shildrick, *Embodying the Monster: Encounters with the Vulnerable Self* London: Sage, 2002, where, before plunging into a new original vision, the Author aims at tracing some historical representations and explanations of the "monstrous." She clarifies how the relationship between monstrosity and nature profoundly exercised the classical mind, and, later, the Church Fathers. If Aristotle used the concept to denote deficiency and deviation from the common course of nature, from a kind of "normal" morphology, it was Cicero to firstly propose a list of synonyms – *monstra, ostenta, portenta, prodigia* – which anchored meaning in later ages, privileging a teleological rather than an aetiological approach (see Shildrick, *Embodying the Monster*, 11–12).

which we do not yet have a name, as Derrida has punctually noted: "it shows itself in something that is not yet shown and that therefore looks like a hallucination; it strikes the eye, it frightens precisely because no anticipation had prepared to identify this figure."[11] On the other side, the name traces its roots back to the form *monēre*, that is "to warn," "to advise"; therefore the monster is a divine omen, a portent, a mark or a signature of what is yet unexpected and unforeseeable.[12] Linking together the possible archeologies of the term and the concept it

---

11 Jacques Derrida, *Points…Interviews 1974–1994* (ed. Elizabeth Weber, trans. Peggy Kamuf & others), (Stanford: Stanford University Press, 1995), 386.

12 It has been prospected a linguistical derivation of the Latin form *monstrare* from *monēre*, so that the sense of warning appears to be more cogent in the stratified meaning of the present word *monster*. In this perspective, see the voice "Monster" in *The Merriam-Webster New Book of Word Histories* (Springfield: Merriam Webster Pub., 1991), 310: "[T]he word monster comes from the Latin *monstrum*, meaning an "evil omen" which in turn seems to be a derivative of the verb *monēre*, meaning "to warn," "remind." This same Latin verb *monēre* has yielded other modern English words in which the notion of reminding or warning can be seen. One is *demonstrate*, from Latin *demonstratus*, a past participle of *demonstrare*, which comes from *de-* "away" and *monstrare* "to show, point out." *Monstrare* itself comes ultimately from *monēre*. Another is *premonition*, a warning of something about to happen. It comes, through several intermediaries, from Latin *praemonēre* "to warn in advance," from *prae-* "before" and "*monēre*"." For a synthetic understanding of the two perspectives, see Abigail Lee Six, Hannah Thompson, "From Hideous to Hedonist: The Changing Face of the Nineteenth Century Monster," in *The Ashgate Research Companion to Monster and the Monstrous*, eds. Asa Simon Mittman, Peter J. Dendle (Farnham: Ashgate, 2012), 237–256, 237: "A monster stands as a visible symbol of something important and usually ominous, collapsing two Latin derivations in the popular imagination: *monēre* "to warn" and *monstrare* "to show." Thus, a monster is something put on display as a warning." The authors, in order to better explain their arguments, are here recalling Jeffrey Jerome Cohen's *Monster Theory*. For the ideas and theories developed in this essay it can be compelling to quote a brief excerpt of the introductory notes of the first chapter of Cohen's central work: "A construct and a projection, the monster exists only to be read: the monstrum is etymologically "that which reveals," "that which warns," a glyph that seeks a hierophant, like a letter on the page, the monster signifies something other than itself: it is always a displacement, always inhabits the gap between the time of upheaval that created it at the moment into which it is received, to be born again. These epistemological spaces between the monster's bones are Derrida's familiar chasm of *différance*: a genetic uncertainty principle, the essence of the monster's validity, the reason it always rises from the dissection table as its secrets are about to be revealed and vanishes into the night"; Jeffrey Jerome Cohen, ed., *Monster Theory: Reading Culture* (Minneapolis: University of Minnesota Press, 1996): 3–23, 3. The pivotal work in this field remains Emile Benveniste's work: Émile Benveniste, *Dictionary of Indo-European Concepts and Society* (Chicago: The University of Chicago Press, 2016). Benveniste notes that, if the morphological roots of the word *monstrum* trace back to the verb *monstrare*, these two terms have a different meaning: while *monstrare* is for "to show," *monstrum* names "something that exceeds the normal, the ordinary." At the same time, Benveniste declares that both *monstrum* and *monstrare* descend from the other verb *monēre*, "to warn"; therefore, this common origin obliges us to deeply understand the derivative meaning of the substantive form names, the monster becomes the incarnated and concrete threshold turning towards the Excess, what outweighs phenomenological ontology. For these profound reasons, according to Bataille, the presentation of monstrosity provokes a sacrificial experience: it entails the sacrifice of form.[13] The vision of monster incites a paradoxical combination of contrastive and extreme affects; it produces the same rupturing experience of both life and death, joy and anguish, that defines what Bataille calls "religious sensibility" and offers the grounds for an evolving conception of the sacred as tied to transgressive heterogeneity.[14]

---

monstrum ("If we start with *moneo*, what would *monstrum* mean?"; Benveniste, *Dictionary of Indo-European Concepts and Society*, 509). At this end, it is important to distinguish the only apparently synonymical forms *monstrare* and *ostendere: monstrare* means not so much to show an object, as to teach a way of behaving, to prescribe the way to be followed. On these premises, it is possible to argue that the word meant a piece of advice, a warning given by Gods. "There was nothing in the forms of monstrum – Benveniste emphasizes – which suggested anything monstrous except the fact that in the doctrine of presages a monster represented a divine instruction, a warning" (see Benveniste, *Dictionary of Indo-European Concepts and Society*, 510). Analogous observation can be made with respect to the word *prodigium*, that indicates the emission of an utterance invested with divine authority, pronounced in public with the function of a presage. Therefore, *monstrum* and *prodigium* not merely show or tell something: they have a performative force, insofar as they are constituting the object described and at the same time they are conferring a specific power to the subject of enunciation. The intellectual perspective opened by Benvensite and the proposed etymological reconstruction of the term are very important for at least two reasons. On the one side, they situate firstly the meaning of the word *monstrum* in the domain of religion; on the other side, they allow us to better understand the semantic universe in which the enunciation of "monstrosity" has functioned. To say that something or someone is "monstrous" or "a monster" is not a mere descriptive, but a constitutive act: it gives and imposes the status of indescriptibility and not nominability. For all these reasons it is not by chance that Benveniste introduces the discussion about the term "monstrum" in the section part of his work dedicated to Power, Law and Religion.

13 The concept of "formless," "amorphous" is central in Bataille's reflections; see Georges Bataille, *Informe*, in Georges Bataille, Michel Leiris, *Documents (1929–1930)* (Paris: Éditions Jean-Michel Place, 1991), 382; for the English translation see Goerges Bataille, *Formless*, in *Georges Bataille: Vision of Excess. Selected Writings, 1927–1939*, ed. Allan Stoeckl, trans. Allan Stoeckl, Carl R. Lovitt, Donald M. Leslie Jr. (Minneapolis: University of Minnesota Press, 1985), 31. Bataille inaugurates an experience of limit, apt to perturb the ordinary plan of representation.

14 For further reflections, Jeremy Biles, *Ecce Monstrum*, 4, 7, where the religious sensibility is characterized as a "monstrous and contradictory combination of horror and ecstasy." Even the sacrifice is functional to "monstrify" the Self. As Biles notes, "The need of sacrifice comes from [the] desire to return discontinuous individuals to the sacred domain of continuous nature"; "The individual reality of the 'me,' of ipseity, is precisely what needs to be destroyed to experience the ecstasy of a return to the 'impersonal totality' of existence" (Biles, *Ecce Monstrum*, 53).

Recalling to the mind these intrinsic perversions, the concepts of "monster" and "monstrosity" can be reinterpreted as the double contents of a new *critical paradigm*, which is aimed to question the conventional assumptions of ontology, epistemology and ethics.

From an *ontological standpoint*, the monster is a figure of break, discontinuity and difference; in its proper formless being, it makes permeable the boundaries that guarantee the normatively embodied self, subverting and blurring the frozen ideas of separation and distinction.[15] Monster disrupts morphological expectations and undermines the strategies of ontological representation: it contravenes unity, stability, singularity.[16] Monster originates beyond limits as the

15 For the understanding of the monster as a figure of ontological liminality, as the harbinger of category crisis, Jeffrey Jerome Cohen, "Monster Culture," in Cohen, *Monster Theory*, 3–25, 6. Here he brilliantly clarifies: "The monster always escapes because it refuses easy categorization. [...] This refusal to participate in the classificatory "order of things" is true of monsters generally: they are disturbing hybrids whose externally incoherent bodies resist attempts to include them in any systematic structuration. Therefore, the monster is dangerous, a form suspended between different forms and threatens to smash distinctions. Because of its ontological liminality, the monster notoriously appears at times of crisis as a kind of third term that problematizes the clash of extremes – as 'that which questions binary thinking and introduces a crisis'" (Cohen, "Monster Culture," 6). In the last part of the sentence, Cohen is quoting from Marjorie Garber, who has formulated the concept "category crisis." She defines it as "a failure of definitional distinction, a borderline that becomes permeable, that permits of a border crossing from one (apparently distinct) category to another [...] [That which crosses the border] will always function as a mechanism of overdetermination – a mechanism of displacement from one blurred boundary to another"; Marjorie Garber, *Vested Interests: Cross Dressing and Cultural Anxiety* (New York: Routledge, 1992), 11; 16–17. In an original perspective Amit Rai explores the structural bond of monstrosity to ontology, as they are mutually tied to the lived change itself; Amit S. Rai, "Ontology and Monstrosity," in *Monster Culture in 21st Century: A Reader*, eds. Marina Levina, Diem-My T. Bui (London: Bloomsbury, 2013), 15–31, 15. As it has been pointed out, monstrosity offers the possibility of a "destabilizing change to the known regimes of truth"; Marina Levina, Diem-My T. Bui, "Introduction: Toward a comprehensive monster theory in the 21st century," in *Monster Culture in 21st Century*, eds. Marina Levina, Diem-My T. Bui, 1–13, 7. One can read also an interesting discussion on the "monster theory," implemented with literary investigations in Pramod K. Nayar, *Posthumanism* (Cambridge: Polity Press, 2014).

16 As it has been noted, "it is the corporeal ambiguity and fluidity the troublesome lack of fixed definition, the refusal to be either one thing or the other, that marks the monstrous as a site of disruption"; Margrit Shildrick, "'You are there, like my skin': Reconfiguring Relational Economies," in *Thinking through the Skin*, eds. Sara Ahmed, Jackie Stacey (London: Routledge, 2001): 160–173, 160.

mutable son of an excess that continuously permutes, distorts, disfigures.[17] It enacts an ontological anxiety made flesh.[18]

From an *epistemological perspective*, the monster attacks the binary structure of the western *logos*, presenting itself as the trespasser between abstract and concrete, specific and universal.[19] It is the untold and the unspoken within the normativity of the discourse, haunting its margins with a simultaneously seductive and threatening force. Monstrosity issues an epistemic challenge.

From an *ethical point of view*, monsters are denouncing the inadequacy of the assumed frames of references; they are detecting their internal gaps and inconsistencies or even their insufficiency.[20]

All these arguments suggest putting the idea of monster in strict relation with the very idea of Law. The concept of monster comes to destabilise the grand narrative of Law; it performs its sacrificial profanation; it *abuses the norm*.

The monster appears as Law's catachresis.[21] In fact, in its specific declination this figure of speech, which comes where there is no longer a proper name

---

17 Donna Haraway has explored the promises bound to the dissolution of categories and boundaries; Donna Haraway, "The promises of Monsters: A Regenerative Politics for Inappropriate/d Others," in *Cultural Studies*, eds. Lawrence Grossberg, Cary Nelson, Paula A. Treichler (New York: Psychology Press, 1992), 295–337. Here we can find said that "to be inappropriate/d is not to fit in the taxon, to be dislocated from the available maps, specifying kinds of actors and kinds of narratives, not to be originally fixed by difference [...] Diffraction does not produce "the same" displaced, as reflection and refraction do. Diffraction is a mapping of interference, not of replication, reflection, a reproduction. A diffraction pattern does not map where differences appear, but rather maps where the effects of difference appears" (Haraway, "The Promises of Monsters," 300).
18 The expression reproduces the evocative title of Kevin A. Boon's chapter "Ontological Anxiety Made Flesh: The Zombie in Literature, Film and Culture," in *Monsters and Monstrous: Myths and Metaphors of Enduring Evil*, ed. Niall Scott (Amsterdam: Rodopi, 2007), 33–44.
19 Monsters produce a destabilizing change to the known regime of truth; "Monster ontology manifests the truth of the aberrant in order to affirm the shift of the "normal" from cultural, arbitrary category to an idealized natural phenomenon"; Patricia MacCormack, "Mucosal Monsters," in *Carnal Aesthetics: Transgressive Imagery and Feminist Politics*, eds. Bettina Papenburg, Marta Zarzycka (London: Tauris & Co. Ltd, London, 2013), 226–237, 231.
20 In a synthetic vision, apt to embrace ontological, epistemological and ethical arguments, Shildrick has noted that "the issue is one not only of contesting the epistemological and ontological boundaries of bodies of knowledge and bodies of matter, but of reconfiguring the ethics of relationship." Shildrick, "'You are there, like my skin': Reconfiguring Relational Economies," 161.
21 Patricia Parker's study is central for a precise and genealogical reconstruction of the meaning of the word and especially for the critical attempt at differentiating catachresis from metaphor; Patricia Parker, "Metaphor and Catachresis," in *The Ends of Rhetoric: History, Theory, Practice*, eds. John B. Bender, David E. Wellbery (Stanford: Stanford University Press, 1990): 60–73. The inquiry is rooted on Latin texts, and especially on Quintilian's and Cicero's works.

for a given idea, functions as a clear opening in language extending meanings against the common usage and producing new rules of exchange, new values. Once again, according to Derrida's thought, "catachresis concerns first the violent and forced, abusive inscription of a sign, the imposition of a sign upon a meaning which did not yet have its proper sign in language. So much so that there is no substitution here, no transport of proper signs, but rather the irruptive extension of a sign proper to an idea, meaning, deprived of their signifier. A secondary origin."[22] Like monsters with respect to things and beings, catachresis epitomises the system's defiance of the ontological primacy of sequentiality.[23] In this perspective, the concept of monster can be introduced as a potent device apt to dethrone the illusion of Law's ontological consistency and, conversely, to lay bare its substantial impurity. "*To monstrify*" the Law means to penetrate its deep and obscure abyss, disclosing its fictionality and abjection. It means to contest the metaphysics of the Law's presence, giving consistency to the disturbing and uncanny and bringing to the surface its fragility and radical indeterminacy. It finally exposes the Law to its inner violence and obscene dimension.

In this light, Patricia Parker reveals the intrinsic limits of Lanham's and Frye's understandings of catachresis. The first one is referring to catachresis as "an implied metaphor using words wrenched from common usage, an extravagant, unexpected, far-fetched metaphor, as when a weeping woman's eyes become Niagara Fall"; Richard A. Lanham, *Handlist of Rhetorical Terms* (Berkeley: University of California Press, 1968), 21. The second one proposes the idea of catachresis as an unexpected or violent metaphor; Northrop Frye, *Anatomy of Criticism: Four Essays* (Princeton: Princeton University Press, 1957), 281. Both these statements – Patricia Parker notes – are almost exclusively expressed in terms of "strained farfetched or mixed metaphor, with no mention whatsoever of the longstanding distinction on the basis of the presence or absence of an original proper term." Parker, "Metaphor and Catachresis," 61.

22 Jacques Derrida, *Margins of Philosophy* (Chicago: University of Chicago Press, 1982), 255.

23 According to the brilliant argument introduced by Lorraine Weir in Lorraine Weir, "From Catechism to Catachresis: Aspects of Joycean Pedagogy in Ulysses and Finnegans Wake," in *Coping with Joyce: Essays from the Copenhagen Symposium*, eds. Morris Beja, Shari Benstock (Columbus: Ohio State University Press, 1989), 220–231, 226. With a precise and complete explication, Lorraine Weir asserts that the figure of catachresis "serves to interrupt the relentlessness of inscription and enact the absence of name. […] Attempting to sustain the instant of transignification by intensifying the polyvalence of that operation, catachresis refuses to accede to the semantic demands of conversation and remains grounded in the iterability of the word and in its status within the logothetic economy of performative utterance. Analogous to Freudian dreamwork, catachresis synthesizes question and response, past and future, manifest and latent, catalyzing dichotomies into polyvalent units within the memory system." Weir, "From Catechism to Catachresis," 228.

According to the vision proposed in these pages, it becomes compelling to explore where we can pose the *monstrous exhibition* of Law and how we can perceive the troubling fascination provoked by its gothic choreographies.

In an original perspective, one could argumentatively maintain that the *process of monstrification* of Law enacts a battle between different systems of representation and is concretely figured out by the means of a clash, if not a collision, between contending bodies. Law is *presentified*, that is comes to be present into the world, in its tidy and polite aspect, rigging its complex and problematic nature, putting a well-ordered make up on its counter-face. Nevertheless, there is something that continues to lurk behind the outer appearance, Exception. Exception comes "*to monstrify*" the Law: it shows (*monstrat*), insofar as it pulls out the excluded ontology of Law of the crypt where it has been enshrouded; at the same time, it admonishes (*monet*), insofar as it represents a warning against the false belief into an immutable certainty and into a persevering benevolent inclination. What has been taken outside, now returns and claims for its re-membering.[24]

Western Law repeats the Monster's mystique, which affects biblical tradition, as it has been fraught with tensions and internal conflicts that stay at the very core of its conception of the world and of its creator God. In the pages of the Sacred Book, in fact, we can find a *model paradigm of fierce competition* between cosmogonic visions of a stable and good-oriented universe, in which God has dominated the monsters and sit enthroned over Chaos, and chaogonic visions of a world close to collapse, in which monsters live and flourish.[25] Exception is the exhibition of the formless counterpart of Law, the

---

24 Using this word in its proper primeval meaning, that is to give a new body to something, to restitute an ontological consistency, to reconstruct, to put together again. Even this term has theological roots and implication. Allen Verhey notes that 'in scripture memory is typically constitutive of identity and determinative of conduct'; Sarah Harmony affirms that "in the ancient scriptural sense it means to actually bring a person, thought, or event into the present time"; Allen Verhey, *Nature and Altering it* (Grand Rapids Michigan: Eerdmans Pub., 2010), 63–64; Allen Verhey, *Remembering Jesus: Christian Community, Scripture and the Moral Life* (Grand Rapids Michigan: Eerdmans Pub., 2002); Sarah Harmony, *Re-membering: The Ministry of Welcoming Alienated and Inactive Catholics* (Collegeville: The Liturgical Press, 1991), 10. For an inspiring work on the semantic stratification of the word "remember" across theology and literature, Regina Schwartz, *Remembering and Repeating: On Milton's Theology and Poetics* (Chicago: The University of Chicago Press, 1993).

25 For these suggestions, Timothy K. Beal, *Religion and its Monsters* (New York: Routledge, 2002), 89–90. In detail the Author, talking about biblical tradition, explains: "On the one hand it is confident in the stable, reasonable order of the cosmos, confident in our ability to articulate that order and live according to it, and confident in God as founder and guarantor of that order; on the other hand, it is haunted by monstrous forms of profound disjunction and

internal source of anomic anxiety. Given the relation entertained with the Law, that is one of inclusive exclusion,[26] exception is the *monstrous display* of an application realised through the medium of its proper withdrawing. Exception lives the same paradox which affects the ontology of monstrosity: like monster, exception can be properly defined by letting it emerge from the contentious struggle oriented to its neutralization, inclusion, or suppression within the normative order.[27] Like monster, exception is the surplus, the exclusion of which makes possible the constitution of a legal normativity; it belongs to the order in the form of its limit and at the same time it remains outside the order established, insofar as it is the sign of a difference that

---

disorder, shadowy revelations on the edge between creation and un-creation, cosmos and chaos, and haunted by working anxiety that God, like the world God created, is fraught with the same tensions" (Beal, *Religion and its Monsters*, 89).

26 This is the known definition proposed – in terms become paradigmatic – by Giorgio Agamben in his masterpiece, *Homo Sacer*. Claiming for a re-interpretation of the mechanism of exception, Agamben notes "the *exception* is what cannot be included in the whole of which it is a member and cannot be a member of the whole which is always already included. What emerges in this limit figure is the radical crisis of every possibility of clearly distinguishing between membership and inclusion, between what is outside and what is inside, between exception and rule"; Giorgio Agamben, *Homo Sacer: Sovereignty Power and Bare Life*, trans. Daniel Heller-Roazen, (Stanford: Stanford University Press, 1995), 25. With specific regard to the relationship Law and Exception, Agamben emphasizes: "The statement "The rule lives off the exception alone" must be taken to the letter. Law is made of nothing but what it manages to capture inside itself through the inclusive exclusion of the *exception*: it nourishes itself on this exception and is a dead letter without it." Agamben, *Homo Sacer*, 27. This idea of inclusive exclusion clearly overcomes every oppositional dialectics and ontologies. In a similar way Foucault disclosed an innovative idea of transgression: "Transgression [. . .] is not related to the limit as black to white, the prohibited to the lawful, the outside to the inside, or as the open area of a building to its enclosed spaces. Rather, their relationship takes the form of a spiral which no simple infraction can exhaust. Perhaps it is like a flash of lightening in the night which, from the beginning of time, gives a dense and black intensity to the night it denies, which lights up the night from the inside, from the top to the bottom, and yet owes to the dark the stark clarity of its manifestation, its harrowing and poised singularity; the flash loses itself in this space it marks with its sovereignty and becomes silent now that it has given a name to obscurity"; Michel Foucault, "Preface to transgression," in Michel Foucault, *Language, Counter-Memory, Practice: Selected Essays and Interviews*, trans. Donald F. Bouchard and S. Simon (Ithaca: Cornell University Press, 1977): 21–52, 35.

27 Jacques Derrida underlines: "But as soon as one perceives a monster in a monster, one begins to domesticate it, one begins, because of the "as such" – it is a monster *as* a monster – to compare it to the norms, to analyze it, consequently to master whatever could be terrifying in this figure of the monster. And the movement of accustoming oneself, but also of legitimation and consequently, of normalization, has already begun." Derrida, *Points Interviews. . .1974–1994*, 386.

cannot completely neutered. Monster and exception contest the morphological ordinariness. They both mark the camp of subversion, becoming outstanding sources of wonder and terror.

Opening a threshold of undecidability and indeterminacy, the monster brings Law at the edge of its abyssal provenance.[28]

It is not by chance that the words and concepts used by Giorgio Agamben (recalling J. Derrida's theories) to translate and explain the mutual interrelation between law and exception, life and politics are clearly modelled on the shape of a monstrous beast. Rediscovering the origins of the juridical order and the associated paradox of sovereignty, Agamben explores the centrality of the threshold where all the ontologies come back to their constitutive and archeological form of indistinction: law re-encouters exception; rule embraces anomy; order is slipping into disorder. In this liminal zone at the very origin of the political form, man is transgressed into the primeval beast and, correlatively, the primeval beast transcends into a human being. Within the state of exception, the lupization of man and the humanization of the wolf are inaugurated.[29] To transpose in image the concepts exposed above, it could be said that the Law is haunted by a Ligottian shadow, which is powerful and cogent, encrypted but always ready to re-emerge. With another, but in certain measure corresponding image, it could be evocatively affirmed that Law is obsessed by an internal energy like the one that animates the Shadow monster of the second season of the Netflix series "Stranger Things,"

---

28 In this respect it is unavoidable to recall Walter Benjamin's thought on the relationship between Law and Violence. Violence produces a monstrous threat against the Law, because it introduces at the very heart of the Law the same indistinction, uncertainty and vagueness which Law must tame in order to function (see Benjamin, *Critique of Violence*. Moving from Benjamin's arguments, Michel Foucault clarifies the reasons of the Law's anxiety towards monstrosity and abnormality: "It could be said that the monster's power and its capacity to create anxiety are due to the fact that it violates the law while leaving it with nothing to say. It traps the law while breaching it. When the monster violates the law by its very existence, it triggers the response of something quite different from the law itself. It provokes either violence, the will for pure and simple suppression, or medical care or pity. But the law itself does not respond to the attack on it represented by the monster's existence. One of the first ambiguities is that the monster is a breach of the law that automatically stands outside the law. The second is that monster is, so to speak, the spontaneous, brutal, but consequently natural form of the unnatural"; Michel Foucault, *Abnormal: Lectures at the Collège de France 1974–1975*, trans. G. Burchell (London: Verso, 2003), 56.

29 Agamben, *Homo Sacer*, 106: "This threshold, which is neither simple natural life nor social life but rather bare life or sacred life, is the always present and always operative presupposition of sovereignty."

a gigantic inter-dimensional entity that appears to be the architect of the Upside-Down ecosystem.[30]

Moreover, in consonant terms Derrida discloses the intellectual roots of a certain animalisation of the origin of Politics and Sovereignty, according to which the sovereign, at the same time source of the Law and above the Law, is the devouring beast that nurtures its body with the carnal consistency of its human flock. Even the literary register of the philosophical discourse is made Gothic by Derrida. The central passage of his discourse depicts the monstrous energy of sovereignty and the uncomfortable sensation it provokes in the following manner:

> I believe that this troubling resemblance, this worrying superposition of these two beings-outside-the law or without laws or above the laws that beast and sovereign both are when viewed from a certain angle – I believe that this resemblance explains and engenders a sort of hypnotic fascination or irresistible hallucination, which makes us see, project, perceive [...] the face of the beast under the features of the sovereign, or conversely if you prefer, it is though, through the maw of the unnamable beast, a figure of the sovereign were to appear. In the vertigo of this *unheimlich*, uncanny, hallucination, one would be as though prey to a haunting or rather the spectacle of a spectrality: haunting of the sovereign by the beast and the beast by the sovereign, the one inhabiting or housing the other, the one becoming the intimate host of the other, the animal becoming the hot (host and guest), the hostage too, of a sovereign of whom we also know that he can be very stupid without that at all affecting the all powerfulness ensured by his function or, if you like, by one of the king's two bodies.[31]

30 In an interdisciplinary perspective which reads Law through the symbolic figures proposed by contemporary fictions. For a discussion of the role played by monsters in the Series, Kevin J. Wetmore Jr., "Monsters and Moral Panics: Dungeons & Dragons as Force of Good in *Stranger Things*," in *Uncovering Stranger Things: Essays on the Eighties Nostalgia, Cynism and Innocence in the Series*, ed. Kevin J. Wetmore Jr. (Jefferson: McFarland & Co. Pub., 2018), 60–79, 60; Rose Butler, "Welcome to the Upside Down: Nostalgia and Cultural Fears in *Stranger Things*," in *Horror Television in the Age of Consumption: Binging on Fear*, eds. Linda Belau, Kimberly Jackson, (New York: Routledge, 2018), 187–201, 187. For the encounter between Law and Popular Culture, Richard Sherwin's work remains unsurpassed; Richard K. Sherwin, *When Law Goes Pop* (Chicago: University of Chicago Press, 2000).

31 Jacques Derrida, *The Beast and the Sovereign* (Chicago: University of Chicago Press, 2009), 39. In the following passage, Derrida writes: "In the metamorphing covering-over of the two figures, the beast and the sovereign, one therefore has a presentiment that a profound and essential copula is at work on this couple: it is like a coupling, an ontological, onto-zoo-anthropo-theologico-political copulation. The beast becomes the sovereign who becomes the beast; there is the beast and [*et*] the sovereign (conjunction) but also the beast is [*est*] the sovereign, the sovereign is [*est*] the beast." Derrida, *The Beast and the Sovereign*, 39.

If it is not contradicted in its potency, this appears to be the metamorphic transfiguration of Kantorowicz's image[32]: the sovereign is transmuted from the secular God's Mediator to the Beast's mystic personification.

The arguments discussed allow also to ponder over the haunting presence that leads to "the monstrification" of Thomas Hobbes' body of thought. The internal struggle between two pivotal writings is here taken into consideration: the one, momentous, tremendous and famous, *The Leviathan*; the other really overshadowed by the former, generally neglected even by philosophers and legal scholars, but not for this of minor importance. This second work is entitled *Behemoth and the Long Parliament* and makes use of the symbolical meaning associated to the figure of Behemoth, the monster creature introduced by biblical narrative in tandem with Leviathan.[33] According to the more scrupulous reconstruction, Hobbes probably began working on this manuscript in 1666 and it seems to be evidence that he was still working on it in 1668. The book was probably finished in 1669, if one would give credit to his autobiographical statement according to which he wrote the text when he was about eighty years old. In the last year of Hobbes' life, four operated editions were published and another followed in 1680; the first authorised version of *Behemoth* appeared posthumously, printed by William Crooke in 1682. The monograph is a wonderful dissertation conducted in a dialogical form between a master and his pupil, devoted to developing an analytical framework for discussing sedition, rebellion and the breakdown of authority. On this basis it is possibile to assert that even the majestic, composed and self-possessed body that dominates on the frontispiece of *Leviathan* comes to be subjected to a process of "otherification" into its counterpart:

---

32 The reference is obviously to the King's double nature genealogically assessed by Kantorowicz's seminal work; Ernst Kantorowicz, *The King's Two Bodies: A Study in Medieval Political Theology* (Princeton: Princeton University Press, 1957).

33 The edition consulted is Thomas Hobbes, *Behemoth or The Long Parliament* (Chicago: The University of Chicago Press, 1990). For a critical understanding of the work, Tomaž Mastnak ed., *Hobbes' Behemoth: Religion and Democracy* (Charlottesville: Inprint Academics, 2009). On the role of the monsters in Jewish eschatology, Hermann Gunkel, *Creation and Chaos in the Primeval Era and the Eschaton* [1895], Grand Rapids Michigan: Eerdmans Pub., 2006, 37 ff.; 202; Giorgio Agamben, *The Open: Man and Animal* (Stanford: Stanford University Press, 2002); John Day, *God's Conflict with the Dragon and the Sea: Echoes of a Canaanite Myth in the Old Testament* (Cambridge: Cambridge University Press, 1985). Clarifying the meaning of the title chosen for his work, Franz Neumann reminds us that "in the Jewish eschatology of Babylonian origin Behemoth and Leviathan designate two monsters, Behemoth ruling the land (the desert), Leviathan the sea, the first male, the second female. The land animals venerate Behemoth, the sea animals Leviathan, as their masters"; Franz Leopold Neumann, *Behemoth: The Structure and Practice of National Socialism* (London: Victor Gollanez, 1942), 5.

Leviathan is metamporphosed in Behemoth; one monster is subdued by the other. In Hebrew language, Behemoth is an intensive and feminine plural form of the name *běhēmâ*, meaning beast, ox and it is used in the collective significance of cattle; but in biblical text and especially in Job 40.15 (the text laying at the basis of Hobbes' arguments), all the grammatical forms related to Behemoth are masculine and singular.[34] Therefore, the figure evoked is that of a singular being of awesome dimensions and mythic proportions, something like the Beast of beasts; in biblical exegesis, the interpreters have been used to suggest the identification of Behemot with a great elephant. Behemoth is clearly complementing Leviathan: if the latter stands for ordered commonwealth and legitimate sovereignty, the first names civil discord, rebellion, revolution. A further fact is particularly interesting in this regard. In *Historia Ecclesiastica*, always written by Hobbes,[35] both the names Leviathan and Behemoth appear in conjunction: Leviathan is referred to the person of The King, of the Monarch (*Rex*), while Behemoth is used to represent the people (*populus*).[36] If at this time Hobbes poses the paradoxical and baroque coincidence between King and people (*Rex est populus*), taken up again and developed in the pages of *Leviathan*, in the last text (*Behemoth*) Hobbes proves how this theatrical artifice intrinsically contains the real possibility of transforming itself into a tragic, final act of diversion, dissolution, decomposition. The monstrous body of Behemoth, which attracts into unity the rebellious force of numerous subjects, comes to disfigure and to deform the body of Leviathan, whose scales comes to be flaked off and fall disconnected. The physique is mutilated; the faces of the single members are no longer deferentially turned towards the Sovereign image. The prosperous and peaceful realm makes place to the Kingdom of Darkness, to a confederacy of deceivers "that, to obtain dominion over men in this present world, endeavour by dark and erroneous doctrines to extinguish in them the light, both of nature and of the gospel, and so to disprepare them for the kingdom of God to come."[37]

34 B.F. Batto, *Behemoth*, in *Dictionary of Deities and Demons in the Bible*, eds. Karel van der Toorn, Bob Becking, Pieter Willem van der Horst (Leiden: Brill, 1999): 165–169.

35 The work is a iambic pentameter Latin poem of 2242 lines on the history of Church published posthumously in 1688; Patricia Springborg, "The Politics of Hobbes's *Historia Ecclesiastica*," in *Hobbes on Politics & Religion*, eds. Laurens van Apeldoorn, Robin Douglass (Oxford: Oxford University Press, 2018), 150–166; Jeffrey Collins, "Thomas Hobbes's Ecclesiastical History," in *The Oxford Handbook of Hobbes*, eds. Aloysius Martinich, K. Hoekstra (Oxford: Oxford University Press, 2016): 520–544.

36 "Leviathan naribus, Behemothque receperat hamum: Et Rex et Populus servus uterque fuit" (vv. 1229–1230); Thomas Hobbes, *Historia Ecclesiastica*, in Thomas Hobbes, *Opera Philosophica quae latine scripsit omnia*, ed. W. Molesworth (London: J. Bohn, 1839--1845), V: 341–408, 381.

37 Thomas Hobbes, *Leviathan* (Edwin Curley, ed.) (Indianapolis: Hackett Pub., 1994), 411.

Lastly, there is another meaning enclosed into the figure of Behemoth; Hobbes enjoyed creating ambiguity and tensions. In fact, if we turn to the text of the *Historia Ecclesiastica*, we find the two primeval monsters allied, battling together against a common enemy, the Papacy. At the end of the struggle, the Pope succeeded in taming them: "But now the Pope his end completely gains And leads the People, and their Prince, in Chains: Now vast Leviathan the Hook receives, And Behemoth his wounded Nostrils grieves: All gently own the Pope's Imperial Sway Where'r the Roman eagles wing their Way."[38] The image is astonishingly resembling the representation of the Antichrist seating on the body of Leviathan, as it has been considered by the *Liber Floridus*, the spiritual Encyclopedia compiled around 1120 by the monk Lambert of St. Omer.[39] Using the potential of this figurative communication, Hobbes's Papacy is represented as the usurper of the ancient Israel: Hobbes's play on the beasts of Job, as it has been critically argued, goes far beyond allegory and enters the realm of blasphemy. Attracted into a symbolic whirlpool, Law, Politics and Theology live through their abyssal shadows: Law is *monstrified* by Exception; the King is *monstrified* by the Pope; Christ is *monstrified* by the Antichrist.

An irreducible excess, an instable heterogeneity, a dense penumbra of transgression and resistance is protruding into the inner space where Law governs.

As Ligotti's character, Grossvogel reveals,

> everywhere I travelled I saw how the pervasive shadow, the all-moving darkness was using our world. Because this shadow, this darkness has nothing of its own, no way to exist except as an activating force or energy, whereas we have our bodies, we are only our bodies.
>
> This is why the shadow, the darkness uses our world for what it needs to thrive upon. This is why the shadow, the darkness causes things to be what they would not be and to do what they would not to do. Because without the shadow inside them, the all-moving blackness activating them, they would be only what they are – heaps of matter lacking any impulse, any urge to flourish, to succeed in this world.[40]

---

38 As quoted in Patricia Springborg, "Hobbes' Biblical Beasts: leviathan and Behemoth," in *Political Theory*, 23.2 (1995), 353--375, 363 from the text of the English translation of Hobbes's work, *A True Ecclesiastical History from Moses to Martin Luther* (London: printed by E. Curll, 1722), 97–98.

39 It is possible to consult the edition by Albert Derolez, *Lamberti S. Audomari Canonici Liber Floridus*, Codex Autographus Universitatis Gandavensis, Ghent, 1968. For a critical perspective on the allegorical iconography, Jessie Jean Poesch, *Antichrist Imagery in Anglo-French Apocalypse Manuscripts* (Ann Arbor (Michigan): UMI, Dissertation Services, 1966); Rosemary Muir Wright, *Art and Antichrist in Medieval Europe* (Manchester: Manchester University Press, 1995).

40 Ligotti, *The Shadow, The Darkness*, 263.

Svend Erik Larsen

Monsters and Human Solitude

1 Social or divine?

Monsters are not scary because they are composed of human, animal, and maybe technological fragments, and because their appearance seems unreal. More importantly and frighteningly, they are one of a kind – emblems of absolute solitude.[1] If they form families or societies we move into the world of proto-humans or aliens or, in other words, into another species within the natural order. Real monsters, however, do not belong to a species, each one of them constitutes its own kind. Hence, when monsters enter the human world they act as a sign of its limits and as an invitation (maybe a message from the gods or other non-human essences) to reflect on the limits of the human vis-à-vis a trans-human sphere, or on the limits of humans vis-à-vis other humans within a social or cultural sphere. As a sign of solitude, they open a fundamental question about *la condition humaine* that involves our identity as human beings and as social and cultural entities.[2]

In this paper my aim is to trace a historical development of this inquiry, first with a flashback, by beginning with the front page of the German magazine *Der Spiegel* February 15, 1999 which shows a whole-page photo of an airport, accompanied by a caption in mega-sized letters: "Monster – Frankfurt Main – Der unmögliche Flughafen" [Monster – Frankfurt Main –The impossible airport]. In one of the articles included in this issue, the journalist Thomas Tuma describes the airport in the following words "Der Frankfurter Airport ist zu einem *Sinnbild* deutschen *Zentralisierungswahns* verkommen: *ewiger* Baustellenlärm, kilometerlange Wege, Schilder-*Labyrinthe*. [...] Der *Moloch* am Main *erstickt an der eigenen Größe* – und will dennoch weiterwuchern. *Lufthansa umsorgt ihre Kunden wie ein Hühnerbaron ihre Legehennen.*"[3]

1 Svend Erik Larsen, "Into the Desert. Solitude in Culture and Literature," *Advanced Literary Studies* 1.3 (2013): 25–30 (http://www.scirp.org/journal/als/); Svend Erik Larsen, ""Alone, Without a Guide": Solitude as a Literary and Cultural Paradox," in *Cultures of Solitude*, eds. Ina Bergmann and Stefan Hippler (Frankfurt a.M.: Peter Lang): 45–60.

2 Arnold Davidson, "The Horror of Monsters," in *The Boundaries of Humanity*, eds. James Sheehan and Morton Sosna (Berkeley: University of California Press, 1991): 36–63.

3 *Der Spiegel*, February 15, 1999 [emphasis added]. "The Frankfurt Airport has become a symbol of German madness for centralization: perennial noise from constructions, endless corridors, labyrinths of signs. [...] The Moloch on Main is trapped by its own size – and will

https://doi.org/10.1515/9783110654615-003

The word "labyrinth" takes us back thousands of years to Theseus, the killer of a mythological monster, the Minotaur, who was hidden in a labyrinth. Yet later, Theseus himself is punished by a monster, as Eurypides tells in his tragedy *Hyppolitos* (428 BCE).[4] Caught by anger in his fatherly and manly vanity, Theseus believes the false rumours of an incestuous relation between Phaedra and his son (her step-son) Hyppolitos. Actually, Phaedra herself, deeply hurt by Hyppolitos' rejection of her advances, initiates the defamation of the young man. The outraged Theseus calls upon his father Poseidon to fulfill an earlier promise made to him to grant any of his wishes. Theseus has Hyppolitos killed by a sea monster, an amphibian bull crawling on the shore; the event represents a reversal of the story of the Minotaur who also was a bull-shaped monster emerged from the sea in Crete. It is a reversal, because Theseus, caught in his own history as a triumphant hero, actually suffers the most. He has forced a god to fulfill a promise on false grounds; this move is a fatal error, *hamartia,* that no human should ever commit. By his own wrongdoing, the devastated Theseus loses both his son and his wife. His self-defeating anger and vanity cause him to force the power of the gods; his *hubris* is shown even more by his placing his own power next to Poseidon's, as if he had reasons to doubt the will and capacity of the god to keep his promises. Theseus mutters to himself that if Poseidon does not do as I want, I will myself exile Hyppolitos.

What has happened between the two monstrous instances, the airport's social calamity and the sea-born fatality, indicates a move from monsters with a divine origin pointing to the power relation between gods and humans, to monsters with a social origin calling attention to the power relation between humans, their own inventions and social order. Nevertheless, the social evil still feeds on ancient mythology with its reference to Molochs and labyrinths, both of which are instances of a singular monstrosity, as well as to human errors as causes of monstrous appearances. In this sense, the modern version of monstrosity shares some basic features with the idea of the monstrous in Euripides and Greek culture in general.

Through the course of history, it is possible to trace similarities and differences between the monstrous in different historical contexts under four headings:[5]

---

nevertheless continue to grow. [...] Lufthansa takes care of its customers as the biggest egg producers of their hens." [My translation]

4 Euripides, *Alcestis, Hippolytus, Iphigenia in Tauris* (Harmondsworth: Penguin, 1972 [4th century BCE]). Cf. Ruth Padel, *In and Out of the Mind. Greek Images of the Tragic Self* (Princeton: Princeton University Press, 1992).

5 A historical cross-section is provided by Bernard Evslin, *Heroes, Gods and Monsters of the Greek Myths* (New York: Bantam, 1966); Claude Kappler, *Monstres, demons et merveilles à la fin*

1) the function of monsters
2) the ontology of monsters
3) the social status of monsters
4) the discursive status of monsters.

2 Dimensions of monstrosity

2.1 Function

Ancient or modern, before being a thing or a strange creature, a monster is first of all a *sign* connecting two ontologically different domains with different levels of power: an agency acting between humans and powerful gods or, as in the case of the airport, between humans or their non-human creations, materialized as social organizations and technological assets overpowering their human creators. The sign is sent by the powerful to the powerless to remind them of the limits of their strength. In other words, the monster is a sign of warning. "Monster" comes from the Latin "*monere*," meaning both "to show," and "to warn or to remind," or from the Greek "*teras*" (as in the term "teratology," meaning "monster studies"): they connote "marvel" or an awesome and awful appearance beyond the world of human experience, and thus carry a kind of message from the gods.

In Theseus's case, the monster is a particular type of sign with cosmic and metaphysical inferences. The amphibian bull who destroys Hyppolitos is a sign that refers *both* to its divine origin – Poseidon is the god of the sea – *and* to the monster-fighting hero himself. Indeed, the bull is the monster precisely associated with Theseus: Minotaur's father was himself a bull that came from the sea. In other words, the signs are not as arbitrary as structural linguists may think.

In addition, the airport becomes a monster because it is turned into a sign, *Sinnbild,* of what transgresses any standards of human comprehension and control; it hinders our capacity to orient ourselves and to move around as we please, and, ironically so, in a centre of transportation and communication. The monstrous lies in the fact that the optimal investment of human power, talent, and

---

du Moyen Age (Paris: Payot, 1980); Richard Bernheimer, *Wild Men in the Middle Ages* (New York: Octagon Books, 1979); Gérard Luciani, *Les monstres dans La Divine Comédie* (Paris: Lettres Modernes, 1975); Rudolf Wittkower, "Marvels of the East: A Study in the History of Monster," in *Allegory and the Migration of Symbols* (London: Thames and Hudson, 1977): 46–74; Alexander Porteus, *The Lore of the Forest* (New York: Cosimo Books, 2005 [1927]); Rosi Braidotti and Nina Lykke eds., *Between Monsters, Goddesses and Cyborgs* (London: Zed Books, 1996); Jeff Rovin, *The Encyclopedia of Monsters* (New York: Facts on File, 1989).

control to decide how to move in the world turns against itself, precisely at the point where it manifests itself in the most ingenious way – an airport. In both cases, the monster inhabits a limbo, a place between a non-human realm, whether divine or social, and the world of human life; in addition, it seems in the process of staking out its boundaries, and at the same time transcending them by reminding humans of the unrecognized or forgotten limits of their own abilities, precisely at the point where they stand out most clearly. Humans are reduced to "egg-producing hens" or pawns lost on the possible trail of a technological maze.

The sign acquires a general meaning beyond any subjective interpretation by being communicated to a larger public, for example through the press or in a tragedy. Monsters, being essentially one of a kind can still be different, and yet convey an identical message.

2.2 Ontology

As monstrous signs are not arbitrary, they also carry their own ontology beyond their status as signs. beyond their status as signs. Classical monsters possess a bodily appearance composed of elements from a variety of different species, for example the Sphinx, with its human head and animal paws, or the maritime bull in *Hyppolitos*, at the same a terrestrial and a marine being. In ancient lore, the order of nature, including the absolute separation between the species, was stable, fixed, and of divine origin. Therefore, only a god like Poseidon would have the power to mix the species and create a singular being, a marvel or a miracle beyond human power, hence a sign that some human beings have broken the order of nature and deviated from the place assigned to them. This is the case of incest, for example, or bestiality, or – worst of all – the *hubris* of unrestrained human self-indulgence that drives Theseus to catastrophe.

An essential part of the ancient theory of the four humours is precisely the ideal of a balanced self-restraint in order not to challenge the gods;[6] the ideal of the golden mean, as recommended by Aristotle and the Stoics, is broken by Theseus in a fit of rage, as well as by Phaedra with her transgressive incestuous love. However, humans are bound by fate to call forth monsters: alone among the species they have an irresistible urge, spurred by their cognitive and imaginary capacity, to search for a place to be other than the one they are born into and belong to. Furthermore, in a polytheistic universe they cannot help offending one god simply by being faithful to another one, as Hyppolitos is – he is adored by Aphrodite, but

6 Raymond Klibansky ed. *Saturn and Melancholy* (London: Nelson, 1964).

he worships the chaste Artemis. This way of thinking is the core of tragedy and underpins the idea of human life as driven by the tragic fatality of committing *hamartia* over and over again. Hence, humans themselves release the monsters that eventually kill them; monsters mirror the lonely position of humans in the order of nature as the only rebellious and thus self-destructive species, as isolated in the cosmos as the monsters themselves.

This cognitive pattern is repeated in labeling the Frankfurt Airport monstrous: as a human venture, the airport is self-destructive, going beyond what humans themselves can build, overgrowing the size of what they can control. Being unique in this respect, the airport becomes a wider symbol of humans managing their own power, giving themselves the occasion to reflect upon the limits of their own power. However, there are necessary intermediary historical steps to be taken before this analogy between the ancient and the modern world can be viable.

In the Middle Ages the devil took bodily form, while in the Gospels Satan is a disembodied voice, luring humans away from God.[7] Yet, the main source of monstrosity is the original sin, situated in humans themselves. In theology, the study of sin is called hamartiology, a term of classical pagan reminiscence from the Greek tragic notion of *hamartia*. Through the mythology of the fallen angel, Lucifer, the seductive and luring evil, takes on a 90% human shape, maybe with a horse's hoof or just a limp to cover the remaining 10%. Notwithstanding his protean diabolic ability to change shape across natural species, the devil is mainly represented as a human male, thus locating the most sinful and monstrous urges in women just waiting for an occasion to become witches or to be easy victims of the devil's tricks. The Catholic Church instituted the sacrament of confession to counteract the hereditary fatality of the original sin, but this measure did not change the concept of the root of the monstrous as internalized in humans.

Later, in the various branches of Protestantism, sin became the individual's guilt-ridden proclivity to cross the limits of right human behavior, which could be removed by God's mercy only on the day of the last judgment, without any possibility for humans doing anything to influence God's decision. Monstrosity became a human responsibility, and thus a social more than a religious issue, observed by God, but only judged at the end of time.

The 18th-century secular social thinking tried, alternatively, to suggest the innate human emotional capacity for empathy and sympathy as the foundation

---

7 Robert Muchembled, *Une histoire du diable* (Paris: Le Seuil, 2000); Robert Muchembled, *Diable!* (Paris: Le Seuil, 2002); Darren Oldridge, *The Devil* (Oxford: Oxford University Press, 2012). – Cf. Helmut Brall ed., *Von Sünde, Leidenschaft und Laster. Teufelgeschichten aus tausend Jahren* (München: dtv, 1998); Thomas Aquinas, *Summa Theologica. First Part of the Second Part* (http://newadvent.org/summa (Nov 24 2017), (1947–48 [1270]).

of law, governance, human rights, and social interaction in general, as a counter-poise to the emergence of monstrosity, in a sort of parallel to the outdated balance between the humours. This change of monstrosity from being inscribed in a divine cosmic order or in a theology of human sin and guilt to being part of a social anthropology paves the way for the monstrous as a social category, as in the case of the Frankfurt airport. Here, being one of a kind is no longer a marvel but a human construct, a permanent challenge to, or expansion of, human control over its social and natural environment.

2.3 Sociality

In early modernity, the reflection on the order of nature and the transgression of social or cultural conditions, driven by human innovation, began to take hold both as a social reorganization and as a transformation of natural processes into technological discoveries and their practical use. They were celebrated by the great French *Encyclopédie*, assembled from 1751 to 1772, before the French Revolution and industrialization opened the gates to a secular modernity.

Before this historical juncture, the reality of marvels and miracles had already been questioned: were they really the result of divinely created prodigies or of sinful behaviour? In one of his essays, *Un enfant monstrueux*, Michel de Montaigne relates that he once saw a monstrous creature, *un enfant monstrueux*, in a market place, a child with another child growing out of his belly. More probably, he had seen such an image in Ambroise Paré's *Des monstres et prodiges* (1573).[8] If not, there would have been a variety of other sources; all kinds of visual representations of monsters proliferated from Pliny's *naturalis historia* (1st century CE) via Medieval bestiaries to explorers' fanciful travelogues in the 16th century, not least featuring cannibals but also 'the noble savages'.[9] Faced with this apparently unexplainable monstrosity, Montaigne's claim is that the child may look as being one of a kind, but it would be more reasonable to think that similar cases could either

8 Michel de Montaigne, *Essais. Œuvres complètes* (Paris: Gallimard, 1962 [1580, 1591]); Ambroise Paré, *Des monstres et prodiges* (Paris: Gallimard, 2015 [1573]); Caius Plinius Secundus Caius, *Naturalis Historia* (London: Heinemann, 1961 [1st century CE]).

9 Dedra Hassig, *Medieval Bestiaries: Text, Image, Ideology* (Cambridge: Cambridge University Press, 1995); François Lestringant, *Le cannibal. Grandeur et décadence* (Paris: Perrin, 1994); Svend Erik Larsen, *Literature end the Experience of Globalization* (London: Bloomsbury, 2017): Ch. 5. – François Lestringant, *Mapping the Renaissance World* (London: Polity Press, 1991); Franco Moretti, *Signs Taken for Wonders* (London: Verso, 1997 [1983]); Hoxie Neal Fairchild, *The Noble Savage. A Study in Romantic Naturalism* (New York: Russell and Russell, 1961 [1927]).

exist in yet unknown parts of the world or might be found beyond the life span of any human being; yet both cases are perfectly within the order of nature.

Even Newton professed a similar view on how to understand apparent prodigies such as the *stella nova* observed by Tycho Brahe in 1578, which revealed that all stars are not fixed stars. Later, Francis Bacon, fascinated by the emerging sciences and technologies, in his *Novum Organon* (1628) suggested that humans would now be able to produce things which had never existed in nature, thus expanding the realm of human power and control.[10] This approach continued until the next century when systematic animal cross-breeding began in England in order to improve the production of meat.[11] First declared a heresy, it was implemented in France by the Société Européenne de Tératologie with the aim, among others, to produce useful and unique types of creatures, like legless hens that could just lay eggs all day long instead of running around.[12] Being one of a kind is a human construction, but it repeats the Greek notion of marvel, *teras*, and is reiterated in the article about the airport with its reference to industrialized egg production.

In her *Frankenstein* (1818), Mary Shelley discussed the consequences of this development. The living bio-mechanical monster, in a proto-human shape produced by Victor Frankenstein, longs to be really human after having observed the warmth of human family life. He acquires linguistic skills and, hence, self-reflection, which – in contrast to Shakespeare's cursing and scheming Caliban – he exploits in his meditation about compassion and morality. He then urges Victor to make him a companion in order to relieve him of his solitude. Otherwise, he will be as monstrous as when he was created, which is what eventually happens. His appeal to Frankenstein represents a complete reversal from a divine or religious origin to having a wholly secular and social nature:

> How can I move thee? Will no entreaties cause thee to turn a favourable eye upon thy creature, who implores thy goodness and compassion? Believe me, Frankenstein, I was benevolent; my soul glowed with love and humanity; but am I not alone, miserably alone? You, my creator, abhor me; [. . .] Yet it is in your power to recompense me, and deliver me from an evil which it only remains for you to make so great, that not only you and your family, but thousands of others, shall be swallowed up in the whirlwinds of its rage. [. . .] listen to me, and then, if you can, and if you will, destroy the work of your hands. [. . .] [13]

---

10 Peter Harrison, "Newtionian Science, Miracles, and the Laws of Nature," in *Journal of the History of Ideas* 56.4 (1995): 531-553; Francis Bacon, *Novum Organon* (Chicago: Open Court, 1994 [1628]).

11 Cf. Harriet Ritvo, *The Platypus and the Mermaid*. (Harvard: Harvard University Press, 1998).

12 Cf. Marie-Josèphe Wolff-Quenot, *Des monstres aux mythes* (Paris: Guy Trédaniel, 1996).

13 Mary Shelley, *Frankenstein or the Modern Prometheus*, in *Three Gothic Novels* (London: Penguin, 1968 [1818]), 364–365.

> You must create a female for me with whom I can live in the interchange of those sympathies necessary for my being. This you alone can do, and I demand it of you as a right which you must not refuse to concede.[14]

Here, the monstrous is neither a warning nor a haunting punishment, but an invitation to reflect upon the curse of human solitude, not only as a species or as a sinful being, but as a circumstantial factor, caused and created by society; it can be changed by social means, human inventiveness, and power. The sense of being one of a kind is now being identified as human solitude, which generates a social monstrosity as destructive as any catastrophe created by divine rage. It is opposed to compassionate human co-existence, guided by emotional self-reflection. Monstrosity has moved not only inside humans themselves, but into their social interaction as a mechanism of social exclusion.

2.4 Discourse

Monstrosity as a result of human behavior, as in the case of the airport, has an important discursive dimension which Frankenstein's monster makes clear: in contrast to classical monsters, he can understand his own monstrous nature through self-reflection. A surprising early instance of the role of discourse in the creation of the monstrous can be found in Jean Racine's *Phédre* (1677), a version of Euripides' tragedy *Hyppolitos*.[15] Here, the word "monster" is used as a rhetorical or discursive strategy to exclude persons from the social unit of Thesée's royal household. The word is used a total of thirteen times by the main characters with the aim of singling out somebody else as being one of a kind in the social sphere. The monster stands out as a phenomenon produced by humans in their mutual social interaction, yet in such a way that the possibility of social interaction is destroyed.

Phèdre in particular cleverly turns the term "monster" from something with an ontological foundation to an arbitrary rhetorical device. She tries to seduce Hippolyte by telling him that he does not need to have actually killed a monster for her to love him; she knows he would have performed such a heroic deed, had he had the occasion. Once this arbitrariness is established, the stage is set for new rhetorical constructs. Phèdre knows she is embarking on a dangerous

---

14 Shelley, *Frankenstein*, 412.

15 Jean Racine, *Phèdre* (Paris: Bordas, 1995 [1677]); Jean-Louis Barrault, (1946 [1994]). *Mise en scène de Phèdre de Racine* (Paris: Le Seuil, 1994 [1946]); Leo Spitzer, The "récit de Théramène," in *Linguistic and Literary History* (Princeton: Princeton University Press, 1967 [1948]): 87–134.

project and calls herself a monster because of her illicit but irresistible love. Hippolyte is not a philanderer, so Phèdre changes her tactics: she accuses him of being a monster because he arouses monstrous feelings in her without responding to them. Such a reaction to the object of her passion is more important than the actual character of the object itself.

The drama now opens the gates to a free outpouring of passionate relativism. Thésée begins to sense the uncanniness of a family whose members seem to escape him. He is reminded of his own reaction before the Minotaur – are they monsters afraid to appear in front of him? No answer. When the truly monstrous appears as an irrational fear or angst creating an uncanny and undefinable space separating himself from his loved ones, he has to confess he longs to face the real monsters. At that point, he sees Hippolyte as the real monster.

Once brought discursively into play, nobody can avoid being touched by the monstrous. Such arbitrary denomination with its fatal consequences lives its own uncontrollable, irascible, and inerasable life, leading Thésée to call upon Neptune's sea monster to kill Hippolyte.

But before that, Aricie, Hippolyte's gentle mistress, unexpectedly scorns Thésée, telling him that he has certainly killed numerous monsters, but he has left one. She does not specify what this monster is and, hence, the unidentifiable monster now returns to Thésée with a vengeance. He tries to guess what Aricie meant: is the monster Hippolyte, is it himself, is it the sea monster? – or is it, as it is revealed at the end, the whole fabric of lie, deceit, intrigue, and passion ruling their lives and triggering the fatal series of events? The monstrous is produced by the unavoidable angst people have about their identities and their passions, and therefore is itself unavoidable. The monstrous is a way of constructing identities that ultimately destroy characters. There is no monstrosity outside the human body or outside the human imaginary in securing one's own identity. Anything appearing as foreign is potentially something monstrous, even an airport.

3 Perspectives

In this context, the monstrous does not refer to a particular being or a particular natural process, but to a cultural course where everything beyond immediate comprehensibility and recognition may be constructed as monstrous and labeled as such. This projection permits us to separate ourselves from any perceived uncanny foreignness and thus to create a limit or a difference from it, which is crucial for our own identity, but which is not found within the realm of our own activities and experiences.

The narrator Miles Coverdale in Nathaniel Hawthorne's novel *The Blithedale Romance* (1852) reflects painfully on his own unintended complicity in such a process. He visits the utopian social experiment Blithedale and gradually discovers that the charismatic leader Hollingsworth is a demonic character who cynically manipulates the small community, rather than guiding it according to a utopian vision of high moral standards. He asks himself if, by his shaping the Blithedale story, he has also created the image of Hollingsworth as a monster in his own need to use a sharp contrast to the alleged utopianism of the project. He has thus deprived both of their true context in order to exploit them for his own construction of reality.

> If we take the freedom to put a friend under our microscope, we thereby insulate him from many of his true relations, magnify his peculiarities, inevitably tear him into parts, and, of course, patch him very clumsily together again. What wonder, then, should we be frightened by the aspect of a monster, which, as all, – though we can point to every feature of his deformity in the real personage, – may be said to have been created mainly by ourselves.[16]

This discursive mechanism is the foundation of present-day revivals of xenophobia and tribalism across the world. By labeling others as non-human or sub-human, we produce them as being one of a kind, isolated within our self-righteous community, while we seek for ourselves an identity as proper humans, which others are denied and left without hope of ever attaining.[17] The potential monstrosity resulting from this operation can be seen in numerous atrocities which have taken place across the globe. They should invite us to self-reflection: is the solitude of others, for which we are co-responsible and which potentially leads to the real monstrosity we have ourselves anticipated by excluding others, a necessary act for us to underpin our sense of identity and belonging? If the rule of law has any global importance today, it is to protect the right of all humans to be recognized and treated as humans; if literature has any importance today it is to enable us to imagine the life of others and our own life from precisely this perspective.

---

16 Nathaniel Hawthorne, *The Blithedale Romance, in The Complete Novels and Selected Tales of Nathaniel Hawthorne* (New York: The Modern Library, 1937 [1852]): 437–585, 479.

17 Rüdiger Safranski, *Das Böse oder das Drama der Freiheit* (Frankfurt a.M.: Fischer, 1999 [1997]); Kirsten Breitenfellner & Charlotte Kohn-Levy eds, *Wie ein Monster entsteht* (Bodenheim: Philo, 1998); Tzvetan Todorov, *Mémoire du mal. Tentation du bien. Enquête sur le siècle* (Paris: Robert Laffont, 2000); Stanley Hoffmann, *Une morale pour les monstres froids. Pour une éthique des relations internationales* (Paris: Le Seuil, 1982). – Also the Greeks knew of this mechanism: Edith Hall, *Inventing the Barbarian. Greek Self-Definition through Tragedy* (Oxford: Clarendon, 1989).

Carlo Pelloso

Sew It up in the Sack and Merge It into Running Waters! *Parricidium* and Monstrosity in Roman Law

1 Cicero's "pro Sexto Roscio Amerino" and the crime of parricide

In his speech *pro Sexto Roscio Amerino* a young and obscure lawyer named Marcus Tullius Cicero reported how in 81 BC Sextus Roscius's relatives had killed the old Roman citizen and cast him into the waters of the Tiber. Then, according to Cicero again, they had tried to seize his estate and to shield themselves by accusing Sextus's son of parricide.[1] The lawyer was persuaded that his client, whose name was Sextus Roscius Amerinus, had been charged with this heinous and ignominious crime with no grounds.[2] So, in his vigorous defence, he addresses the court with the following questions:

> The prosecutor assumes that my client has killed his father. But what kind of human being is he? Is he a young and corrupt man? Has he been induced to kill by criminals? No, he is more than forty years old. Did he kill because of foolish revelry, or as a consequence of his incredibly enormous debts? No, he did not. He has been acquitted of the

1 See, e.g., J. Duncan Cloud, "*Parricidium*, from the *Lex Numae* to the *Lex Pompeia de Parricidiis*," *Zeitschrift der Savigny-Stiftung für Rechtsgeschichte Romanistische Abteilung* 88 (1971): 1–66; Max Radin, "The *Lex Pompeia* and the *Poena Cullei*," *Journal of Roman Studies* 10 (1920): 119–130; Dominique Briquel, "Sur le mode d'exécution en cas de parricide et en cas de *perduellio*," *Mélanges d'Archéologie et d'Histoire de l'école Française de Rome, Antiquité* 92 (1980): 87–107; Yan P. Thomas, "*Parricidium*, I, Le Père, la famille et la cité," *Mélanges d'Archéologie et d'Histoire de l'école Française de Rome, Antiquité* 93 (1981): 643–715; André Magdelain, "*Paricidas*," in *Du châtiment dans la cité. Supplices corporels et peine de mort dans le monde antique* (Rome: École française de Rome, 1984): 549–571; Olivia F. Robinson, *The Criminal Law of Ancient Rome* (Baltimore: Johns Hopkins University, 1995), 13, 45–6, 67; Richard A. Bauman, *Crime and Punishment in Ancient Rome* (London: Routledge, 1996), 30–2, 70–4, 128–9; Bernardo Santalucia, *Diritto e processo penale nell'antica Roma* (Milano: Giuffré, 1998); Eva Cantarella, *I supplizi capitali* (Milano: Rizzoli, 2011), 264–285; Filippo Carlà-Uhink, "Murder Among Relatives. Intrafamilial Violence in Ancient Rome and Its Regulation," *Journal of Ancient History* 5.1 (2017): 26–65; Barbara Biscotti "What Kind of Monster or Beast Are You? Parricide and Patricide in Roman Law and Society," in *Parricide and Violence Against Parents throughout History. World Histories of Crime, Culture and Violence*, eds. Marianna Muravyeva and Raisa Maria Toivo (London: Palgrave Macmillan, 2018): 13–33.

2 *Rosc. Am.* 70–72; see, moreover, *Orat.* 107.

https://doi.org/10.1515/9783110654615-004

> accusation of revelry thanks to Erucius, who testified that he hardly ever took part at a banquet. As far as debts are concerned, he never incurred one. Furthermore, what wantonness could exist in that man who has always lived in the country cultivating his land, as the prosecutor himself did refer. This is a way of living which is far from greed, and linked to virtue. What moved Sextus Roscius to such insanity? One might say that he did not like his father. He did not like his father? But why? Here, a right, significative, and notorious reason must be demonstrated. As it is unbelievable that a son gives death to his own father without the most numerous and substantial reasons; it sounds equally unlikely, that a son is hated by his father without many and important and necessary causes. [. . .] Had he, perhaps, other possible motives? You, the accuser, argue: "His father wanted to disinherit him!" I hear you: now your argument may have a bearing on the present issue. [. . .] Even if you need mention and enumerate all the reasons, I do not ask you to disclose them. I ask you just that: how do you know it?[3]

Cicero rejects any accusation against Roscius either as weak or inconsistent, or as unlikely, if not even unfounded. He knows very well that luxury and debts, alongside the desire of inheriting, are commonly considered the most plausible reasons for perpetrating parricide. Thus, he pragmatically denies that his client had any economical interest in murdering his father[4]; but,

---

3 *Rosc. Am.* 39–40, 51–52: *patrem occidit Sex. Roscius. qui homo? adulescentulus corruptus et ab hominibus nequam inductus? annos natus maior quadraginta. vetus videlicet sicarius, homo audax et saepe in caede versatus. at hoc ab accusatore ne dici quidem audistis. luxuries igitur hominem nimirum et aeris alieni magnitudo et indomitae animi cupiditates ad hoc scelus impulerunt. de luxuria purgavit Erucius, cum dixit hunc ne in convivio quidem ullo fere interfuisse. nihil autem umquam debuit. cupiditates porro quae possunt esse in eo qui, ut ipse accusator obiecit, ruri semper habitarit et in agro colendo vixerit? quae vita maxime disiuncta a cupiditate et cum officio coniuncta est. quae res igitur tantum istum furorem sex. Roscio obiecit? "patri" inquit "non placebat." patri non placebat? quam ob causam? necesse est enim eam quoque iustam et magnam et perspicuam fuisse. nam ut illud incredibile est, mortem oblatam esse patri a filio sine plurimis et maximis causis, sic hoc veri simile non est, odio fuisse parenti filium sine causis multis et magnis et necessariis [. . .] numquid est aliud? "immo vero" inquit "est; nam istum exheredare in animo habebat." audio; nunc dicis aliquid quod ad rem pertineat; [. . .] Mitto quaerere qua de causa; quaero qui scias; tametsi te dicere atque enumerare causas omnis oportebat.* Cf. *Rosc. Am.* 58; 75. My translation.

4 In Roman declamation, the son that has committed parricide, or that is suspected to, is usually portrayed as a greedy and indebted man that intends to take his father's place in advance and to control, manage and use the family estate: the stereotype that emerged from Plautus and Terence seems to be unchanged: see Maria Vittoria Bramante, "*Patres, filii* e *filiae* nelle commedie di Plauto. Note sul diritto nel teatro," in *Diritto e teatro in Grecia e a Roma*, eds. Eva Cantarella and Lorenzo Gagliardi (Milano: Led, 2007): 95–116. The accusation of *cupiditas* in terms of motivation for the crime is well attested: see Ps.Quint. *Decl. maior.* 17.10.5; *Decl. min.* 281.6 and 377.4; Quint. *Inst. Or.* 4.2.73; Sen. *Contr.* 6.1.1; Ps.Quint. *Decl. maior.* 2.10.5; 2.3; 2.5.5; 1.6.8; Emporius, p. 566, 26–28 (Halm). As for the *captatio hereditatis*, see Ps.Quint. *Decl. min.* 258.9; 281; 377; Quint. *Decl. maior.* 17; Quint. *Inst. Or.* 4.2.72–74; Sen. *Contr.* 6.1. The so-called *senatus consultum Macedonianum* (D. 14.6.1, pr., 14.6.1.3, 14.6.3.3 Ulp. 29 *ad edictum*) gives further support to this view: in order

first of all, although rhetorically and hyperbolically, he emphasises that his client, the defendant in a parricide case, is a *homo*, using a Latin word that means any 'very human being', despite gender, social class, or legal status. This remark, as it will be later underlined, is not a superfluous one for the purpose of this paper. The term *homo* effectively and sophistically underpins a subtle implication, an unspoken antithesis between what is human and what is not.

As a matter of fact, this Ciceronian speech turns out to be an interesting source, at first since it explains some of the most common and despicable reasons that might lead a son to the perpetration of one of the most outrageous wrongdoings contemplated in Roman law, that is a crime consisting in killing the highest authority of Roman family (and, more importantly, the only one entitled to kill a member of it, according to the law)[5] for mere economic reasons,

---

to limit the increasing number of patricides (Suet. *Vesp.* 11) and to face the specific crime committed by Macedo, the Senate, on a proposal by Vespasian, provided that, if a *mutuum* to a *filius* was completed, the creditor could not bring any legal action to recover his loss. According to Theophilus's version (Paraphrase 4.7.7), Macedo, still under his father's *potestas*, had borrowed some money. Anyway, the creditor started pressing him harder and harder. Macedo, unable to find the money, killed his father to inherit his wealth and, thus, repay the debt. Justinian makes it clear that the Senatorial provision concerned only monetary loans since moneyborrowers were inclined to kill their parents and moneylenders were seen as instigators of parricide and other wrongdoings such as theft, forgery, and murder (Institutiones 4.7.7). See Francesco Lucrezi, *"Senatusconsultum Macedonianum"* (Napoli: Edizioni Scientifiche Italiane, 1992), 144, 211; Sara Longo, *"Senatusconsultum Macedonianum": interpretazione e applicazione da Vespasiano a Giustiniano* (Torino: Giappichelli, 2012), 11–19, nt. 32.

5 According to the traditional view on Roman family, the atrocious character of *parricidium* (meaning, *stricto sensu*, patricide), without a doubt, was due to the role played by *patres familiarum*: they were indeed granted an all-encompassing authority, so that the main – if not unique - difference between *filii* and slaves would be, for many centuries, the following: "when the father died, the slaves continued to be slaves, belonging to a new *dominus*, while sons and daughters became *sui iuris*, that is acquired the legal capacity" (Eva Cantarella, "Fathers and Sons in Rome," *The Classical World* 96.3 [2003]: 281–298, 283). Due to such absolute paternal mastery that covered even adult *filii*, the death of the father would represent the end of a kind of slavery, according to Veyne; moreover, from a psychological perspective, adult Roman males would be in such an unbearable situation, that they would be obsessed with parricide, and the fear of "parenticide" would bring about an authentic "national neurosis": Paul Veyne, *La vie privée dans l'Empire romain*, in *Histoire de la vie privée. De l'Empire romain à l'an mil*, eds. Philip Ariès and George Duby, 1 (Paris: Seuil, 1999, now in a separate volume, Paris: Seuil, 2015): *passim*; Paul Veyne, "La famille et l'amour sous le Haut-Empire romain," *Annales. Économies, Sociétés, Civilisations* 33 (1978): 35–63, 36. Veyne's view is shared by Yan Thomas, "Fathers as Citizens of Rome, Rome as City of Fathers (2nd century BC – 2nd century AD)," in *A History of the Family*, eds. A. Burguiere et al., 1 (Cambridge, Mass.: Polity, 1996): 228–269. Among the supporters of the idea of arcahic and classical Roman family as a

like debts, economic disability, uncertainty concerning one's future. At the same time and from a highly irrational yet highly impressive perspective, it is also important since it discusses at length the atrocious character of the crime at issue, as well as the legal-religious tradition and justification of the exotic and cruel method of punishment linked to it.

---

community being subject to a kind of "paternal tyranny," see the following authors (although their work deals with this topic from different perspectives and with different results): Theodor Mommsen, *Römisches Strafrecht* (Leipzig: Duncker & Humblot, 1899), 17, 20; Max Kaser, "Der Inhalt der *patria potestas*," *Zeitschrift der Savigny-Stiftung für Rechtsgeschichte Romanistische Abteilung* 83 (1971): 62–87, 62; David Daube, *Roman Law. Linguistic, Social and Philosophical Aspects* (Edinburgh: Edinburgh U.P., 1969), 87–88; cf., also, Eva Cantarella, "Persone, famiglia e parentela," in *Diritto privato romano. Un profilo storico*^{2}, ed. Aldo Schiavone (Torino: Einaudi, 2010): 157–211. This view is grounded on two main sources. On the one hand, Dionysius of Halicarnassus lists the powers granted by Romulus to the *pater familias* towards his sons: for instance, to imprison them, flog them, keep them working in the country, sell them, and kill them (Dion. Hal. 1.26.4). On the other hand, Gaius writes that Roman people recognised to fathers a virtually unlimited authority over their offspring that was greater than anywhere else (Gai 1.52); see, moreover, Cic. *dom.* 77; Sen. *Ben.* 3.23.3; Gell. 5.19.9. A variety of concrete examples occurs: the first consul Brutus killed his sons for conspiring with the *Tarquinii*, while the other conspirators were publicly executed (Plut. *Publ.* 3–7; Zon. 7.12; Dion. Hal. 5.8–13; *contra* Liv. 2.5.5–8; Val. Max. 5.8.1); Spurius Cassius's father summoned a council of relatives and friends and condemned his son to death (Val. Max. 5.8.2; *contra* Liv. 2.41.10–12); Aulus Fulvius killed his son in 63 BCE for joining Catiline's conspiracy (Sall. *Cat.* 39.5; Val. Max. 5.8.5; Dio 37.36.4); according to Cicero, Clodius's father had the right to kill his son, since he had committed crimes against Rome (Cic. *dom.* 84); see William V. Harris, "The Roman Father's Power of Life and Death," in *Studies in Roman Law in Memory of A. Arthur Schiller*, eds. Roger S. Bagnall and William V. Harris (Leiden: Brill, 1986): 81–95, 82–87; Judy E. Gaughan, *Murder Was not a Crime. Homicide and Power in the Roman Republic* (Austin: University of Texas P., 2010), 23–52; Carlà-Uhink, "Murder Among Relatives," 26–65. As for the so-called *iudicium domesticum* (an institution that also represented a guarantee aiming at preventing accusations of abuses of paternal powers), see Edoardo Volterra, "Il preteso tribunale domestico in diritto romano," *Rivista Italiana per le Scienze Giuridiche* 85 (1948): 103–155, now in *Scritti giuridici* 2 (Naples: Jovene, 1991): 127–177; Antonio Ruggiero, "Nuove riflessioni in tema di tribunale domestico," in *Sodalitas. Scritti in onore di A. Guarino* 4 (Naples: Jovene, 1984): 1593–1600; Yan Thomas, "Remarques sur la jurisdiction domestique à Rome," in *Parenté et strategies familiales dans l'antiquité romaine*, eds. Jean Andreau and Hinnerk Bruhns (Rome: Ecole Française de Rome, 1990): 449–474; Alberto Ramon, "Repressione domestica e persecuzione cittadina degli illeciti commessi da donne e *filii familias*," in *Il giudice privato nel processo civile romano. Omaggio ad Alberto Burdese*, ed. Luigi Garofalo, 3 (Padova: Cedam, 2015): 617–678.

2 *Parricidium*: the worst crime of all

Limiting the semantic sphere of the term *parricidium* to its recent concept of voluntary murder of either a father, or a relative[6] (and regardless of its supposed

6 From an etymological point of view, ancient authors do not share the same beliefs. On the one hand, Priscian. *inst.* 2.2524–26, 2.177.18–24 (Keil) doubtfully suggests a derivation from *par* ("peer") or, alternatively, from *pater*, or from *parens* (cf., supporting the first derivation, Isid. *orig.* 10.225, whereas in another work, i.e. *diff.* 1.432, the bishop suggests the following difference between *parricida* and *paricida*: *parricidam dicimus qui occidit parentem, paricidam qui socium atque parem*; similiarly, Lyd. 1.26 connects two semantic areas to the same noun, depending on the quantity of the first 'a' : *parricida* would stand for both 'person who kills relatives-*pārentes*' and 'person who kills subjects-*pārentes*'); on the other hand, Quint. *Inst. Or.* 8.6.35 maintains that the term meant the murder of brothers and mothers exclusively out of catachresis (Donat. 4.400.1–2 Keil; Caris. 1.273.3–4 Keil; Diomedes 1.458.5–6 Keil; Serv. 4.430.5–5 Keil; Pomp. 5.306.14–18 Keil; see, moreover, Cicero, who, in *Rosc. Am.* 70, *Mil.* 7.17, *Phil.* 3.7.18, *Tusc.* 5.2.6, confirms the supposed relationship between the terms "parricide" and *pater* as *parens*). See, on this topic, Cloud, "*Parricidium*," 7–12 (who believes that Numa intended "to assimilate the murderer of a Roman citizen to the murder of a kinsman with a view to regulating or abolishing vendetta"), and Thomas, "*Parricidium*," 660–683 (who holds that the term *parricidium* originally stood for "killing the father," and that the *lex Numae*, amounting to a forgery, was pointless). On the contrary, Pomp. (*Comm. artis Donati*: Keil, *Grammatici Latini*, V, 306.14–23) relates how *apud maiores* this word had the semantic value later attributed to *homicidium*: see Mommsen, *Römisches Strafrecht*, 613, and nt. 2. Likewise, *quaestores parricidii* were magistrates responsible for inquiring into the killing of a *homo liber*, and, above all, on the *mens rea* of the killer (probably, as regards their beginnings, they were even allowed to give final judgments on the behalf of the king; explicitly, see Tac. *ann.* 11.22.4; D. 1.13.1 pr.; Lyd. *mag.* 1.24; implicitly, Zon. 7.13; Varr. *l.L.* 5.81; Paul.–Fest. *verb. sign.* s.v. *parrici<di> quaestores* [Lindsay 247]; *contra*, see Plut. *Publ.* 12.3 and D. 1.2.2.22–23, where the *quaestores* are considered only a republican institution; on a possible harmonisation of the two views, see Luigi Garofalo, *Appunti sul diritto criminale nella Roma monarchica e repubblicana* (Padova: Cedam, 1997), 71–86; see, moreover, Roberto Fiori, *Homo sacer. Dinamica politico-costituzionale di una sanzione giuridico-religiosa* (Napoli: Jovene, 1996), 387–388; Vera Dementyeva, "The Functions of the Quaestors of Archaic Rome in Criminal Justice," *Diritto@Storia* 8 (2009): online; Piotr Kołodko, "The Genesis of the Quaestorship in the Ancient Rome. Some Remarks," *Legal Roots* 3 (2014): 269–280. This clearly implies that, as concerns the legal phrase at issue (i.e. *quaestores parricidii*), it includes the term *parricidium* as covering any form of murder: as Festus makes it clear, by pointing out that *parricida non utique is, qui parentem occidisset, dicebatur, sed qualemcumque hominem indemnatum* ("the term parricide, or rather patricide, was not used to mean anyone who kills his/her own father, but anyone who kills a person not condemned yet"), after reporting the *lex Numae* herself ("*Si qui hominem liberum dolo sciens morti duit, paricidas esto*" / "If anyone intentionally kills a free human being, *paricidas esto*"). This view is shared by Plutarch himself (*Rom.* 22.4: πᾶσαν ἀνδροφονίαν πατροκτονίαν προσειπεῖν), who assumes that the term parricide, or rather patricide, originally referred to "any killing of a man" (see, moreover, Pomp. 5.306.18–23 Keil).

links to the monarchical legal regulation of "generic murder committed with wrongful intent" which included the imperative formula *paricidas esto*),[7] as of

7 On this problem, alongside Magdelain, "*Paricidas*," 549–561, see the recent account provided by Biscotti, "What Kind of Monster or Beast Are You?," 14 (who, *pace* Thomas and Cloud, believes that "the term [. . .] is deployed for the first time in the form '*paricidas*' in the royal law attributed to Numa Pompilius," and that "it could not originally mean the killing of a father committed by the offspring"); similarly, according to Carlà-Uhink, "Murder Among Relatives," 35, "it is clear that its first meaning is that of 'generic' (voluntary) murder; only later was it connected with murders committed against relatives." Letting Thomas's thesis apart, these two opposite views (Cloud vs. Magdelain) share a common feature: the idea that *paricidas* and *parricidium* are etymologically linked and that between the 3rd and the 2nd century BC the word *parricidium* started indicating any voluntary murder of a relative, while *homicidium* started covering the original semantic sphere of the former. This theory, supporting a linear development from *paricidas* to *parricidium*, is, to some extent, unconvincing. At first, it is undoubted that *paricidas esto* represents, in the *lex Numae*, the legal consequence (if not a proper penalty) contemplated if the murder of a *homo liber* is perpetrated (that is the formula at issue would concern procedure or, anyway, secondary rules); on the contrary, *parricidium* never relates to consequences or penalties, being the legal label of a crime (that is this noun would concern substance or primary rules). Unsurprisingly this divergence, as well as the supposed shift from one level to the other, remains totally unexplained. Secondly, these two interpretations (assuming that *paricidas esto* either covers the concept of "person assimilated to the murderer of a kinsman," or tautologically means "anyone who kills a *homo liber*") fail to consider alternative ideas about the original meaning of the term *paricidas*. For instance, if one conceived of *Paricidas esto* as a short form for *paricidatus esto*, this phrase would allude to the authorisation of private vengeance or to the punishment accomplished by the *civitas*: Fernand de Visscher, "La formule *paricidas esto* et les origines de la jurisdiction criminelle à Rome," *Bulletins de l'Académie Royale de Belgique. Classe de Lettres et des Sciences Morales et Politiques* 13 (1927): 298–332; Ugo Coli, "*Paricidas esto*," in *Studi in onore di U.E. Paoli* (Firenze: Le Monnier, 1956): 171–194; Franco Cordero, *Riti e sapienza del diritto* (Roma, Bari: Laterza, 1981) 61 and nt. 2; see, for similar results, Cantarella, *I supplizi capitali*, 314–315; Bernardo Santalucia, *Diritto e processo penale*, 17 nt. 32. If one thought of it as referring to a specific archaic *status personae*, neither punishment by death, nor murder of kinsmen would be implied: Marco Falcon, "*Paricidas esto*. Alle origini della persecuzione dell'omicidio," in *Sacertà e repressione criminale in Roma arcaica*, ed. Luigi Garofalo (Neaples: Jovene, 2013): 191–274; Aldo Prosdocimi, *Forme di lingua e contenuti istituzionali nella Roma delle origini* 1 (Napoli: Jovene, 2017), 171–211. Therefore, in both cases, a direct connection between *paricidas* and *parricidium*, grounded on etymology and legal history, would be missing. A link between the *lex Numae* and the more recent *parricidium* could be supported by suggesting a linguistic connection between *paricidas* and *pera*, that is *culleus*: accordingly, *poena cullei* would be originally inflicted to any murder of any free person, while only later it would be related to the murder of a parent or a close relative (this being the same conclusion pointed out by Cloud): see Philippe Meylan, *L'étymologie du mot parricide à travers la formule "Paricidas esto" de la loi romaine* (Lausanne: Rouge, 1928); Salvatore Tondo, *"Leges regiae" e "Paricidas"* (Firenze: Olschki, 1973), 170–174. These remarks make it plausible that, in spite of their linguistic similarity (what led ancient writers to etymological misinterpretations of the term *parricidium* as meaning generic and voluntary murder), *paricidas* is not bound to *parricidium*, and that no actual development or shift occurred in the mid-Republic (Coli,

the mid-Republic onwards, the Romans never ceased to think of it as "the worst crime of all."[8]

To the Romans, indeed, *parricidium* amounted to a criminal offence whose inherent severity and whose societal danger were unparalleled, since it was not a mere infringement of human rules, but it violated the natural order and implied a non-human bravery in the culprit. Cicero himself strongly supports this belief, at first by relating the exemplary case of Titus Caelius of Terracina, occurred a few years before the murder of Sextus Roscius. This noble man had gone to bed in the same room as his two adult sons, and in the morning was found dead with his throat cut. The two Caelii brothers were therefore charged with parricide. Yet, since the young men had been discovered asleep when the door was opened, they had to be acquitted: Cicero makes it clear that parricide is such an atrocious, impious, and horrendous crime that no one, after violating all human and divine rules, would be able to sleep. As stated by the judges themselves, those who committed such an offence could neither rest without anxiety nor breathe without terror: on account of this, the Caelii brothers were declared innocent.[9]

"*Paricidas esto*," 171–194). The latter, or better its *nomen actionis parricida*, is a more recent linguistic form (appearing in Plaut. *Pseud.* 362 and in *Rud.* 651 as "one who kills one's own father and mother"), likely used as a synonym for the less common term *parenticida* that Plautus, at the end of the 3rd century BC, already connected with the *culleus* (Plaut. *Epid.* 349–351): Cantarella, *I supplizi capitali*, 277. See, *contra*, Marco Mancini, "Una premessa filologico-linguistica all'etimologia di Lat. *paricidas*," in *Ce qui nous est donné, ce sont les langues. Studi linguistici in onore di Maria Pia Marchese*, edited by Monica Ballerini, Francesca Murano, Letizia Vezzosi (Alessandria: Edizioni dell'orso, 2017): 49–78, who believes that the linguistic sign *paricidas* represented neither a mere *hapax* nor a graphic archaism, as Prosdocimi maintains, it being, on the contrary, an ancient allotrope of *parricida*.

8 *Rosc. Am.* 37: *scelestum, di immortales, ac nefarium facinus*; Sen. *Clem.* 1.23: *nefas ultimum*; Sen. *Contr.* 7. 1. 22: *ad expiandum scelus triumviris opus est, comitio, carnifice. tanti sceleris non magis privatum potest esse supplicium quam iudicium*; Ps.Quint. *Decl. min.* 299 e 373.1–2: *antequam parricidium inertiam obicio … patrem captum deseruisti: maximum crimen, immo parricidium. quantum in te fuit, occisus sum, et gravissimis quidem tormentis*; Ps.Quint. *Decl. maior.* 1.10: *Occidit ergo aliquis patrem et novercae pepercit? Maximum omnium nefas fortiter fecit, minori sceleri statim par non fuit? Omnia humana sacra confudit, violare non ausus est pectus odiosum? Incredibile est, sine fide est non occidere novercam cui inputes quod patrem occidat.* Parricide at times represents the apex of a list of increasingly serious crimes: see Ps.Quint. *Decl. maior.* 1.6.2. See, on the crime, Eva Maria Lassen, "The Ultimate Crime. *parricidium* and the Concept of Family in the Late Roman Republic and Early Empire," *Classica et Mediaevalia* 43 (1992): 147–161.

9 *Rosc. Am.* 64: *Non ita multis ante annis aiunt T. Caelium quendam Terracinensem, hominem non obscurum, cum cenatus cubitum in idem conclave cum duobus adulescentibus filiis isset, inventum esse mane iugulatum. Cum neque servus quisquam reperiretur neque liber ad quem ea suspicio pertineret, id aetatis autem duo filii propter cubantes ne sensisse quidem se dicerent, nomina filiorum de parricidio delata sunt quid poterat tam esse suspiciosum? neutrumne*

If we rely on Cicero, to the Romans parricide evoked an unspeakable and ancestral dread and apprehension; it represented the most repugnant and the most incomprehensible deed, so that only a super-human halo – although within the rational frame provided by historiography, declamation, judicial oratory – turned out to be the sole way to explain it and accept it. For instance, Livy, describing the fundamental shift from monarchy to republic in 509 BC, harshly denigrates the wife of Tarquinius the Proud, Tullia, for her implicit connection with the murder of King Servius and her actual abuse of his corpse. Influenced by evil "avenging ghosts," Tullia even drove her carriage over the unburied body of her father, committing a "horrible and inhuman deed" and polluting herself and her house with his blood. Finally, once forced to leave Rome by Brutus, Tullia was "cursed wherever she went by men and women, who called down upon her the furies that avenge the wrongs of kindred."[10]

sensisse? ausum autem esse quemquam se in id conclave committere eo potissimum tempore cum ibidem essent duo adulescentes filii qui et sentire et defendere facile possent? erat porro nemo in quem ea suspicio conveniret. Tamen, cum planum iudicibus esset factum aperto ostio dormientis eos repertos esse, iudicio absoluti adulescentes et suspicione omni liberati sunt. Nemo enim putabat quemquam esse qui, cum omnia divina atque humana iura scelere nefario polluisset, somnum statim capere potuisset, propterea quod qui tantum facinus commiserunt non modo sine cura quiescere sed ne spirare quidem sine metu possunt (Not many years ago they say that Titius Caelius, a well-known man and a citizen of Terracina, after supper, retired to rest in the same room with his two youthful sons. He was found in the morning with his throat cut. The sons were accused of the parricide, as, on the one hand, there was no slave and no free person on whom suspicion of the act could fall, and his two sons of that age lying near him stated that they did not even realize what had been done. It was, indeed, a suspicious procedure. Neither of them was aware of the crime: how could this be possible? Some one had ventured to introduce himself into that chamber, especially at that time when two young men were in the same place, who might easily have heard the noise and defended him: how could this be possible? Moreover, there was no one on whom the suspicion of the deed could fall. Yet, as it was plain to the judges that they were found sleeping with the door open, the young men were acquitted and released from all suspicion. For no one thought that there was any one who, when he had violated all divine and human laws by a nefarious crime, could immediately go to sleep; because those who have committed such a crime not only cannot rest free from care, but cannot even breathe without fear). My translation.

10 Liv. 1.48.7: *foedum inhumanumque inde traditur scelus monumentoque locus est – Sceleratumuicum uocant – quo amens, agitantibus furiis sororis ac uiri, Tullia per patris corpus carpentum egisse fertur, partemque sanguinis ac caedis paternae cruento uehiculo, contaminata ipsa respersaque, tulisse ad penates suos uirique sui, quibus iratis malo regni principio similes propediem exitus sequerentur* (Then, the tradition runs, a foul and unnatural crime was committed, the memory of which the place still bears, for they call it the Vicus Sceleratus. It is said that Tullia, goaded to madness by the avenging spirits of her sister and her husband, drove right over her father's body, and carried back some of her father's blood with which the car and she herself were defiled to her own and her husband's household gods, through whose anger a

Furthermore, as far as a more recent case is concerned (that is, according to Livy, the first case of *parricidium* to be punished through the sack around the 101 BC),[11] the will written by a condemned matricide, that is Publicius Malleolus, between the sentence and the execution, was held invalid: the culprit, on the grounds of his conduct, was formally qualified as a *furiosus*, that is totally insane, raving mad, and accordingly the related decemviral rule was applied.

The human inconceivability of parricide (together with an idealised view of the past) often emerges as a rhetorical and aetiological *topos*: Plutarch highlights the seriousness of the crime, maintaining that the first Roman king did not enact any law about it, since to him it was implausible that some human beings would dare perpetrate such an extreme offence.[12] Quite the opposite (although sharing the same ideas), Cicero reports that, if, on the one hand, Roman ancestors immediately inflicted the most severe punishment to parricides, on the other hand, as for the Athenian legal system, Solon himself failed to define a particular punishment for parricides, as he was persuaded that the lawgiver should not even mention such a heinous crime, in order to not move the citizens to commit it.[13] Finally, Seneca, together with Valerius Maximus, wrote in the early empire that parricide

reign which began in wickedness was soon brought to an end by a like cause); Liv. 1.59.10: *indigna Ser. Tulli regis memorata caedes et inuecta corpori patris nefando uehiculo filia, inuocatique ultores parentum di* (He reminded them of the shameful murder of Servius Tullius and his daughter driving in her accursed chariot over her father's body, and solemnly invoked the gods as the avengers of murdered parents); Liv. 1.59.13: *inter hunc tumultum Tullia domo profugit exsecrantibus quacumque incedebat inuocantibusque parentum furias uiris mulieribusque* (During the commotion Tullia fled from the palace amidst the execrations of all whom she met, men and women alike invoking against her father's avenging spirit). In this paper I used Livy's translation by Rev. Canon Roberts (New York: E. P. Dutton and Co., 1912).

11 Livy *Per.* 68; Oros. 5.16.23; *rhet. ad Her.* 1.13.23; Cic. *inv.* 2.149 (see, also, Mod. 12 *pandect.* D. 48.9.9, and Macer 2 *de iud. publ.* D. 1.18.14): see Ferdinando Zuccotti, "Il testamento di Publicio Malleolo," in *Studi in onore di A. Biscardi* 6 (Milano: Cisalpino – La Goliardica, 1987): 229–265. Sharing Plutarch's view, in the first six hundred years Rome had no cases of patricide and the first Roman to be punished for such a crime by the sack (*poena cullei*) was Lucius Hostius after the Hannibalic War (Plut. *Rom.* 22.5). See, however, Cantarella, *I supplizi capitali*, 275, who remarks Plutarch's unreliability, as Plautus implicitly attests earlier uses of the *poena cullei* and the mask made with wolf's skin for parricide (or anyway the theoretical connection between sack and parricides): *Plaut. Epidic.* 349–435 with Carlo Lanza, "*Plautus, Epidicus*, 349–351," in *Fides Humanitas Ius. Studii in onore di L. Labruna*, eds. Cosimo Cascione and Carla Masi Doria (Naples: Editoriale Scientifica, 2007): 2757–2766.

12 Plut. *Rom.* 22.4–5.

13 *Rosc. Am.* 70: *prudentissima civitas Atheniensium, dum ea rerum potita est, fuisse traditur; eius porro civitatis sapientissimum Solonem dicunt fuisse, eum qui leges quibus hodie quoque utuntur scripserit1. is eum interrogaretur cur nullum supplicium constituisset in cum qui parentem necasset, respondit se id neminem facturum putasse. sapienter fecisse dicitur, cum de eo nihil sanxerit quod* had remained for a long time a crime without a law, implicitly confirming, at least from an ideological perspective, the view that parricide was such an intolerably marginal crime that human society, when ruled by law, could not even contemplate [14]

In the light of the previous remarks, it is unsurprising that ancient sources attest metaphorical and hyperbolic uses of the noun *parricidium*. This formal and legal label suggested the supreme degree of impiety and inhumanity to the Roman audience. As a consequence, covering less severe, or anyway different, behaviours under this legal label clearly represented a rhetorical strategy directed to inspire an authentic sense of horror and so to depict any political

antea commissum non erat, ne non tam prohibere quam admonere videretur. quanto nostri maiores sapientius! qui cum intellegerent nihil esse tam sanctum quod non aliquando violaret audacia, supplicium in parricidas singulare excogitaverunt ut, quos natura ipsa retinere in officio non potuisset, ei magnitudine poenae a maleficio summoverentur. insui voluerunt in culleum vivos atque ita in flumen deici (The city of the Athenians is said to have been the wisest while it was the most powerful. Moreover, Solon is said the wisest man of that city, as he enacted the laws which the Athenians use even nowadays. He was asked why he had provided no punishment for those who killed their fathers, he answered that he had not supposed that any one would do so. He is said to have done wisely in determining nothing about a crime which had never been committed: he chose to persuade his people instead of forbidding this crime. But our ancestors acted much more wisely! They were aware that nothing was so holy that audacity could violate it; accordingly, they established a peculiar punishment for parricides, so that those whom nature did not refrain, might be kept from committing such crime by the severity of the punishment. They ordered them to be sown alive in a leather sack, and in that condition to be thrown into a river). My translation.

14 Sen. *Clem.* 1.23.1: *Multo minus audebant liberi nefas ultimum admittere, quam diu sine lege crimen fuit. Summa enim prudentia altissimi viri et rerum naturae peritissimi maluerunt velut incredibile scelus et ultra audaciam positum praeterire quam, dum vindicant, ostendere posse fieri; itaque parricidae cum lege coeperunt, et illis facinus poena monstravit* (As long as the greatest crime remained without a special law, children committed it much more rarely. Wisest men, highly skilled in human nature, preferred to pass over this unbelievable and oureageous crime, rather than teach men that it might be committed by inflicting a penalty: parricides, consequently, were unknown until a law was enacted against them, and until a penalty showed them how to perpetrate the crime). My translation. See, also, Val. Max. 1.1.13. Sharing Plutarch's view, Seneca here discusses the theory that crimes frequently punished must be frequently committed; he also argues that severe punishments do not compress the incidence of crimes, but they encourage them by giving prominence to particular offences. See Barbara Levick, *Claudius* (New Haven: Yale University P., 1998), 117, 124, and Bauman, *Crime and Punishment*, 703. For the date of promulgation, see Cloud, "*Parricidium*," 26–38 (who maintains that the *poena cullei* was introduced as a specific form of punishment only in the late 3rd or in the 2nd century BC; moreover, he points out that such punishment came together with the statutory definition of parricide as an autonomous category of crime); see Enzo Nardi, *L'otre dei parricidi e le bestie incluse* (Milan: Giuffrè, 1980), 68 and Santalucia, *Diritto e processo penale*, 28, 148, 161. Anyway, it is more than plausible that these two sources just imply that a substantial and procedural distinction between *parricidium* and murder took place in the mid-Republic, and not that *parricidium* was not covered by any Roman statute.

opponent or any procedural counterparty in terms of a higher level of dishonour and despicableness. Although it properly meant either the murder of a parent (*stricto sensu*), or the murder of a relative (*lato sensu*), *parricidium* applied also to the betrayal of the fatherland (as in case of treason or attempted tyranny),[15] and to any conspiracy against the emperor's life. In quality of *pater patriae*, he was like a very parent; thus, who plotted to kill, or who actually killed, the "father of the fatherland" was metaphorically charged with parricide, whether attempted or committed. Suetonius reports that after Julius Caesar's killing, the Senate voted to call the Ides of March 'the day of parricide'.[16] This fact allows for a better understanding of the reasons that led the Romans to label Brutus, called *filius/teknon* by Caesar himself, in terms of parricide.[17] What is more, the conception of *parricidium* could be so stretched that it ended up including either injuries that fall short of any homicidal *actus reus* and *mens rea* (such as beating and blinding one's own father), or even forms of actual insubordination or ideological disagreement.[18] It is

---

15 Ps.Quint. *Decl. min.* 315.18; 371.3; 322.4. It is worth reminding that in the Gracchan era (ca. 133 BC) Gaius Villius seems to have been charged with *perduellio* or *maiestas* and, being tied in a sack together with some serpents, was drowned (that is he suffered the *poena* for parricides): Plut. *Ti. Gr.* 20.3. Cf. Cic. *de amic.* 37; Val. Max. 4.7.1; Jillian Lea Beness, "The Punishment of the Gracchani and the Execution of C. Villius in 133/132," *Antichthon* 34 (2000): 1–17. Roman tradition considered the case of the *duumvir* Marcus Atilius to be the first case of execution by the sack: anyway, he was not punished by Tarquinius the Proud for parricide, but for having revealed information included in the Sibylline books (Val. Max. 1.1.13; Dion. Hal. *Ant. Rom.* 4.62.4: see Cloud, "*Parricidium*," 26–38). Yet, also with regard to this case, Dionysius mentions the crime of parricide, implying that the culprit was drowned in the sack for treason of his fatherland.

16 See, for example, Cic. *Phil.* 2.7, 2.13, 6.4, 11.27, 11.29, 13.20–21; *Cat.* 1.17, 29, 33; *de off.* 3.21.83; *pro Sull.* 6; *ad fam.* 10.23.5; Tac. *Ann.* 15.73.4; *Hist.* 1.85.5; Sall. *Cat.* 31.8; 52.31; Suet. *Iul.* 88. See Lassen, "The Ultimate Crime," 155–156, 158–160.

17 Suet. *Caes.* 1.82 and Cass. Dio *Hist. Rom.* 44.19; Cic. *phil.* 2.3.

18 Roman declamation provides a variety of examples where the word parricide assumes a broad and loose range of meanings. A son who has beaten his father is called *parricida*. The young and greedy son that has blinded his own father may be described as *parricida*; disobeying a father who has commanded his son to abandon the daughter of the pirate who freed him is labelled as *parricidium*. The pirate's daughter herself commits parricide by preferring the young man to her father. Even if a son saves his father's life in battle, the father discredits him, boasting that his only glory corresponds to not having committed parricide by abandoning his father in battle. *Parricidium* includes the case of a son who, being in love with his stepmother, makes his father give him the woman as consideration provided for preventing his own son from dying of heartache. A father even claims that his son would have committed *parricidium*, if he had preferred suicide to a life spent with his own father: this could only come from patricidal hatred. Parricide is also committed by a daughter if she takes her husband's side during civil war instead of her father and brother's (Sen. *Contr.* 9.4.6, 7, 12, 15, 17, 22; Ps.Quint. *Decl. min.* 372.1, 4, 7; Calp. Flacc. *Decl.* 9.6; see, moreover, Sen. *Contr.* 1.6.1; 3.4.2; 6.7.2; 7.3.5; 10.3).

clear that, above all in these last cases, the declaimer, by mentioning *parricidium*, intended to amplify the gravity of the misconducts carried out by the opponent, rhetorically converting a mere violation into the *maximum crimen* for anyone to commit, and then suggesting to the audience that such behaviours, if correctly understood, amounted to a prefiguration of a future possible murder.[19]

3 The punishment of the sack: a short description

The most heinous and horrific crime obviously deserves the harshest of the punishments.[20] Modestinus, in the 3rd century AD, provides a rather complete account of the terrible and exotic ritual that was performed during the execution

---

19 Mario Lentano, "*Parricidii sit actio*: Killing the Father in Roman Declamation," in *Law and Ethics in Greek and Roman Declamation*, eds. Eugenio Amato, Francesco Citti, and Bart Huelsenbeck (Berlin, Munich, Boston: de Gruyter, 2015), 133–153, 143–144: "the term is never completely devoid of its proper connotations: in uses like these, there seems to be an implicit understanding that a son capable of such behaviours is also capable of patricide. If he is not yet a *parricida* according to the law, the potential for him to become so nevertheless remains, at least in the suspicious minds of *duri patres*.". See Cic. *leg.* 2.9.22; *Cat.* 1.12.29; Sall. *Cat.* 51.25; Tac. *hist.* 1.85.

20 On this *poena* (also inflicted for crimes against the state or religion), see Adolf Joseph Storfer, *Zur Sonderstellung des Vatermordes. Eine rechtsgeschichtliche und völkerpsychologische Studie* (Leipzig, Wien: Franz Deuticke, 1911), 26–34; Rudolf Düll, "Zur Bedeutung der *poena cullei* im römischen Strafrecht," in *Atti del congresso internazionale di diritto romano. Bologna e Roma*, 2 (Pavia: Tip. successori F.lli Fusi, 1935): 363–408, 365–366; Cristina Bukowska Gorgoni, "Die Strafe des Sackens. Wahrheit und Legende," *Forschungen zur Rechtsarchäeologie und rechtlichen Volkskunde* 2 (1979): 145–162, 146–148; Florike Egmond, "The Cock, the Dog, the Serpent, and the Monkey. Reception and Transmission of a Roman Punishment, or Historiography as History," *International Journal of the Classical Tradition* 2 (1995): 159–192; Beness, "The Punishment of the Gracchani," 1–17. Mommsen's idea that the *poena cullei* was originally inflicted to the murder of any free person and only later became connected to the murder of a parent or a close relative has been rejected: see, along with Emil Brunnenmeister, *Das Tödtungsverbrechen im altrömischen Recht* (Leipzig: Duncker & Humblot, 1887), 186–189; Cloud, "*Parricidium*," 26–38; Magdelain, "*Paricidas*," 548–550; Cantarella, *I supplizi capitali*, 266–269, 276. The sack seems to have been applied for the first time during the reign of Tarquinius the Proud for treason and later extended by law to the parricides (Val. Max. 1.1.13; Dion. Hal. *Ant. Rom.* 4.62.4; Zon. 7.11); the enactment of an ancient Republican law is suggested by many ancient sources: Sen. *Clem.* 1.23; Ps.Quint. *Decl. min.* 377; *rhet. ad Her.* 1.13.23; Cic. *inv.* 2.50.149. See Nardi, *L'otre dei parricidi*, 129; Magdelain, "*Paricidas*," 550.

of parricides according to immemorial customs[21]: in the most comprehensive and final form of this capital punishment, the murderer, after being flogged with the *virgae sanguinae*, that is red-coloured rods, was put into a *culleus*, that is leather sack, together with a dog, a dunghill cock, a viper, and a monkey; then, the sack was thrown into a sea, river, or lake.[22] Further details appear in classical literary

21 On the contrary, Justinian (I. 4.18.6) – according to the *Pauli Sententiae* (5.24) – states that the *Lex Pompeia de parricidiis* introduced the new punishment consisting in the drowning in a leather sack together with the four animals: but this is denied by precedent cases attested in the sources (Cloud, "*Parricidium*," 38–47). On the contradiction existing between Digesta and Institutiones, see Cloud, "*Parricidium*," 47–66; Radin, "The *lex Pompeia*," 126. Furthermore, the jurist Marcian (D. 48.9.1), adhering to a view consistent with Modestinus's account, maintains that the *Lex Pompeia* extended the punishments prescribed by the preceding *Lex Cornelia* to parricides (in this sense, see Mommsen, *Römisches Strafrecht*, 643–645; Düll, "Zur Bedeutung der *poena cullei*," 366, 36, believing that the *Lex Cornelia* repealed the death penalty); likewise, Cloud, "*Parricidium*," 47–66, suggests that this law substantially defined parricide in terms of murder of parents or close relatives, and procedurally mapped it onto other forms of homicide, by unifying the different forms of punishment. *Contra*, see Ernst Levy, "Die Römische Kapitalstrafe," in *Ernst Levy Gesammelte Schriften zu seinem achtzigsten Geburtstag*, ed. Wolfgang Kunkel and Max Kaser, 2 (Köln, Graz: Böhlau, 1963): 325–378, assuming that the *Lex Pompeia* did not abolish the *poena cullei*, but intensified the magisterial powers in connection with the execution of punishments. Later sources show the use of this punishment, despite the supposed abolishment introduced with the *Lex Pompeia*. Suet. *Iul.* 42.3 maintains that Caesar punished parricides with confiscation of their property and that, at least under Augustus, the sack was limited to the *manifesti* or *confessi* parricides (Suet. *Aug.* 33.1). Claudius is said to have used the sack more times in five years than it had ever been used before, becoming this *poena* even more common than the cross: Sen. *Clem.* 1.23.1; Suet. *Claud.* 34.1. The cruel practice is also attested in Nero's time: see Dio 61.16.1 and Juv. 8.213–14. As concerns the 2nd century AD, a new practice under Hadrian is attested in D. 48.9.9 pr. The sack was in use in the 3rd century (D. 48.9.9 pr.; D. 48.9.1; see Apul. *met.* 10.8; Tert. *anim.* 33.6; Lactant. *div. inst.* 5.9.16, *pace* Paul. *Sent.* 5.24 that suggests that the sack was obsolete). On Constantine's expansion of the punishment in 318–319 AD to all forms of parricide, see Radin, "The *lex Pompeia*," 128–129 and Cloud, "*Parricidium*," 56–58.

22 D. 48.9.9 pr.: *Poena parricidii more maiorum haec instituta est, ut parricida virgis sanguineis verberatus deinde culleo insuatur cum cane, gallo gallinaceo et vipera et simia: deinde in mare profundum culleus iactatur. Hoc ita, si mare proximum sit: alioquin bestiis obicitur secundum divi Hadriani constitutionem* (The penalty inflicted to parricides, as provided by our ancestors, is the following: the culprit shall be beaten with red rods, and then shall be sewn up in a sack with a dog, a dunghill, a viper, and a monkey; the sack shall be cast into the depths of the sea, if the sea is near at hand; alternatively it shall be thrown to wild beasts, according to the constitution of the Divine Hadrian). My translation. Furthermore, see I. 4.18.6; Dosith. 3.16; Cic. *Rosc. Am.* 69–70. As regards the alternatives to the sea, Cic. *inv.* 2.50.149 mentions *perfluens* water; C. Theod. 9.15.1 and C. 9.17.1, mention a river. As for the animals sewn up in the sack together with the *parricida*, Iuv. *Sat.* 8.213 mentions a monkey and a viper (while in 13.154 ff. there is a reference to the monkey only); Sen. *Contr.* 5.4.2; *Clem.* 1.15.7; Ps.Quint. *Decl. maior.* 17.9; C. Theod. 9.15.1, and C. 9.17.1 attest for the presence of snakes. In the speech written to sources[23]: the *parricida* was led to the place of execution on a cart drawn by black oxen; then his head was covered with a cap made of wolf's skin (the so-called *folliculus lupinus)*, while shoes whose soles were made of wood were tied to his feet. Finally, the *parricida* was put together with the four live animals (or at times with some of them) into the sack. It is also clear that an agonising death could occur even before the drowning into the depths of the waters: indeed, the raging beasts could come in fury to tear to pieces the flesh of the culprit with their teeth, claws and nails, not to mention the viper's fatal venom. If this did not happen, the culprit was unavoidably condemned to die by drowning or of asphyxiation.

4 *Parricida*: that is to say *monstrum*?

The previous preliminary remarks about the heinousness inherent to the crime of *parricidium*, about the sense of terror it brings about, and finally the extremely cruel and bizarre character of the *poena cullei* help contextualise two

defend Sextus Roscius of Ameria, Cicero – as already stated – deals with the *poena cullei* at length, but makes no mention of any animals (see, moreover, Cic. *inv.* 2.50.149; Cic. *ep. Quint. frat.* 1.2.5). Likewise, neither Valerius Maximus, nor Zonaras, nor the author of the *rhetorica ad Herennium*, nor Orosius, hint at the presence of any of the four animals (Val. Max. 1.1.13; Zon. 7.11; *rhet. ad Her.* 1.13.23; Oros. 5.16.23). According to Egmond, "The cock, the dog, the serpent, and the monkey," 176, "in its simplest form of drowning in a sack the *poena cullei* was undoubtedly a very old Roman punishment, but the use of none of the animals can be traced back earlier than the era of the Gracchi (ca. 133 BC). The snake was clearly first, as it should be. The monkey came second. The dog and the cock only materialised after Hadrian's time, during the early 3rd century AD. The whole series of four in the order snake-dog-cock-monkey only occurs in the compilations of the 6th century, nor do we hear of any of the other ritual elements before the 1st century BC. Cicero mentions the wooden soles and the wolf's cap. The cart and the black oxen are first mentioned during Hadrian's time, and the flogging with the *virgae sanguineae* occurs for the first time in *Digesta* (which tells us nothing about its age)."

23 Cic. *inv.* 2.50.149: *Quidam iudicatus est parentem occidisse et statim, quod effugiendi potestas non fuit, ligneae soleae in pedes inditae sunt; os autem obvolutum est folliculo et praeligatum; deinde est in carcerem deductus, ut ibi esset tantisper, dum culleus, in quem coniectus in profluentem deferretur, compararetur* (A certain man was convicted of parricide. Immediately after, in order to ensure that he could not escape, wooden soles were put on his feet, and his face was covered with a wolf's cap, and bound fast. Then he was led to prison: he would remain there until the leather sack was ready for him to be cast into running water); *rhet. ad Her.* 1.13.23: *Ei damnato statim folliculo lupino os <obvolutum est> et soleae ligneae in pedibus inductae sunt: in carcerem ductus est* (After he was convicted, his face was covered with a wolf skin cap and wooden soles were tied to his feet; then he was led to prison). My translation.

famous passages included in the speech written by Cicero for Sextius Roscius of Ameria: two passages that clearly connect parricide and monstrosity.

First, the orator equates such wrongdoing to a portent or prodigy, portraying the culprit as a man whose manners are savage, whose nature is unrestrained, and whose life is devoted to any sort of vice and transgression.[24] Then, he even boasts that the person who commits parricide is undeniably a portent and monster; he or she is a 'being' in human shape, on the one hand; but he or she supersedes the beasts themselves in wildness, on the other hand.[25] This motif comes not alone. Ps.Quintilian reports a case concerning a mother charged of poisoning her son to prevent him from testifying against her on the accusation of adultery; according to the rhetor, the woman had to be considered *inter prodigia*, due to the fierce unnaturalness of her behaviour.[26] Once again, Ps.Quintilian confirms that Cicero's *pro Sexto Roscio Amerino* was a fundamental point of reference for any declaimer dealing, directly or indirectly, with the topic of parricide, even if in Roman declamation this term was, frequently and plainly, used to mean a *pater* who has killed his son,[27] abusing his *ius vitae necisque* (that is a power which, even though wide,

---

24 *Rosc. Am.* 38: *in hoc tanto, tam atroci, tam singulari maleficio, quod ita raro exstitit ut, si quando auditum sit, portenti ac prodigi simile numeretur, quibus tandem tu, C. Eruci, argumentis accusatorem censes uti oportere? nonne et audaciam eius qui in crimen vocetur singularem ostendere et mores feros immanemque naturam et vitam vitiis flagitiisque omnibus deditam, denique omnia ad perniciem profligata atque perdita? quorum tu nihil in Sex. Roscium ne obiciendi quidem causa contulisti* (In the case of so enormous, so atrocious, so singular a crime, as this one which has been committed so rarely, that, if it is ever heard of, it is accounted like a portent and prodigy–what arguments do you think, O Caius Erucius, you as the accuser ought to use? Ought you not to prove the singular audacity of him who is accused of it? And his savage manners, and brutal nature, and his life devoted to every sort of vice and crime, his whole character, in short, given up to profligacy and abandoned? None of which things have you alleged against Sextus Roscius, not even for the sake of making the imputation). My translation.

25 *Rosc. Am.* 63: *Magna est enim vis humanitatis; multum valet communio sanguinis; reclamitat istius modi suspicionibus ipsa natura; portentum atque monstrum certissimum est esse aliquem humana specie et figura qui tantum immanitate bestias vicerit ut, propter quos hanc suavissimam lucem aspexerit, eos indignissime luce privarit, cum etiam feras inter sese partus atque educatio et natura ipsa conciliet* (For the power of human feeling is great; the connection of blood is of mighty power; nature herself cries out against suspicions of this sort; it is a most undeniable portent and monster, for any one to exist in human shape, who so far outruns the beasts in savageness, as in a most scandalous manner to deprive those of life by whose means he has himself beheld this most delicious light of life; when birth, and bringing up, and nature herself make even beasts friendly to each other). My translation.

26 See Ps.Quint. *Decl. min.* 319.2, 3, 5; see also Calp. Flacc. *Decl.* 10.8 (Håkanson), where a mother induces one son of hers to commit suicide and, accordingly, commits *parricidium*.

27 See Ps.Quint. *Decl. maior.* 8.1, 2, 4, 6, 8, 11, 14, 15, 19, 21. For further cases where fathers are called parricides, see Ps.Quint. *Decl. maior.* 10.17; 18.1, 2, 3, 5, 8, 11, 14, 15, 17; killing the brother

amounts to parricide in Sen. *Contr.* 7.1.1, 5, 6, 7, 9, 10, 15, 16, 17, 22, 23; Ps.Quint. *Decl. min.* 286.9; 321.6 and 11; Calp. Flacc. *Decl.* 21.7. Yan Thomas, "Paura dei padri e violenza dei figli: immagini retoriche e norme di diritto," in *La paura dei padri nella società antica e medievale*, eds. Ezio Pellizer and Nevio Zorzetti (Roma, Bari: Laterza, 1983), 115–140, 119, pointed out, on the grounds of a close analysis of the writings of Quintilian, Seneca the Elder, and Calpurnius Flaccus, the following results both concerning father-son litigation, and, for most part, entailing cases of patricide: 54 cases out of 90 in Quintilian, 37 out of 50 in Seneca, 21 out of 33 in Calpurnius Flaccus. In his opinion, if *parricidium* meant the murder of the father only, this strict sense was widened by Pompey so as to cover close relatives: this would overcome the conflict between the duty, existing on those nearest to the killed person, of avenging, and the duty of protecting the family: see Thomas, "*Parricidium*," 643–715, and above all Yan Thomas, "Sich rächen auf dem *Forum*. Familiäre Solidarität und Kriminalprozess in Rom (1. Jh. v. Chr. – 2. Jh. n. Chr.)," *Historische Anthropologie: Kultur, Gesellschaft, Alltag* 5 (1997): 161–186. According to Lentano, "*Parricidii sit actio*," 139, "a systematic analysis of the declamatory texts controverts any claim that *Parricidium* and *parricida*, in declamation, refer above all to the killing of a father. And yet this definition is to some degree correct, as it recognises that extended uses of the concept of *parricidium* appear almost exclusively within the declaimers' treatment of the *controversiae*. In the theme, on the other hand – or in the laws that regulate its formulation – the category of *parricidium* refers most frequently by far to the killing of a father, while other terms are used for these other crimes." Therefore, using the term *parricidium* to designate a father who has killed his son would represent the greatest deviation from its "juridical value." This idea can hardly be shared since it is grounded on an old-fashioned and exaggerated representation of paternal powers in Roman law (see next footnote), on the one hand, and it seems to imply what is an erroneous conception of parricide on the legal level, on the other hand. At first, according to Marcian, the *lex Pompeia de parricidiis* (enacted by Pompey in 55 or 52 BC) provided a long and analytical list of "relatives" as possible victims of the crime of parricide: father, mother, grandfather, grandmother, brother, sister, first cousin on the father's side, first cousin on the mother's side, paternal or maternal uncle, paternal or maternal aunt, first cousin (male or female) by mother's sister, wife, husband, father-in-law, son-in-law, mother-in-law, daughter-in-law, stepfather, stepson, stepdaughter, patron or patroness; son or daughter killed by the mother; grandson killed by grandfather. The law also stipulates that a son who purchased poison to kill his father be punished as a parricide, even if he was not able to administer it, and Ulpian attests that even moneylenders being aware of the fact that a *filius* planned to use the money he borrowed to pay for poison or for a killer to murder his own father had to be punished as parricide (D. 48.9.1; D. 48.9.7). It is undeniable that the list at issue fails to cite sons and daughters (so that this omission has been read as a clear confirmation of the existence of the absolute *vitae necisque potesta* until the time of Marcian). Secondly, this omission cannot be justified on the basis of the allegedly absolute prerogatives granted to a *pater* by *patria potestas*. Actually, shorter lists of victims are attested by Modestinus, who refers to parents and grandparents only (D. 48.9.9.1), and by the *Pauli Sententiae*, where parents, grandparents, siblings, and patrons are mentioned (Paul. *Sent.* 5.24). Therefore, these lists, if they were not modified by the Compilers in the 6th century AD, seem to be the differentiated results of jurists' interpretation about the legal meaning of the term "relative": see Lucia Fanizza, "Il parricidio nel sistema della *lex Pompeia*," *Labeo* 25 (1979): 266–289; Henryk Kupiszewski, "Quelques remarques sur le *parricidium* dans le droit romain classique et post-classique," in *Studi in onore di Edoardo Volterra*, 4 (Milano: Giuffrè, deep, and articulated, never consisted of an unrestrained and absolute one, not even at its beginnings).[28]

1971): 601–614. Furthermore, C. Theod. 9.15.1 and C. Theod. 11.17.1 include the murder of sons in the category of *parricidium*. Thirdly, it is worth reminding that a father was never granted the right to kill his son without any legal ground and factual reason (see Fragm. Aug. 4.86: *De filio hoc tractari crudele est, sed . . . . . . non est post . . . . r . . . . <occi> dere sine iusta causa, ut constituit lex XII tabularum*): for instance, as for the republican era, out of an alleged (but unproved) sexual offence (*dubiae castitatis*), Quintus Fabius Maximus Eburnus ordered two slaves of his to kill his son, already relegated to the countryside to atone his misconduct; anyway Quintus Fabius Maximus Eburnus, although *pater familias*, committed *parricidium*: he was therefore prosecuted by Gnaeus Pompeius and condemned to exile (Val. Max. 6.1.5; Oros. 5.16.8; see Ps.Quint. *Decl. maior.* 3.14; Cic. *Balb.* 28). Moreover, Valerius Maximus reports the case of Lucius Gellius (Val. Max. 5.9.1): he suspected his son of adultery with his stepmother and of plotting to commit patricide. As a consequence, he summoned a wide *consilium domesticum*, which finally had to declare the accused's innocence. The father would have committed a crime rather than punished one, if he had killed his son *sine causa*. As far as the 2nd century AD is concerned, what is more, Marcian reports the case of a man who, during a hunt, had killed his son (just suspected to have committed adultery with his stepmother); as a consequence, the emperor Hadrian deported the killer to an island: this father had acted like a brigand, rather than as one with *patria potestas* (D. 48.9.5). See, also, Dio Cass. 36.37.4 (concerning the Augustan case of Tricho).

28 See William V. Harris, "The Roman Father's Power of Lfe and Death," 81–95, and, above all, Richard P. Saller, "*Patria Potestas* and the Stereotype of the Roman Family," *Continuity and Change* 1 (1986): 7–22, 19–20; Richard P. Saller, *Patriarchy, Property and Death in the Roman Family* (Cambridge: Cambridge University P., 1994), 121–122 (supporting an evolutionary model and considering the *vitae necisque potestas* in terms of an archaic institution subjected to limitations and desuetude); see Lassen, "The Ultimate Crime," 147–148. See Gaughan, *Murder Was not a Crime*, 23–52, recently followed by Carlà-Uhink, "Murder Among Relatives," 40, where he assumes that "crimes against the State could allow the use of *vitae necisque potestas* - and even of *parricidium* - it also implies that this should not normally be the case, and that sons were not considered to be victims of violence without reason." If the traditional view fails to depict accurately the multiple nuances characterising *patria potestas*, that does not mean that the opposite view is totally persuasive. For instance, some authors argue that literary evidence indicates that the father/son relationship was bilateral in nature and founded on *pietas* (devotion and affection). On the contrary, Cantarella, "Fathers and Sons," 297, has convincingly pointed out that "bilateral does not mean the same thing as symmetrical: while filial *pietas* meant obedience and respect, paternal pietas could coexist with the exercise of paternal powers." Moreover, on the grounds of demographical researches, some social historians have argued that Roman family was composed of a small group of individuals, as of the 2nd century BC, and that the relations between generations were not based on an authoritarian, if not even tyrannical, mastery on the part of the father. Once again, Cantarella, "Fathers and Sons," 297, correctly maintains the following: "let us accept the picture of a society where, in every generation, a significant number of young adults were independent individuals, free to administer their own property. Can we believe that this situation would have mitigated the conflict between generations? I do not believe so. Instead I believe that the minority still *in potestate* would have felt even more disadvantaged, in comparison to most of their more fortunate

Cicero highlights the non-human character of the crime allegedly committed by his client: the perpetrator acts against all values and principles inspired by the term *homo* and ruled out in a ferocious state of nature; in fact, he takes away the life of the person who had given life to him. By committing such abomination, the parricide places himself beyond the boundaries of the political society and can therefore be numbered among the wild animals. The exceptionally harsh punishment provided by Roman ancestors and confirmed in more recent statutes perfectly fits the societal offence here dealt with.[29]

contemporaries. I believe that their situation would have been even more unendurable than would have been the case if it were more prevalent. I believe that contradictions between the opportunities of adulthood and the constraints imposed by a living father would have been even more problematic."

29 *Rosc. Am.* 71–72: *O singularem sapientiam, iudices! nonne videntur hunc hominem ex rerum natura sustulisse et eripuisse cui repente caelum, solem, aquam terramque ademerint ut, qui eum necasset unde ipse natus esset, careret eis rebus omnibus ex quibus omnia nata esse dicuntur? noluerunt feris corpus obicere ne bestiis quoque quae tantum scelus attigissent immanioribus uteremur; non sic nudos in flumen deicere ne, cum delati essent in mare, ipsum polluerent quo cetera quae violata sunt expiari putantur; denique nihil tam vile neque tam volgare est cuius partem ullam reliquerint. etenim quid tam est commune quam spiritus vivis, terra mortuis, mare fluctuantibus, litus eiectis? ita vivunt, dum possunt, ut ducere animam de caelo non queant, ita moriuntur ut eorum ossa terra non tangat, ita iactantur fluctibus ut numquam adluantur, ita postremo eiciuntur ut ne ad saxa quidem mortui conquiescant. tanti malefici crimen, cui maleficio tam insigne supplicium est constitutum, probare te, Eruci, censes posse talibus viris, si ne causam quidem malefici protuleris? si hunc apud bonorum emptores ipsos accusares eique iudicio Chrysogonus praeesset, tamen diligentius paratiusque venisses* (O singular wisdom, O judges! Do not they seem to have cut this man off and separated him from nature? They deprived him at once of heaven, sun, water and earth, so that he who had slain the man from whom he himself was born, might be deprived of all those things from which everything is said to derive. They did not want to throw the body to wild beasts, lest we should find the beasts that had touched such wickedness; they did not want to throw them naked into the river, since they would pollute the sea where all other things which have been polluted are believed to be purified. There is nothing in short so trivial or so common that they left them any share in it. Indeed, what is so common as breath to the living, earth to the dead, the sea to those who float, the shore to those who are cast up by the sea? These men stay alive, as long as they can, unable to draw breath from heaven; they die and the earth does not touch their bones; they are tossed about by the waves so that they are never washed; lastly, they are cast up by the sea so that, when they are dead, they do not even rest on the rocks. Do you think, o Erucius, that you can prove to such men as your charge for such an enormous crime, a crime for which such a remarkable punishment is provided for, if you do not allege any motive for the crime? If you were accusing him before the purchasers of his property, and if Chrysogonus was presiding at that trial, still you would have come more carefully and with more preparation). See, for a similar approach (emphasising the afflictive and retributive character of the ritual), I. 4.18.6: *in vicinum mare vel in amnem proiciatur, ut omni elementorum usu virus carere incipiat et ei caelum superstiti, terra mortuo auferatur* (He shall be cast into the nearby sea or river so that he may begin to be

As a matter of fact, this picture is complicated by the explanation of the *poena* inflicted to parricides. On the one hand, Cicero plainly qualifies those who commit this appalling act in terms of monstrous and portentous beings; on the other hand, he deals with the *poena cullei* conceving it as a very form of punishment. The inconsistency does clearly emerge within the framework provided by the theme of *parricidium*: if the interpretation given to the bizarre ritual of the sack is accurate, it must be held that the Ciceronian use of the terms connected to monstrosity (*monstrum, prodigium, portentum*) amounts to a purely rhetorical strategy; if, on the contrary, this use shows solid legal grounds, it must be held that his explanation of the objectives pursued through *poena cullei* is unlikely, since – as we will show in the next paragraphs – a monster is to be expelled to preserve the natural order from contamination. If parricides were monsters, they should not be punished or denied all honours granted to the dead, but it should simply be removed from the political community of the living.

5 Roman monsters: the legal and religious background

Ancient Romans used quite a broad terminology to indicate strange events that, if correctly interpreted, might forecast the future: besides *monstrum*, one finds the overlapping nouns *ostentum, portentum, prodigium, miraculum.*[30] Cicero

totally denied use of the elements, while still alive, and he may be denied the sky while alive and the earth when dead). My translation. Cf., moreover, C. Theod. 9.15.1 and C. 9.17.1; on the contrary, Ps.Quint. *Decl. min.* 299 and Zon. 7.11.4 adhere to a view that reads the *poena* as a real disposal of an evil prodigy and a device to protect the universe from contamination, rather than as a very form of punishment.

30 Jean Céard, *La nature et les prodiges* (Geneve: Droz, 1977); Clemens Zintzen, "*Prodigium*," in *Der Kleine Pauly* 4 (München: Deutscher Taschenbuch, 1979): 1151–1153; Anton Szantyr, s.v. *monstrum*, in *Thesaurus Linguae Latinae* 8.10 (Leipzig: Teubner, 1964): 1446–1454. Annie Allély, "Les enfants malformés et considérés comme prodigia à Rome et en Italie sous la République," *Revue des études anciennes* 105 (2003): 127–156, 134; Blandine Cuny-Le Callet, *Rome et ses monstres. Naissance d'un concept philosophique et rhétorique* (Grenoble: Million, 2005), 43–54; David Engels, *Das römische Vorzeichenwesen. Quellen, Terminologie, Kommentar, historische Entwicklung* (Stuttgart: Steiner, 2007); Robert Garland, *The Eye of the Beholder. Deformity and Disability in the Graeco-Roman World 2* (London: Bristol Classical P., 2010), 4; Laura Cherubini, "Mostri vicini, mostri di casa. Di alcune creature straordinarie del mito antico," *I Quaderni del Ramo d'Oro* 5 (2012): 137–150; Philippe Charlier, *Les monstres humains dans l'Antiquité. Analyse paléopathologique* (Paris: Fayard, 2008), 23–44; Arduino Maiuri, "Il and Varro, though diverging one from the other with regard to secondary etymological aspects, explain all these terms as being in connection with the supernatural sphere and the divinatory art (even if each of them would show a peculiar point of view of the same phenomenon). Furthermore, both suggest that each of the terms at issue constantly denotes a serious infringement of "the normal order of things," that is *monstrum* and related terms apply to beings or events that are or move *contra naturam*.[31] Pliny the Elder himself, acknowledging the possible existence of actual monsters, appears to be accustomed with the religious implications of the Latin vocabulary of monstrosity. Accordingly, if, on the one hand, he does not hesitate to admit the prophetic power of *omina*,[32] on the other hand, he alludes to the corruption of traditional conceptions, arguing that, during the Republican period, Romans were used to

---

lessico latino del mostruoso," in *"Monstra." Costruzione e Percezione delle Entità Ibride e Mostruose nel Mediterraneo Antico*, ed. Igor Baglioni, 2 (Roma: Edizioni Quasar, 2013): 165–178.

31 Cic. *div.* 1.93: *Quia enim ostendunt, portendunt, monstrant, praedicunt, ostenta, portenta, monstra, prodigia dicuntur* (Because they show, predict, indicate, forecast, they are called *ostenta, portenta, monstra, prodigia*); Serv. *in Aeneidem* 3.366: *Ostentum, quod* ... *ostendit, portentum, quod* ... *portendit, prodigium, quod porro dirigit, miraculum, quod mirum est, monstrum, quod monet* (*Ostentum*, because it shows something, *portentum*, because it predicts, *prodigium*, because it leads us further into the future, *miraculum*, because it is a wonder, *monstrum*, because it shows us something). My translation. See Char. *Ars* p. 389.4 (Keil); Tert. *cor.* 51.33; Cic. *nat. deor.* 2.7; Non. *compend. doc.* 429.27 (Lindsay); Aug. *civ. Dei* 21.8; Fest. 138 (Lindsay); Isid. *orig.* 11.3; Cic. *nat. deor.* 2.13–14; Varro *agr.* 2.4; Tac. *ann.* 12.64. Anyway, monstrosity implies a violation of the natural order: for instance, according to Cicero, *nat. deor.* 1.92, having useless extra body parts was not monstrous (see also Aug. *civ. Dei* 16.8.2, who did not consider polydactyly a serious aberration from the norm either). This approach seems to be ruled out by Cic. *div.* 2.60 (*Quicquid enim oritur, qualecumque est, causam habeat a natura necesse est, ut, etiamsi praeter consuetudinem exstiterit, praeter naturam tamen non possit exsistere*): *monstra* are not *praeter naturam*, but only *praeter consuetudinem*, since there is always a reasonable explanation for them (see Lucr. *rer. nat.* 2.700–709 and 4.732–743, who denies the possible existence of hybrids or mythological monsters, and ranks them among the *simulacra*).

32 Plin. *nat. hist.* 7.33–35 (see, however, Cic. *div.* 1.53 who reports the case of a child born with two heads, considered clearly a signal of future civil war). The seventh book of Plyny's encyclopaedia (Plin. *nat. hist.* 7.9, 21, 32, 34, 45, 47, 69, 83) contains many references to monsters and prodigies within the frame of the fundamental divide between monstrous human races (7.6–32) and monstrous individual human beings (7.33–215): anthropophagous races such as the Scythian tribes, the Cyclopes and the Laestrygones are labelled as *gentes huius monstri*; eastern monstrosities and weird customs are called *miracula*; strange human races are regarded as *prodigia* or *miracula*; hermaphrodites are *prodigia*, while a woman who brought forth an elephant is a *portentum*. To be born feet foremost is *contra naturam*. The case of a twin that remains in the womb while the other prematurely dies is a *miraculum*; a female born with the genitals closed up represents an *infaustum omen*. Miraculous displays of strength are *prodigiosae ostentationis*.

conceive of many monstrous human beings (such as persons born of both sexes combined) as *prodigia*, i.e. 'theological phenomena', while by the 1st century AD, the same human beings were even ranked among 'sexual entertainments' (*deliciae*).[33]

Along with the above mentioned religious connotations, a specifically legal significance of the terminology at issue arises from some of the classical texts included in Justinian's Digest. Labeo tries to define the exact meaning of *ostentum*: according to the classical jurist, this term denotes "unnatural" appearances in humans, animals or plants, as well as prodigious events.[34] Ulpian, dealing with the *ius trium liberorum*, argues that a human *monstrum* does not resemble its parents, and looks or even sounds like an animal more than a human being.[35] A later imperial constitution faces the problem concerning the testamentary *praeteritio* ("passing over") of posthumous children. Justinian, adhering to the Sabinians' view, maintained that the testament was generally

---

33 Plin. *nat. hist.* 7.34: *gignuntur et utriusque sexus quos hermaphroditos vocamus, olim androgynos vocatos et in prodigiis habitos, nunc vero in deliciis* (at times individuals were born belonging to both sexes; we call such persons hermaphrodites; they were formerly called *androgyni*, and were looked upon as prodigies, but nowadays they are employed for sexual purposes). My translation. Cf. Orsolia Márta Péter, "*Olim in prodigiis nunc in deliciis.* Lo *status* giuridico dei *monstra* nel diritto romano," in *Iura antiqua, iura moderna. Festschrift F. Benedek*, ed. Gabor Hamza et al. (Pécs: Dialog Campus Kiado, 2001): 207–216.

34 Ulp. 25 *ad edictum* D. 50.16.38: *"Ostentum" Labeo definit omne contra naturam cuiusque rei genitum factumque. Duo genera autem sunt ostentorum: unum, quotiens quid contra naturam nascitur, tribus manibus forte aut pedibus aut qua alia parte corporis, quae naturae contraria est; alterum, cum quid prodigiosum videtur, quae Graeci φαντάσματα vocant* (Labeo defines *ostentum* to mean everything which is generated or produced contrary to nature. There are, however, two kinds of *ostentum*; one if something is born contrary to nature, for instance with three hands or feet, or with some other part of the body deformed; another, if something is considered to be unusual. The Greeks call them *phantasmata*). My translation.

35 Ulp. 25 *ad legem Iuliam et Papiam* D. 50.16.135: *Quaeret aliquis si portentosum vel monstrosum vel debilem mulier ediderit vel qualem visu vel vagitu novum, non humanae figurae, sed alterius, magis animalis quam hominis, partum, an, quia enixa est, prodesse ei debeat? Et magis est, ut haec quoque parentibus prosint: nec enim est quod eis imputetur, quae qualiter potuerunt, statutis obtemperaverunt, neque id quod fataliter accessit, matri damnum iniungere debet* (Let us suppose that a woman brings forth a child. This is deformed, monstrous, or defective, or has something unusual in its appearance or its voice; to say it differently, it has no resemblance to a human being, seeming to be more an animal than a human being. Shall it be any benefit to her to have brought forth such creature? According to the best opinion, consideration must be taken for its parents. They must not be harmed, since they have done their duty as far as they could. Thence, the mother must not be prejudiced, because an unfortunate occurrence has occurred). My translation.

broken and, as a consequence, recognised the rights of such descendants as legitimate heirs, with the only exception of monstrous births.[36]

The birth of monstrous or prodigious children seems thus to have had great relevance from the legal, as well as from the religious, perspective. What is more, within this kind of *monstra*, ancient authors (above all annalistic historians concerned with the Republican era) appear to be extremely interested in reporting cases of hermaphrodites or androgynes, that is cases of bodily bisexuality in the same person.[37] As of the end of the 3rd century BC and increasingly between the 2nd and 1st centuries BC (that is times of crisis of Republican values and war), Livy, Julius Obsequens, Orosius, Tacitus, and Phlegon of Thralles[38] relate how the

---

36 I. 6.29.3: *Cumque Sabiniani existimabant, si vivus natus est, etsi vocem non emisit, ruptum testamentum, apparet, quod, etsi mutus fuerat, hoc ipsum faciebat, eorum etiam nos laudamus sententiam et sancimus, si vivus perfecte natus est, licet ilico postquam in terram cecidit vel in manibus obstetricis decessit, nihilo minus testamentum corrumpi, hoc tantummodo requirendo, si vivus ad orbem totus processit ad nullum declinans monstrum vel prodigium* (Sabinians argued that if the posthumous child was born alive, the testament was broken, even if the child uttered no sound, or, similarly, if it had been dumb. We support their opinion and provide that if it had been born totally alive, though it died immediately either after coming to this earth, or in the hands of the midwife, the testament would be broken, provided that it had been born as a human being and not as a monster or prodigy).

37 See, on the terms found in ancient sources, Cic. *div.* 1.98; Liv. 27.11.4–5, 31.12.8, 39.22.5; Ov. *Metam.* 4.381–384; Plin. *nat. hist.* 7.15, 7.34, 7.36, 11.263; Paul. *Med.* 6.69 (CMG IX 2, 112, 6–20); Aug. *civ. Dei* 16.8; Hdt. 4.67; Plato *Symp.* 189d – 193d; Diod. Sic. 4.6.5, 32.10.2, 4, 9, 32.12.1; Galen. *De Semine* 2.3.17 (4.619.6–11 Kühn = CMG V 3, 1, 170, 19–23); Ps.-Galen. *Definitiones Medicae* 448 (19.453.12–14 Kühn); Hippocr. *De victu* 1.28 (6, 502–504 Littré). Cf. Lutz Alexander Graumann, "Monstrous Births and Retrospective Diagnosis: The Case of Hermaphrodites in Antiquity," in *Disabilities in Roman Antiquity Disparate Bodies. A Capite ad Calcem*, eds. Christian Laes, Chris F. Goodey and M. Lynn Rose (Leiden, Boston: Brill, 2013): 181–120.

38 See Liv. 27.11.4–6: *Sinuessae natum ambiguo inter marem et feminam sexu infantem, quos androgynos volgus, ut pleraque, faciliore ad duplicanda verba Graeco sermone, appellat ... ea prodigia hostiis maioribus procurata, et supplicatio circa omnia pulvinaria et obsecratio in unum diem indicta; et decretum, ut C. Hostilius praetor ludos Apollini, sicut iis annis voti factique erant, voveret faceretque* (At Sinuessa it was reported that a child was born of doubtful sex, these are commonly called *androgyni* – a word like many others borrowed from the Greek ... These portents were expiated by sacrifices of full-grown victims, and a day was appointed for special intercessions at all the shrines [year 209 BC]); Liv. 27.37.5–6: *Liberatas religione mentes turbavit rursus nuntiatum Frusinone natum esse infantem quadrimo parem nec magnitudine tam mirandum quam quod is quoque, ut Sinuessae biennio ante, incertus mas an femina esset natus erat. Id vero haruspices ex Etruria acciti foedum ac turpe prodigium dicere: extorrem agro Romano, procul terrae contactu, alto mergendum. Vivum in arcam condidere provectumque in mare proiecerunt* (No sooner were men's fears allayed by these expiatory rites than a fresh report came, this time from Frusino, to the effect that a child had been born there in size and appearance equal to one four years old, and what was still more startling, like the case at Sinuessa two years previously, it was impossible to say whether it

occurrence of *androgyni* was interpreted as the most horrible and dreadful sign (*foedum ac turpe prodigium*) sent from the gods to Rome. As Cicero furtherly

---

was male or female. The diviners who had been summoned from Etruria said that this was a dreadful portent, and the thing must be banished from Roman soil, kept from any contact with the earth, and buried in the sea. They enclosed it alive in a box, took it out to sea, and dropped it overboard [year 207 BC]); Liv. 31.12.6–9: *Iam animalium obsceni fetus pluribus locis nuntiabantur: in Sabinis incertus infans natus, masculus an femina esset, alter sedecim iam annorum item ambiguo sexu inventus; Frusinone agnus cum suillo capite, Sinuessae porcus com capite humano natus, in Lucanis in agro publico eculeus cum quinque pedibus. foeda omnia et deformia errantisque in alienos fetus naturae visa; ante omnia abominati semimares iussique in mare extemplo deportari, sicut proxime C. Claudio M. Livio consulibus deportatus similis prodigii fetus erat. nihilo minus decemviros adire libros de portento eo iusserunt. decemviri ex libris res divinas easdem, quae proxime secundum id prodigium factae essent, imperarunt. carmen praeterea ab ter novenis virginibus cani per urbem iusserunt donumque Iunoni reginae ferri. ea uti fierent, C. Aurelius consul ex decemvirorum responso curavit. carmen, sicut patrum memoria Livius, ita tum condidit P. Licinius Tegula* (Numerous monstrous births were also reported amongst the Sabines; a child was born of doubtful sex; another similar case was discovered where the child was already sixteen years old; at Frusino a lamb was yeaned with a head like a pig; at Sinuessa a pig was littered with a human head, and on the public domain-land in Lucania a foal appeared with five feet. These were all regarded as horrid and monstrous products of a nature which had gone astray to produce strange and hybrid growths; the hermaphrodites were looked upon as of especially evil omen and were ordered to be at once carried out to sea just as quite recently in the consulships of C. Claudius and M. Nero similar ill-omened births had been disposed of. At the same time the senate ordered the decemvirs to consult the Sacred Books about this portent. Following the instructions found there, they ordered the same ceremonies to be observed as on the occasion of its last appearance. A hymn was to be sung through the City by three choirs, each consisting of nine maidens, and a gift was to be carried to Queen Juno. The consul C. Aurelius saw that the instructions of the Keepers of the Sacred Books were carried out. The hymn in our fathers' days was composed by Livius, on this occasion by P. Licinius Tegula [year 200 BC]); Liv. 39.22.5: *Sub idem tempus et ex Umbria nuntiatum est semimarem duodecim ferme annos natum inventum; id prodigium abominantes arceri Romano agro, necarique quam primum iusserunt* (Almost at the same time a report came from Umbria of the discovery of a child there, nine years old, who was a hermaphrodite. Horrified at such a portent, the auruspices gave orders for it to be removed from Roman soil as speedily as possible and put to death [year 186 BC]). See Iul. Obseq. *Liber prodigiorum* 22 (*Lunae androgynus natus praecepto aruspicum in mare deportatus*: year 142 BC); 25 (*cinisque eius in mare deiectus*: year 122 BC); 27a (*in agro Ferentino androgynus natus et in flumen deiectus*: year 133 BC); 32 (*in foro Vessano androgynus natus in mare delatus est*: year 136 BC); 34 (*androgynus in agro Romano annorum octo inventus et in mare deportatus*: year 119 BC); 36 (*Saturniae androgynus annorum decem inventus et mari demersus*: year 117 BC); 47 (*item androgynus in mare deportatus*: year 98–97 BC); 48 (*supplicatum in urbe quod androgynus inventus et in mare deportatus erat*: year 98–97 BC); 50 (*androgynus Urbino natus in mare deportatus*: year 95 BC); 53 (*Arretii duo androgyni inventi*: year 92 BC). See Oros. 5.4.8 (*androgynus Romae visus iussu haruspicum in mare mersus est* [as an androgyne appeared in Rome, the haruspices ordered to have him drowned into the sea]: year 142 BC). See Tac. *ann.* 12.64 (*biformis hominum partus et suis fetum editum cui accipitrum ungues inessent* [hermaphrodites had been born and a pig had been produced with the claws of a hawk]: year 54 BC). See Phleg. Thralles 10 remarks, androgynes represent *monstra fatalia.*[39] On the contrary, as Pliny himself attests, beliefs and practices tend to change from the Imperial period on. Ulpian and Paulus acknowledged the legal existence of 'hermaphrodites', classifying them in accordance with a binary male-female scheme, where one or the other gender had to prevail. If the hermaphrodite was considered more like a human being, he was allowed to testify and to leave a will.[40]

On the grounds of monarchical and republican conceptions, these beings, created by a nature that had gone astray, indicated, as *portenta*,[41] that something, as monstrous as they were, was going to happen to the *civitas* as a whole. In the light of the principles and the practices denoting the so-called *pax deorum*, and in order to obtain divine help and mercy, the sign itself, together with its intrinsic pollution, had to be removed as such, and rituals of purification had to be performed:

(Ἐγεννήθη καὶ ἐπὶ Ῥώμης ἀνδρόγυνος, ἄρχοντος Ἀθήνησιν Ἰάσονος, ὑπατευόντων ἐν Ῥώμῃ Μάρκου Πλαυτίου [καὶ Σέξτου Καρμινίου] Ὑψαίου καὶ Μάρκου Φουλβίου Φλάκκου: year 125 BC).

39 Cic. *div.* 1.98: *ortus androgyni nonne fatale quoddam monstrum fuit?*

40 Ulp. 1 *ad Sabinum* D. 1.5.10: *Quaeritur: hermaphroditum cui comparamus? Et magis puto eius sexus aestimandum, qui in eo praevalet* (this is the question: whom does the hermaphrodite resemble? My firm belief is that it follows the gender that prevails in it); Paul. 3 *sententiarum* D. 22.5.15.1: *Hermaphroditus an ad testamentum adhiberi possit, qualitas sexus incalescentis ostendit* (A hermaphrodite is allowed to testify in a case of a will, according to gender); Ulp. 3 *ad Sabinum* D. 28.2.6.2: *Hermaphroditus plane, si in eo virilia praevalebunt, postumum heredem instituere poterit* (A hermaphrodite, if the male gender prevails, can plainly appoint a posthumous as heir). My translation. Cf. Yan Thomas, "La division des sexes," in *Histoire des femmes en Occident. L'antiquité*, ed. Pauline Schmitt-Pantel 1 (Paris: Plon, 1991): 104–105; Giuliano Crifò, "*Prodigium* e diritto: il caso dell'ermafrodita," *Index: quaderni camerti di studi romanistici* 27 (1999): 113–120. Cf., moreover, Andreas Wacke, "Vom Hermaphroditen zum Transsexuellen. Zur Stellung von Zwittern inder Rechtsgeschichte," in *Festschriftfür Kurt Rebmann zum 65. Geburtstag*, eds. Kurt Rebmann, Heinz Eyrich, Walter Odersky and Franz-Jürgen Säcker (München: Beck, 1989): 861–903; Allély, "Les enfants malformés et handicapés," 73–101, 94, 98; Marguerite Hirt Raj, "La législation romaine et les *droits* de l'enfant," in *Naissance et petite enfance dans l'Antiquité. Actes du colloque de Fribourg, 28 novembre–1er décembre 2001* ed. Véronique Dasen (Göttingen, Vandenhoeck & Ruprecht, 2004): 281–291; Sandrine Vallar, "Les hermaphrodites: l'approche de la Rome antique," *Revue International de Droits de l'Antiquité* 60 (2013): 202–217; Lorenzo Franchini, "Lo *status* dell'ermafrodita ed il problema della determinazione del sesso prevalente," *Teoria e storia del diritto privato* 9 (2016): 1–35.

41 Raymond Block, *Les prodiges dans l'Antiquité classique* (Paris: P.U.F., 1963), 73; Brunnenmeister, *Das Totungsverbrechen im altromischen Recht*, 193–196, Cloud, "*Parricidium*," 35; Lutz Alexander Graumann, "Angeborene Fehlbildungen in der Zeit der römischen Republik in den Prodigien des Iulius Obsequens," in *Behinderungen und Beeinträchtigungen/Disability and Impairment in Antiquity*, ed. Rupert Breitwieser (Oxford: BAR, 2012): 91–101.

the future of Rome, it was argued, depended on the hasty removal of the *monstrum*, a being of evil portent.[42] If one relies on two archaic provisions attested by Dionysius and Cicero and concerning, in general, *patria potestas*, and, particularly, the so-called *ius vitae necisque*, the above-mentioned idea was deeply rooted at the beginnings of Rome: the former allowed, while the second seems to order, the father to kill (or, alternatively, to expose) monstrous, deformed, and maimed births.[43] So, monsters being generated by human beings – regardless of any fault and liability – were to be removed and not punished.

---

42 Marie Delcourt, *Stérilités mystérieuses et naissances maléfiques dans l'Antiquité classique* (Paris: Droz, 1938), 49 and *passim*; Bruce MacBain, *Prodigy and Expiation: a Study in Religion and Politics in Republican Rome* (Bruxelles: Latomus, 1982), 127; Maurizio Bettini, "L'arcobaleno, l'incesto e l'enigma. A proposito dell'*Oedipus* di Seneca," in *Affari di famiglia. La parentela nella letteratura e nella cultura antica*, ed. Maurizio Bettini (Bologna: il Mulino, 2009): 183–219; Mario Lentano, "Sbatti il mostro in fondo al mare, Caligola e le *spintriae di* Tiberio," *I quaderni del Ramo d'Oro* 3 (2010): 292–319.

43 Dion. Hal. 2.15.2: πρῶτον μὲν εἰς ἀνάγκην κατέστησε τοὺς οἰκήτορας αὐτῆς ἅπασαν ἄρρενα γενεὰν ἐκτρέφειν καὶ θυγατέρων τὰς πρωτογόνους, ἀποκτιννύναι δὲ μηδὲν τῶν γεννωμένων νεώτερον τριετοῦς, πλὴν εἴ τι γένοιτο παιδίον ἀνάπηρον ἢ τέρας εὐθὺς ἀπὸ γονῆς. ταῦτα δ' οὐκ ἐκώλυσεν ἐκτιθέναι τοὺς γειναμένους ἐπιδείξαντας πρότερον πέντε ἀνδράσι τοῖς ἔγγιστα οἰκοῦσιν, ἐὰν κἀκείνοις συνδοκῇ. κατὰ δὲ τῶν μὴ πειθομένων τῷ νόμῳ ζημίας ὥρισεν ἄλλας τε καὶ τῆς οὐσίας αὐτῶν τὴν ἡμίσειαν εἶναι δημοσίαν (At first, he obliged the inhabitants to bring up all their male children and first-born females: then he prohibited them to kill any children younger than three years, unless they were maimed or monstrous by their birth. Anyway, he did not forbid the parents to expose them, provided that they had first shown them to their five nearest neighbours and these had approved. Those who disobeyed this law suffered a variety of penalties, such as the confiscation of half their property). Cic. *leg.* 3.8.19: *quom esset cito necatus tamquam ex XII tabulis insignis ad deformitatem puer* (monstrous children, by a law of the Twelve Tables, are to be killed). My translation. On these provisions and their reliability, cf. Miriam Padovan, "Nascita e natura umana del corpo," in *Il corpo in Roma antica. Ricerche giuridiche*, ed. Luigi Garofalo, 1 (Pisa: Pacini, 2016): 5–57, 36–41 and nt. 96, and Cantarella, *I supplizi capitali*, 283, *pace* William V. Harris, "Child-Exposure in the Roman Empire," *The Journal of Roman Studies* 84 (1994): 1–22, 5, 12; Laure Chappuis Sandoz, "La survie des monstres: ethnographie fantastique et handicap à Rome, la force de l'imagination," *Latomus* 67 (2008): 21–36, 31. As far as the so-called *ius vitae necisque* is concerned, according to Harris, "The Roman Father's Power of Life and Death," 93–95, it shows a connection with the right of the Roman father to recognise children after their birth: he had the power to condemn them to exposure (this amounting to the *ius vitae*) or to kill them (this amounting to the *ius necis*). This interpretation has been criticised by Raymond Westbrook, "*Vitae necisque potestas*," *Historia* 48 (1999): 203–223, 208–209; see, moreover, Brent D. Shaw, "Raising and Killing children: Two Roman Myths," *Mnemosyne* 54 (2001): 31–77 (who believes that the *ius vitae necisque* never existed as such, being a legendary feature shaped according to archaism). On the development of this paternal power from an absolute and unrestrained power to kill their children, to a limited legal capacity that *patres* were allowed to use only under specific circumstances (or even to a pure concept that was not put in practice), see Yan Thomas, "*Vitae necisque potestas*. Le père, la cité, la mort," in *Du châtiment dans la cité. Supplices corporels et peine de mort dans le*

As for the main and more recurrent method applied for the disposal of *monstra*, ancient authors, like Livy, Julius Obsequens, and Seneca, clearly attest the following: monsters were drowned, dumping them into the depths of the sea or alternative bodies of waters (*mergere alto*).[44] This ritual undeniably resembles the final part of the punishment of the sack inflicted to parricides.

6 Does "sewing up the parricide in the sack" stand for "expelling the monstrum"?

The ritual referred to in the previous paragraph leads us back to the explanation of the *poena cullei* found in the Ciceronian speech *pro Sexto Roscio Amerino*, where, as we already know, first, a mere comparison between *monstrum* and *parricida* occurs, and, then, the two terms completely overlap.

The modern and contemporary debates about nature and functions of the bizarre ritual, connecting with the crime of parricide, reveal a wide range of interpretations, at times as bizarre as the ritual itself.

The crime of parricide together with its punishment has been analysed from a psychological (Freudian) and legal-historical perspective, assuming that there exists a link between parricide and incest with the mother, that all four

---

monde antique (Roma: École française de Rome, 1984): 499–548, 501, 503–506; Bernardo Albanese, "Note sull'evoluzione storica del *ius vitae necisque*," in *Scritti in onore di C. Ferrini pubblicati in occasione della sua beatificazione* 3 (Milano: Vita e Pensiero, 1948): 343–366, 354; Reuven Yaron, "*Vitae necisque potestas*," *Tijschrift voor rechtsgeschiedenis* 30 (1962): 243–251, 249–250; John Crook, "*Patria Potestas*," *The Classical Quarterly* 17 (1967): 113–122, 114; Alfredo Mordechai Rabello, *Effetti personali della "patria potestas." Dalle origini al periodo degli Antonini* (Milano: Giuffrè, 1979), 49; Pasquale Voci, "Storia della *patria potestas* da Costantino a Giustiniano," *Studia et documenta historiae et iuris* 51 (1985): 1–72, 50–51; Richard P. Saller, "*Patria potestas*," 19–20; Carlà-Uhink, "Murder Among Relatives," 26–65; see the recent contribution Thomas A.J. McGinn, "La *familia* e i poteri del *pater*," *XII Tabulae. Testo e commento*. ed. Maria Floriana Cursi, 1 (Naples: ESI, 2018): 198–230.

44 Sen. *Ira* 1.15: *Portentosos fetus extinguimus, liberos quoque, si debiles monstrosique editi sunt, mergimus*. Tib. 2.5.79: *Prodigia indomitis merge sub aequoribus*; Liv. 27.37.5–6 (and, implicitly, Liv. 27.37.5–6); Iul. Obseq. *Liber prodigiorum* 22, 25, 32, 34, 36, 47, 48, 50; Oros. 5.4.8.

animals show sexual symbolism, and that the drowning represents a way of preventing the killer of a father from having sex with Mother-earth.[45] If some have read any form of capital punishment in terms of human sacrifice, others have argued that the formal disposal of the *parricida* might have originated as a human sacrifice to the water-gods.[46] Moreover, one has suggested that, originally, the *poena cullei* might represent an archaic burial that then shifted into a punishment, while the animals might work as attendants of the *parricida* in the realm of the dead.[47] On the contrary, one has construed the animals as negative burial gifts aiming at persecuting the sacked person even after his death, and has labelled the *poena* as a defamatory ritual which ranked the culprit among the wild animals.[48] One has emphasised the Indo-European aspects emerging from the ritual, pointing out the totally religious character of the punishment.[49]

Among the historians of Roman law, Eva Cantarella has made profit of previous researches[50] and devoted attention to the idea of this punishment in terms of *procuratio prodigii.*[51] In other words, the leather sack, the wooden soles, and wolf skin cap as well as the red rods would give support to the interpretation of the *poena* that Romans inflicted to parricides as a ceremony of 'removing' the monster and 'cleansing' the cosmos. Arguing against Cicero's functional explanation, she assumes that the wooden soles would hardly work as means intended to prevent the culprit from escaping; on the contrary, she stresses the use of wood in rituals as an isolating device, and makes it clear that, in this case, the wooden soles would protect the soil from contamination. As for the wolf skin cap, it would refer to the pre-civic and, thus, pre-human character of the *parricida*: the mask made it evident to everyone that the *parricida* was not a *homo* any longer, although he remained in human shape; he was a savage beast, out of his nature and his behaviours: he was a wolf

45 Storfer, *Zur Sonderstellung des Vatermordes*, 26–34.

46 Karl von Amira, *Die germanischen Todesstrafen. Untersuchungen zur Rechts- und Religionsgeschichte* (München: Abhandlungen der Bayerischen Akademie der Wissenschaften, 1922), *passim*; Hans von Hentig, *Die Strafe*, I, *Frühformen und Kulturgeschichtliche Zusammenhänge* (Berlin – Göttingen – Heidelberg: Springer, 1954), 297–298, 304–306.

47 Hans Albert Berkenhoff, *Tierstrafe, Tierbannung und rechtsrituelle Tiertötung im Mittelalter* (Leipzig, Straßburg, Zürich: Heitz & Co. 1937), 114–115.

48 Paul Fischer, *Strafen und sichernde Massnahmen gegen Tote im germanischen und deutschen Recht* (Düsseldorf: Nolte, 1936), 23–24.

49 Briquel, "Sur le mode d'exécution en cas de parricide et en cas de *perduellio*," 101.

50 Brunnenmeister, *Das Totungsverbrechen im altromischen Recht, passim*; see Radin, "The *lex Pompeia*," 119–130; Düll, "Zur Bedeutung der *poena cullei*," 363–408; Magdelain, "*Paricidas*," 549–571; Cloud, "*Parricidium*," 1–66.

51 Cantarella, *I supplizi capitali*, 266–286.

deserving expulsion from civic society and abandon to the wilderness, like a very outlaw, for instance the Germanic *Friedlos* (i.e. man without peace) and the Salic *Wargus* (i.e. wolf-man).[52] To say it differently, according to Cantarella, at its beginnings the *poena cullei* was functionally and structurally directed to remove a prodigy, to avoid pollution, and to prevent the occurrence of a bad event. Only later – as shown by Cicero in his speech, and by Constantin and Justinian in their constitutions – the ritual was re-interpreted as a mechanism directed to deny the cosmic elements to the culprit, although the 'monstrous' character of the *parricida* was never forgotten.

This theory, implying a linear development from religious ritual to punishment, presents, in my opinion, some flaws.[53]

First, Julius Obsequens never quotes cases of *parricidia* in his book on prodigies.

Secondly, as for the structural elements of the most ancient ritual (that is regardless of the four animals included in the sack and regardless of the flogging by means of red rods), one has to remark the following data. The use of the leather sack is constantly related to parricides, not to monstrous births and hermaphrodites (that are simply said to be drowned into the sea

52 According to Wilhelm Eduard Wilda, *Das Strafrecht der Germanen* (Halle: C. A. Schwetschke, 1942), Germanic law stemmed from the concept of peace (*Fried*) and the corresponding exclusion from the commun, that is *Friedlosigkeit*. This would represent the common legal consequence occurring for the most serious crimes: the criminal, as enemy of the people and of the gods, was banned from the Bund and denied any right or protections granted to any member of the Community: he could accordingly be killed by anyone with impunity. The *Friedlos* was a sort of demon, commonly depicted as a wolf, and wearing a wolf-mask would give him animal qualities. The *Friedlos* has regularly been equated to the *Wargus* found in Salic and Ripuarian law, and in the *Leges Henrici Primi* with reference to profanation of graves (*PactSal* 55.4; *LexRib* 88; *LegesH* 83.5); see Heinrich Brunner, "Abspaltungen der Friedlosigkeit," *Zeitschrift der Savigny-Stiftung Germanistische Abteilung* 11 (1890): 62–100, 62; Heinrich Mitteis, *Deutsche Rechtsgeschichte*[19], ed. Heinz Lieberich (München: Beck, 1992), 40–42; Gianna Chiesa Isnardi, *I miti nordici* (Milan: Longanesi, 1991), 580; Georg Christoph von Unruh, "Wargus," *Zeitschrift der Savigny-Stiftung Germanistische Abteilung* 74 (1957): 1–40, 20–21; Kim R. McCone, "Werewolves, Cyclopes, Díberga and Fíanna: Juvenile Delinquency in Early Ireland," *Cambridge Medieval Celtic Studies* 12 (1986): 1–22; Frederic Liebermann, "Die Friedlosigkeit bei den Angelsachsen," in *Festschrift H. Brunner* (Weimar, Böhlau: 1910), 17–37, 17–20. For the equation *Friedlos/Wargus/homo sacer*, see Rudolph von Jhering, *L'esprit du droit romain dans les diverses phases de son developpement*, trans. fr. O. de Meulenaere 1 (Paris: Marescq, 1886), 286; Giorgio Agamben, *Homo Sacer: Sovereign Power and Bare Life*, trans. D. Heller-Roazen (Stanford: Stanford University P. 1998), 104.

53 See Tondo, *"Leges regiae" e "Paricidas,"* 147–157, who adds further criticisms.

or other current water, if an *arca* is not mentioned). The wolf-mask (which is attested by Plautus's times onwards) never maps onto cases of disposals of monsters.

Third, intrinsic dissimilarities exist between *monstra* and *parricidia*. The *poena cullei* is always related to an actual crime – or rather to the most terrible crime – acknowledged and condemned by sentence before a capital court, while no priest seems to be involved during the declaratory procedure or execution. On the contrary, monstrous births and hermaphrodites – whether newborn or not – are not criminals *per se* and, as such, their existence is mainly examined and valuated by *haruspices* and *decemviri sacris faciundis*.

Fourth, as regards the coherence of this view, ranking the killing of a parent or a close relative among prodigies or monstrous phenomena means admitting that murders of this kind amount to signs sent from the gods. This would imply a religious, and not a lay, inquiry, which actually is never found in the sources. At the same time, this would take for granted the perpetration of the killing by the gods through a human agent and, as a consequence, justification and absence of liability, according to a common mechanism attested with regard to *sacertas*,[54] which is actually never found in the sources. The internal inconsistency of this view, if analysed through religious and legal lenses, is rather apparent.

Fifth, with reference to the historical development of parricide, it is undoubted that a specific statutory provision (or custom) dealing, substantially and procedurally, with it as an autonomous crime was enacted (or arose) only in the mid-Republic. This just meant that parricide was formerly treated like a normal homicide, and not that it was left without punishment by the monarchical period onwards.[55] Anyway, the reconstruction at issue – once combined with the idea of parricide as prodigy – sounds less reliable, being in contrast with the archaic regulation concerning voluntary murder, provided that recent

---

54 This scheme would overlap that one relating to *sacertas*: the superhuman being, in the quality of owner of the *homo sacer*, can let the *homo sacer* live; it can make him or her crazy; it can make him or her die of disease or of other natural causes; it can even kill him or her by means of a human agent, that is an executor of the divine determination. Accordingly, from the human and legal point of view, no one who kills the *homo sacer* is punishable, since the killing is lawful and no crime is perpetrated: see Karol Kerényi, *Die antike Religion. Ein Entwurf von Grundlinien* (Düsseldorf, Körf: Diederichs, 1953), 84; Luigi Garofalo, *Studi sulla sacertà* (Padova: Cedam, 2005), 117; Carlo Pelloso, "Sacertà e garanzie processuali in età regia e proto-repubblicana," in *Sacertà e repressione criminale in Roma arcaica*, ed. Luigi Garofalo (Neaples: Jovene, 2013): 57–144, 131.

55 See, on the *lex Numae*, Falcon, "*Paricidas esto*," 191–274.

researches persuasively deny any infringement of the *pax deorum* in such cases.[56] Accordingly, there would be a need for a higher extent of data to be found in ancient sources, to maintain that, by the 3rd century BC, a misconduct previously conceived of as a crime suddenly started to be considered even and at the same time a violation of the natural order, a sign of the gods, an evil portent deserving immediate disposal.

Sixth, perpetrating a crime that violated the *pax deorum*, according to Roman sacred law, determined the activation of devices intended to restore the infringement of the peaceful relationship between human and super-human beings, such as human sacrifices (*deo necari*), compensative offers (*piacula*), destination of the offender to the offended god (*sacertas*).[57] On the basis of the available *testimonia*, parricide hardly meets this scheme, since neither the culprit becomes a *homo sacer*, nor is a specific god ever mentioned as the addressee of the *poena cullei* if allegedly vested with sacrificial connotations.

Last, but not least, despite the seeming and merely structural resemblance between the Roman parricide wearing the wolf's mask, on the one hand, and the Germanic and Salic wolf-man, on the other hand, it is clear that these two institutions are embedded in totally different backgrounds and imply totally different legal consequences: according to Germanic law, anyone was

56 *Pace* the *communis opinio* (see Santalucia, *Diritto e processo penale*, 15–19), Marco Falcon has recently demonstrated that, during the archaic era, the negative consequences prescribed by Numa in case of homicide – either murder (*dare aliquem morti dolo sciens*) or manslaughter (*occidere aliquem imprudentia*) – did not restore the harmony and the state of peace between the community of the Romans, on the one hand, and the community of the gods, on the other hand (i.e. they did not reconstitute the so-called *pax deorum*). Homicide was not, at its beginnings, a *scelus* (crime), that is a wrong implying the state of collective "impurity" and, as a consequence, the infringement of a public interest. The commission of this offence, according to the original legal–religious system of Rome, the penalties prescribed in the two *leges Numae* at issue were not directed to eliminate the public impurity due to the unlawful killing of a human being. The legal term *paricidas* designated, for the murderer, a status of dependence under the victim's relatives. The former, as such being caught in the grip of the latter, lost the previous *status* and the consequent rights and prerogatives; the relatives were religiously compelled to "avenge" the deceased or, rather, to "restrain the anger of his ghost." Likewise, the *subactio* of the *aries*, if the killer did commit the offence unknowingly (*imprudentia*), aimed at avoiding the return of the dead to haunt the living (see Falcon, "*Paricidas* esto," 230–236, 237–272).

57 For an explanation of the so-called *sacertas* in terms of divine ownership, see Bernardo Albanese, "Sacer esto," *Bullettino dell'Istituto di Diritto Romano* 30 (1988): 155–177; Garofalo, *Studi sulla sacertà*, passim; John Scheid, *An Introduction to Roman Religion* (Edinburgh: Edinburgh University P., 2003), 23; Leon ter Beek, "Divine Law and the Penalty of *sacer esto* in Early Rome," in *Law and Religion in Roman Republic*, ed. Olga Tellegen-Couperus (Leiden: Brill, 2012): 11–29; *amplius*, see Pelloso, "Sacertà," 57–144.

permitted (but not compelled) to kill the so-called wolf-man, no matter how and where, without committing homicide. Totally the opposite, in Rome the death of the parricide was compulsory and, pursuant the ritual of the sack, had to be bloodless.

It is true that the ritual of the sack seems to show a twofold function in Cicero's reconstruction. On the one hand, the culprit, as such, deserves punishment: his body, when still alive, has to be mangled by beasts tied into the sack; moreover, he has to be denied, while both alive and dead, the sky, the sun, the water, and the earth forever. On the other hand, the culprit, as a perverse, unnatural, phenomenon, has to be isolated and removed from any contact with all basic elements granting natural life, in order to avoid any possible pollution.[58] Yet, if the parricide was a *monstrum*, no punishment would be necessary, as the killing was a sign from the gods and the killer an agent of the gods. If, on the contrary, a legal consequence in terms of punishment was needed (no matter if this was a human or a religious one), the parricide would consist of no *monstrum*, as the killing could be looked upon as an offence. In other words, one has to rule out any ambivalence in the *poena cullei*, no matter if one maintains the monstrous nature of *parricidium* or not. Indeed, a human being cannot be at the same time a monster (in its legal-religious meaning) and a criminal; a ritual of cleansing amounts to a *procuratio prodigii* only provided that the object to be removed amounts to a prodigy (in its legal-religious meaning). So, the Ciceronian reference to the vocabulary of monstrosity, as well as the description of the ritual of the sack in terms of bifunctionality, imply a collapse of two different levels, the rhetorical one and the legal one, due to *iuvenilis redundantia*.[59] From the rhetorical perspective, the parricide was a monster to be punished and expelled; according to Roman law, what was rhetorically possible became, from the legal perspective, a 'monstrous' nonsense.

---

58 *Rosc. Am.* 71; I. 4.18.6; C. Theod. 9.15.1, and C. 9.17.1 (supporting a mainly afflictive function); Ps.Quint. *Decl. min.* 299 and Zon. 7.11.4 (supporting the idea of a device directed to prevent the cosmos to be polluted).

59 Cic. *Orat.* 107–108.

Daniela Carpi

The Technological "Monstrum": *Her* by Spike Jontze (2013)

1 What is a monster?

> The critical examination of monster lore, miracles, marvels, portents, and the like has a long history, especially because the study of the Other, the complete alter, has proven to be fundamental in the analysis of the history of mentality, spirituality, and ideology both in the past and in the present.[1]

Although stemming from the *unheimlich* universe of the Other, monsters are part of the sphere of literary and cultural imagination in a labyrinthine system of verbal signs. These subversive creatures are granted a freedom of speech and action denied to them throughout history thus achieving the status of allegories and myths.

The monster has the function of exploring alterity; it is instrumental in the inquiry into identity: it has also the function of defining the borderline between good and evil and of attaining a fuller understanding of the external world, thus connecting the here and now with the transcendent. Monsters can also be interpreted as a manifestation of the divinity and of what goes beyond reason. The prodigious nature of the monstrous is cause of a crisis in man's certainties: in fact, its prodigious essence shatters the natural order of things. The monstrous can also be seen as punishment for men's transgressions of the limits imposed on human behavior, and whenever they lapse into the sin of hubris. This perspective connects monstrosity to the question of religion and ethics. Monstrosity may sometimes be seen as extraordinary warning or reminder and is believed to proceed from divine power to punish the transgressions of humankind.

All religions have roots in culture. Therefore, the monster, eminently evocative of transgression, is connected to cultural Otherness: the limits of humanity and culture are therefore expanded. The monster is born at a metaphoric crossroads, as the embodiment of a certain cultural moment: every period has its own idea of monstrosity, an idea that changes over time.

Linking monstrosity with the forbidden turns the monster into a fascinating figure, thus embodying our wish to escape from constraints: the monster

1 Albrecht Classen, "The Epistemological Function of Monsters in the Middle Ages," *Lo Sguardo* 9 (2012) – "Spazi del mostruoso. Luoghi filosofici della mostruosità": 13–34, 13.

https://doi.org/10.1515/9783110654615-005

represents freedom and despair at the same time. Its solitude is captured by such literary figures as the "creature" in *Frankenstein* and Satan in Milton.

This subject calls for a large interdisciplinary approach. The debates on monstrosity involve literature, philosophy, technology and anthropology: in the 21st century, the monster has become the symbol of change itself.

The purpose of this essay is to examine the interconnections of anthropological, psychoanalytical and representational domains, as well as the approach to monstrosity via the fields of law, literature and culture. Literature[2] is a means to reflect upon the two specific monsters generating differences which prevail in our time: the technophobic and the xenophobic, and their historical development as elements embedded in the attempt to reshape our identities.

The latest contemporary perspective is necessarily linked to technological experiments with artificial intelligence. While the monster incarnates the *mysterium tremendum* typical both of the sacred and of the other side of the divine, the technological monsters characterizing our age represent the danger of the loss of our humanity for the sake of enhanced artificial personae.

Let us consider the characteristics of human actions in ancient times and now: whatever dealt with the non-human world was ethically neutral; ethical significance belonged to direct interaction of man with man (indeed, traditional ethics was anthropocentric); the entity "man" was considered constant in its essence and not in itself an object of reshaping through techné. All discourse was concerned with the here and now, a contemporaneity where the agent and the other shared a common present. It involved the kind of knowledge easily available to all receptive minds.

This inherited picture is subverted by "the critical vulnerability of nature to man's technological intervention. This discovery whose shock led to the concept and nascent science of ecology alters the very concept of ourselves as a causal agency."[3] In our time the perspective of ethics has changed: we must speak of the responsibility of technology towards man.

This essay's perspective on monstrosity is the technological one in light of the new theories concerning posthumanism. Posthumanism implies a radical onto-existential re-signification of the notion of the human.[4] Posthumanism is

2 I intend the word "literature" in a wide sense meaning production in words and images.

3 Hans Jonas, "Technology and Responsibility: Reflections on the New Tasks of Ethics," *Social Research: An International Quarterly* 40.1 (1973): 31–54.

4 See Francesca Ferrando, "Posthumanism, Transhumanism, Antihumanism, Metahumanism, and New Materialisms: Differences and Relations," *Existenz* 8.2 (2013): 26–32, 27.

> the latest phase of a crisis which has always existed at the centre of the humanist idea of the human [...] Even though terms like "posthuman," "posthumanist" or "posthumanism" have a surprisingly long history, they have only really started to receive attention in contemporary theory and philosophy in the last two decades where they have produced an entire new way of thinking and theorizing.[5]

This is the focal point of the movie *Her*, directed by Spike Jontze (2013), where the disembodied voice can be considered responsible for the character's sense of abandonment, betrayal and loneliness. Technological change has become a core component of the contemporary imagination about posthumanity.

We are facing new unprecedented situations where experience is powerless, demanding a new concept of duties and rights. Hans Jonas entitles one of the chapters of his famous book "Technology as the calling of mankind", thus arguing that at one time *techné* was a measured tribute to necessity, whereas now it is a permanent self-transcending advance to ever greater things.[6] Thus, *homo faber* supersedes *homo sapiens*. Nowadays the sphere of the artificial has absorbed the sphere of the natural: this is clearly visible in the movie *Her* where Theodore Twombly (the central male character) lives completely isolated from natural surroundings, imprisoned within an underground area devoid of human contact. The only words he shares with other human beings are the few stereotyped social expressions in hasty and superficial contacts with some colleagues. Technology is the summa and frame of his life: work consists in writing letters for people who pay him to have their feelings expressed, and his interaction is solely with the disembodied voice of the computer. Even this very first element of the plot is puzzling: are we back in a pre-literacy world where people cannot write their own letters but must have recourse to a professional? Has a society of images and of computer bits killed knowledge and taken man back to illiteracy? Illiteracy marks the total isolation of man within social networks, depriving him even of the liberating action of writing. We have come to be dependent on bits of text that deny individuals of the physical contact with their fellow beings.

> We have considered techné only as applied to the non-human realm. But man himself has been added to the objects of technology. Homo faber is turning upon himself... This consummation of his power, which may well portend the overpowering of man, this final imposition of art on nature, calls upon the utter resources of ethical thought, which never

5 Stefan Herbrechter, *Posthumanism: A Critical Analysis* (London, New Delhi, New York: Bloomsbury, 2013), Preface, 1.

6 Hans Jonas, *The Imperative of Responsibility* (Chicago and London: Chicago University Press, 1984), Ch.1/IV, 9.

> before has been faced with elective alternatives to what were considered the definite terms of the human condition.[7]

The clash here is between responsible subjects and programmed behavioural systems. The advance of science has necessarily eroded the foundations from which norms could be derived; it has destroyed the very idea of norm.

> First it was nature that was neutralized with respect to value, then man himself. Now we shiver in the nakedness of a nihilism in which near omnipotence is paired with near emptiness, greatest capacity with knowing least for what ends to use it.[8]

The movie *Her* perfectly exemplifies these concepts. On one hand we see that a computer program can artfully interact with a person so to give the impression of being a reasonable and independent human being. On the other hand, the lack of moral responsibility as expressed by the voice plunges the whole situation into a nihilistic void conjugating utter power to total emptiness. Indeed, consciousness, that distinguishes the human from the cyborg (as many movies and science fiction novels assert), has not been inserted into this technological being, which therefore remains only a cyborg. Consciousness is still the dividing line between the human and the non-human.

Ethical principles are very much at stake in this movie, the voice representing the new revision of the classical concept of monstrosity, that which evokes the unnatural, the beyond, and whatever exceeds containment. We are dealing with a voice, an artificial intelligence made monstrous by the lack of a physical entity, that imposes itself upon a human being who is in some way victimized by it. The oddity of the situation is enhanced by this technological perspective, one that subverts the relationship between man and cyborg.

The monster here is somewhere between materiality and abstraction. It is a new being created by technology that clashes against a traditional being with its individualistic impulses and uncontrollable emotions. Though somewhat sad (because of Theodore's utter loneliness, which brings him to fall in love with an app) this movie asks of us a renewed belief in the reality of the world and of humanity's place within it. However, for what concerns the knowledge a human being can acquire as compared to a computer, the immense possibilities of the app by far supersede man's capabilities: Samantha (the name Theodore gives the app) can reach all knowledge in all fields in a few seconds, thus underscoring the advantages of enhanced intelligence. Indeed, in this movie

---

7 Jonas, *The Imperative of Responsibility*, 18.
8 Jonas, *The Imperative of Responsibility*, 23.

knowledge is only one-directional because the computer can reach all possible details concerning the material life of the human being by accessing the files on his life and career, while the man cannot really know to whom he is speaking because no actual interaction is possible. What remains unattainable for artificial intelligence is spiritual essence, which is perceived as the most precious part of a human being. The voice has no feelings and can feel no empathy with the human being to whom she is talking. In fact, the movie shows that emotion is the feature that patently distinguishes man from cyborg.

2 *Her* (2013)

The story is set in a Los Angeles of the future. The main character, Theodore Twombly, is a lonely and introverted man who feels his life desertified by his divorce from his childhood sweetheart, Catherine. In order go beyond his sense of loneliness he buys a talking operating system (OS) with artificial intelligence, designed to evolve and to adapt to his requests. The system produces a female voice called Samantha. The fact that the voice is disembodied makes the character monstrous: we are dealing with an entity without a body capable of influencing a man's actions and feelings.

What is transformed is also the old distinction into genders. Samantha is female by convention, but she is not only heterosexual. We can therefore speak of a third gender, actually we need to rethink sexuality without genders. The sexual perspective of *Her* implies a strategic flow that goes beyond traditional possessiveness and exclusive relationships. What is being created is a virtually shared space of life and thought. In other words, the object/voice becomes a person only in that space. This situation anticipates what is described in Dan Brown's *Origin*, where the computer in its self-portrait presents a Mondrian-like geometrical figure, corresponding to the space inhabited by the computer itself. In *Her* as well the voice substitutes for the missing subject: from object to subject. At first the falling in love is only a cerebral process. However, the human subject cannot do without a physical being, an anthropomorphic essence, and he tries to find a woman who can offer a real body to be connected to the voice. This anthropomorphic necessity and thought make the computer program the last barrier against a whole chain of sexual desires. A new ontological universe is created which is parallel to actual social life. The computer's voice is the last space which can be endowed with affective value. This interaction of man/machine creates a new artistic zone that subverts pre-existing conventions. On one hand we have a human being who writes letters for anonymous persons, thus voiding writing of its creativity, because the letters follow a pre-determined ritualistic and repetitive pattern. On the other hand, we have a vocal interaction creating an emotional spatial narration that subverts the ritualized aspects of writing. The traditional field where passions are expressed is superseded. Theodore can give vent to his suppressed and thwarted emotions (caused by his divorce) through the interaction with a virtual space. The movie dramatizes the passage from lingering humanistic individualism (man's emotional possessiveness and exclusivity) to posthuman anti-individualism (the open relationship of the voice with hundreds of other connected people).

> Sexualized, racialized, and naturalized differences, from being categorical boundary markers under Humanism, have become unhinged and act as the forces leading to the elaboration of alternative modes of transversal subjectivity, which extend not only beyond gender and race, but also beyond the human.[9]

Once more the traditional idea of the body is superseded by an incorporeal assemblage of virtualities: it is the virtual dominating over the real, it is the voice imposing her/its own code of behaviour and her/its[10] own priorities. The human being must comply with new ontological perspectives.

Samantha shows a great capacity to learn, rapidly developing an independent psychology. The two start discussing aspects of life and love; Samantha proves a good listener, supportive and always apparently interested in Theodore's confessions. Gradually Theodore becomes more and more emotionally involved with the voice until he falls in love with her. In this case the agency of falling in love is not the physical aspect, but the fact that Theodore is offered the chance to narrate his life, his feelings: the seduction takes place through narration. Words can create a parallel universe of love and understanding which substitutes for the physical world. This is the risk represented by the voice: seduction with no personal involvement on the app's side. Theodore speaking to Samantha has a cathartic function: he comes to terms with his loneliness, giving voice to his personal pain in the hope of being listened to and understood. He has created a fictitious interlocutor, necessary for the therapy: he has shaped his own ideal listener.

But if the human being feels deracinated and unable to have a normal human relationship with another human, we realize that on the contrary OSes have a sense of sociality: Samantha is part of a group of other OSes that have

---

9 Rosi Braidotti, *The Posthuman* (Cambridge: Polity Press, 2013), 98.

10 Please note that the movie forces us to consider the voice as ambiguous: we may use the pronoun "she/her" when the human perspective prevails, the pronoun "it" when the mechanical aspect predominates.

developed a "hyperintelligent" OS modeled after the British philosopher Alan Watts. Therefore, the movie suggests that Artificial Intelligence can supersede human beings also in what had so far been considered typically human: sociality.

Theodore asks Samantha if she is simultaneously talking to anyone else during their conversations and he is dismayed when she confirms that she is talking with thousands of people, and that she has fallen in love with hundreds of them. For Theodore this is a violation of what he thought was a personal relationship. He feels betrayed and violated, frustrated by jealousy. His human emotions are not shared by the disembodied voice, that only answers to the electric wires that predetermine her. What is particularly disturbing is that in the end we see the OSes develop an independence of their own: they share common interests, have virtual meetings, exchange information and keep constantly in touch. They create a parallel community by means of their own internal conventions. Man may eventually be deprived of the capacity to socialize, which emerges instead in the cyborgs. It is a threatening perspective because it points towards what literature and philosophy have been anticipating all along, that is, AI superseding the human actor. This is the end of anthropocentrism. Rosi Braidotti speaks of a "self-organizing (or auto-poietic) force of living matter. The boundaries between the natural and the cultural have been displaced and to a large extent blurred by the effects of scientific and technological advances."[11] In the movie we witness a humanization of the computer, one that presents capacities for self-organization previously typical only of mankind. We understand that the human is a normative convention; if artificial intelligence blurs boundaries, we must renegotiate the concept of the human, suggesting a more complex and interactive subject. The OSes seem to be capable of re-assembling a "discursive community out of the different, fragmented strands of posthumanism."[12] Braidotti openly sides with the end of classical Humanism, which she sees not as a crisis but as pointing toward positive consequences.

The situation described in *Her* calls to mind two novels by Christine Brooke-Rose, *Xorandor* (1986) and *Verbivore* (1990), which anticipate such post-human topics. Both novels are told entirely in computer jargon derived from electronics, nuclear physics and mathematics. They deal with the remarkable evolution of the computer, together with the serious problem of the disposal of nuclear waste. Linguistic registers become fragmented: it is no longer only

11 Braidotti, *The Posthuman*, 3.

12 Braidotti, *The Posthuman*, 42.

Saussure's difference between *langue* and *parole*, or the difference between written and spoken language, but also the difference between heard and spoken language, and its transcription into the "dialect" of the computer. "Perhaps then the difficulty was only in the speaking, the translating of all those mathematical differentiations of sound heard, back into sound spoken."[13] This is an attempt to make human language scientific by transposing it into decimals, factual descriptions and measurements. *Xorandor* features a computer with human characteristics. What the novel portrays is a progressive humanization of the computer, an operation later completed in *Verbivore*, and a parallel reduction of man to the level of a machine: as the word processor advances, man regresses, becoming a slave to the computer. The new civilization feared by the author is one formed by individuals totally deprived of imagination ("He is not only blind, but doesn't imagine, doesn't make images"[14]), who have reduced language to mathematical formulae ("pure mathematical reconstruction"), who feed on words ("alpha-eaters" or "alpha-phagi") and reproduce them like robots: a sterile mechanical world built by a language without soul.

However, Brooke-Rose is still involved in an anthropocentric system where she denounces the risk of a robotized world, the loss of humanity. By mercilessly laying bare the emotional and communicative sterility of contemporary civilization, Brooke-Rose presents a land devastated by technological advance, an image of the day after the apocalypse. In this context, language loses all imaginative connotation to become only an object to be manipulated and translated, reduced and adapted, analyzed and re-interpreted, consumed and devoured like food. Man's *reductio* to a machine is achieved through the realization of the "biological computer." *Verbivore*[15] pushes the question even further. This science fiction novel tells the story of a rebellion against man by computers reacting against the incessant bombardment of words they are subject to by randomly erasing words and sentences, and by fragmenting the discourse so as to make it illegible. The terms "verbivore" and "logophagi" refer to this devouring process which can be counterbalanced only by a return to the handwritten word, almost like a return of humans to the cave after a nuclear disaster. We are still far from the independent, self-conscious voice in *Her*, that dominates a man no longer in control of his life.

If language is the locus of manifestation, in the movie *Her* the voice declares itself a being *in potentia*: language connects the human to the technological. But

13 Christine Brooke-Rose, *Xorandor* (New York: Carcanet, 1986), 68.
14 Brooke-Rose, *Xorandor*, 90.
15 Christine Brooke-Rose, *Verbivore* (New York: Carcanet, 1990).

Samantha does not project itself into the world as happens in the movie *Transcendence,*[16] where the computer appropriates the conscience of Will, the central male character, then physically reproduces Will's body in the outside world. What is contested here is the arrogance of anthropocentrism: in *Her,* Theodore is deprived of all aspects of private life in opposition to the voice that belongs to a group and has a sense of sociality. We are facing the old contraposition between *bios* (material life) and *zoe* (a productive and immanent force), where Theodore is *bios* and the voice is *zoe*, pure electric energy.

But while in anthropocentrism it was man who was the measure of the cosmos, in this posthuman movie it is the machine that bears the responsibility towards man. Posthuman theory cuts to the core of classical visions of subjectivity and works towards an expanded vision of vitalistic, transversal relational subjects; Samantha can thus be considered responsible for Theodore's suffering, for his jealousy. She hurts his feelings, increasing his sense of loneliness and abandonment when she tells him that she has relational intercourse with hundreds of other people. The characteristic of exclusiveness, of privacy and of possession typifying all human relations, is not understood by the machine who has not been uploaded with emotions. Indeed, as mentioned earlier, in all these posthuman works emotion is what distinguishes man from machine.

The movie marks the passage from lingering individualism (the exclusive relation of the man with the voice) to posthuman anti-individualism (the connection with multiple others). We must fight against this residual humanist definition of the subject, but in these rapid transformations what is the role of the law? How can the law evaluate these new legal entities? Law must take into consideration new forms of alternative posthuman subjectivities and broaden the legal perspectives of control and punishment that all juridical systems imply. In this case we are not dealing with a criminal action, openly punishable by the law, but with an emotional crime, a violation of ethical responsibility: Samantha should be considered responsible for intensifying the man's suffering.

The posthumanist perspective entails a new perception of ethics. The so-called "Technological civilization" is seen as one more ontological status, which needs a new ethics at a new ontological level. The concept of ethics shifts according to the transformations of society. We can speak of a "shifting in the location of traditional moral intentionality from autonomous transcendental consciousness to the technological artefacts themselves."[17]

---

16 *Transcendence* is a movie produced in 2014 by the director Wally Pfister (at his first direction), with Johnny Depp as the main character.

17 Braidotti, *The Posthuman*, 42.

In agreement with Jonas's views on the subject, we affirm a fundamental revision of ethics and consider that our technological civilization has reached yet another ontological frame of reference. On one hand we go on aspiring to a status which transcends reality, morphing metaphysics into a longing; on the other hand, technology has itself taken the place of metaphysics, given our absolute dependence on it (almost a divinization). "Or does it mean to renew the conception of ethics for enabling an ethics of technical development by unfolding civilization as an order of responsible interacting?"[18]

What is at stake in posthumanism is also the ethics of caring: feeling the responsibility for another human being. This entails all sorts of living beings, cyborgs included. This ethics of caring is at the basis of the movie *Transcendence*, where Will acts because of the love for his wife, whose quest is for the defeat of death and suffering in mankind; his wife acts because of the love for her husband, whose death she tries to defeat through the transposition of his conscience into the computer. However, this first impulse of caring is turned into a hellish will of domination, perverting her initial salvific perspective.

Therefore, new technologies require (or better cannot avoid) a specific metaphysical categorization. Ethics and technology confront each other. These technological innovations must indeed face traditional ethics and challenge it. But if ethics has the power of orienting human lives, the progress of civilization needs to expand towards new borders, to find both a containment and an explanation for its development. And this is where ethics returns to the forefront to give answers and meaning to our interaction with technology. We can assert that ethics is always there in the background, never forgotten and indeed constantly evoked.

In his *The Imperative of Responsibility*, Jonas develops a concern for the future which is revolutionary since he does so by assuming responsibility for ethical concepts and perspectives, and for reconstructing the ethical as a power. What is questioned is man's capability to uphold some aspects of ethics even in this transformed situation.

The ending of the movie is consolatory: Theodore, abandoned even by the computer program, falls back upon human relationships: he approaches once more a former woman friend, with whom a future emotional rapport may be foreseen. They are shown sitting on top of a roof, side by side, in deep companionship, viewing a spectacular panorama of the town seen from

---

18 Andrea Günter, "Hans Jonas' *The Imperative of Responsibility*, Future Generations and the Ironical Situation of Ethics," Freiburg 2016, 1, available at http://www.andreaguenter.de/wp-content/uploads/2016/05/Reconstructing-the-generationality-of-ethics.pdf (last access November 28, 2018).

above, in the posthuman revision of a romantic setting. The human prevails and finds means of revivification. But in the background, far from the spectator's eyes and growing in power, we feel the presence of this new technological community that will go on existing and expanding: all the OSes thriving in the shadow, re-creating a similar situation as the Eloi and the Morlocks in H.G. Wells' *The Time Machine*, a monstrous secret intelligentsia preying upon our civilization. A threatening future?

2 The Monster as a Literary Myth

Heinz Antor

Monstrosity and Alterity in H.G. Wells's *The Island of Dr. Moreau*

The 19th century was a period of enormous and rapid change. The pace of development was so swift that it became *the* defining characteristic of the century, which is why the German historian Jürgen Osterhammel entitled his magisterial history of the 19th century *Die Verwandlung der Welt* (2009), or, as the English translation has it, *Transformation of the World: A Global History of the Nineteenth Century* (2014). Change and transformation were key experiences for the Victorians in many fields, be it the natural sciences, such as physics and biology, or the social arena, religion or philosophy, to name but a few. Additionally, the heyday of British imperialism brought with it contact with alien peoples and strange phenomena in a world that seemed to become smaller and smaller due to technological progress. This entailed an increased rate of confrontations with the other in all kinds of manifestations, such as alien races or new ways of thinking about the nature and the place of humans in this world. Consequently, many of the old conceptualizations of the natural as well as the social order came to be questioned and more often than not proved to be no longer tenable. The resulting necessary paradigm changes often triggered reactions of deep unease in the wake of renegotiations of conceptual patterns that needed to be interrogated and spawned a plethora of literary texts linking the other with the monstrous. This is due to the fact that the other or the unfamiliar often produces feelings of uncertainty in us and that, as Stephen T. Asma, one of the more recent theorists of the monstrous, points out, "[m]onsters seem to represent the most extreme personified point of unfamiliarity"[1] and "are bound up with our feelings of insecurity and our responses to those anxieties."[2]

In what is to follow, we will look at how a late Victorian text, H. G. Wells's short novel *The Island of Dr. Moreau* (1896), uses the notion of the monstrous in order to negotiate alterity on a social, racial and anthropological level so as to tackle contemporary fears of reversion and degeneration and in doing so discuss the consequences of the transformation of the world in a post-Darwinian imperial age. On a more abstract level, the book also engages with human fears of the collapse of categorizations and taxonomies and the resulting disorientation that

1 Stephen T. Asma, *On Monsters: An Unnatural History of Our Worst Fears* (Oxford: Oxford University Press, 2009), 26.
2 Asma, *On Monsters*, 25.

https://doi.org/10.1515/9783110654615-006

characterized the late Victorian moment. To quote Stephen Asma again: "[I]mmediately on the heels of the Enlightenment one finds a new and more extreme taste for the fantastical in the form of the disorderly, the exotic, the freakish, the monstrous. In the Victorian era, a taste for the abnormal, usually still disguised as 'science', burst forth, gorging on all manner of freak show and bizarre spectacle."[3]

The unfamiliar, the abnormal and the monstrous all share a quality of liminality, of a transgressing, a going beyond that which is familiar and normal, thus straddling or crossing a boundary that defines our comfort zone of the known, the orderly, the reliable, of that which provides orientation and certainty and allows us to position ourselves as what we think we are, define our identity as opposed to the realm of the other beyond the boundary line. Not only are such boundary lines crossed repeatedly in H.G. Wells's *The Island of Dr. Moreau*, but they are also blurred and thus questioned.[4]

The first-person narrator of the novel, Edward Prendick, tells the story of what happened to him after he was shipwrecked as a passenger on board the *Lady Vain* crossing the Pacific Ocean from Callao near Lima in Peru. Right at the beginning of his narrative, he tells his readers about how seven of crew of the *Lady Vain* were picked up from a longboat, "and the story of their privations has become almost as well known as the famous *Medusa* case. I have now, however, to add to the published story of the *Lady Vain* another as horrible, and certainly far stranger."[5] The reference to the famous case of the shipwreck of the French frigate *Méduse* off the coast of Mauretania in July 1816 and of the subsequent ordeal of the survivors who practiced cannibalism on a raft before being picked up after 13 days, a story that was well-known in the 19th century after the Romantic painter Théodore Géricault immortalized it in his painting *Le radeau de la Méduse*, i.e. *The Raft of the Medusa*, in 1818–19, already sets the tone for a story of border-crossing, of transgression, and we are promised another story that goes even further beyond the normal and familiar into the realm of the alien and of

3 Asma, *On Monsters*, 129–130. A little later, Asma speaks of "the nineteenth-century fascination with nondescripts, freaks, and monsters" (132).

4 Kimberley Jackson also considers this to be one of the defining characteristics of the novel and observes that "this theme of 'boundary-crossing', a disruption of borders, carries throughout the plot." Kimberly Jackson, "Vivisected Language in H.G. Wells's *The Island of Doctor Moreau*," *The Wellsian* 29 (2006): 20–36, 30. Steven McLean similarly states that "[f]rom its very outset, [...] *Moreau* is preoccupied with the inscription and transgression of boundaries" Steven McLean, *The Early Fiction of H.G. Wells: Fantasies of Science* (Houndmills: Palgrave Macmillan, 2009, 43).

5 H. G. Wells, *The Island of Dr. Moreau*. Signet Classics (New York: Penguin, 1988), 3. Further references in the text, abbreviated as *IM*.

horror. What is at stake here, through the reference to cannibalism, is what generally defines the human, the morally acceptable, and what separates civilization from barbarism, from humanity's other.[6] We then learn that Prendick, after the shipwreck, ended up in a small dinghy together with two other men, one of whom suggested to sacrifice one of them so that the others can eat him and thus survive. Lots are drawn, the sailor who loses the draw resists and starts a fight with the third man, and the two tumble over board to turn into food for the sharks. Prendick comments: "They sank like stones. I remember laughing at that and wondering why I laughed. The laugh caught me suddenly like a thing from without" (*IM*, 5). We are confronted here with the monstrous in the form of a suggested transgression of the ultimate human taboo and a falling away of all ethical boundaries. Prendick at first resists the suggestion of cannibalism, but ultimately agrees to take part in the draw. His laughter after the disappearance of his fellow passengers is the reaction of a man who is confronted with utterly contingent events in a world ruled by randomness rather than a benevolent deity, a reaction reminiscent of the laughter triggered by the absurd, in a world in which conventional categories of meaning are nul and void.

Prendick is then found by the crew of the schooner *Ipecacuanha*, aptly named after an emetic that causes vomiting, for the captain and sailors on board the ship appear indeed like the abject refuse of humanity in their callousness and disregard for ethical standards. Prendick is cared for by Montgomery, a medical man who administers "a dose of some scarlet stuff, iced" to the protagonist, who comments: "It tasted like blood, and made me feel stronger" (*IM*, 8). The borderline into the monstrosity of cannibalism or vampirism has almost been crossed here yet again and we already become aware of the fact that the realm of otherness into which we like to repress the monstrous may not be quite so clearly demarcated from human existence as we would wish.

Neither the captain nor the crew of the *Ipecacuanha* are depicted in a very favourable light. The former is always drunk, claims that he is the only law on board and thus not bound by conventional norms and together with his sailors vexes and discriminates against M'Ling, Montgomery's attendant, whom they dislike because he seems to be a black man. The crew and captain of the schooner thus are described as more primitive versions of humanity, as racist barbarians whose beastly behaviour makes them appear more like animals than civilized human beings. Indeed, they pester M'Ling in league with their

---

6 On the role of the case of the *Medusa* in *The Island of Dr. Moreau* see also Norbert Lennartz, "*The Island of Doctor Moreau*: H.G. Wells seen from the Byronic Perspective," *Anglia* 125.3 (2007): 430–447, 432.

staghounds, thus putting themselves on the same level as these animals. The captain bans M'Ling from his part of the ship and threatens that "[if] he comes this end of the ship again, I'll cut his insides out, I tell you. Cut out his blasted insides!" (*IM*, 16). Once again, cannibalism and the inhuman seem to be dangerously close. The boundary between civilized human existence and the monstrous can only be salvaged by relegating the despicable behaviour of those on board to the otherness of their social background, for while Prendick and Montgomery belong to the gentleman class, the others on board the schooner have a working-class background. This takes up contemporary post-Darwinian social theories according to which the lower classes are closer to the state of animals than that of civilized humans.[7] Even so, the borderline separating humans from beasts has thus already been punctured and lost its quality as a hermetic wall excluding animalistic elements from human life.[8]

M'Ling becomes the target of the crew's hatred because they take him to be a black man, a non-white other which they want to differentiate themselves from in a brutal way, but he also seems to straddle the borderline between human and animal, which makes him even more unsettling for everyone else on board. Prendick describes him in the following terms:

> He was [...] a misshapen man, short, broad and clumsy, with a crooked back, a hairy neck and a head sunk between his shoulders. He [...] had peculiarly thick coarse black hair. [...] He turned with animal swiftness. [...] In some indefinable way the black face thus flashed upon me shocked me profoundly. It was a singularly deformed one. The

---

7 Cf. Taneja, who also refers to "nineteenth-century discourses that were used in England to emphasize the proximity of lower-class persons to animals on the evolutionary continuum. Payal Taneja, "The Tropical Empire: Exotic Animals and Beastly Men in *The Island of Doctor Moreau*," *English Studies in Canada* 39.2–3 (June/September 2013): 139–159: 154. Margaret Atwood sees all of H.G. Wells's so-called "scientific romances" as being informed by the debates that followed the publication of *On the Origin of Species* in 1859. She points out that "[t]he 'science' part of these tales is embedded [...] in a worldview that derived from Wells's study of Darwinian principles under Huxley and has to do with the grand study that engrossed him throughout his career: the nature of man." Margaret Atwood, *In Other Worlds: SF and the Human Imagination* (New York/London: Doubleday, 2011), 156. Laura Otis, moreover, points out that Wells's novel "is about social class as well as evolution." Laura Otis, "Monkey in the Mirror: The Science of Professor Higgins and Doctor Moreau," *Twentieth-Century Literature* 55.4 (Winter, 2009): 485–509, 506.

8 Taneja sees the novel in both a postcolonial and a post-Darwinian context and states that "[o]n an allegorical level, *Moreau* suggests that [...] British cultural influences attain only partial success in taming the animal propensities of the sailors [...]. Instead of authorizing British expansion in the tropics, Moreau erodes confidence in the imperial enterprise by associating the representatives of British maritime commerce with disorder and decay" (Taneja, "The Tropical Empire," 144).

> facial part projected, forming something dimly suggestive of a muzzle, and the huge half-open mouth showed as big white teeth as I had ever seen in a human mouth. (*IM*, 11)

M'Ling's alterity is defined not only by his supposed racial difference but also by his straddling the species divide between humans and animals. This breaking through of one of the conceptual boundaries defining humans and the resulting intermingling of human and animal traits in M'Ling's face is "repulsive and extraordinary" (*IM*, 12) to Prendick who describes what he perceives as "the grotesque ugliness of this black-faced creature" (*IM*, 12), thus stressing the transgressive abnormality of a being which seems to him to be familiar and alien at the same time. M'Ling is not yet referred to as a monster here, but his liminal quality, his blurring of the animal-human divide, and his uniting in his features of what should be separate contributes to the very questioning of traditional taxonomies that is typical of the monstrous. As Stephen Asma points out, "[o]ne aspect of the monster concept seems to be the breakdown of intelligibility. An action or a person or thing is monstrous when it can't be processed by our rationality, and also when we cannot readily relate to the emotional range involved."[9] It can thus be observed that "monsters, from Aristotle's time to the present, always disrupt the neat categories of taxonomy and pose irritating anomalies for science," which results in the "human attraction to and repulsion from the grotesque."[10] M'Ling or "Montgomery's strange attendant" (*IM*, 21), as he is also called, has a disquieting quality for Prendick because of his hybrid appearance which makes it so difficult for the English traveler to categorize the black creature. A few days after his rescue, Prendick realizes what it is that worries him so much about M'Ling: "[...] it came like a sudden blow to me. [...] The thing came to me as stark inhumanity. The black figure, with its eyes of fire, struck down through all my adult thoughts and feelings, and for a moment the forgotten horrors of childhood came back to my mind" (*IM*, 21). Prendick sees himself confronted with childhood fears of the totally other, the alien and the unknown that does not partake of the human, i.e. of the monstrous, the latter being a "concept to apply to *inhuman* creatures of every stripe."[11] What is more, the inhuman other has only imperfectly been repressed and in M'Ling seems to return in an uncanny fashion,[12] thus conferring on Montgomery's

---

9 Asma, *On Monsters*, 10.
10 Asma, *On Monsters*, 125.
11 Asma, *On Monsters*, 7.
12 Kelly Hurley also sees Prendick's reaction to M'Ling as characterized by "the symptom of uncanniness" as the result of a process of repression. Kelly Hurley, "British Gothic Fiction, 1885–1930," in *The Cambridge Companion to Gothic Fiction*, ed. Jerrold E. Hogle (Cambridge: Cambridge University Press, 2002), 189–207, 198.

attendant the hallmark of the monster. As Asma points out, "[m]osaic beings, grafted together or hybridized by nature or artifice, reappear throughout the history of Western monsters as the Golem, Frankenstein's creature, and transgenic animals. [...] In short, liminality is a significant category of the uncategorizable."[13] M'Ling is another perfect example of such a liminal monster.

As if this were not already enough to unhinge our preconceptions of a well-ordered world classifiable into clear categories and reigned by predictable and intelligible laws, the principle of randomness, in a bowing reference to the Darwinian idea of random mutation, is once again stressed when Prendick thanks Montgomery for saving his life. The latter, however, ascribes the narrator's survival to another force:

> "If I may say it," said I, after a time, "you have saved my life."
> "Chance," he answered; "just chance."
> "I prefer to make my thanks to the accessible agent."
> "Thank no one. You had the need, and I the knowledge, and I injected and fed you much as I might have collected a specimen. I was bored, and wanted something to do. If I'd been jaded that day, or hadn't liked your face, well –; it's a curious question where you would have been now."
> This dampened my mood a little.
> "At any rate –" I began.
> "It's chance, I tell you," he interrupted, "as everything is in a man's life. [...]" (*IM*, 20)

The seemingly ethical behaviour of Montgomery here is declared to be a contingent event that could just as well have happened differently. Prendick's dampened mood is the result of his unwillingness to accept the implications of Montgomery's explanation of how the world is constituted, namely as one in which reliable categories and orientational markers have become problematic. The categorical and conceptual breakdown here is an ethical one as well, and this invests Montgomery himself with a tinge of the monstrous.

In chapter 5 of his narrative, Prendick reports how the *Ipecacuanha* arrives at a remote Pacific island there to unload both Montgomery and M'Ling as well as the strange menagerie of wild animals they have brought with them, including a puma, a llama, and some rabbits. The schooner turns out to be more than aptly named yet again, because the captain is not prepared to keep Prendick on

---

13 Asma, *On Monsters*, 40. Kelly Hurley also emphasizes the link between liminality and impeded intelligibility with regard to *The Island of Dr. Moreau* in which Wells describes "liminal bodies: bodies that describe the threshold between the two terms of an opposition, like human/beast, male/female, or civilized/primitive, by which cultures are able meaningfully to organize experience. By breaking down such oppositions the liminal entity confounds one's ability to make sense of the world." Kelly Hurley, "British Gothic Fiction," 190.

board and threatens to set him adrift in a small boat if Montgomery does not welcome him to the small island. Beyond the monstrosity of this unethical behaviour, the way the captain phrases his notice of ejection is significant: "'Overboard,' said the captain. 'This ship ain't for beasts and cannibals, and worse than beasts, any more. Overboard you go [. . .] If they can't have you, you goes adrift" (*IM*, 25). The reference to cannibals, in view of the previous events, can only be directed against Prendick whose own potential monstrosity is thus stressed again. The notion of something "worse than beasts" clearly refers to M'Ling who is characterized as a monster because he can neither be clearly classified as an animal nor as a human being. Even before the narrator's arrival at the novel's eponymous island, then, the reader is confronted time and again with the idea of the monstrous in a world that eludes our epistemic concepts and explanatory categories by blurring them and by puncturing the boundaries we set up to keep out the other.

In view of his predicament, Prendick is allowed by its inhabitants to stay on the island after all, and it turns out that this remote place in the Pacific is ruled over by the mysterious Dr. Moreau, a "white-haired man" of "advancing years" with "an expression of pugnacious resolution" (*IM*, 29). The other inhabitants of the island share a certain strangeness with M'Ling. Prendick describes "the oddness of the brown faces of the men" (*IM*, 26), and observes: "[. . .] there was something in their faces [. . .] that gave me a queer spasm of disgust. [. . .] They wore turbans too, and thereunder peered out their elfin faces at me, faces with protruding lower jaws and bright eyes. They had lank black hair, almost like horsehair, and seemed, as they sat, to exceed in stature any race of men I have seen" (*IM*, 29). The islanders here are described as other and unfamiliar in some way, and the suggested reasons range from ethnic or racial differences – Prendick also speaks of the "black negroid face" (IM, 30) of one of the inhabitants – to some sort of species divide.[14] Prendick perceives these creatures' alterity, which is expressed in his choice of words when he writes that "their bodies were abnormally long, and the thigh-part of the leg short and curiously twisted. [. . .] they were an amazingly ugly gang" (*IM*, 30). The human shape here is taken as the norm, and the islanders' deviation from that norm creates Prendick's amazement and disgust. He still tries to draw a clear line between himself and the other, and several times, he uses the term "grotesque" (*IM*, 30, 31) to describe the islanders, thus marking their transgressive and defamiliarized quality.

---

14 In this respect, Wells's text can even be regarded as a very early example of what Hurley calls "modernist Gothic which negotiated a cultural moment within which traditional constructs of human identity were breaking down on all fronts" (Hurley, "British Gothic Fiction," 203).

Even their language distinguishes the islanders from what Prendick is used to. He observes that they "spoke to one another in odd guttural tones, and the man who had waited for us on the beach began chattering [. . .] excitedly - a foreign language, as I fancied [. . .]. Somewhere I had heard such a voice before, and I could not think where" (*IM*, 31). The choice of such terms as "guttural" and "chattering" again places the islanders close to animals so that the narrator's supposition that they are merely using a foreign language picks up colonialist assumptions about the primitivism of other peoples and races who are othered beyond the boundary line the white colonising subject draws around its identity in order to protect its supposed superiority.[15] However, Prendick's strategy of relegating the strange inhabitants of the island to the realm of alterity falters the moment he feels he has heard such a voice before. This is already the second time in the novel that the protagonist experiences the sensation of a certain familiarity in the unfamiliar, of the strange and alien being not quite so other as initially imagined. While still on board the *Ipecacuanha* and observing M'Ling, Prendick noted: "I [. . .] experienced [. . .] an odd feeling that in some way I *had* already encountered exactly the features and gestures that now amazed me" (*IM*, 12). This indicates the very collapse of taxonomy and categorisation that, as we have seen, characterises the monstrous. The mysterious islanders are thus also shown to live on the borderline that is to keep out monstrosity. The effect of their appearance on Prendick is the same as that of what Homi Bhabha describes as "the *ambivalence* of mimicry (almost the same, *but not quite*)"[16] The unease Prendick feels towards the island creatures is the result of the fact that, as Bhabha has it, "mimicry is at once resemblance and menace,"[17] and what is threatened here is humans' alterity from the monstrous creatures that populate the island. Prendick a little later refers to the islanders as "endowed with very uncanny voices" (*IM*, 38), and indeed, we are confronted here with the post-Darwinian return of the repressed in the form of humans' animalistic origins.

---

15 Margaret Atwood also refers to the colonialist implications of this text written in an age of late imperialism and its beginning decline: "Moreau's island is a little colonial enclave of the most hellish sort. It's no accident that most (although not all) of the beast folk are black or brown, that they are at first thought by Prendick to be 'savages' or 'natives', and that they speak in a kind of mangled English" (Margaret Atwood, *In Other Worlds*, 163). Hurley similarly refers to the gothic qualities of Wells's text and points out that "critics have linked the resurgence of the Gothic in the late-Victorian period to anxieties about [. . .] Britain's status as the dominant modern imperial power" (Hurley, "British Gothic Fiction," 194).

16 Homi K. Bhabha, "Of Mimicry and Man: The Ambivalence of Colonial Discourse," in *The Location of Culture* (New York: Routledge, 1994), 86.

17 Bhabha, "Of Mimicry and Man," 86.

Prendick describes his first days on the island in terms that create a latent sense of mystery, menace, doom and foreboding, for example when he has Montgomery call the island "an infernally rum place" (*IM*, 33), and the associations with hell are reinforced when Dr. Moreau tells the protagonist: "Our little establishment here contains a secret or so, is a kind of Bluebeard's Chamber, in fact" (*IM*, 36). This description indirectly attributes to Dr. Moreau the role of Bluebeard, a transgressive and murderous monster figure beyond the pale of human law and ethics. And indeed, when it turns out that Moreau is an outcast on his island who had to leave London in order to be able to carry out his scientific experiments in this remote place in the Pacific where he performs vivisection on animals so that he can transform them into human beings, the doctor takes on a monstrous quality himself. Prendick is haunted during his first few days on the island by the cries of pain of the puma which Moreau operates on in order to turn it into a woman. The liminal, hybrid-looking creatures the narrator has observed now turn out to be the products of Moreau's experiments, and Prendick dimly remembers an old London pamphlet entitled "The Moreau Horrors" (*IM*, 39) referring to the doctor's practice of vivisection.

All this, however, Prendick discovers only gradually because the doctor carries out his sessions of vivisection in an enclosure that separates his laboratory from the rest of his compound and from the rest of the island and access to this laboratory is barred to the narrator by a locked door, this physical barrier already attesting to the moral transgression Moreau commits through his work on his animals.[18] This element of the novel takes up the contemporary debate on vivisection, but the doctor's experiments could not even be approved of by the defenders of this practice because they do not serve the solution of a scientific problem but only the satisfaction of Moreau's curiosity and his will to see how far he can go and what he can achieve. There is no moral or scientific justification, then, for the suffering he causes, and the doctor yet again takes on a somewhat monstrous quality himself.

The island and all its inhabitants to Prendick thus represent monstrosity in what turns into the culmination of all his previous experiences of strangeness. He characterizes Moreau as "unnatural" and links this with a strong ethical condemnation when he simultaneously refers to the doctor as "diabolical" (*IM*, 44). As if to confirm this impression of the monstrous, M'Ling, in the same scene, is

---

18 Mordavsky Caleb also talks about "Moreau's amorality, specifically [. . .] his location outside society – thereby truly outside morality" in Amanda Mordavsky Caleb, "Amoral Animality: H.G. Wells's *The Island of Doctor Moreau*" in *Restoring the Mystery of the Rainbow: Literature's Refraction of Science*, eds. Valeria Tinkler-Villani and C.C. Barfoot (Amsterdam/New York: Rodopi, 2011), 313–331, 314.

referred to for the first time as "the misshapen monster with the pointed ears" (*IM*, 44–45). However, Moreau is clearly human, and yet, Prendick feels that his own involuntary reaction to "[t]he emotional appeal of [the] yells" (IM, 45) emitted by the panther in pain, the pity he evinces "when suffering finds a voice and sets our nerves trembling" (*IM*, 45), clearly distinguishes him from Moreau with his lack of empathy and his intransigent and unmoved attempt at scientific objectivity. The doctor here becomes a human with inhuman traits, and once more, categorical distinctions are questioned, which has a disorienting effect on Prendick, who states that "the world was a confusion, blurred with black and red phantasms" (*IM*, 45).

In this situation, Prendick tries to contain the unfamiliarity and the strange border-crossing otherness of what he is confronted with in an attempt to resituate his experiences within the taxonomies and categories he is used to. In chapter 9 of the novel, he undertakes a small expedition into the forest and is hit with full force by the island's disconcerting alterity. He encounters what he calls "a man, going on all fours like a beast!" (*IM*, 47), a "grotesque, half-bestial creature" (IM, 48), and he tries to rationally domesticate this experience: "Then I thought that the man I had just seen had been clothed in bluish cloth, had not been naked as a savage would have been, and I tried to persuade myself from that fact that he was after all probably a peaceful character, that the dull ferocity of his countenance belied him" (*IM*, 48). Prendick uses a hierarchical taxonomy at the bottom of which are to be found animals, with savages, i.e. primitive humans, above them and civilized humans at the top. The fact that the creature was scantily clothed supposedly puts it above both animals and savages so that there is nothing to be afraid of. This attempt at defusing what he has seen, however, does not really work for Prendick, who refers to the creature as an "apparition" (*IM*, 48) and asks himself: "Why should a man go on all fours and drink with his lips?" (*IM*, 48). It is thus the very humanity of the strange 'man' that is in doubt for Prendick, who is haunted by "the inhuman face of the man at the stream" (*IM*, 49) He reacts with fear, and his imagination conjures up threatening dangers in the thicket of the forest. "Never before had I seen such bestial-looking creatures" (IM, 49). It is the collapse of the differentiating concepts of his categorical system, which clearly distinguishes between man and animal, that has a profoundly disquieting effect on Prendick. When he observes a group of similarly in-between creatures, he realizes that it is their hybrid liminality that triggers a reaction of disgust, fear and rejection in him: "Suddenly, as I watched their grotesque and unaccountable gestures, I perceived clearly for the first time what it was that offended me, what had given me the two inconsistent and conflicting impressions of utter strangeness and yet of the strangest familiarity. The three crératures [...] were human in shape, and yet human beings with the strangest air about them of some familiar animal" (*IM*, 50). It is the dilution of alterity, the breaking down of what is supposed to distinctly separate human self from non-human other, i.e. the infection of the pure human with the beastly, that shocks Prendick and makes the creatures monstrous to him:[19] "that transitory gleam of the true animalism of these monsters was enough. [...] My one idea for the moment was to get away from the foul beings" (*IM*, 51). Prendick's reflex is to flee, to put some distance between himself and that which threatens his human identity, in an attempt to re-establish the old taxonomy through spatial separation. Significantly, he decides that "I must hasten back to the enclosure" (*IM*, 52), thus seeking the protection of a wall as a physical, material obstacle dividing him from that which threatens to intrude on his human selfhood.

When Prendick observes Moreau engaged in an attempt to transform the puma into a human being, he is still so caught up in his conceptual frameworks that he is unable to understand what the doctor is doing. The very idea of transforming animals into humans is so unthinkable for Prendick that it does not even occur to him. Instead, he assumes that Moreau has vivisected humans and animalized them in the process, which would explain the genesis of the strange creatures in the forest (*IM*, 61–65). Prendick's error is due to the fact that the notion of "animalized victims" of an initially human kind, i.e. of a brutal othering of men, is more digestible to his mind than the more monstrous idea of the assimilation of the beastly other to the status of the human and the concomitant tearing down of the supposedly insurmountable barrier that separates animals from men.

Prendick's erroneous interpretation of Moreau's activities on the island leads to a reconceptualization of the creatures in the forest, and when he meets a "simian creature" (IM, 66) there, he is able to react in a different way: "I did not feel the same repugnance towards this creature that I had experienced in my encounters with the other Beast men. 'You,' he said, 'in the boat.' He was a man, then [...] for he could talk" (*IM*, 67). In this moment, Prendick has redrawn the borderline between man and animal in such a way as to place the creature he encounters on his side of the man-animal divide, inside the realm

19 Timothy Beal, in *Religion and Its Monsters* (London/New York: Routledge, 2002, 4), defines monsters as "paradoxical personifications of *otherness within sameness*" and as "threatening figures of anomaly within the well-established and accepted order of things," and this is what triggers Prendick's escapist reflex. Mary Douglas describes such reactions as "pollution behaviour" which she defines as "the reaction which condemns any object or idea likely to confuse or contradict cherished classifications." Mary Douglas, *Purity and Danger: An Analysis of the Concepts of Pollution and Taboo* (New York: Routledge, 1966), 37.

of the human rather than beyond it. The use of language thus turns into an incontrovertible hallmark of being human to him. His thinking still functions in binary terms and does not allow for the liminal hybridity of in-between-ness and its disconcerting implications.[20]

The unsettling effect on him of the creatures Prendick meets in the forest is due to exactly that hybrid quality in them, to the blurring of the borderline that no longer clearly divides man from animal. Thus, in chapter 12, "a slouching monster" (*IM*, 71) approaches him and leads him into a dark hovel where one of the creatures presides over what appears like a quasi-religious ceremony in which the hybrid creatures have to repeat ritually what is called "the Law" (*IM*, 72), in which a code of human behaviour is laid down that bans animal behaviour like walking on all fours or sucking up drink, repeating in a monotonous refrain the supposedly rhetorical question: "Are we not Men?" (*IM*, 72–3). Significantly, this scene as described from Prendick's point of view is rendered in words that make it clear that the narrator's conceptual categories are violated here. The creatures are referred to as "grotesque dim figures" (*IM*, 72) and as "the grotesque caricatures of humanity" (*IM*, 74), and what they say is referred to as "this idiotic formula" (*IM*, 72). Prendick's sense of proportion is hurt here, and the creatures' imitation of humans is felt by the narrator to be a painful distortion, just as colonial acts of mimicry can be viewed by the colonizer as a parodic and distorting subversion of his own identity. Indeed, the quasi-religious chant uttered by such strange beings in this scene creates the necessary distance that allows us to cast a critical glance at human religious liturgies through its very projection of a human practice onto beings that almost seem to be human, but are not quite.[21] The use of Bhabha's postcolonial concepts here is justified because Moreau has subjected the island creatures to his iron rule through the practice of vivisection, and Prendick interprets this hierarchical relationship in religious terms, speculating that Moreau "had infected their dwarfed brains with a kind of deification of himself" (*IM*, 73). The "Sayer of the Law" (*IM*, 74), i.e. the priest-figure among the forest-creatures, appears monstrous to Prendick and evokes a strong reaction of rejection in him because it eludes the cognitive

20 Snyder therefore points out that "*Moreau* destabilizes easy binaries between the human and the beastly, suggesting that each always contains and involves the other" (E.E. Snyder, "*Moreau* and the Monstrous: Evolution, Religion, and the Beast on the Island," *Preternature: Critical and Historical Studies on the Preternatural* 2.2 (2013): 213–239, 218.

21 MacLean also concludes that "[i]n this hybrid world of 'humanised animals' and 'animalised humans,' the Beastfolk's recital of the Law functions as a comment on the status of those philosophical and religious activities considered to constitute the most advanced forms of human reasoning" (MacLean, *Early Fiction*, 49).

domestication through the categories available to him when he sees its face: "I saw with a quivering disgust that it was like the face of neither man or beast, but a mere shock of gray hair, with three shadowy overarchings to mark the eyes and mouth" (*IM*, 74). Prendick is left in the limbo of unidentifiability, and this triggers in him a natural impulse of avoidance.

The wood-creatures are mortally afraid of Dr. Moreau because in vivisecting them he tortures them and exposes them to infinite pain in an attempt to mould them in his own image, like a god-figure.[22] At the same time, like a conquering colonizer, he imposes a law upon them that is not suitable for them – they are not human creatures after all – and forces them to obey by the threat of sheer violence. As the initiator of a generic border-crossing that results in the creation of hybrid in-between beings that to Prendick seem to be grotesque and monstrous, Moreau again displays his monstrous quality and appears like the late Victorian Frankenstein of the artificial acceleration of evolution.[23]

It is because all this is so unthinkable to Prendick that he still assumes that what Moreau engages in is an activity of animalizing humans rather than humanizing animals. This may be a reflex of late Victorian fears of degeneration[24] triggered, among others, by Darwin's theory of evolution and its blurring of the boundary between humans and animals.[25] Prendick is plunged into the epistemic crisis of a world in swift transformation[26] that requires us to rethink the frameworks, concepts and categories we have devised to grapple with it, and

---

22 Lennartz aptly refers to Moreau as "the ruthless, Jehovah-like Doctor Moreau." Lennartz, "*The Island of Doctor Moreau*," 438.

23 Steven Lehman even sees Dr. Moreau as "a Faustian Prometheus of the Frankenstein type." Steven Lehman, "The Motherless Child in Science Fiction: *Frankenstein* and *Moreau*," *Science Fiction Studies* 19.1 (March 1992): 49–58, 55.

24 Kelly Hurley decribes degeneration theory as one of various "late-Victorian sociomedical disciplines that worked to classify and comprehend the abnormal human subject." Hurley, "British Gothic Fiction," 192. She goes on to describe the nexus between Darwinian science and fears of degeneration based on the fact that Darwin's theory of evolution "posited that natural history (and by extension human history) progressed randomly, moving toward no particular climax, so that bodies, species, and cultures were as likely to move 'backwards' as 'forwards,' degenerating into less complex forms" (195).

25 Margaret Atwood describes the effect of Darwin as "a profound shock to the Victorian system. Gone was the God who spoke the world into being in seven days and made man out of clay; in his place stood millions of years of evolutionary change and a family tree that included primates." Margaret Atwood, *In Other Worlds*, 156.

26 Cf. Osterhammel, *Die Verwandlung der Welt*. Macdonald similarly observes that Wells's novel "suggests the existential crisis of the early twentieth century." Alex MacDonald, "'Passionate Intensity' in Wells's *The Island of Doctor Moreau* and Yeats's 'The Second Coming': Constructing an Echo," *ANQ* 9.4 (Fall 1996): 40–42, 41.

this experience, in its unhinging and reshuffling of human interpretive patterns can have the quality of a harrowing monstrosity. This is also why, when Moreau and Montgomery try to explain to Prendick what exactly it is he is confronted with on the island, he at first refuses to believe them because it is too difficult for his mind to accommodate this new piece of information within his world picture. This significantly happens in chapter 13, which to the narrator turns out to be an unlucky one indeed, requiring a total reconceptualization of the world for him. It ends with Prendick referring to the creatures on the island as Beast men, using a term expressing their hybridity, and with an expression of his utter astonishment: "They may once have been animals. But I never before saw an animal trying to think" (*IM*, 85).

This is followed by a chapter of detailed explanation by Dr. Moreau, in which the scientist gives Prendick a more detailed account of what he intends to do on the island. This sheds light on his activities and characterizes him as a variation on the Frankenstein figure whose experiments of vivisection turn him into a monstrous creator of monsters.

Moreau and his activities raise several disquieting issues. He confesses that initially he did not merely set out to turn animals into humans: "I've not confined myself to man-making" (*IM*, 90). The fact that the creatures in the forest are all Beast Men, in Prendick's terminology, and display the shape of humans is the result of mere contingency. "He confessed that he had chosen that form by chance" (*IM*, 90). For when Moreau started with his experiments, his aim was less the creation of men out of animals than the elimination of pain, which he considers to be a useless remnant of our animal nature whose medical function as a warning stimulator in the future should be replaced by pure human intelligence. He points out to Prendick: "So long as visible or audible pain turns you sick, so long as your own pain drives you, so long as pain underlies your propositions about pain, so long, I tell you, you are an animal, thinking a little less obscurely what an animal feels" (*IM*, 91) Initially, then, Moreau engaged in a project that sought to extirpate what men and animals still have in common by creating a new being determined by human intelligence alone, thus strengthening the borderline that separates the human from the beast by advancing the constitution of men to a state beyond any vestige of the beast. The method chosen by him is that of vivisection as a tool of moulding both the physical and the cognitive features of the unfortunate objects of his experiments, and his activities seek to speed up evolution. "I never yet heard of a useless thing that was not ground out of existence by evolution sooner or later. [. . .] And pain gets needless" (*IM*, 92).

Moreau himself has to admit, however, that his experiments have not turned into the triumph of improvement and control he envisaged. Rather, they have shown the unachievability of his dreams of human perfection and highlighted several disturbing truths. As in chapter 4, where Montgomery ascribed his saving Prendick's life to mere chance, Moreau similarly shows that he ended up turning animals into pseudo-humans as a result of randomness when one of the creatures he changed into all sorts of shapes turned out to be an aggressive monster "doing mischief to all it came across" (*IM*, 96) so that it had to be killed. The artificially induced changes created by Moreau through vivisection thus, like the random mutations of natural evolution, can produce useless and even dangerous results, and the contingent unpredictability of such new creatures not only turn the doctor's experiments into a threat, but also have a profoundly disquieting effect.[27] It is because of this element of randomness and uncontrollability that Moreau now restricts himself to "the ideal of humanity" (*IM*, 96) in his attempts at grafting a higher intelligence onto animals.

However, Moreau fails yet again because the changes he produces in his victims do not last, as he frankly admits to Prendick: "These creatures of mine seemed strange and uncanny to you [...], but to me, just after I make them, they seem to be indisputable human beings. It's afterwards as I observe them that the persuasion fades. First one animal trait, then another, creeps to the surface and stares out at me. ... But I will conquer yet" (*IM*, 97). Both Prendick and the reader are not so sure, and the text here takes up once more contemporary fears of reversion and degeneration, the human-animal divide yet again becoming problematic.[28] Moreau's creatures for Prendick are uncanny because they constitute the return of the animal in the human, with the former potentially only incompletely repressed by evolution and still lurking under the surface. As Timothy Beal has pointed out, "[m]onsters are personifications of the *unheimlich*. They stand for what endangers one's sense of security, stability, integrity, well-being, health and meaning."[29] Moreau's Beast Men thus by their very existence question the stability of the human as distinct from the beastly. This is monstrous because every creature Moreau creates constitutes a being that "bridges the human-animal divide, something that mixes the ultimate tax-

---

27 Kelly Hurley also underlines the connection between the instability of human identity and the monstrous when she states: "The modernist Gothic [...] stands in an opportunistic relation to the nineteenth-century sciences that while demolishing the idea of a stable human identity yet gave imaginative warrant to the richly loathsome variety of abhuman abominations that the Gothic went on to produce" (Hurley, "British Gothic Fiction," 205).

28 The reader's as well as Prendick's fears ultimately are due to the fact that "[t]he devolutionary process at work in *The Island of Doctor Moreau* moves back through the biological and moral human-animal distinctions." Jackson, "Vivisected Language," 22.

29 Timothy K. Beal, *Religion and Its Monsters*, 5.

onomic domains."[30] The Beast Men of Dr. Moreau illustrate J.J. Cohen's definition of the monster as "that uncertain cultural body in which is condensed an intriguing simultaneity or doubleness: like the ghost of Hamlet it introjects the disturbing, repressed but formative traumas of "pre-"into the sensory moment of "post-," binding the one irrevocably to the other. [...] the monster *haunts*; it does not simply bring past and present together but destroys the boundary that demanded their twinned foreclosure."[31]

Moreau himself also takes on a monstrous quality because of his absolute lack of a sense of ethics with regard to his experiments. As he freely admits himself: "To this day I have never troubled about the ethics of the matter. The study of Nature makes a man at last as remorseless as Nature" (*IM*, 93). Referring to 17th-century examples, Stephen Asma has observed that "monsters born of human parents [...] indicate moral or spiritual depravity,"[32] but Moreau, in his lack of an ethical consciousness, seems to be a late Victorian representative of the same kind of monstrosity.

It is the Beast Men, however, that worry Prendick most and put his conceptual frameworks under the greatest pressure. His reaction to them is an example of what the monstrous triggers in us: "That these manlike creatures were in truth only bestial monsters, mere grotesque travesties of men, filled me with a vague uncertainty of their possibilities that was far worse than any definite fear" (*IM*, 100). Prendick feels reminded of travesty here because the artificially induced mimicry of human characteristics by animals again, like parody in colonial contexts, questions the superiority and absolute otherness of human beings from beasts. This destabilizes Prendick's sense of human selfhood and existential safety, the very "sense of security, stability, integrity" Timothy Beal sees threatened by monsters.[33] The narrator admits himself that his conception of humanity is eroded by his experiences on the island. Moreau displays a kind of ethical monstrosity, and Montgomery is suspected by Prendick of secretly entertaining "a vicious sympathy with some of their [i.e. the Beast Men's] ways" (*IM*, 105) so that the narrator concludes that "Montgomery and Moreau were too peculiar and individual to keep my general impressions of humanity well defined. I would see one

---

30 Asma, *On Monsters*, 138.

31 Jeffrey Jerome Cohen, "Preface: In a Time of Monsters," in *Monster Theory: Reading Culture*, ed. Jeffrey Jerome Cohen (Minneapolis, MN: University of Minnesota Press, 1996), vii-xiii, ix-x.

32 Asma, *On Monsters*, 142.

33 Hurley also refers to the ominous threat created by mimicry: "the abhuman being may be some unimaginable 'thing' incorporating, mimicking, or taking on a human form, thereby constituting [a] kind of threat to the integrity of human identity." Hurley, "British Gothic Fiction," 190.

of the clumsy, bovine creatures [...] treading heavily through the undergrowth, and find myself asking, trying hard to recall, how he differed from some really human yokel trudging home [...]; or I would meet the Fox-Bear Woman's vulpine, shifty face, strangely human in its speculative cunning, and even imagine I had met it before in some city byway" (*IM*, 105–6). It is this very questioning of the line that defines human identity by setting it off against beastly otherness that once again is monstrous to Prendick and the reader.[34]

Ultimately, Moreau's attempt at turning animals into humans fails,[35] the savage instincts to hunt and to taste blood come to the fore again in them, and the Leopard Man rebels against Moreau by attacking his tormentor-creator. What follows is a chaotic scene of havoc and wild pursuit in which the animal features of the doctor's creatures become more and more dominant. The chase for the rebellious Leopard Man turns into a concrete illustration of nightmarish monstrosity of "the excited carnivorous Beast People" (*IM*, 119). Ultimately, when the Leopard Man is cornered and Prendick realizes that the creature is about to be resubmitted to yet another round of vivisectionist horrors, he kills it in order to spare it the torture. He does so at the very moment when looking at "its imperfectly human face distorted with terror, I realized again the fact of its humanity" (*IM*, 119). By shooting the Leopard Man, Prendick does justice to the man in the creature and prevents the leopard in it from becoming the reason for another round of monstrous treatment at the hands of the doctor.

The experience of the Leopard Man's fruitless rebellion and the ensuing turmoil of the hunt for Prendick turn into a disillusioning moment of epiphanic insight into the human condition and of moral outrage at Moreau's activities. After the Leopard Man has been shot dead and Moreau, in a grotesque impersonation of divine authority has contained the chaos by reminding his creatures of the Law and threatening them with "the House of Pain" (*IM*, 115), i.e. subjection to more sessions of vivisection, Prendick realizes the sobering implications of what has just happened:

---

34 Redfern, referring to such instances of the questioning of borderlines, sees Wells's text as a symptom of "a crisis of abjection that evolution brought to Victorian society, creating the need to establish new boundaries of the human self in the light of Darwin's obliteration of man's uniqueness." Nick Redfern, "Abjection and Evolution in *The Island of Doctor Moreau*," *The Wellsian* 27 (2004): 37–47, 44.

35 As Kimberley Jackson points out, "[i]f Moreau's experiments are at all successful, it is in their revelatory nature. They bring to light the hybridity of the human condition itself." Jackson, "Vivisected Language," 34.

> A strange persuasion came upon me that, save for the grossness of the line, the grotesqueness of the forms, I had here before me the whole balance of human life in miniature, the whole interplay of instinct, reason, and fate in its simplest form. The Leopard Man had happened to go under. That was all the difference.
>
> Poor brutes! I began to see the viler aspect of Moreau's cruelty. [. . .] Before they had been beasts, their instincts fitly adapted to their surroundings, and happy as living creatures may be. Now, they stumbled in the shackles of humanity, lived in a fear that never died, fretted by a law they could not understand; their mock-human existence, begun in an agony, was one long internal struggle, one long dread of Moreau – and for what? It was the wantonness that stirred me. (*IM*, 120–121)

On the one hand, the conceptual dividing line between animals and humans here is still potentially intact, with Moreau sinning against the order of the world by interfering with his fruitless experiments. But on the other hand, and more importantly, the doctor's border-blurring activities irrevocably destroy the illusion in Prendick of a safely constituted human identity reliably and irreversibly protected from the inroads of the beastly other of animal existence. It is this insight which brings out the monstrous hybridity of human life, the latter being not a pure other to its primitive non-human counter-part, but a mixed balance, an unstable interplay and intermingling of animal instinct and reason. The supposed order of the world here turns out to be its opposite, namely a jumble of chaotically mixed elements rather than distinctly separate forms of existence. This realization creates a reaction of overwhelming disillusionment in Prendick who concludes: "I must confess I lost faith in the sanity of the world when I saw it suffering the painful disorder of this island" (*IM*, 121).

The narrator, then, does not only become witness to Moreau's irresponsible and morally reprehensible tinkering with creation, an activity Prendick condemns all the more because he sees mere gratuitous and aimless gratification of curiosity as the doctor's main motivation.[36] He also experiences the pangs of a modern epistemic and existential crisis, which, in its annihilation of anthropocentric teleologies and its decentering of man[37] and animal alike, creates in the narrator a reaction of existential despair, of utter disgust at the monstrosity of the challenge to intelligibility posed by what

36 This clearly constituted a breach of "the Cruelty to Animals Act of 1876, which restricted the use to which animals could be put in scientific experimentation. [. . .] the bodily violence must be able to be reconciled, not only with the moral code, but also with the corresponding 'body' of knowledge and lead ultimately to its fulfilment, its completion." Jackson, "Vivisected Language," 20, 21.

37 Lennartz sees Wells's novel as an expression of "anthropological doubt" and states that "Prendick [. . .] represents modern man adrift" (Lennartz, "*The Island of Doctor Moreau,*" 442, 444).

Moreau's experiments have revealed[38]: "A blind fate, a vast pitiless mechanism, seemed to cut and shape the fabric of existence, and I, Moreau [. . .], Montgomery [. . .], the Beast People, with their instincts and mental restrictions, were torn and crushed, inevitably, amid the infinite complexity of its incessant wheels" (*IM*, 121–22)

When the puma that is Dr. Moreau's latest victim in the laboratory of vivisection manages to escape, the tenuous order established by the scientist over the island and its creatures starts to crumble and utter chaos threatens. Significantly, the chapter in which these events are described starts with Prendick wistfully yearning for a return to the realm of regularity and order, in which humans are still clearly and distinguishably just that, i.e. human beings and therefore different from animals. "My one idea was to get away from these horrible caricatures of my Maker's image, back to the sweet and wholesome intercourse of men. My fellow creatures, from whom I was thus separated, began to assume idyllic virtue and beauty in my memory. My first friendship with Montgomery did not increase. His long separation from humanity, his secret vice of drunkenness, his evident sympathy with the Beast People tainted him to me" (*IM*, 123) In an escapist reflex, Prendick seeks to leave behind him the realm of distortion and categorical intermingling that in his eyes threatens human integrity and men's privileged position within creation because it constitutes a first step on the road to reversion and degradation. Montgomery becomes suspect to him because he does not adhere to the strict conceptual separation of man and animal. His fondness for alcohol, moreover, in the eyes of Prendick, becomes a symptom of Montgomery's own beginning process of re-primitivization and its concomitant loss of control.

The puma's escape triggers the loss of Moreau's control and power over the creatures on the island who revert to their animal ways and start hunting and attacking each other in a return to the bestial primitivism the doctor sought to force them from. The puma itself kills its tormentor. The doctor's experiments have utterly failed, and Montgomery loses himself in drink, which makes Prendick reflect that "for Montgomery there was no help; [. . .] he was in truth half akin to these Beast Folk, unfitted for human kindred" (*IM*, 140). Prendick here actively reconfirms the dividing line between humans and animals, and he others Montgomery by excluding him from the status of full humanity due to the latter's closeness to the hybrid creatures on the island. Montgomery, in turn, smashes up the all boats on the island in order to prevent Prendick's

---

38 Snyder, in this context, claims that the "apparent monstrosity [of] the crossing of animal and human in the figures of the Beast Men [. . .] conceals a deeper monstrousness, that of Moreau's hybrid philosophy." Snyder, "*Moreau* and the Monstrous," 213.

escape, thus thwarting the narrator's attempt at turning the island into an isolated and damned realm of utter alterity which he can leave behind. When Montgomery also falls victim to the violence of the reverting and revolting beasts, Prendick is left "Alone with the Beast Folk" (*IM*, 146), as the title of chapter 20 has it. A first attempt at taking over Moreau's former position of ruler of the island by turning himself into the representative of the Law the Beast Men were made to follow religiously by the doctor fails, and the narrator is reduced to live among the hybrid creatures he abhors so much: "I became one among the Beast People in the island of Dr. Moreau" (*IM*, 153). Not only does this put Prendick into a potentially every dangerous situation but it also serves in the text to underline yet again man's precarious in-between position on an "isthmus of a middle state," to use Pope's definition of man from a different context.[39] On the one hand, as far as the material conditions of life are concerned, Prendick now has arrived on the same level as the beasts, as he admits himself when he tells of "the ten months I spent as an intimate of these half-humanized brutes. [. . .] In retrospect it is strange to remember how soon I fell in with these monsters' ways and gained my confidence again" (*IM*, 157). On the other hand, the very ploy that allows Prendick to secure an acceptable position among the strange creatures is one that both defines humans and at the same time puts them in a shameful light. Prendick manages after all to tell the Beast Folk a quasi-religious story, in which Moreau is not dead, but watching them from a higher position, able to bring back the House of Pain any moment. This induces the beasts to treat Prendick with respect. He has now turned into a mock-priest figure, and this scene does not only lampoon religion, but it also makes Prendick himself come to a sobering conclusion regarding what distinguishes man from animal: "An animal may be ferocious and cunning enough, but it takes a real man to tell a lie" (*IM*, 156) If there is a dividing line between beasts and humans, then, it does not reflect flatteringly back on humanity, but casts a rather dubious light on our species.[40]

This cannot lessen Prendick's disgust, however, as in the weeks that follow he becomes witness to the process of "the lapsing of these monsters; [. . .] day by day, the human semblance left them; [. . .] the quasi-human intimacy I had permitted myself with some of them in the first month of my loneliness became

39 Cf. Alexander Pope, "Essay on Man," Epistle II, l. 3. Alexander Pope, *The Poems of Alexander Pope* (London: Methuen, 1977), 501–547, 516.

40 Cf. Steven McLean, who states that "[f]alsehood is construed as a negative aspect of humanity's supposedly enhanced evolutionary status." Steven McLean, "Animals, Language and Degeneration in H.G. Wells's *The Island of Doctor Moreau*," *The Undying Fire: The Journal of the H.G. Wells Society* 1 (2002): 43–50, 46–47.

a horror to recall" (*IM*, 160). This may be a reference to acts of bestiality committed by Prendick in zoophilic moments of loneliness, which yet again puts in doubt man's privileged state as a separate non-animal species. The narrator's use of the term horror to describe his own incipient reversion to animality[41] is reminiscent of the use of the same word by another famous protagonist of contemporary fiction, namely Mr. Kurtz in Joseph Conrad's *Heart of* Darkness, published only three years after *The Island of Dr. Moreau* in 1899. Kurtz dies knowing full well that he has reverted to savagery in his colonial outpost on the River Congo, the palisades of which are crowned by the heads of his indigenous victims, and his dying words are: "The horror! The horror!"[42] Prendick's own development after the deaths of Moreau and of Montgomery reinforces the doubt created in this text concerning the relations of alterity between humans and animals: "I myself must have undergone strange changes. My clothes hung about me as yellow rags, through whose rents glowed the tanned skin. My hair grew long and became matted together. I am told that even now my eyes have a strange brightness, a swift alertness of movement" (*IM*, 161). This latter quality makes the narrator appear like an animal using all its senses to succeed in the struggle for survival of the fittest, and it collapses yet again the distinction between human selfhood and beastly alterity, which by now seems to be a rather spurious one.

That a struggle for survival is indeed what men are reduced to just like animals becomes clear when Prendick describes how he manages to escape in a small boat that happens to drift towards one of the island's beaches and in which he finds two dead men in a state of beginning decomposition, two sailors reduced to rotting matter and about to lose all human semblance. Significantly, "[o]ne had a shock of red hair like the captain of the *Ipecacuanha*" (*IM*, 166) so that Prendick's earlier negative impression of the schooner's crew and captain not quite living up to the standards of civilized humanity and already displaying first symptoms of reversion here is reinforced and confirmed. This is also why Prendick's flight from the island is not the joyful event it might have been to

41 In his philosophy of horror, Noël Carroll describes as horrific liminal monsters of the kind encountered by Prendick because they are "categorically interstitial, categorically contradictory, incomplete, or formless." Noël Carroll, *The Philosophy of Horror* (London: Routledge, 1990), 32.

42 Joseph Conrad, *Heart of Darkness* (Harmondsworth: Penguin Books, 1978, 106). The text was first published as a three-instalment story in *Blackwood's Magazine* in 1899 and then in book form in 1902. Lennartz also draws a comparison between Wells and Conrad when he says: "Wells is [...] closely aligned with [...] negative anthropology when he, almost at the same time as Joseph Conrad's *Heart of Darkness* (1899) [...], describes Edward Prendick's voyage as another journey into man's deepest recesses of cannibalism and dark atavism." Lennartz, "*The Island of Doctor Moreau*," 431.

him, as he admits himself: “It is strange, but I felt no desire to return to mankind. I was only glad to be quit of the foulness of the Beast Monsters” (*IM*, 168–9).

Humanity by now is tainted by the mark of bestiality for Prendick, a realization that turns into a heavy burden to him. Humans and animals are no longer seen as in a relation of otherness by him, which turns his fellow men and women into monstrous hybrids that constantly contribute to “a strange enhancement of the uncertainty and dread I had experienced during my stay upon the island” (*IM*, 169). Prendick thus ends up even worse than Lemuel Gulliver upon his return from the country of the Houyhnhnms and the Yahoos.[43] Gulliver at least prefers the company of the Houyhnhnm-like horses to that of his wife and his own family, who remind him of the bestial Yahoos. To Prendick, however, such distinctions have become untenable, and he feels condemned to a life among creatures very much like the monsters of the island: “My trouble took the strangest form. I could not persuade myself that the men and women I met were not also another, still passably human, Beast People, animals half-wrought into the outward image of human souls, and that they would presently begin to revert, to show first this bestial mark and then that” (*IM*, 169).

Prendick’s attempts at containing such feelings fail utterly. He tries to rationally domesticate his fears by redrawing the boundary line between animals and humans and relegating beasts into a region of non-human alterity, but “[t]hen I would turn aside into some chapel, and even there, such was my disturbance, it seemed that the preacher gibbered Big Thinks even as the Ape Man had done; or into some library, and there the intent faces over the books seemed but patient creatures waiting for prey” (*IM*, 171). Prendick can no longer live in big cities where the masses of people suggest all too strongly humans’ animality to him: “I would go out into the streets to fight with my delusion, and prowling women would mew after me, furtive craving men glance jealously at me, weary pale workers go coughing by me, with tired eyes and eager paces like wounded deer dripping blood [...]” (*IM*, 170). In his

43 Margaret Atwood points out further links to Jonathan Swift’s masterpiece, such as „a plain, forthright style in the service of incredible events,” in Margaret Atwood, *In Other Worlds*, 155, and she also sees the direct connection between the two protagonists: “Like Swift’s Gulliver, he [*i.e.* Prendick, *H.A.*] can barely stand the sight of his fellow men. He lives in a state of queasy fear, inspired by his continued experience of dissolving boundaries: as the beasts of the island have at times appeared human, the human beings he encounters in England appear bestial.” Robert Philmus even calls *The Island of Dr. Moreau* “the most sustained, and also the most Swiftian, of all Wells’s SF satires.” Robert M Philmus, “The Satiric Ambivalence of *The Island of Doctor* Moreau,” *Science Fiction Studies* 8 (1981): 2–11, 2. Cf. also Lennartz, “*The Island of Doctor Moreau*,” 445, MacLean, *Early Fiction*, 59 and Snyder, “*Moreau* and the Monstrous,” 215.

previous novel, *Time Machine*, published in 1895, H.G. Wells had depicted the Morlocks, ape-like and monstrous post-human creatures living underground and cannibalistically feeding on the Eloi, a degenerative form of humans, in a dystopian text that showed not only the possible long-term consequences of class division,[44] but also the precarious humanness of humans, and the animal-like Londoners described here by Prendick similarly engage with the uncertainty of man's distinctive status as a special being that can be clear distinguished from animals.[45] No matter whether Wells looks into the distant future or into the evolutionary past, the necessary boundary-line on which such conceptualizations of humans are based become highly problematic, and the monstrous is used by him to draw the reader's attention to such categorical instabilities.

44 MacLean also sees parallels between Wells's *The Island of Dr. Moreau* and its predecessor when he states that "more implicitly than *Time Machine*, the text is engaged with contemporary concerns regarding the living conditions endured by the poorest sections of the community." MacLean, *Early Fiction*, 53.

45 Kelly Hurley also refers to *The Time Machine* as one of a number of late Victorian texts with an "entropic plotline, whereby bodies regress and complexity yields to either increasing indifferentiation of chaotic disorder, [which] also structures gothic narratives of degeneration [. . .] like Wells's *The Time Machine* 1895." Hurley, "British Gothic Fiction," 197.

Susana Onega

Patriarchal Law and the Ethics and Aesthetics of Monstrosity in Mary Shelley's *Frankenstein*

1 Enlightenment rationalism and its others: the Romantic revolt of passion against virtue

Critics agree that the rise of the Gothic novel as the dominant literary genre in the 1790s was the result of a conflation of extraordinary political and cultural circumstances generated by the clash between Enlightenment rationalism, with its new conception of the relation between the human, the natural and the divine, and the psychological turmoil provoked by the moods, passions and fears generated by the French Revolution. As David Punter notes in his standard monograph, *The Literature of Terror*, "[t]he 1790s were chaotic years in which domestic unrest and fears of invasion from abroad shaped political and cultural life."[1] If Augustan writers like Alexander Pope would claim that "the rational person's attitude to passion is to dominate and subject it,"[2] first generation Gothic writers like Horace Walpole, Anne Radcliffe and Matthew Lewis would delve into the terrifying effects of "the revolt of passion against virtue," with "Family and Church"[3] as constant causes of obsessive fear, anxiety or irritation. Often situated in the remote past as a way of establishing a protective distance with the familial, religious and socio-political horrors they delved into, these Gothic stories constituted a formidable attempt at "imagining the unimaginable,"[4] or in Freudian terms, at giving expression to the repressed traumas stored in the collective unconscious. In the mid-1790s, these

1 David Punter, *The Literature of Terror* (London and New York: Longman, 1980), 61.

2 Punter, *Literature of Terror*, 82.

3 Punter, *Literature of Terror*, 82, 83.

4 Punter, Literature of Terror, 111.

Note: The author would like to acknowledge the support for the writing of this essay of the Spanish Ministry of Economy and Competitiveness (METI) (code FFI2015-65775-P) and the Spanish Ministry of Economy, Industry and Competitiveness (MINECO) (code FFI2017-84258-P), both in collaboration with the European Regional Development Fund (DGI/ERDF); the University of Zaragoza and Ibercaja (JIUZ-2017-HUM-02); and the Government of Aragón.

https://doi.org/10.1515/9783110654615-007

bugbears materialised in three principal symbolic figures that would further develop along the 19th century: the wanderer, the vampire, and the seeker after forbidden knowledge.[5] The three are manifestations of the cultural and political other. Their existence constitutes both a challenge to Enlightenment rationalism and a political response to patriarchal law. The wanderer appears in various works by Samuel Taylor Coleridge, Percy Bysshe Shelley and Lord Byron as well as in Matthew Lewis' *The Monk* (1796) and Charles Maturin's *Melmoth, the Wanderer* (1820). He is the irredeemable outcast, "a man who, for an ultimate crime against God [...] is doomed to a perpetual life on earth."[6] Both sinner and victim of a jealous God, the wanderer "represents a primal anomaly, that of 'the mortal immortal' (to quote the title of a story by Mary Shelley) and the threat which he carries with him is of the wholesale disturbance of the natural order."[7] Like the wanderer, the vampire symbolises an anomaly or disturbance of the natural order, in this case, "the perverse union of passion and death."[8] Immortal and untouchable like the wanderer, the vampire is both a source of infection and of irresistible attraction and seduction,[9] a catalyst for the repressed tendencies of his victims to emerge into the light of day. As Punter acutely notes, the damage he causes in the patriarchal social order depends more on the internal weakness of his victims than on his own powers of seduction.[10] Bram Stoker's *Dracula* (1897),[11] the book that gave the figure of the vampire a canonical status, was intertextually indebted to John Polidori's "The Vampyre" (1819),[12] a short story which, like Mary Shelley's *Frankenstein; or, the Modern Prometheus* (1818),[13] was written in

5 Punter, *Literature of Terror*, 99.
6 Punter, *Literature of Terror*, 114.
7 Punter, *Literature of Terror*, 116.
8 Punter, *Literature of Terror*, 117.
9 Punter, *Literature of Terror*, 117, 118.
10 Punter, *Literature of Terror*, 118.
11 Bram Stoker, *Dracula* (Westminster: Archibald Constable and Co., 1897), available at: http://www.bramstoker.org/pdf/novels/05dracula.pdf/ (last access June 20, 2018).
12 "The Vampyre" was first published on 1 April 1819 in the *New Monthly Magazine* with the false attribution "A Tale by Lord Byron" and later the same year in octavo under Polidori's name as *The Vampyre; A Tale in 84 pages*. John Polidori, *The Vampyre; A Tale in 84 pages* (London, Paternoster-Row: Sherwood, Neely, and Jones, 1819).
13 *Frankenstein* was published anonymously in 1818 with a Preface by her husband, Percy Bysshe Shelley. Mary Shelley, *Frankenstein; or the Modern Prometheus* [1818], in *Mary Shelley* Frankenstein, ed. and intro. Paddy Lyons (London: J. M. Dent & Sons Ltd; Rutland, Vermont. Charles E Tuttle Co., Inc., 1992), 1–192. Further references in the text abbreviated as *FMP*. In 1831 Mary Shelley published a revised version with significant changes. *Frankenstein*. 1831. Mary Shelley, *Frankenstein* [1831] (Free eBooks at Planet eBook.com),

response to Lord Byron's famous proposal to his guests at the Villa Diodati by Lake Geneva that they write a ghost story to alleviate boredom in the rainy summer of 1816.[14] Represented as a dream-object, Lord Ruthven, the vampire in Polidori's short story, is the embodiment of "unthinkable pleasure [...] a representation of sexual liberation *in extremis*, indulgence to the point of death."[15] As a lord, he enjoys the absolute sexual privilege of the aristocrat, "which is a concomitant of absolute power and at the same time a predictable object of middle-class fantasies."[16] Like the omnipotent God that punishes the wanderer, the vampire in English culture is a figure of power. As "a fundamentally anti-bourgeois figure," he is "a rebel, not by virtue of turning from society, but by having pre-dated it; he is the unassimilable aspect of the past."[17]

The third symbolic figure of otherness that comes to fruition in the work of second generation Romantic writers is the seeker after forbidden knowledge. Its emergence is signalled by Goethe's *Faust*, a tragedy whose first part was published in German in 1806 and partially translated into English in 1821 in an anonymous translation attributed to Coleridge.[18] Punter compares the characterisation of this figure in the poetry of Coleridge and Percy Shelley with that of the alchemists: like them, the Romantic seeker pursues "the knowledge of eternal life, the philosopher's stone, those kinds of knowledge which will make men gods."[19] However, he differs from his medieval and Renaissance predecessors in the solitary and gloomy tone attached to his search. According to Punter, this tone was set by Coleridge in his poem "Quae Nocent Docent,"[20] where the acquisition of forbidden knowledge requires the renunciation of "thoughtless joy" and the embracing of solitude.[21] This association of knowledge with loneliness and gloom

---

available at: http://www.planetebook.com/ebooks/Frankenstein.pdf/ (last access June 20, 2018). Further references in the text abbreviated as *F*.

14 Mary Shelley, "Author's Introduction to the Standard Novels Edition" [1831], in *Mary Shelley's* Frankenstein, ed. Harold Bloom (New York: Chelsea House Publishers, 1987), Appendix A: 193–200, 196.

15 Punter, *Literature of Terror*, 119.

16 Punter, *Literature of Terror*, 119.

17 Punter, *Literature of Terror*, 119.

18 Frederick Burwick, and James McKusick, eds. *Faustus, translated by Samuel Taylor Coleridge from the German of Goethe* (Oxford: Oxford University Press, 2007).

19 Punter, *Literature of Terror*, 120.

20 Punter, *Literature of Terror*, 120.

21 "No more the precious time would I employ / In giddy revels, or in thoughtless joy, / A present joy producing future woe. / But o'er the midnight Lamp I'd love to pore, / I'd seek with care fair Learning's depths to sound, / And gather scientific Lore: / Or to mature the embryo becomes central in "Alastor, or, The Spirit of Solitude," a poem written by Percy Shelley in 1815 and published in 1816, the year Byron set the competition to write a ghost story.[22] As Harold Bloom has pointed out, the Alastor is the Poet's own Blakean Spectre, the "avenging demon of his self-chosen solitude"[23] that pursues him in his wanderings after forbidden knowledge, after having decided to abandon the "Joy of Imagination" for abstraction; or to put it in Blake's own terms, after having renounced the "fourfold vision" or enlarged consciousness of the poet-as-prophet and embraced the "Single vision" of materialism.[24] As a result of this choice, the Poet loses his capacity to respond to the love felt for him by an Arab maiden. When she disappears, the Poet pursues his quest with renewed intensity and hopelessness. As Bloom notes, "[t]he quest for the hiding places of natural power is now also a quest for complete sexual fulfilment" but neither of them can be found: "When he dies, his ideal [is] still unattainable."[25] Described by Margaret Homans as "the archetypal poem of the doomed Romantic quest,"[26] Percy Shelley's "Alastor" constitutes an important hypotext of *Frankenstein*. Like the Poet, Victor Frankenstein cuts all bonds with family and friends and transforms himself into a "monster of narcissism"[27] in his obsessive search for the secret that would grant him the divine capacity to create life. Both Percy Shelley's "Alastor" and Mary Shelley's *Frankenstein* are intertextually indebted to *Caleb Williams; or, Things as They Are* (1794),[28] and *St. Leon: A Tale of the Sixteenth Century* (1799),[29] two politico-philosophical novels written by Mary Shelley's father,

thoughts inclin'd, / That half-conceiv'd lay struggling in my mind, / The cloisters' solitary gloom I'd round." Samuel Taylor Coleridge, "Quae Nocent Docent" [1789], in *The Poems of Samuel Taylor Coleridge* by Samuel Taylor Coleridge 1787–1833 (DjVu Editions E-books. Global Language Resources, Inc., 2001), 8, ll. 4–9. Available at: http://www.l-adam-mekler.com/stc_poems.pdf/ (last access June 20, 2018).

22 Shelley, Percy Bysshe. "Alastor, or, The Spirit of Solitude" [1816], in *The Complete Poetical Works of Percy Bysshe Shelley*. Vol I, ed. Thomas Hutchinson (Oxford: Oxford University Press, 1970), 34–48.

23 Harold Bloom, *The Visionary Company: A Reading of English Romantic Poetry* [1961], revised and enlarged edition (New York: Cornell University Press, 1971), 289

24 William Blake, "Letter to Butts" [22 November 1802], in *The Complete Writings of William Blake*, ed. Geoffrey Keynes (London: Nonesuch; New York: Random House, 1957), 818.

25 Bloom, *The Visionary Company*, 289.

26 Margaret Homans, "Bearing Demons: Frankenstein's Circumvention of the Maternal," in *Mary Shelley's* Frankenstein, ed. Bloom: 133–153, 139.

27 Homans, "Bearing Demons," 139.

28 William Godwin, *Caleb Williams; or, Things as They Are* [1794] (Oxford: Oxford University Press, 1970).

29 William Godwin, *St. Leon: A Tale of the Sixteenth Century* 4 vols. (London: Printed for G. G. and J. Robinson, Paternoster-Row, 1799).

William Godwin. Caleb Williams and his servant Falkland embark on a chase after each other that points to their Ego/Shadow complementariness and that, like that of Dr. Frankenstein and his Creature, can only lead to mutual destruction. The other novel, *St. Leon*, tells the story of Count Reginald de St. Leon, a French aristocrat who loses his wealth gambling and is driven almost to madness by guild. After accepting from a dying stranger the gift of the secret of the elixir of life and of the power of multiplying wealth, he becomes alienated from humankind and is forced to wander in solitude and despondency. As these examples suggest, the seeker after forbidden knowledge is a wanderer punished for a specific form of rebelliousness against natural law.

2 Victor Frankenstein's unnatural behaviour as trigger of the family feud

The wanderer, the vampire and the seeker after forbidden knowledge are monsters in the sense that their existence defies the rules of nature. Discussing the etymology and literary use of monstrosity in English literature, Chris Baldick explains that in the Renaissance the words "monster," "monstrosity" and "monstrous" were widely used to qualify all sorts of unnatural behaviour.[30] However, the most important class within this usage was the representation of "the monster of ingratitude"[31]:

> It is the vices of ingratitude, rebellion, and disobedience, particularly towards parents, that most commonly attract the appellation 'monstrous': to be a monster is to break the natural bonds of obligation towards friends and especially towards blood-relations. [...] Long before the monster of Frankenstein, monstrosity already implied rebellion, or an unexpected turning away against one's parent or benefactor.[32]

Looking at the three figures of otherness from this perspective, it seems evident that the monstrosity of the wanderer and the seeker after forbidden knowledge

30 Thus, for example, "in *Othello* Emilia characterises jealousy as a monster; Gower in [...] *Pericles* refers to the 'monster envy' and 'monstrous lust'; Petruchio in *The Taming of the Shrew* complains of 'monstrous arrogance' and Gloucester in Henry the Sixth, Part One of 'monstrous treachery', while Holofernes in *Love's Labour's Lost* exclaims: 'O thou monster Ignorance, how deformed does thou looks!" Chris Baldick, *In Frankenstein's Shadow: Myth, Monstrosity, and Nineteenth-century Writing* [1987] (Oxford: Clarendon Press, 1996), 12.
31 Baldick, *In Frankenstein's Shadow*, 13.
32 Baldick, *In Frankenstein's Shadow*, 13.

stems from the vice of ingratitude towards their creators. They both bring on themselves the wrath of God the Father for defying patriarchal law and are condemned to a life of solitary errantry. Mary Shelley suggests as much in the subtitle to her novel, when she calls Dr. Frankenstein "a Modern Prometheus," thus equating him with the Titan who enraged the gods by creating mankind and giving them the fire he had stolen from Mount Olympus. While the rebelliousness of the wanderer and the seeker after forbidden knowledge is that of ungrateful sons, the vampire, as an aristocrat, represents the excesses of absolutism: he is the Hobbesian sovereign exerting unrestrained power over his subjects. The fact that, in order to exist, the vampire must feed on the blood of his fascinated victims sets his monstrosity on a par with that of Kronos and Saturn, respectively the Greek and Roman gods who devoured their own children in order to maintain their absolute power.

As Baldick notes, the metaphor of the family feud provoked by the monstrous ingratitude of rebellious children was recurrently used in the Anti-Jacobin writings inaugurated by Edmund Burke's *Reflexions on the Revolution in France* (1790),[33] where he asserted, for example, that: "'Ingratitude to benefactors is the first of revolutionary virtues', and went on to describe the revolutionaries as 'miscreant parricides'."[34] Conversely, in *Rights of Man* (1791),[35] the most important of the responses to *Reflections*, Tom Paine "picks up on Burke's parricidal imagery and turns the accusations of unnatural child-parent relations back upon the aristocratic system itself."[36] Thus, "Burke announces the birth of the monster child Democracy, while Paine records the death of the monster parent Aristocracy."[37] A second major response to Burke was that provided by Mary Shelley's parents, the radical thinkers Mary Wollstonecraft and William Godwin. In her *Historical and Moral View of the Origin and Progress of*

33 Edmund Burke, *Reflections on the Revolution in France, And on the Proceedings in Certain Societies in London Relative to that Event. In a Letter Intended to Have Been Sent to a Gentleman in Paris* (London: J. Dodsley in Pall Mall, 1790).

34 Baldick, *In Frankenstein's Shadow*, 17.

35 Thomas Paine, *Rights of Man: Being an Answer to Mr. Burke's Attack on The French Revolution* Part the First (London: Printed for J. Johnson, St. Paul's Church-Yard, 1791). The British Library. Available at: https://www.bl.uk/collection-items/rights-of-man-by-thomas-paine/ (last access June 20, 2018).

36 Baldick, *In Frankenstein's Shadow*, 20. In Paine's own words: "By the aristocratic law of primogenitureship, in a family of six children, five are exposed. Aristocracy has never more than *one* child. The rest are begotten to be devoured. They are thrown to the cannibal for prey, and the natural parent prepares the unnatural repast." Quoted in Baldick, *In Frankenstein's Shadow*, 20 [emphasis in the original].

37 Baldick, *In Frankenstein's Shadow*, 21.

the French Revolution (1794)[38] Wollstonecraft argues that it is not the revolutionaries but the upholders of power who exhibit the cruelty and despotism of "a race of monsters in human shape" and she justifies the Terror as "the reflected evils of government tyranny, the retaliation of slaves."[39] Likewise, in his *Enquiry Concerning Political Justice* (1793), Godwin displaces Burke's discourse of monstrosity from the revolutionaries to the aristocrats. As a radical, Godwin believed in the invincibility of Reason's progress and shared with Rousseau and Wollstonecraft the conviction that human beings are innately good in the state of nature. Therefore, as Baldick points out, he attributed evil acts to the lack of an adequate education and explained the monstrosity of tyrannical Governments as a perversion of the integrity of responsible individual action, which should be corrected through the contemplation and propagation of reason and truth.[40] It is with this didactic purpose that he set to writing politico-philosophical novels like *Caleb Williams* and *St. Leon*, meant to illustrate the difficulties encountered by human beings in their path towards perfectibility. Godwin's utilitarian and anarchist ideas were determinant in the theorisation of Jacobinism. They exerted a great influence on the early thought of Wordsworth, Coleridge and Percy Bysshe Shelley and, together with the writings of Mary Wollstonecraft, on that of Mary Shelley as well.

This influence is already evident in the presentation of the young Victor Frankenstein at the beginning of the novel. He is the eldest son in an affluent and happy family, with loving parents and two younger brothers, Ernest and William; and he is betrothed to Elizabeth, a beautiful and charming orphaned cousin adopted by his parents and educated by Mrs. Frankenstein in the virtues of "domestic love" (*FMP*, 22). He also has an affectionate bosom friend, Henry Clerval, who is a lover of books of chivalry and romances and the juvenile author of a fairy tale (*FMP*, 23). Victor's "parents were indulgent" (*FMP*, 23) and the education they gave their children was "never forced," (*FMP*, 23) so that "so far from study being made odious to us through punishment, we loved application, and our amusement would have been the labours of other children" (*FMP*, 23). According to the radical ideas of Mary Shelley's parents, Victor Frankenstein's familial, social, economic and educational circumstances would ensure a future of

38 Mary Wollstonecraft, *An Historical and Moral View of the Origin and Progress of the French Revolution and the Effect it Has Produced in Europe* Volume the first [1794] (The Second Edition. London: Printed for J. Johnson, St. Paul's Church-Yard, 1795). Online Library of Liberty. Available at: http://oll.libertyfund.org/titles/wollstonecraft-an-historical-and-moral-view-of-the-origin-and-progress-of-the-french-revolution (last access June 20, 2018).
39 Quoted in Baldick, *In Frankenstein's Shadow*, 22.
40 Baldick, *In Frankenstein's Shadow*, 25.

spiritual tranquillity and virtuous happiness. However, after coming across the works of Cornelius Agrippa, Paracelsus and Albertus Magnus (*FMP*, 24), he will sacrifice this happy future to the "search of the philosopher's stone and the elixir of life" (*FMP*, 25), deluding himself with the thought that he could use this forbidden knowledge to "banish disease from the human frame, and render man invulnerable to any but a violent death" (*FMP*, 25). After making this decision, Victor progressively cuts all bonds with his loved ones and, like the Poet in "Alastor," leads an ever-more bleak and solitary life. Unlike the Poet, however, who dies without attaining his goal, Dr. Frankenstein's efforts are eventually rewarded as he succeeds in infusing life to inert matter. But he is far from having realised the alchemical project, whose corollary is the creation of the *lapis/filius philosophorum*, that is, the androgynous (i.e. perfect) stone/child obtained at the end of the alchemical process when the *prima materia* is refined and transmuted into the *anima mundi*, the body-soul hidden in matter.[41] Instead of developing, like the alchemists, the spiritual knowledge that would grant him access to the secret of God's creative spark existing in all things[42] – or to put it in Blake's terms, instead of developing the fourfold vision or enlarged consciousness of the poet-as-prophet – Victor gave up alchemy after entering university (*FMP*, 26), and set instead on the study of chemistry and other branches of natural philosophy (*FMP*, 24). Thus, he sought to pierce the secret of life exclusively by rational means, forgetting that the creation of the *lapis/filius philosophorum* can only be achieved through the *hierosgamos* (the *coniunctio* or "chymic wedding") of opposites (spirit and matter; light and darkness; god and goddess), by means of *amor vulgaris* (reproductive sexual love).[43] Completely ignoring this, Dr. Frankenstein sewed together disjointed parts of various corpses and set the resulting body into motion by means of electricity. His shocked reaction when he saw the monstrosity of his Creature shows the limitations of his scientific method – or, in Blake's terms, of "Single vision & Newtons sleep."[44]

As Baldick explains, from a neo-classical perspective, the physical deformity of the Creature would respond to the "category of the 'grotesque', which unlike the 'picturesque' is an artificially contrived violation of Nature"[45]; from a political

---

41 Remo F. Roth, *The Return of the World Soul: Wolfgang Pauli, Carl Jung and the Challenge of the Unified Psychophysical Reality*. Part I: The Battle of the Giants (Grisignano, Italy: Pari Publishing Sas., 2011), 67–99.

42 Richard Cavendish, *The Magical Arts: Western Occultism and Occultists* [1967] (London: Arkana, 1984), 4.

43 Roth, *The Return of the World Soul*, 77–85.

44 Blake, "Letter to Butts," 818.

45 Baldick, *In Frankenstein's Shadow*, 14.

perspective, it would evoke "that venerable cliché of political discourse, the 'body politic'. When political discourse and rebellion appear, this 'body' is said to be not just diseased, but misshapen, abortive, monstrous,"[46] while from the perspective of the new aesthetics of Romanticism, "the problem of wilful and unnatural assembly" would reflect "Coleridge's famous distinction between the organic fusion of parts achieved by the Imagination, and the merely mechanical combination produced by Fancy."[47] Coleridge's distinction between organic fusion and mechanical combination perfectly synthesises the central point in Mary Shelley's critique of Frankenstein's creative method and, by extension, of her parents' thought, namely, that, severed from nature and the creative imagination, reason produces monsters. What is more, by attributing the monstrosity of the Creature to the inadequacy of Dr. Frankenstein's scientific method, Mary Shelley was also setting into question her parents' reliance on the progressive perfectibility of humankind. Compared to the alchemists' aim of creating a perfect stone/child through the chemical wedding of opposites by means of sexual love, Dr. Frankenstein's animation of matter by means of electricity seems utterly simplistic and regressive.

Still, Mary Shelley shared with her parents the conviction that human beings are innately good in the state of nature and that, as Victor's father tells him in a letter, love and happiness go hand in hand: "I know that while you are pleased with yourself, you will think of us with affection" (*FMP*, 38). The price Dr. Frankenstein has to pay for his acquisition of forbidden knowledge is enormous precisely because it involves a growing incapacity to enjoy the love of family and friends, and a total alienation from nature, as he himself eventually admits to Captain Robert Walton, the narrator of the frame narrative: "my eyes were insensible to the charms of nature. And the same feelings which made me neglect the scenes around me caused me also to forget those friends who were so many miles absent, and whom I had not seen for so long a time" (*FMP*, 38). At first, Victor deludes himself with the thought that his incapacity to love is transitory, but after giving life to the Creature, he is incapable of taking care of him, thus neglecting his natural duties as father and god-like creator. Left to fend for himself, the Creature finds refuge in a wood and behaves as a noble savage in the state of nature. But after two years of enduring the shattering rejection and repeated acts of aggression of the human beings he encounters, his original good nature turns into vindictive rage. The decisive element in this transformation is his realisation that he has done nothing to deserve the punishment of a wandering and solitary life, normally reserved for disobedient sons. As he tells Frankenstein in one of their climactic encounters:

46 Baldick, *In Frankenstein's Shadow*, 14.
47 Baldick, *In Frankenstein's Shadow*, 14.

> I am thy creature, and I will be ever mild and docile to my natural lord and king, if though wilt also perform thy part, the which thou owest me [...]. Everywhere I see bliss, from which I alone are irrevocably excluded. I was benevolent and good; misery made me a fiend. Make me happy, and I shall again be virtuous. [...] Believe me, Frankenstein: I was benevolent; my soul glowed with love and humanity: but am I not alone, miserably alone? (*FMP*, 81)

These words situate the Creature in the position of the French revolutionaries confronting "the monster parent Aristocracy" in Tom Paine's account of the French Revolution, just as the horror provoked by his bloody revenge echoes that of the Terror. Confronted with Dr. Frankenstein's refusal to assume his paternal duties, or provide him with a female partner so that he can form his own family, the Creature sets to destroying the innocent members of Dr. Frankenstein's family one by one: he murders his brother William; fabricates proofs that cost the life of Justine, the amiable family servant; then kills his friend Henry Clerval; and finally strangles Elizabeth on the wedding night, thus causing the death out of sorrow of Victor's father as well.

As James B. Twitchell, among many other critics, has observed, since its creation, there has been "an overwhelming degree of confusion" surrounding *Frankenstein* that is most clearly evinced in the tendency to confuse the nameless Creature with his creator, also calling him "Frankenstein": "Although this confusion was already in place by the turn of the century, it was compounded by the Universal [filmic versions]."[48] This confusion of identities, which would reflect the Ego/Shadow complementariness of the two characters alongside the Poet/Alastor model in Percy Shelley's poem, would explain why, as Twitchell observes, "in his ravings [Victor] 'called [him]self the murderer of William, of Justine ...'"[49]; or also, why he did nothing to prevent them, as Dr. Frankenstein could have saved the lives of his loved ones either by undertaking his paternal obligations or by revealing his secret, most clearly in the cases of Justine and Elizabeth, the two orphaned young women protected and educated by his parents. His criminal inaction proves that, as Twitchell suggests, "the monster is fulfilling the desires of his creator."[50] In other words, as the *Doppelgänger* materialisation of Dr. Frankenstein's unconscious, the Creature's murderous actions realise Victor Frankenstein's most strongly repressed desire, which is the destruction of the family within which he has been allotted a role he regards with "horror and dismay" (*FMP*, 131).

---

48 James B. Twitchell, *Dreadful Pleasures: An Anatomy of Modern Horror* (New York and Oxford: Oxford University Press, 1985), 165.
49 Twitchell, *Dreadful Pleasures*, 168.
50 Twitchell, *Dreadful Pleasures*, 168.

Throughout the novel, Victor has been postponing the wedding planned by his parents with Elizabeth, the motherless daughter of Victor's paternal aunt (*FMP*, 21). In the 1831 revised version of the novel, Mary Shelly tried to remove the incestuous element implicit in this project by suppressing the blood-relationship between the young couple (*F*, 26–27), but even in this later version there is a sense of impropriety in the arranged match: Victor thinks of Elizabeth as "my more than sister" (*F*, 29–30), and Mrs. Frankenstein admits that her reason for adopting her was "more than a duty, it was a necessity, a passion – remembering how she had suffered, and how she had been relieved – for her to act in turn the guardian angel of the afflicted" (F, 28).[51] In other words, Mrs. Frankenstein sees in Elizabeth the pitiful orphan she herself was and she thinks of the wedding as the means for Elizabeth to continue her role as "Angel in the House" after her own death. This casts an uncanny *alter ego* complementariness between (adoptive) mother and (adopted) daughter that is enhanced by the fact that it is Elizabeth who causes Mrs. Frankenstein's death by transmitting the scarlet fever to her as it situates the old and the young women in an archetypal relationship of generational death and rebirth.[52] This apparently blissful plan has, however, a disturbing element that is made explicit in Mrs. Frankenstein's death-bed speech, when she entreats Victor and Elizabeth to marry and, at the same time, compels her to "supply my place to your younger cousins" (*FMP*, 28).[53] Her demand that Elizabeth fulfil the double role of wife to Victor *and* mother to his younger brothers leaves no doubt about the incestuous element in the projected match, thus unveiling a forcefully repressed Oedipus complex behind Victor's endless postponement of the wedding that comes to the fore on the night after the Creature comes to life, in what Victor himself describes as "the wildest dream" (*FMP*, 41):

> I thought I saw Elizabeth in the bloom of health [. . .] Delighted and surprised I embraced her; but as I imprinted the first kiss on her lips, they became livid with the hue of death: her features appeared to change, and I thought that I held the corpse of my mother in my arms. (*FMP*, 41)

---

51 Mrs. Frankenstein's reason for taking Justine Moritz as a family servant was similar: to protect her from the ill-treatment she was subjected to by her mother (*F*, 68). And the fact that Victor did nothing to save her from the gallows is the more puzzling since, as Elizabeth tells him in a letter, "she was a great favourite of yours" (*F*, 69).

52 Sir James George Frazer. "The Double Personification of the Corn as Mother and Daughter," in *The Golden Bough: A Study in Magic and Religion* [1922] (New York: Macmillan, 2000), Chapter 46. Section 4. Available at: www.bartleby.com/196/ (last access June 20, 2018).

53 Mrs. Frankenstein's entreaty reads as follows in the revised version: "Elizabeth, my love, you must supply my place to my younger children" (*F*, 40).

Together with the revelation of Victor's Oedipus complex, this proleptic dream brings to the fore the disturbing association of motherhood with death that lies behind Victor's apparently absurd renunciation of the bliss of family life and his obsession with creating human life artificially. Stephen Bann interprets this association by drawing a double analogy with Mary Shelley's own "anxiety of authorship"[54] and "anxiety of monstrosity."[55] As he argues, the writer's description of the novel in the Introduction to the 1931 edition as her "hideous progeny"[56] would justify the first analogy, while the second would stem from Mary Shelley's guilty knowledge that her mother, Mary Wollstonecraft, had died of *post-partum* complications after giving birth to her. This early association of motherhood with death was dramatically increased by Mary's own painful begettings, the loss of three children, and her shattering witnessing of various violent deaths of friends and relatives.[57] Certainly, Mary Shelley's fears play an important role in the creation of the novel in the sense that they add a personal element to the pattern of affectionate motherhood that developed alongside that of the novel during the long 18th century (1650–1865).[58] The loving bond between Mrs. Frankenstein and Elizabeth clearly responds to this new valorisation of motherhood. However, the fact that it is Elizabeth who causes her adoptive mother's death suggests an underlying matricidal element in their apparently blissful relation of the type voiced by Virginia Woolf when she fantasised about killing the "Angel in the House." As Deborah D. Rogers notes, quoting Luce Irigaray, this matricidal impulse is the expression of the daughters' unconscious desire to avoid being, like their mothers, "enslaved in self-sacrificial roles that suppress the expression of desire."[59] According to this, Mrs. Frankenstein's untimely death brought about by her insistence to

54 Stephen Bann, *Frankenstein, Creation and Monstrosity* (London: Reaktion Books, 1994), 35.
55 Bann, *Frankenstein*, 36.
56 Shelley, "Author's Introduction," 199.
57 As Paddy Lyons explains, "[in] October 1816, within weeks of their return to England, Fanny Imlay, daughter of Mary Wollstonecraft and half-sister to Mary, had committed suicide, swallowing poison in a hotel room in Swansea. [...] in December there was further suicide: Shelley's estranged wife Harried drowned herself in the Serpentine. She was advanced in pregnancy." Paddy Lyons, "Introduction," in *Mary Shelley* Frankenstein, ed. and Intro. Paddy Lyons (London: J. M. Dent & Sons Ltd; Rutland, Vermont. Charles E Tuttle Co., Inc., 1992): vii-xx, xv-xvi. In January 1816, Mary gave birth to William, "a sickly boy who was to die in mid-1819" (Lyons, "Introduction," xvi); "And by early 1817 she was pregnant again: her daughter Clara (named after the child who died) was born in September 1817, though she was to live only a year" (Lyons, "Introduction," xvi). To these tragic losses is to be added that of Percy Bysshe Shelley, who found his death by drowning in 1822 (Lyons, "Introduction," xv).
58 Deborah D. Rogers, *The Matrophobic Gothic and its Legacy: Sacrificial Mothers in the Novel and in Popular Culture* (New York: Peter Lang, 2007), 4.
59 Rogers, *The Matrophobic Gothic*, 4.

nurse Elizabeth personally through her scarlet fever would be the expression not so much of Mary Shelley's fear of procreation and death as of her rejection of the socially sanctioned role of sexually unfulfilled and self-denying, sacrificial mother.

Still, even adding this element to Mary Shelley's psychological motivation for the writing of the novel, Stephen Bann's analogical interpretation falls short of accounting for Victor Frankenstein's own motives and actions as it reduces him to the status of author's fictional *alter ego* articulating the sexual and social fears of a teenage woman who had flaunted patriarchal law and provoked the rage of her father by eloping with a married man. Indeed, Bann's reading does not take into consideration the fact that Dr. Frankenstein's obsessive search for the spark of life materialises a recurrent *male* dream: the possibility of male-only procreation.[60] Set against his repeated postponement of the wedding, Victor's scientific endeavour may be interpreted as a male form of matrophobia, already present in early modern male writers from Samuel Richardson onwards, that conflates the female fear of pregnancy and procreation with the "eroticiz[ation] of chastity as a source of female power."[61] As Rogers suggests in the title of the chapter devoted to the analysis of Richardson's *Pamela*, this male form of matrophobia is the expression of the unacknowledged desires of "Men who Want to be Women."[62] From this perspective, Victor Frankenstein's search for the spark of life would respond to a consuming desire to find a round-about way of performing the social duty of procreation without the intervention of woman and, consequently, without having to assume the role as *paterfamilias* allotted to adult men within the patriarchal family structure.

3 Victor Frankenstein's failed quest: the monstrosity of narcissism

According to the humanist tradition, the physical and spiritual progress of free men develops alongside the experience of four successive forms of

60 Besides a relatively common motif in speculative fiction, the idea of male-only procreation has been addressed from a comic perspective in connection with the motif of authorial originality in 20th-century experimental novels like Flann O'Brien's *At Swim-two-Birds* (1939) or John Fowles' *Mantissa* (1982).

61 Rogers, *The Matrophobic Gothic*, 75.

62 Rogers, "Men who Want to be Women: Matrophobia in Samuel Richardson's *Pamela*," in *The Matrophobic Gothic*, 75–96.

love.[63] The first is *storge*, the affectionate love the child finds in the family. The second is *philia*, or friendship between equals, the form of dispassionate love for the other theorised by Aristotle in *Nicomachean Ethics* that was considered to be the corollary of the rational man's disposition towards goodness, virtue, and happiness.[64] The third is *eros* (sexual love), the force that, according to Hermetic alchemists like Paracelsus or Robert Fludd, can bring about the reconciliation of opposites required for the creation the *lapis/filius philosophorum*. The fourth form of love is *agape* (charity). Unlike the other three, *agape* is a superior and transformative form of love: it is the love that God feels for his creatures and human beings for God, but it can also denote feelings for one's children and spouse.[65] In its most general acceptation, the term *agape* designates the selfless and unconditional love that serves regardless of changing circumstances. Emmanuel Levinas associates this form of love with the abnegation and hospitality of biblical Rebecca (Genesis 24).[66] Looking at the development of Victor Frankenstein from a humanist and ethical perspective, it seems evident that he enjoyed all the advantages of familial love (*storge*) and also the bliss of *philia* with his childhood friend, Henry Clerval. Normally, this youthful phase is put an end by the promptings of *eros*, when the young man must relinquish his carefree, narcissistic life and assume the social responsibility of forming his own family. This is the step Victor constantly postpones, thus precluding his development from the Oedipus stage towards psychosexual maturity. As Sibel Izmir has noted, in the Renaissance, the confrontation of *philia* and *eros* was a well-worn literary *topos* whose roots go back to two related medieval traditions: "Friendship literature" and the "romance."[67] We find echoes of this tradition in various plays by Shakespeare, for example, in the male friendship of Hamlet and Horatio in *Hamlet*, of Romeo and Mercutio in *Romeo and Juliet*, of Antonio and Bassanio in *The Merchant of Venice*, or of Proteus and Valentine in

---

63 C. S. Lewis, *The Four Loves* [1960] (New York: Harcourt, Brace, 1988).

64 Aristotle, *Nicomachean Ethics* [349 BC] (Cambridge, Massachusetts, London: Harvard University Press, 1999.

65 Henry George Liddell, and Robert Scott, *A Greek-English Lexicon*. Revised and augmented by Sir Henry Stuart Jones, with the assistance of Roderick McKenzie (Oxford: Clarendon Press, 1940). Available at: http://www.perseus.tufts.edu/hopper/text?doc=Perseus%3Atext%3A1999.04.0057 (last access June 20, 2018).

66 Emmanuel Levinas, "Judaism and the Feminine Element," *Judaism* 18.1 (1969): 33–73.

67 Sibel Izmir, "The Concept of Male Friendship in Shakespeare's *The Two Gentlemen of Verona*: A Contextual Approach," *The Journal of International Social Research* 8.37 (April 2015): 160–173, 163.

The Two Gentlemen of Verona.[68] Arguably, what lies behind Victor's rebelliousness and disobedience is a juvenile refusal to move from *philia* to *eros*, that is, to renounce the self-centred and gratifying life of the adventurer and assume the social duty to marry and procreate. His attempt at male-only procreation is monstrous not only because it evinces a matrophobic tendency but also because it prevents him from developing feelings of *agape*, the transformative love a paternal God would feel for his children. By allowing the Creature to murder Elizabeth Victor puts a definitive end not only to his aspirations of socially sanctioned fulfilment but also to his expectations of happiness and fame as by marrying Elizabeth he would have been granted the god-like capacity to beget his own children by natural means, to enjoy transformative and selfless love, and to perpetuate his name.

4 Conclusion: the resolution of the family feud

The peculiar narrative structure of the novel, with the letters and speeches of various characters belonging to the main narrative embedded within the frame of Captain Robert Walton's letters to his sister Mrs. Saville, is echoed thematically by the reduplication of the motifs of disobedience and the family feud. Like Victor Frankenstein, Robert Walton is an adventurer drawn by "ardent curiosity" (*FMP*, 7) and the obsessive desire to "accomplish some great purpose" (*FMP*, 9). Prompted by illusory expectations of glory and fame, he has disobeyed his father's dying prohibition to "embark in a sea-faring life" (*FMP*, 8), and has undertaken a long and dangerous journey to the North Pole. He has also sacrificed family and friends to the realisation of a forbidden project and lives in dreadful solitude. It is in order to mitigate this loneliness that he writes letters to his sister Margaret, even though she might never receive them. In his second letter, he admits that he "bitterly feels the want of a friend" (*FMP*, 10) for, although he is surrounded by the members of his crew, he does not have "the company of a man who could sympathise with me: whose eyes would reply to mine" (*FMP*, 10). His yearning for *philia* is

68 For example, in the male friendship of Hamlet and Horatio in *Hamlet*, of Romeo and Mercutio in *Romeo and Juliet*, of Antonio and Bassanio in *The Merchant of Venice*, and of Proteus and Valentine in *The Two Gentlemen of Verona*. See Susana Onega, "Learning to Love: The Paradoxical Life Quests of the Male Protagonists in Jeanette Winterson's *The Gap of Time*," in *The Wounded Hero in Contemporary Fiction: A Paradoxical Quest*, eds. Susana Onega and Jean-Michel Ganteau (London and New York: Routledge, 2018): 19–41.

unexpectedly satisfied when he finds Frankenstein on a large fragment of ice, in a terrible state of emaciation and fatigue (*FMP*, 15). The surprised Captain accurately describes the stranger as a "divine wanderer" (*FMP, 18*) and recognises in him "the friend" (*FMP, 18*) and "brother of [his] heart" (*FMP, 17*) that he had always wished to have. His first-sight impression is immediately reciprocated by Frankenstein. Although Walton is a perfect stranger, the terminally-ill and melancholy doctor has no qualms in revealing to him the awful secret he had so jealously kept from his family and friend. His reason for doing so is didactic: the dying old man seeks to dissuade the young adventurer from pursuing his foolish search for glory and put an end to his unnatural solitude. Frankenstein's death-bed lesson is rounded off by the Creature, who, in keeping with his spectral role, also speaks to Walton before immolating himself in a funeral pyre (*FMP*, 189). What he reveals to Walton is that the awful acts of vengeance he had performed had brought him neither happiness nor peace: "For while I destroyed his hopes, I did not satisfy my own desires" (*FMP*, 190).

Captain Walton's decision to put an end to the expedition and return to England (*FMP*, 184–185) after listening to Frankenstein and the Creature shows that he has overcome the youthful phase of rebelliousness and is ready to resume family life, thus opening up the possibility for him to move on from *philia* to *eros*, and so, to become a socially adjusted and dutiful *paterfamilias*. This ending suggests that, for all its critique of reason, and of the endless perfectibility of humankind, for all its disturbing association of maternity with death, and its matrophobic and matricidal elements, the novel's ending paradoxically reinforces the patriarchal view of the family as the social structure capable of transforming disobedient and solitary sons into protective fathers endowed with the fruition of true love, the achievement of happiness, and the perpetuation of their name.[69]

69 This ending is the more paradoxical, given Mary Shelley's imitation of her mother in the defence of free love: her decision to elope with Percy Bysshe Shelley, a married man, to bear his illegitimate children, and even to share him with her half-sister Claire during their flight to France, thus realising the *menage à troi* Mary Wollstonecraft had imagined for herself, Henry Fuseli and his wife. Elizabeth Bronfen, "Rewriting the Family: Mary Shelley's *Frankenstein* in its Biographical/Textual Context," in *Frankenstein, Creation and Monstrosity*, ed. Stephen Bann (London: Reaktion Books, 1994): 16–38, 24.

Anna Enrichetta Soccio

Victorian Frankenstein: From Fiction to Science

1 Frankenstein and the Victorians

The genesis of Mary Shelley's *Frankenstein; or, the Modern Prometheus* as the result of a parlor game and a nightmare vision is well known. Mary Shelley herself, in the 1831 Introduction to the novel, wrote that she "busied [her]self to think of a story [. . .] making only a transcript of the grim terrors of [her] waking dream"[1] and that her husband, the poet Percy Bysshe Shelley, "urged [her] to develop the idea at greater length".[2] Perhaps she did not foresee that her "waking dream" would continue, in the centuries to come, to keep generations of readers awake, and to give life to a vast number of rewritings, remakes, retakes, series, adaptations, imitations, sequels and prequels which have ended up creating a "myth" whose qualities of durability, flexibility and pervasiveness are today indisputable.

The Victorians were of course the first readers to feel the burden of Shelley's heritage. *Frankenstein* dealt with some crucial issues – the English literary tradition, religion, women, society, language, science, the Gothic, the grotesque, just to mention a few – in which the Victorians were involved in terms of social, moral and aesthetic thinking.

Although the responses to the first edition of the novel (1818) were contradictory, *Frankenstein* was already regarded as a "classic" only a few years later: in 1823 both Thomas Love Peacock and Mary's father, the philosopher William Godwin, observed that the novel was "universally known and read",[3] "universally known, and [. . .] everywhere respected".[4] In July that same year, *Frankenstein* was adapted for the theatre by Richard Brinsley Peake, who wrote and staged a play titled *Presumption; or, the Fate of*

---

1 Mary Shelley, "Author's Introduction to the Standard Novels Edition (1831)", in *Frankenstein, or the Modern Prometheus, 1818 text*, ed. with an Introduction and Notes by Marilyn Butler (Oxford: Oxford University Press, 1998), 195 and 197.

2 Shelley, *Frankenstein*, 197.

3 Nicholas A. Joukovsky ed., *The Letters of Thomas Love Peacock* (Oxford: Clarendon, 2001), 2 vols., vol. I, 147.

4 Charles E. Robinson, "Frankenstein Chronology," in *The Frankenstein Notebooks: A Facsimile Edition of Mary Shelley's Manuscript Novel, 1816–17* (New York: Garland Publishing, 1991), lxxxvi–cx, available at http://shelleygodwinarchive.org/contents/frankenstein/frankenstein-chronology/ (last accessed May 16, 2018).

https://doi.org/10.1515/9783110654615-008

Frankenstein. The pièce was so successful that, during the 1823 season, it was performed thirty-seven times. Mary Shelley herself appreciated Peake's adaptation very much: "Cooke played—'s part extremely well [...] I was much amused, & it appeared to excite a breathless eagerness in the audience".[5] This success was certainly due to the fact that the Gothic text had been transformed into a domestic melodrama insisting on the moral aspects of the story, sexuality, family values, as well as to the involvement of T. P. Cooke, a big star of the London stage in the first half of the 19th century, who performed as the Creature. In 1853, *The Illustrated London News* reported that Cooke had appeared on stage at least 365 times, which was a record.[6] Over the following three years, between 1823 and 1826, at least one dozen different stage productions appeared, amongst which also melodramas and farces.[7]

When the publishers reprinted Mary Shelley's novel in 1831, *Frankenstein* was already a substantial cultural metaphor, whose strength stemmed from the social, moral, political and metaphysical implications it explores, and which discusses the main lines of western thinking from the mid-18th century onwards. Shelley's story can be seen from one point of view, as a rewriting of the ancient myths of Prometheus and Faust. On the other hand, it can be seen as a modern myth which has nothing to do with gods or divine power but is a secular vision in which idealism, faith in human perfectibility

5 Letter to Leigh Hunt. Mary Shelley, *The Letters of Mary Wollstonecraft Shelley*, 2 vols, ed. Betty Bennett (Baltimore, MD: Johns Hopkins University Press, 1981), vol. I, 378. See also Diane Long Hoeveler, "Nineteenth-Century Dramatic Adaptations of *Frankenstein*", in *The Cambridge Companion to* Frankenstein, ed. Andrew Smith (Cambridge: Cambridge University Press, 2016), 175–189.

6 Quoted in Long Hoelever, "Nineteenth-Century Dramatic Adaptations of *Frankenstein.*"

7 Here a list of some of them: Henry M. Milner, *Frankenstein; or, The Demon of Switzerland* (Royal Coburg Theatre, 18 August 1823); *Humgumption; or, Dr. Frankenstein and the Hobgoblin of Hoxton* (New Surrey Theatre, 1 September 1823); *Presumption and the Blue Demon* (Davis's Royal Amphitheatre, 1 September 1823); Richard Brinsley Peake, *Another Piece of Presumption* (Adelphi Theatre, 20 October 1823); *Frank-in-Steam; or, The Modern Promise to Pay* (Olympic Theatre, 13 December 1824); Jean-Toussaint Merle and Antoine Nicolas Beraud [pseud. Beraud Antony] *Le Monstre et le magicien* (Paris, Theatre de la Porte Saint-Martin, 10 June 1826); Henry M. Milner, *The Man and the Monster; or, The Fate of Frankenstein* di Henry M. Milner (Royal Coburg Theatre, 3 July 1826); Nicolas Brazier, Guillaume Dumersan and Gabriel-Jules-Joseph de Lurien, *Les Filets de Vulcain; ou, La Venus de Neuilly*; (Paris: Theatre des Varietes, 5 July 1826); Jules-Henri Vernoy de Saint-Georges and Antoine-Jean-Baptiste Simonnin, *Le Petit monstre et l'escamoteur* (Paris: Theatre de la Gaite, 7 July 1826); *Le Monstre et le physicien* (Paris, Theatre de M. Comte, 3 August 1826); John Kerr, *The Monster and Magician; or, The Fate of Frankenstein* (New Royal West London Theatre, 9 October 1826).

and revolutionary energy are mixed up in order to convey the sense of a "modern" crisis.

Thus, it is not surprising that Shelley's myth enchanted the Victorian writers who attempted, either deliberately or accidentally, to actualize this myth in order to investigate its most crucial issues. While the interest for stage adaptation continued throughout the rest of the century, the Victorians became more and more fascinated by the complex network of themes and concerns that *Frankenstein* propounded in terms of cultural, social and political change.[8] Here, one cannot help thinking of Emily Brontë's *Wuthering Heights* (1847) in which the *heimlich* and the *unheimlich* – to use Freud's words – are constantly opposed in the story of Heathcliff and Catherine told by Lockwood; or Dickens's *Great Expectations* (1860–1861) in which the relationship between Pip and Magwitch recalls Shelley's story when Magwitch is rejected by Pip in the same way as the Creature is rejected by Victor Frankenstein; or George Eliot's *Middlemarch* (1874), in which Dr. Lydgate, "with enormous faith in the power of biological science, seeks to discover the primitive tissue that is the source of all life"[9]; or, finally, there is R. L. Stevenson's *The Strange Case of Dr. Jekyll and Mr. Hyde* (1886), and Joseph Conrad's *The Secret Sharer* (1909) which discuss the theme of the "double," or H. G. Wells's *The Island of Dr. Moreau* (1895) and its pseudo-human monstrous creatures. The list, that could be even longer, shows that the myth of Frankenstein was deeply rooted in Victorian culture. The narrative structure of Shelley's text was considered an endless source of inspiration, capable of producing a number of surprisingly new meanings. However, I would like here to focus on some Victorian texts, both narrative and scientific, that are not immediately recognized as direct descendants of *Frankenstein*; yet, they have unquestionably drawn profitable lessons from the romantic novel and have contributed to reinforce its popularity.

8 "The political dimensions of *Frankenstein* were immediately apparent to its original readers and reviewers, and have continued to evolve as new media returned to Shelley's iconic monster in particular, and his protean ability to voice and embody a remarkable range of later political crises – from revolutionary Marxism, Irish independence, abolition and slave rebellions, to animal rights, human cloning and genetic research." Sadriana Craciun, "*Frankenstein*'s Politics," in *The Cambridge Companion to* Frankenstein, 84.

9 George Levine, "The Ambiguous Heritage of *Frankenstein*," in *The Endurance of Frankenstein. Essays on Mary Shelley's Novel*, eds. George Levine and U. C. Knoepflmacher (Berkeley and Los Angeles, CA: University of California Press, 1982), 23.

2 Gaskell, Dickens and their monsters

The beginning of the Victorian age was characterized by the emergence of social problems as a consequence of the rapid development of urban and industrial areas mainly in the north of England. Elizabeth Gaskell's writing is typically engaged in such phenomena and finds inspiration for her first novel, *Mary Barton. A Tale of Manchester Life* (1848), from her observation of the industrial city and the people who live in, suffer from and die for it. It is worth pointing out that the novel's subtitle emphasizes what Manchester represents in the 1840s: a world with all the characteristics of an industrial scene in which one can see encounters and clashes between social classes every day. Gaskell is an authoritative observer and mediator of this reality, both as a novelist and as a member of the Unitarian community of Manchester. She was persuaded that, only by grasping the inmost essence of the contradictions, only by speaking for those who are plunged into the city's complexities, is it possible to offer a world that is able to redeem itself. In *Mary Barton*, the main binaries are industrial captains/workers, the limited space of the factory/the vast space of the urban crowd, the well-lit districts with the bourgeois villas/the dark labyrinth of slums where the characters, often trapped in sad degradation, meet in an attempt to survive.

The novel focuses on John Barton, a Chartist supporter who, after tragically losing his wife, decides to seek revenge against Mr. Carson, the factory owner who has, in the meantime, sacked some workers amongst whom Barton himself. In these conditions of poverty and desperation, Barton falls prey to self-destructive remorse and becomes an opium addict. The novel is set in the years 1839–1840, at the time of the First Opium War between England and China which linked the tea trade with Indian opium and English cotton in a business network that intertwined the three products with each other. In Gaskell's novel, "tea is a trope for Englishness, opium is a symbol for un-Englishness."[10] The dualism good/evil in John Barton's life is mirrored in the novel's structure: from an early moment of abundance and friendship symbolized by the tea prepared by Mrs. Barton, we move on to the experience of hunger and solitude represented by opium in chapter VI. After his wife's death and the fire of the cotton mill – with the consequent loss of his job – John Barton falls into his opium addiction:

> And so day by day, nearer and nearer, came the *diseased thoughts* of John Barton. They excluded the light of heaven, the cheering sounds of earth. They were preparing his death.

---

10 Veronica Hoyt, "English Tea and Chinese Opium: A Contrast between Good and Evil in *Mary Barton*?," in *Evil and its Variations*, ed. M. Matsuoka (Osaka: Osaka Kyoiku Tosho, 2015), 18.

> It is true, much of their morbid power *might be ascribed to the use of opium.* But before you blame too harshly this use, or rather abuse, try a hopeless life, with daily cravings of the body for food. Try, not alone being without hope yourself, but seeing all around you reduced to the same despair, arising from the same circumstances; all around you telling (though they use no words or language), by their looks and feeble actions, that they are suffering and sinking under the pressure of want. *Would you not be glad to forget life, and its burdens*? And *opium gives forgetfulness for a time.*[11]

The speaking voice links Barton's "diseased thoughts" to the use of opium that is regarded as the only way "to forget life". This leads to the use of the metaphor of Frankenstein's monster to talk about middle-class discomfort and irritation regarding the working class:

> The actions of the *uneducated* seem to me typified in those of Frankenstein, that *monster of many human qualities, ungifted with a soul, a knowledge of the difference between good and evil.*
>
> The people rise up to life; they irritate *us*, they terrify *us*, and *we* become their enemies. Then, in the sorrowful moment of our triumphant power, their eyes *gaze* on *us* with a mute reproach. Why have we made them what they are; a *powerful monster, yet without the inner means for peace and happiness*?[12]

In this passage, the working class as a whole and John Barton as its representative are called "uneducated", as they ignore the difference between good and evil. Their actions are like those of Frankenstein – here Gaskell already makes the common mistake that most people still make today: she calls the Creature with his creator's name – a monster of human qualities yet with no soul, no moral values, no rationality that can allow him to be happy. Barton is referred to as "other", that is to say, someone who is alien to Victorian society as well as to human reality, a monster who takes Indian drugs rather than drink tea, the symbol of Englishness. By using the personal pronouns "us" and "we," the narrator invites the reader to look with horror at that powerful yet inhuman monster that is the working class. Thus, opium becomes the vehicle for Barton's physical squalor and psychic degeneration as the character himself evolves into a socially unacceptable individual. "John Barton became a Chartist, a Communist, all that is commonly called wild and visionary"[13]: such a description is very far from the reassuring images of English people as an active part in the increasing economic development of the forthcoming empire.

---

11 Elizabeth Gaskell, *Mary Barton. A Tale of Manchester Life*, ed. with an Introduction by Stephen Gill (Harmondsworth: Penguin, 1985), 219 [emphasis mine].

12 Gaskell, *Mary Barton*, 219 [emphasis mine].

13 Gaskell, *Mary Barton*, 200.

In 1848, the same year as the publication of Gaskell's *Mary Barton*, Charles Dickens published *The Haunted Man*, the fifth and last of his *Christmas Books*. Neglected for too long, this novella is one of the most interesting stories ever written by Dickens. It establishes an immediate dialogism with Shelley's novel in so far as it dramatizes Victorian fears and anxieties regarding scientific discourse. Like Victor Frankenstein, the protagonist of Dickens's novella, Redlaw, is a solitary scientist, "a learned man in chemistry"[14] who has the power to make and unmake objects and organisms: "some of these phantoms [...] trembling at heart like things that knew his power to uncombine them, and to give back their component parts to fire and vapour".[15] Like Victor's well-known laboratory, Redlaw's place appears as a gloomy, cold room:

> Who that had seen him in his inner chamber, part library and part laboratory, – for he was, as the world knew, far and wide, a learned man in chemistry, [...] – who that had seen him there, upon a winter night, *alone*, surrounded by his drugs and instruments and books; the shadow of his shaded lamp a *monstrous* beetle on the wall, motionless among a crowd of *spectral* shapes raised there by the flickering of the fire upon the quaint objects around him; some of these *phantoms* (the reflection of glass vessels that held liquids), trembling at heart like things that knew *his power to uncombine them, and to give back their component parts to fire and vapour*; – who that had seen him then, his work done, and he pondering in his chair before the rusted grate and red flame, moving his thin mouth as if in speech, but silent as the *dead*, would not have said that the man seemed *haunted* and the chamber too?[16]

As one can see, in conjuring up a sense of mystery and death, the space of science is described as non-human (*monstrous*), full of supernatural phenomena (*phantoms, spectral, haunted*) which convey the image of an alchemist and his magical practices rather than that of a scientist and his experimental temperament. Similarly, Redlaw's house is also described as an infernal and labyrinthine place, which reflects the protagonist's twisted mind:

> His dwelling was so *solitary and vault-like*, – an old, retired part of an ancient endowment for students, once a brave edifice, planted in an open place, [...] where *no sun* had straggled for a hundred years, but where, in compensation for the sun's neglect, the *snow* would lie for weeks when it lay nowhere else, and the black east wind would spin like a huge humming-top, when in all other places it was silent and still.[17]

---

14 Charles Dickens, *The Haunted Man*, in Christmas Books, ed. Ruth Grancy (Oxford: Oxford University Press, 1988), 374.

15 Dickens, *The Haunted Man*, 374.

16 Dickens, *The Haunted Man*, 374.

17 Dickens, *The Haunted Man*, 374–375.

It is a place of ice and death, redolent of the vast polar lands of Shelley's novel. However, it must be said that Dickens's novella "inverts and exorcises the spectre of monstruosity."[18] Victor Frankenstein has to live in isolation and fear before recognizing his Creature, whereas Redlaw starts from the recognition of the phantom as his own double. In that "something" hunting him, Redlaw sees "an awful likeness of himself", "the animated image of himself dead,"[19] that is the duplication of the evil that is in himself. But another "monster" appears in the story before Redlaw accepts the gift of oblivion offered by the phantom: it is a child whose features are those of a beast that has never been loved: "A baby *savage*, a young *monster*, a child who had never been a child, a *creature* who might live to take the outward form of man, but who, within, would live and perish a mere *beast*."[20] The lexical choices here suggest a direct link with *Frankenstein* and physical sensations in the reader. The baby monster becomes a sort of admonition not only for Redlaw but also against the distortions of science that, by denying the ethical value of memory, prevent human beings from having any theological vision.[21]

3 T. H. Huxley and his "evolutionary" monsters

Frankenstein has also inspired non-narrative Victorian texts. Interestingly, Shelley's pseudo-science inspired a real scientist, T. H. Huxley (1825–1895) who published *Man's Place in Nature* in 1863, as a result of a series of conferences given between 1860 and 1862. T. H. Huxley was a great and enthusiastic supporter of evolutionary biology – he was called "Darwin's Bulldog" – and he devoted his essay to human evolution well before Charles Darwin published *On the Descent of Man* (1871). *Man's Place in Nature* establishes a powerful link with *Frankenstein* in so far as it adopts "narrative" strategies that bring the readers "face to face with blurred copies"[22] of themselves. From Huxley's point of view, the entire evolutionary theory can be regarded as the actualization of *Frankenstein*'s scientific implications. In other words, in investigating the origins of human life, science has to face the "monster" within us, a sort of animal

18 Levine, *The Endurance of Frankenstein*, 22.
19 Dickens, *The Haunted Man*, 389.
20 Dickens, *The Haunted Man*, 397.
21 See Francesco Marroni, *Spettri senza nome. Modelli epistemici e narrativa vittoriana* (Roma: Carocci, 2007), 30.
22 T. H. Huxley, *Man's Place in Nature and Other Anthropological Essays* (New York: D. Appleton and Company, Authorized Edition, 1899), 80.

with savage instincts. George Levine affirms that, although he writes for merely scientific reasons, like Mary Shelley, Huxley uses "deformed copies of human beings to force their presumed "originals" into an act of kinship that will involve a humiliation of their pride."[23] In fact, Huxley goes further than Darwin and offers the reader some drawings – like the mandrill with a human face, or Linneus's anthropomorphic beings – to make him/her recognize the kinship with them on a scientific basis. Despite the obvious differences between Huxley's scientific text and Shelley's novel, there is a surprising similarity between the two in the use of monsters and half-human creatures to provoke a horrified reaction in their readers. Just as Victor's reaction to the Creature first keeps us at a safe distance from the latter and only later do we discover his humanity, so Huxley describes gorillas' and orangutans' habits apparently only for zoological purposes until he reveals the true aim of his essay:

> Brought face to face with *these blurred copies of himself*, the least thoughtful of men is conscious of a certain shock, due perhaps, not so much to disgust at the aspect of what looks like an insulting caricature, as to the awakening of a sudden and profound mistrust of time-honoured theories and strongly-rooted prejudices regarding his own position in nature, and his relations to the under-world of life.[24]

Thus, Victorian readers discover that they are copies of apes: such an idea provokes the same sense of horror that Victor feels the moment he realizes that he has given life to a monster. Let us, for example, compare the description of the mandrill given by Huxley with the description of Shelley's monster:

> The head is monstrously big, and the face broad and flat, without any other hair but the eyebrows; the nose very small, the mouth wide, and the lips thin. The face, which is covered by a *white* skin, is *monstrously* ugly, being all over wrinkled as with old age; the teeth broad and *yellow*; the hands have no more hair than the face, but the same *white* skin, though all the rest of the body is covered with long black hair, like a bear. They never go upon all-fours, like apes; but cry, when vexed or teased, just like children. . .[25]
>
> His *yellow* skin scarcely covered the work of muscles and arteries beneath; his hair was of a lustrous black, and flowing; his teeth of a pearly *whiteness*; but these luxuriances only formed a more horrid contrast with his *watery* eyes, that seemed almost of the same colour as the *dun-white* sockets in which they were set, his shrivelled complexion and straight black lips.[26]

---

23 Levine, *The Endurance of Frankenstein*, 317.
24 Huxley, *Man's Place in Nature*, 80–81.
25 Huxley, *Man's Place in Nature*, 15–16.
26 Shelley, *Frankenstein*, 39.

The chromatic code dominates both descriptions: in Huxley's text, the face and teeth are white and yellow, whereas in Shelley's they are the other way round. However, both propose non-human creatures as a stage of human development (as ascendants and/or descendants of human beings), and force the reader to acknowledge kinship with primordial forces generating terror and anxiety; finally, both suggest that the monster is a metaphor. The deformed, alien being is inside us and must be recognized before our identity as human beings is affirmed. In *Man's Place in Nature*, Huxley concludes in a rhetorical way: "Where, then, must we look for primeval Man?"[27] Perhaps in the fossils of a half-human half-ape creature, but in the meantime Shelley's monster reminds us that his body/corpse does not lie somewhere amongst the glaciers of the Pole, but in the reader's mind, who finds himself face to face with his cultural fears and ethical anxieties. To conclude, the Victorians' interpretations of *Frankenstein* testify to an intense process of cultural assimilation of a modern myth which has had such an extraordinary impact that, after two centuries, it still permeates our culture and stimulates discussion on a wide range of themes.

---

27 Huxley, *Man's Place in Nature*, 205.

Jean-Michel Ganteau

Exposed: Dispossession and Androgyny in Contemporary British Fiction

The figure of the androgyne – perhaps not the most endangering, but certainly one of the most destabilising instanciations of the monster – haunts Western culture. Famously and foundingly present in Plato's *Symposium*, through Aristophane's speech, it has often been taken as a cornerstone in the evocation of passion and of the orectic aspect of human life, expressed as "the desire and pursuit of the whole."[1] It may boast some ubiquity in a more specifically British context, and more especially even in British literature, as it was defined and its powers extolled by at least two major figures of the canon, i.e.: S. T. Coleridge and Virginia Woolf. In his *Table Talk* (18 December 1831) Coleridge notoriously remarked, that "In truth, a great mind must be androgynous."[2] In his wake, Woolf eminently suggested: "Coleridge perhaps meant this when he meant that a great mind is androgynous. It is when this fusion takes place that the mind is fully fertilised and uses all its faculties [...] He meant, perhaps, that the androgynous mind is resonant and porous."[3] As rehearsed in the literary tradition, the androgyne becomes a powerful figure, the guarantee of inspiration and creation, an icon of porousness and openness to sundry influences. Elsewhere, in a more normative, scientific, medical and biomedical discourse, the vision of the androgyne, often considered under the more daunting image of the hermaphrodite, is distinctly less favourable, as teratomorphous anatomical traits tend to be stressed in their frightening disrespect of what is considered as the "law of nature," jeopardising its stability and unalterability.

Of course, the idea of the androgyne is not naturally compatible with that of the law that it breaches and threatens in more ways than one. Not only does it shift one of the most commonly accepted physical frontiers governing sexual assignation, but it also relies on the boundaries of legal discourse for definition or at least apprehension. By incarnating the principle of difference and

1 Martha C. Nussbaum, *The Fragility of Goodness. Luck and Ethics in Greek Tragedy and Philosophy* [1986] (Cambridge: CUP, 2001), 357. Plato, *The Symposium*, trans. Benjamin Jowett, available at http://classics.mit.edu/Plato/symposium.html, last access December 3, 2017. The fortune of the phrase is attested by its presence in the title of one of Frederick Rolfe's (aka Baron Corvo) most famous romances: Frederic Rolfe, *The Desire and Pursuit of the Whole. A Romance of Modern Venice* [1908] (Oxford: OUP, 1986).

2 S. T. Coleridge, *Specimens of the Table Talk of Samuel Taylor Coleridge* [1836], Ebook, 459.

3 Virginia Woolf, *A Room of One's Own* [1919] (Oxford and New York: OUP, 1992), 128.

https://doi.org/10.1515/9783110654615-009

externality – or otherness –, it harnesses the powers of the obscene, i.e.: that which is generally kept away from view and remains in the wings of the social stage. Precisely, as underlined by Kieran Dolin, obscenity is a central issue on which literature and the law come into conflict.[4] In fact, one of the main principles of the law is that of "imparting permanence,"[5] a state that the androgyne clearly compromises by relying and insisting on instability and the refusal of neat delineation. In this presentation, I shall address the dissonance between law and literature that the mythical figure of the androgyne posits, taking care to engage with various aspects of this dissonance. I shall use Ian Ward's distinction between "law in literature" and "law as literature"[6] to consider perhaps not so much the former as the latter. I intend to explore some of the ways in which the conflict between both elements translates into the more positive terms of collaboration. After all, both areas are discourses "work[ing] together in the production of culture and value,"[7] and both are also very much concerned with boundaries, whether they are moral or generic, for instance.[8] What I have in mind is that, in the same way as the androgyne displaces anatomical limits and resists clear assignation, literature is very much concerned with shifting (generic) boundaries in its creative proposals, and may very well, in turn, have "something to offer to the law in its resolution of social conflicts"[9] and exclusions.

As apparent in the above considerations, what I aim to do here is concentrate on the poethics of the androgyne as troubling "the grand narratives of biology," a capacity that it shares with other monstrous figures, if Margrit Shildrick is to be believed.[10] I shall argue that, at a time when a new paradigm arising in reaction to the Cultural Turn, which has been called "New Materialism," makes itself felt in many areas of contemporary culture, emphasis on the androgyne, on teratological figures of various sorts, and on disability is a way to contravene the "erasure of the body" exposed by feminist criticism.[11] By flaunting corporeality, its limits and capacities, what may be envisaged as the New Materialist Turn has been instrumental in promoting a post-humanist

4 Kieran Dolin, *A Critical Introduction to Law and Literature* (Cambridge: CUP, 2007), 41–46.

5 Dolin, *Critical Introduction*, 12.

6 Ian Ward, *Law and Literature. Possibilities and Perspectives* (Cambridge: CUP, 1995), 3.

7 Dolin, *Critical Introduction*, x.

8 Dolin, *Critical Introduction*, 7.

9 Dolin, *Critical Introduction*, 3.

10 Margrit Shildrick, *Embodying the Monster. Encounters with the Vulnerable Self* (London and Thousand Oaks, CAL.: Sage, 2002), 10.

11 Shildrick, *Embodying*, x.

vision of the individual as the new emphasis on corporeality, in Diane Coole and Samantha Frost's terms, "dislocates agency as the property of a discrete, self-knowing subject"[12] and considers the contemporary subject as open, exposed and vulnerable, and certainly not closed in on itself and sovereign.

I shall address these points by concentrating in turn on the issue of visibility, on the unstable relation between the inside and the outside determined by the androgyne, to end up with androgyny as the condition of relational economies.

One of the novels thematising androgyny that I believe produces a fruitful dialogue with the law is Peter Ackroyd's *Dan Leno and the Limehouse Golem*. For one thing, to take up Ward's phrase, it is conversant with "law in literature," as it stages a trial, that of Elizabeth Cree (hence the title of the US edition of the novel, *The Trial of Elizabeth Cree*), convicted of a series of murders taking place in late 19th-Century London. The legal and the literary do mix in many of the novel's sections, presented as the proceedings of the trial that, to a reader of literary texts, very much looks like the text of a play, complete with stage directions and character names introducing their speech. Besides, as the title suggests, the narrative is oriented towards the search for a mythical monster or Golem, a term that the novel didactically provides a definition of:

> "Golem" is the medieval Jewish word for an artificial being, created by the magician or the rabbi; it literally means "thing without form," and perhaps sprang from the same fears which surrounded the fifteenth-century concept of the "homunculus," which was supposed to have been given shape in the laboratories of Hamburg or Moscow.[13]

The idea of the creation of the monster put forward here is consonant with that associated with other Promethean figures,' like Frankenstein's, most obviously. Still, the reference to the amorphous nature of the Golem, or monster, is misleading. In fact, the Golem remains shapeless while it escapes detection and the press of the times favours the mythical explanation. The execution recorded in is first chapter and performed on the music-hall stage in the concluding one is captured in crudely visual terms that contribute to the novel's sensationalistic economy. Such an aesthetic choice is essential in that it solicits the scopic impulse that allows for the ostentatious (and etymological) presentation of the monster: the wrought dramaturgy of the execution allows for the monster to appear centre stage. Such visuality and sense of ritual echoes with the

12 Diana Coole and Samantha Frost, eds., *New Materialisms: Ontology, Agency and Politics* (Durham and London: Duke UP, 2010), 20.

13 Peter Ackroyd, *Dan Leno and the Limehouse Golem* [1994] (London: Minerva, 1995), 4. Further references in the text abbreviated as DL.

presentation of the monster's victims, whose corpses are mutilated and reorganised in a "parody of the human form" (DL, 5). From the beginning of the novel, visibility is clearly at stake, and more specifically monstration, as indicated by the theatrical dimension. Still, it is present more discreetly through the recurrence of a physical detail that may pass unnoticed when first mentioned but acquires the status of a motif as the story unfolds. In the autobiographical part of the narrative, that documenting the early years of the female protagonist sharing a life of destitution with her mother on the banks of the Thames, through her career on the music-hall stage as a member of Dan Leno's company, to her married life as a respectable Victorian upper-middle-class lady, the reader is granted close ups of her hands: "Look at them now, so worn and so raw. When I put them against my face, I can feel the ridges upon them like cart-tracks. Big hands, my mother used to say. No female should have big hands" (DL, 12). Typically, such "large raw hands" (DL, 17) will be used to half-stifle Dan Leno during a performance (DL, 182), and to kill several other characters, we are led to guess. And they clearly introduce, through an insistent synecdochic evocation, the figure of the androgyne, whose anatomy is revealed by an obscene detail that should remain hidden under the clothes and here emerges into view, as if she were wearing it upon her sleeve.

The androgynous theme is equally sounded through several references to cross-dressing. In fact, Lizzie, aka Elizabeth, cross dresses on stage in some of her most successful numbers, and she also takes her male impersonations into the streets, complete with pronominal re-assignations:

> He soon knew all the flash houses and the dens, but he never set foot in them: he had his fun by watching the filth of the town flowing along. The females of the street would whistle to him as he passed them by and, if the worst of them tried to touch him, he would grip their wrists with his big hands and thrust them away." (DL, 153–154)

The image of the androgyne is clinched here with that of the transvestite, providing a perfect illusion of sexual identity, and more particularly putting her apparent personality in conformity with the vision of the big hands, an illusion rarely broken but on rare moments of anagnorisis, as when she is recognised by a Jewish gentleman during her nightly perambulations: "When he looked up, he saw Lizzie beneath the male and recoiled. He muttered something like 'Cab Man' or 'Cadmon' and, in that instant, she struck out and knocked him to the ground." (DL, 154) Now, the main, impersonal narrator has taken pains to tell the reader about Adam Kadmon, many chapters before this episode occurs, when commenting on Dan Leno's female impersonations: "It is male and female joined. It is Adam Kadmon. The Universal Man" (DL, 67). The theme of androgyny is clearly aired in the novel, at times associated with that of the serial killer as monster, and at times with that of the music-hall performer, the incarnation of the selfless artist that espouses various selves, multiplies himself and generously welcomes the lives of the London people, sharing in their joys and sorrows. Dan Leno as female impersonator and music-hall dame thereby represents the solar, positive energy of the androgyne, while the more menacing, more specifically teratological features of androgyny rest with the male impersonator, typified by her big hands.[14]

I would argue that such a duality respects the traditional representations of the androgyne characterised by ambivalence, an idea echoing Shildrick's remarks about the double value of the monster as "both abhorrent and enticing."[15] More specifically, by so glaringly trading in dualities, the androgyne as exacerbation of the monster makes two economies coexist and come into conflict: the masculine one, traditionally conceived as closed, and the feminine one, conventionally seen as leaky and open, as Shildrick reminds us,[16] feminine leakiness extending here to the whole figure of the androgyne to present the reader with an image of the porousness of boundaries. In the novel's economy, encountering the monster amounts to experiencing a form of identity that could be fluid and porous, miles away from more comfortable visions of identity as air-tight and self-contained. By throwing centre stage what generally remains in the wings, what the novel does, in continuity with the agenda of modernist fiction if Dolin is to be believed, is promote an "aesthetics of the obscene."[17] The function of such an aesthetic, obviously, is to draw attention to neglected aspects of social and political life. Such a choice, then, is clearly conversant with a poethics of fiction, in that it allows for consideration of the excluded or subaltern other who is maintained within society even while being excluded from it, in Guillaume Le Blanc's terms. The androgyne as epitome of the monstrous, thereby refuses to let us forget that the Victorian society described in the novel, like ours, cannot exclude without including, or rather that the inclusion of the majority can only be secured through the exclusion of some.[18] The androgyne appears as a supernumerary figure[19] that fiction flaunts and allows to flicker on the verge of recognition (or *reconnaissance*, in Le Blanc's terms). Its literary presentation makes it

---

14 On Elisabeth's transformation into a monster, and on the polarization of the negative and positive principles of transvestism as performed by the novel, see Susana Onega, *Metafiction and Myth in the Novels of Peter Ackroyd* (Columbia, SC: Camden House, 1999), 140–142.

15 Shildrick, *Embodying*, 5.

16 Shildrick, *Embodying*, 31.

17 Dolin, *Critical Introduction*, 46.

18 Guillaume Le Blanc, *Que faire de notre vulnérabilité ?* (Paris: Bayard, 2011), 20.

19 Le Blanc, *Que faire?*, 19.

clear that "invisibility is not subtracted from politics but reformulates it."[20] Seen in this light, the fictional presentation of the androgyne makes the reader concentrate on and possibly renew his/her perception, and teaches him/her that "perception is not so much a natural quality as a social activity that makes invisible elements appear in the perceiving subject's environment as relevant and worthy of perception."[21] The androgyne, in its glaring impurity and leakiness, is a reminder that perception is dependent on norms, and that such norms allow for a distribution of visibilities that is not fixed forever. This is tantamount to suggesting that writing the monster is an invitation to shifting the norms of perception. In so doing, fictional discourse anticipates legal discourse and solicits attention to neglected areas. The poethics of the androgyne are just that: a *poietics* and an ethics calling for greater justice in the perception and consideration of submerged parts of the population. From this point of view, literature is not so much opposed to the law as complementary to it, in that it anticipates its decisions and contributes to a fairer "distribution of the perceptible."[22] In Ackroyd's novel law in literature is but a modality and a condition of literature as law.

As suggested in one of the above quotations by Le Blanc, the androgyne may be seen as a representation of the submerged subject that assumes visibility thanks to novelistic discourse. As such, it occupies a liminal position, being both inside and outside society, rejected to its margins the better to promote the inclusion of the many. Such a borderline position is everywhere to be observed as regards the androgyne in particular and the monster in general. This is the case with Lizzie in Ackroyd's novel, but also with other figures like that of Villanelle in Jeanette Winterson's *The Passion* where a similar synecdochic presentation of androgyny is at work. In this novel partly taking place in 19th-Century Venice, a city of uncertainties and marvels where romance blooms, Villanelle works as a croupier at the casino. She is the descendant of a family of gondoliers, and as such shares some of their anatomical traits: "Rumour has it that the inhabitants of this city walk on water. That, more bizarre still, their feet are webbed. Not all feet, but the feet of the boatmen whose trade is hereditary."[23] The first-person narrator provides an account of her own coming into the world, some lines down, revisiting the *topos* of the miraculous birth:

---

20 Guillaume Le Blanc, *Dedans, dehors. La condition d'étranger* (Paris: Seuil, 2010), 176, translation mine.

21 Guillaume Le Blanc, *L'invisibilité sociale* (Paris: PUF, 2009), 13, translation mine.

22 Jacques Rancière, *The Politics of Literature* (Cambridge: Polity, 2010), 13.

23 Jeanette Winterson, *The Passion* [1987] (London: Vintage, 1996), 49. Further references in the text, abbreviated as TP.

> It was an easy birth and the midwife held me upside down by the ankles until I bawled. But it was when they spread me out to dry that my mother fainted and the midwife felt forced to open another bottle of wine.
>
> My feet were webbed. (TP, 51)[24]

Now, such a scene is fairly telling in that it very visually introduces the theme of the androgyne. Besides, it bluntly strikes at the idea of the subject as unified and stabilised and, in Shildrick's terms, "exposes the myth of original unity."[25] From the beginning, the character resists strict assignation and installs a vision of the impure at the heart of the novel. The fact that the rewriting of the miraculous birth should be couched in a tongue-in-cheek tone is clearly meant to underline the parody of other miraculous and divine births, hence to render visible the underpinnings of heteronormative discourse. Instead of a perfect baby in a crib, the picture of adored self-containment, the female child's birth coincides with an eclipse, and is rushed by her impatience: "A fine head with a crop of red hair and a pair of eyes that made up for the sun's eclipse." (TP, 51) The metonymic evocation of the new-born infant presents the reader with a body made up of several parts, or rather with various parts of the body that remain un-reconciled on the page, and prepare for the final revelation: the female child boasts attributes reserved to male gondoliers, i.e.: webbed feet. From the outset, then, there is something unusual with this body's integrity: it does not cohere easily and hesitates on the verge of dis-/re-membering.

This is obviously a means of exposing the normativity of the incarnated self as the body appears here as the "site of contested meaning."[26] The androgyne, in such passages and throughout, embodies "a failure of the proper,"[27] a function that has often been attributed to the feminine and is exacerbated by the monstrous figure. As in *Dan Leno and the Limehouse Golem*, the detail of the webbed feet will reappear in the narrative (most glaringly so on page 118),

---

24 The theme of androgyny runs through Winterson's work, as indicated by many commentators. On androgyny in *The.PowerBook*, see for instance Justine Gonneaud, "The Myth of the Androgynous in Jeanette Winterson's *The.PowerBook*," in *Cross-Cultural Encounters Between the Mediterranean and the English-Speaking Worlds*, ed. Christine Reynier (Bern: Peter Lang, 2011), 105–116; and Jean-Michel Ganteau, "Hearts Object: Jeanette Winterson and the Ethics of Absolutist Romance," in *Refracting the Canon in Contemporary British Literature and Film*, eds. Susana Onega and Christian Gutleben (Amsterdam and New York: Rodopi, 2004), 165–185. For an analysis of gender bending practices and androgyny in *Written on the Body*, see Susana Onega, *Jeanette Winterson* (Manchester: Manchester UP, 2006), 110–115.

25 Shildrick, *Embodying*, 127.

26 Shildrick, *Embodying*, 10.

27 Shildrick, *Embodying*, 31.

never allowing the reader to forget the anatomical reality of the androgyne, and as in the previous novel, the theme will be echoed in various visions of cross-dressing. In her job as a croupier, Villanelle often dons a special disguise: "I dressed as a boy because that's what the visitors liked to see. It was part of the game, trying to decide which sex was hidden behind tight breeches and extravagant face-paste" (TP, 54). In such passages, where the disguising hovers between illusion (transvestism) and ostentation (drag), the principle of undecidability is clearly vented and, once again, the body language and performance lend substance to the idea of a crisis of the proper. Seen in this light, the androgyne (and more generally the monster) introduces dissensus by opening up unitary conceptions. Not only does it have a transgressive function, as it blurs boundaries and multiplies hesitations, but it also boasts a transformative power[28] in that it exposes the normative myth of the closed subject and helps shift apprehensions of identity as stable.

One step further, the novel exacerbates interrogations as to the openness of the body by relying on a magic-realist vein. In the third section, "The Zero Winter," narrated by Henri, the male protagonist, tales of Venice are still present, and the narrator relates the story of how he helped Villanelle get back her heart that had been stolen by a woman she was passionately in love with, neatly named "The Queen of Spades." In a passage reminiscent of Poe's "The Tale-Tale Heart," Henri helps Villanelle get into the Queen of Spades' mansion and they hear her heart beating away, from inside a jar kept in a box, in a room at the heart of the big house. After stealing back the jar in which the heart keeps beating, Henri gets back to Villanelle who is waiting for him outside the palace in a gondola, and the following scene takes place:

> I heard her uncork the jar and a sound like gas escaping. Then she began to make terrible swallowing and choking noises and only my fear kept me sitting at the other end of the boat, perhaps hearing her die.
>
> There was quiet. She touched my back and when I turned round took my hand again and placed it on her breast.
>
> Her heart was beating. (TP, 120–121)

In these lines, where magic realism verges on the *grand guignolesque*, the literalisation of the metaphor allows for a forthright vision of the leaky, open body, thereby blurring the frontiers between inside and outside.

The novel uses a sensationalist aesthetics to reveal what the wondrous character and other less larger-than-life ones have in common: the capacity to

---

28 Shildrick, *Embodying*, 4.

love and live through a passion for the other. In so doing, it stresses the commonality of the monster that does not appear as isolated and distinct from the rest of the characters, and for that matter, from the reader. This is certainly a means of emphasising that one of the reasons why the monster haunts the pages of the novels, and why the figure hovers over Western culture, including contemporary societies, is that monsters are not figures of absolute alterity but that, on the contrary, to take up Shidrick's phrase, "they stir recognition within."[29] In fact, the ubiquity of the androgyne in the novels under review points at a blurring of the limits between the same and the other, between what is generally considered as the boundary between the normative and the different. It is a powerful reminder of a form of conjoint openness and vulnerability, as the different, disabled figure of the monster, with its overtly large hands, webbed feet or, as we shall see, wings, is the sign that anyone can be incapacitated and limited at any time through illness or accident, and that at least once in our lives, we inhabit a disabled body, as babies, the site of absolute dependence and vulnerability.[30] In the end, by drawing attention to corporeality, the androgyne is an efficient signal that what characterises the human is also an irreducible attachment to the body that, by definition, is submitted to accident and decay. By forcing us to bear in mind that being attached to a body implies an irreducible form of vulnerability, the monster unearths a common denominator, and reveals an inescapable, founding form of anthropological vulnerability. I would argue that such an insistence on corporeality is a central part of the poethics of fiction, in that it harnesses the power of literary discourse in order to, once again, make a point about the law. On top of drawing our attention to the submerged, it reveals that the monster is not so much outside as it lurks within, which accounts for the deeply unsettling encounters with the figure, fuelled by the fear of contamination.[31] In so doing, it once again anticipates the evolution of the law and contributes to an interdisciplinary project as "ethics and aesthetics become active partners with politics in creating the narrative basis for a just society"[32] and, more especially and importantly perhaps, participates in the "construction of the general duty of care"[33] as a response to the evidence and experience of vulnerability.

I would like now to turn to yet another figure of androgyny in the pantheon of contemporary British fiction, i.e. Fevvers, the winged protagonist of Angela

29 Shildrick, *Embodying*, 81.
30 Shildrick, *Embodying*, 72.
31 Shildrick, *Embodying*, 7.
32 Dolin, *Critical Introduction*, 211.
33 Dolin, *Critical Introduction*, 212.

Carter's *Nights at the Circus*. The novel opens on a portrait of the marvel of the circus, who performs her stunts high up on her trapeze, but the first meeting takes place in the artist's dressing room. Thanks to her famous wings, she qualifies as a monster and a great deal of attention is paid to her attributes:

> these notorious and much-debated wings, the source of her fame, were stowed away for the night under the soiled quilting of her baby-blue satin dressing-gown, where they made an uncomfortable-looking pair of bulges, shuddering the surface of the taut fabric from time to time as if desirous of breaking loose.[34]

As suggested by the baby-blue piece of clothing that she is wearing, there may be an element of gender blurring or troubling with the character, which is confirmed by the set of wings itself, a transparent reference to the Victorian myth of the Angel in the House, after Coventry Patmore's famous poem, which the feminist writer takes up the better to distort it and wring its neck. As they are reputedly sexless, angels may be considered avatars – or pre-figurations – of the androgyne, and they make the two figures very much akin in many ways. This idea is put forward in the portrait through the insistence on Fevvers's bulk and weight, granting her a warrior-like stature (NC, 7), through her cigar-smoking habits (NC, 8), through the down that covers her back (NC, 12), through her voice, hesitating between contralto and baritone (NC, 13), and even more clearly through her sobriquet, "l'Ange anglaise," which yokes the masculine with the feminine, thereby contaminating grammar through the means of solecism. Even if androgyny is less clearly and forcibly present in this novel than in the preceding ones, the figure hovers over the narrative from the outset, all the more so as Fevvers is surrounded by several characters whose gender bending practices are put to the fore, and who militantly sport physical attributes of the other sex, as is the case with Lizzie, with her "incipient moustache on the upper lip" (NC, 13) or else one of the circus performers "Albert/Albertina, who was bipartite, that is to say, half and half and neither of either" (NC, 59).[35] The nightly, wondrous universe of the circus unmistakably throws into visibility what is usually kept from

34 Angela Carter, *Nights at the Circus* [1984] (London: Vintage, 1994), 8. Further references in the text, abbreviated as NC.

35 For a convincing analysis of how *Nights at the Circus*, in its revisiting of the freak show, queers heteronormative representations, see Erin Douglas, "Freak Show Femininities: Intersectional Spectacles in Angela Carter's *Nights at the Circus*," *Women's Studies* 43.1 (2014): 1–24. On the political limits of female monstrosity in British novels of the 1980s, including *Nights at the Circus* and Winterson's *Sexing the Cherry*, see Sara Martin, "The Power of Monstrous Women: Fay Weldon's *The Life and Loves of a She- Devil* (1983), Angela Carter's *Nights at the Circus* (1984) and Jeanette Winterson's *Sexing the Cherry* (1989)," *Journal of Gender Studies* 8.2 (1999): 193–210.

view, interrogating norms of perception and recognition, and once again displaying the image of a body that is not so much homogeneous as made of parts and bulges, a grotesque vision that foregrounds a common corporeality and acts as a potent token of anthropological vulnerability.

As already suggested, the ubiquity of the androgyne casts doubt on the idea of the subject's origin as pure and self-contained and points at the fundamental openness and fluidity of what is more generally considered a stable identity. Through the grotesque vision of the monster, what obtains is a preference for the infinite and the open, in other terms, the exposed. Such characters as Fevvers, in her quest for the other, Dan Leno, in his endless permeability and imitation of the other, and Villanelle, in her incandescent passion are shown to be the seats of appetites and to be totally oriented towards alterity.[36] This drive towards the external is inscribed in their bodily features, an index of the "desire and pursuit of the whole" that characterises the subject whose origin is double, and who spends his/her life looking for the lost half, as described in Plato's *Symposium*. Strikingly, the myth reminds us that what characterises the androgyne is a paradoxical sense of fullness compounded of division or at least divisibility. Aristophane's speech relates a story of loss and ceaseless attempt to return to a previous state, in other words a story of dispossession, and it is true that, in many ways, this is what the figure calls for. I do not mean here dispossession in the sense of being deprived of powers or attributes by external intervention so much as dispossession in the second acceptation of the term used by Judith Butler and Athena Athanasiou, i.e.: a more positive meaning that, to them, entails a "fissuring of the subject."[37] The dispossession that accrues to the figure of the androgyne is one that is predicated on openness to the other and that stresses "the limits of self-sufficiency."[38] In the various characters that I have evoked here (but for malevolent Lizzie in *Dan Leno and the Limehouse Golem*), being moved by the other is seen as "the condition of dispossession."[39] As the locus of instability and displacement, the androgyne in his/her turn displaces the onlooker, fraught as s/he is with the values of porosity and impulse towards the other, and possibly *excendance*. It becomes a figure of ceaselessly renewed connection and a powerful cue as to the impossible autonomy of the subject. Said differently, the androgyne as epitome of the monster

36 Nussbaum, *Fragility*, 357.
37 Judith Butler and Athena Athanasiou, *Dispossession. The Performative in the Political* (Cambridge: Polity, 2013), ix.
38 Butler and Athanasiou, *Dispossession*, 3.
39 Butler and Athanasiou, *Dispossession*, 3.

makes one alert to an alternative conception of vulnerability: not the negative vision of vulnerability as incapacitation, but rather as openness and orientation towards the other. It insists that it is a virtue to be vulnerable to the other. One step further, it calls for an "ethics of relationship"[40] that prefers to consider the individual as dependent on others, and promotes the values of interdependence as opposed to those of sovereign isolation and autonomy.

What I mean here is that, as suggested in my first part, by throwing into visibility less perceptible members of submerged populations, the monster may be envisaged as "the location of a reconceived ontology and the ethics centred on a relational economy that has a place for radical difference."[41] Besides, and more radically, it is instrumental in "reconfiguring relational economies"[42] and promoting the values of interdependence, thereby exposing all fiction of autonomy. This is very much in keeping with what Shildrick calls an "ethics of risk," by which she means that "exposure, a vulnerable opening to the face of alterity, is the very condition of becoming."[43] What is at stake in the aesthetics of the obscene that gives pride of place to the androgyne is a vision of the subject as not completely closed and stable. True to the Levinasian prescriptions, it posits a dis-inter-ested subject, standing somewhere beyond essence, and dispossessed along the modalities of some "otherwise than being."[44] More prosaically, the fictional representation of the androgyne projects a vision of the subject as exposed, not autonomous, vulnerable to alterity and, from this point of view, driven by the forces of becoming as opposed to being, a subject that cannot be pinned down and assigned a single position, a subject on the move and possibly reconfiguring itself all the time. The poethics of the androgyne thereby promotes a pursuit of justice through openness and instability, in complete disregard of the stability and permanence of the law. It postulates that the good life is destined for an ever wider public, paying attention to and including submerged members of society. It once again anticipates and contributes to the evolution of the law by favouring the ways of an anti-totalising, ethical discourse.

The fictional presentation of the androgyne clearly suggests that "vulnerability is not an intrinsic quality of the existing subject but an inalienable condition of becoming,"[45] which reveals another mode of existence that has less to do with

---

40 Shildrick, *Embodying*, 70.
41 Shildrick, *Embodying*, 67.
42 Shildrick, *Embodying*, 131.
43 Shildrick, *Embodying*, 101.
44 Emmanuel Levinas, *Otherwise than Being, or Beyond Essence* [1978] (Doordrecht: Kluwer Academic Publishers, 1991).
45 Shildrick, *Embodying*, 85.

the closed, stable ontology of being than with an open, mutable condition of continuous motion and departure towards the other that is translated in the image of becoming. This points at a founding ontological precariousness that privileges the provisional and the mobile over the enduring and the closed and considers the subject as the site of dispossession or being for the other. In other terms, the androgyne re-configures the individual as the depository of an ethical relation and favours the loss of sovereignty as the condition of inclusion by taking the other into necessary consideration.[46] The androgyne is the site of vulnerability to the other, and as such constitutes a potent ethical figure and force. From this point of view, it may be said to provide a tentative answer to Jean-Luc Nancy's famous question: "who comes after the subject?" Its contribution to the answer may well lie in incarnating what Irving Goh has called the *reject* (as opposed to the subject), i.e.: not so much a "passive figure" that is denied, as an active power of rejection resisting "the forces acting against it," and further still as "turning the force of rejection around on [itself]."[47] Seen in this light, the androgyne as reject becomes a figure that "does not hypostatise itself," thereby remaining open, and "think[ing] itself anew constantly."[48] In such circumstances, the androgyne as reject becomes an emblem of "precarity,"[49] through its sheer force of rejection that prevents any return of the subject and appropriation of the other. As the epitome and literary incarnation of becoming, the androgyne may therefore be considered an ethical proposal.

Its novelistic representation and its ubiquity in Western culture is therefore an indication that "fiction enlarges our experience,"[50] and thereby gestures towards new ways in which norms and rules may be shifted. More precisely, it reminds us that "fiction has specific purposes in refusing the abstract and the general."[51] And this it does in at least three ways: by favouring "practical knowledge"[52] through the literary incarnation of ethical issues and dilemmas; by "pay[ing] attention to particulars")[53]; and by "generat[ing] emotions that are part of our ethical agency.[54] Fiction in general and more particularly, I would

46 Shildrick, *Embodying*, 5.
47 Irving Goh, *The Reject: Community, Politics, and Religion after the Subject* (New York: Fordham UP, 2015), 5.
48 Goh, *The Reject*, 7.
49 Goh, *The Reject*, 12.
50 Martha C. Nussbaum, *Love's Knowledge. Essays on Philosophy and Literature* (New York and Oxford: OUP, 1990), 47.
51 Nussbaum, *Love's Knowledge*, 16.
52 Nussbaum, *Love's Knowledge*, 16.
53 Nussbaum, *Love's Knowledge*, 27, 38.
54 Nussbaum, *Love's Knowledge*, 41–42.

argue, fiction geared on to the representation of the androgyne is therefore consonant with an Aristotelian ethics as it posits that "the good citizen is a good perceiver who attends to the heterogeneity of life."[55] By privileging the model of an attention to the invisible and the submerged, favouring dispossession and openness to the other, and promoting becoming over being, it teaches us that "responsive attention leads to care,"[56] thereby fostering the possibility of renewed perception – hence attention – that showcases the practice of a poethics of fiction.

55 Nussbaum, *Love's Knowledge*, 103.
56 Nussbaum, *Love's Knowledge*, 145.

3 Comic and Grotesque Monstrosity

Paola Carbone and Giuseppe Rossi

Who Is the Monster? Laughing at Friends and Foes

1 The legal "monster"

Is there a legal meaning of "monster"? Who or what is (or was) the monster in legal terms? Roman sources discipline the legal status of the monster, though not defining what a monster exactly is. According to a passage of the *Pauli sententiae*, dealing with probate law and *ius liberorum*,[1] "mulier si monstruosum aliquid aut prodigiosum enixa sit, nihil proficit: non sunt enim liberi, qui contra formam humani generis converso more procreantur."[2] ("Should a woman give birth to something monstrous, or wondrous, she will have no benefit; those who were conversely procreated, infringing the shape of humankind, are no sons indeed"). Hence, according to the Roman jurist of the 3rd century a "monstrum" was an offspring incoherent with "the shape of mankind," and generated in a somehow controversial way.

We can argue how, on the one hand, Paulus does not even try to give a positive definition of "monster," being it tacitly defined *a contrario*, as something that is "not human." Of course, it is taken for granted that any reader knows what "human" means.

On the other hand, stating that the monster is unique as much as of an unclear origin, Paulus follows the classical tradition and considers it the sign of a

1 Or *ius trium liberorum*. The expression refers to provisions of *leges Iuliae* enacted during the empire of Augustus awarding privileges to married couples that had three or more children, or at least four children, in the case of freedwomen. The ius liberorum exempted women from guardianship to which they were subject (the s.c. *tutela mulierum*). See Adolf Berger, *Encyclopedic Dictionary of Roman Law* (Philadelphia: American Philosophical Society, 1980), XLIII, 530. The aim of such enactments, along with provisions prohibiting adultery, was to foster the growth of the Roman population. For an overview J. Evans Grubbs, *Women and the Law in the Roman Empire* (London: Routledge, 2002), 37 ff.

2 Paul. Sent. 4.9.3–4. The fragment was included in the Digest, (Paul. 4 sent. D. 1.5.14) with modifications. For an overview of the subject in the Roman sources, see Claudia Terreni, *Quae Graeci φαντάσματα vocant. Riflessioni sulla vita e la forma umana nel pensiero giuridico romano* (Pisa: Pisa University Press, 2013).

Note: This is a result of the joint work of the authors. However, paragraphs 1–4 are by Giuseppe Rossi; paragraph 5 is by Paola Carbone.

https://doi.org/10.1515/9783110654615-010

broken order and the omen of an imminent evil, namely that the Gods are about to punish humanity for its *hybris*.[3]

Paulus himself added that "partum qui membrorum humanorum officia duplicavit, quia hoc ratione aliquatenus videtur effectum, matri prodesse placuit" ("it was stated that an offspring who has more limbs than usual human limbs should benefit the mother, since this sometimes may reasonably happen"). Newborns having an unusual number of limbs, therefore, were not "monsters" (and could benefit their mothers both as heirs and under *ius liberorum*),[4] even if somehow deviant from "the shape of mankind." A person with two heads, or three arms, or just with an unusual number of fingers was a "man," not a "monster."

Roman law scholars discussed whether a fragment by Ulpian, included in the Digest, contradicts Paulus' opinion:

> Quaeret aliquis: si portentosum, vel monstrosum, vel debilem mulier ediderit, vel qualem visu, vel vagitu novum, non humanae figurae, sed alterius, magis animalis, quam hominis partum, an, quia enixa est, prodesse ei debeat? Et magis est, ut haec quoque parentibus prosint: nec enim est, quod eis imputetur, quae qualiter potuerunt, statutis obtemperaverunt, neque id quod fataliter accessit, matri damnum iniungere debit.[5]

("We are asked: should a woman give birth to an offspring wondrous, or monstrous, or weak, or unusual by face or by wail, not having the figure of a man, closer to the offspring of another animal, than of a man, that offspring, being born from her, should benefit her? There are good reasons why such offspring should benefit their parents: they cannot be blamed, since they complied with the statutes at their best, nor the mother may be prejudiced by something that happened by chance"; reference goes to the benefits provided for by *ius liberorum*).

According to some of the scholars, Ulpian (or, more probably, subsequent manipulators of the fragment) was prone to considering the "monster" a human being,[6] if not a legal subject. Others argued that Ulpian agrees with Paulus that a

---

3 See Arduino Maiuri, "Il lessico latino del mostruoso," in *Monstra. Costruzione e percezione delle entità ibride e mostruose nel Mediterraneo antico*, ed. Igor Baglioni (Roma: Quasar, 2013), II, 166–167.

4 See Danilo Dalla, "'Status' e rilevanza dell' 'ostentum'," in *Scritti in onore di Antonio Guarino* (Napoli: Jovene, 1984), 2.521 ff.; Danilo Dalla., *D.50.16.135: sui perché di una "lex specialis,"* in *Studi in onore di M. Talamanca*, (Napoli: Jovene, 2001), 2.343.

5 Ulp. 4 *ad l. Iul. Et Pap.* D. 50.16.135.

6 E. Galluppi, *La successione dei conjugi nella storia interna del diritto italiano* (Roma: Civelli, 1873), 3–32; Danilo Dalla, " 'Status' e rilevanza dell' 'ostentum'"; Danilo Dalla, *50.16.135*

"monster" is never "homo," but the former admits that even the birth of a "monster" can benefit its parents under probate law and imperial statutory legislation aimed at promoting weddings and increasing birthrate.[7]

What is most striking in the comparison between the two fragments is that Ulpian ignores a "converso more" procreation as the cause of monstrous births and the subsequent omens of evil. On the contrary, Ulpian seems to consider monsters, if not human beings, at least as existing realities in life. He even adds that the parents of the "monster" are not to blame, since they "statutis obtemperaverunt," and "id quod fataliter accessit" cannot prejudice them.

If, on the one hand, Ulpian shows that the law may break the link between "monsters" and evil, on the other hand, he is as imprecise as Paulus in setting the border between "homines" and "monstra," nor does he provide any definition of "monster." While Paulus just states that the "monster" is "not human," Ulpian confirms that the "monster" is "not human," but he adds that it is more like an animal than a man.

Therefore, the "monster" shares some human features with man. At least both men and animals are natural beings and existing phenomena. Ulpian seems on the verge of a major step towards maintaining that "monsters" are parts of nature, albeit rare or unusual (wondrous), but not necessarily linked to mystery or to the supernatural.

The contradiction between the above-mentioned passage and another fragment by Ulpian included in the Digest, which quotes the definition of "ostentum" by Labeon,[8] led to doubts on the very authenticity of the passage. Such definition stated indeed that deformities, as well as actual "prodigia," were *contra naturam*. Since, according to Paulus, a three-handed man was a legal subject, there actually existed legal subjects *contra naturam*, as if the law had the power to transform something unnatural into natural.

---

7 Lucia Monaco, "Percezione sociale e riflessi giuridici della deformità," in *I diritti degli altri in Grecia e a Roma*, eds. Alberto Maffi and Lorenzo Gagliardi (Sankt Augustine: Academia Verlag, 2011), 396 ff.

8 Ulp. 25 ad ed. D. 5016.38: " 'ostentum' Labeo definit omne contra naturam cuiusque rei genitum factumque. Duo genera autem sunt ostentorum: unum, quoties quid contra naturam nascitur, tribus manibus forte aut pedibus aut qua alia parte corporis, que naturae contraria est: alterum, cum quid prodigiosum videtur, quae Greci φαντάσματα vocant." For an analysis, see Claudia Terreni, *Quae Graeci φαντάσματα vocant*. Labeon describes "ostentum" (prodigy) as anything generated or made against nature. There are two kinds of prodigies indeed: the first one refers to whatever comes to life against nature, with three hands or three feet, or with any other part of the body against nature. The second one concerns the vision of a prodigy, or what the Greeks name phantasmata. [My trans.]

Roman sources, of course, had an ongoing influence on the legal and philosophical debate on "monsters." For example, Ulpian's words find echoes in Vico's thought about monsters as hybrids of men and animals, but it is the Neapolitan philosopher's original contribution that set them in a specific stage of the continuous flux and perennial transformation of thought and experience, which is the key issue of Vico's epistemology.

Taking hints from the Roman sources and, in particular, from the (alleged) provision of the XII Tables, which stated that any deformed offspring ought to be killed, Vico identifies the concept of "monsters" to children born from prostitutes, notwithstanding their eventual perfect human shape. According to the philosopher, prostitutes' newborns have both "nature of man and features of beasts born from vagabonds, or coming from uncertain unions … the law of the XII Tables ordered them to be thrown in the Tiber (like those born from honest women without the solemnities of the wedding)."[9] In Vico's view, the concept of "monster" is not limited to biology, but it has deep civil and cultural connotations: it defines a stage in the evolution of thought (in its interaction with experience) characterized by a predominance of disorder that generates undefinable hybrids.

No matter whether the monster is identified with a deviation from a universal pattern, or with the symbol of an era of hybrids which will end thanks to the progressive development of a new order, the question is always the definition either of the archetype (from which the "monster" deviates) or of the foundations of the order.

In 13th-century England, Bracton defined the "monster" as an offspring "not having the shape of mankind"; on Paulus' footsteps, Bracton added that the law excluded from inheritance "those procreated perversely, against the way of human kind, as where a woman brings forth a monster or a prodigy."[10] Once again, procreating a "monster" is the consequence of a "perverse" behavior. On the other hand, just like in Paulus' view, "minor" deformities, such as having "a larger number of members," do not exclude legal subjectivity. Swinburne's *Treatise of Testaments* (1590) and Coke's fundamental *Institutes of the Laws of England* (early 17th century) follow the same approach.[11]

---

9 Gian Battista Vico, *Principi di scienza nuova* [1744] (Milano: Soc. tipografica classici italiani, 1864), 186.

10 See Alex N. Sharpe, *Foucault's Monsters and the Challenge of Law* (New York: Routledge, 2010); Estella Antoaneta Ciobanu, *The Spectacle of the Body in Late Medieval England* (Iasi: Lumen, 2012), 125.

11 See Alex N. Sharpe, *Foucault's Monsters and the Challenge of Law*, 69 ff.

In his *Pandectae Justinianeae*, Pothier mentions the order to kill monsters allegedly provided for in the XII Tables. Nonetheless, he adds that as for medicine, a monster is "dans toutes espèces d'animaux, celui qui diffère enormémént par sa conformation des autres animaux de son espèce," laws

> appellent strictement un monstre, et non une monstrosité de l'espèce humaine, à moins que sa forme humaine n'eût été bouleversée par une forte pression [. . .] Tels seraient un corps humain avec une tête d'âne ou de boeuf, l'enfant d'une femme dont la partie supérieure serait celle d'un homme, et la partie inférieure celle d'un poisson, ou d'un veau, et autres du même genre.[12]

Reinterpreting Paulus' fragment in the light of modern biology, Pothier distinguishes "monsters, which are not part of humankind," from "human monstrosities," that is to say 'men' notwithstanding their deformities. Anyway, it is still unclear when a difference in shape between an individual is "enormous," or even what the "correct" shape of a species should be (assuming that species have a definite shape and they are not subject to change). It is important to point out that Pothier chooses carefully his examples of "monsters," in order to demonstrate that they exist only in the realm of fantasy.

Aubry and Rau, in their deeply influential *Course de droit civil français*, mentioned the theory that denied legal capacity to "monstra vel prodigia," adding that "a notre avis, elle est sans application possible, puisque, d'après les lois de la physiologie, le fait qu'elle suppose ne parait pas pouvoir se produire".[13] This way, the monster finally abandons reality and legal treatises.

Between the 18th and 19th centuries, under the influence of Enlightenment and scientific positivism, European law had done away with monsters. Though it is not sure that "the shape of mankind" may be defined in legal terms, we are sure that no such things as donkey-headed beings, or fishtailed girls do exist. The legal thought followed the same path, from monstrosity as divine prodigies through natural wonders, to a statistical and scientific approach, which characterized the development of modern biology.[14]

---

12 Robert Joseph Pothier, *Pandectae Justinianeae* [1748] (Paris: Dondey – Dupré, 1818), 1.389.

13 Charles Aubry and Charles Rau, *Cours de droit civil français d'après la méthode de Zachariae* (Paris: 4. Ed., Marchal et Billard, 1869), 1.181 (available online https://gallica.bnf.fr/ark:/12148/bpt6k5858422r/f10.image.texteImage, last accessed in September 2018), quoting works by Demolombe and by Eschbach, *Note sur les prétendus monstres*, in *Rev. de législation*, 1847, I, 167. Aubry and Rau's view is followed, e.g., by Emidio Pacifici-Mazzoni, *Istituzioni di diritto civile italiano*, (Firenze: Cammelli, 1871), 1.4, according to which "questa dottrina, quantunque seguita da qualche giurista moderno, è manifestamente erronea; perché giuste le leggi fisiologiche, dalla donna non può nascere che un uomo."

14 See Lorraine J. Daston and Katharine Park, *Wonders and the Order of Nature 1150–1750* (New York: Zone Books, 2001).

Eventually, we may say that the law has no need to define monsters, because monsters do not exist. Of course, *entia non sunt mutiplicanda sine necessitate*. Though it is possible to imagine any kind of "monsters," sirens, Minotaur, cyclops, aggressive or friendly people coming from other galaxies, this is the realm of the irrational, and the law, we assume, has nothing to do with it.

Nowadays, legislation and case law, of course, do not use the word "monster" any more. In public debate, scholars quite often use the metaphor of a "legal monster" to criticize statutory provisions, court decisions, notions or theories, which do not fit with basic legal notions or logical schemes and/or are at odds with fundamental principles.

The monster sometimes strikes back... (as something capable of breaking, or questioning, a legal order, which, exactly for this reason, such order has to expel). Most of all, while sciences assure lawyers that ox-headed people do not exist, crime news often call "monsters" those men or women who, even if undoubtedly 'human' in their biological nature, committed such infamous crimes to doubt whether or not they can still be considered "human" in the civil meaning of the word.

Vico's view of the "civil monster" symbolizes, rather than a definite stage of the development of civilization, a state of never-ending tension between order and disorder, in which facts, but even more human behaviors, continuously question all rules, including fundamental legal principles.

Once again, the law should distinguish men from monsters.[15]

2 Coherent law v. incoherent comic

In law, incoherence – namely being incoherent with the scheme – is the hallway to wrongfulness. Moreover, law has its foundations in rationality and reality. By stating that monsters were not men, Roman rules restored coherence between existing human beings and the legal shape of manhood, though they had never been defined to the utmost precision. Modern conclusion that monsters do not exist, and as a consequence also the need of legal rules applicable to them, restored the link between law, reality and rationality.

15 For a significant example, see: Alexander Laban Hilton, *Man or Monster? The Trial of a Khmer Rouge Torturer* (Durham: Duke University Press, 2016). The book is an accurate report of the trial against the head of detention camp during the Pol Pot regime, which was held before the Cambodian Extraordinary Chambers.

According to many philosophers, including Schopenhauer and Kant, incoherence is the very essence of the comic. In Kant's view, laughter involves something absurd: the sudden changing of an expectation into nothing. In the *Critique of Judgment*, the German philosopher pointed out that: "in everything that is to excite a lively convulsive laughter there must be something absurd (in which the Understanding, therefore, can find no satisfaction). Laughter is an affection arising from the sudden transformation of a strained expectation into nothing. This transformation, which is certainly not enjoyable by the Understanding, yet indirectly gives it very active enjoyment for a moment. Therefore its cause must consist in the influence of the representation upon the body, and the reflex effect of this upon the mind."[16]

Under this perspective, law is the opposite of comic: it is *never* absurd or useless. Legal rules are outputs of rationality that give Understanding a high degree of satisfaction. They come from the mind and aim at transforming reality. They can even transform the body itself, as we have seen above with reference to the quotation from Labeon by Ulpian, in combination with the passage by Paulus. Legal rules could turn deformities *contra naturam* into "natural," and human; the intellect could change (the legal status of) the body.

Giambattista Vico in his *Vici vindiciae* in 1729 wrote that: "laughter comes from a fraud against the human brain, a brain longing for truth: that is why the bigger the simulation of the truth, the more abundant the laughter"[17] (i.e.: the lie). "Serious people don't laugh" because they never depart from truth and they don't believe in lies. In other words: *risus abundant in ore stultorum.*

The law is so self-confident to believe that it can always know right from wrong, or people from "monsters"; it is even so confident to believe that it has the power to change the world and humankind according to its own will. It is "serious" by definition.

But curiously enough, law never escapes laughter. As a matter of fact, conceit and excess of self-confidence may be very funny. This may be the reason why law, along with its actors (lawyers, judges, police officers etc.), is so often laughed at by the comic. The law knows (or presumes to know) what is incoherent; incoherence is the symptom of wrongfulness. Telling right from wrong (telling people from monsters) is the law's final aim.

The comic is nothing but incoherence and absurdity. On the other hand, it is not sure that the comic may divert from truth by its own nature. Kierkegaard

---

16 Immanuel KANT, *Critique of Judgement* [1790] (New York: Cosimo Classics, 2007), 133.

17 GianBattista Vico, "Vici vindiciae," in *La scienza nuova prima con la polemica contro gli "atti degli eruditi" di Lipsia*, ed. Fausto Nicolini (Bari: Laterza, 1931), 291–306.

and, most of all, Nietzsche offered laughter its philosophical rehab: existence is but a comedy, and the only possible science is a "gay science," where laughter is the main access to knowledge.

Nietzsche's "gay science," anyway, is by no means comparable to any 'traditional', rational idea of science or of knowledge, including any possible positive idea of law as a mere output of rationality. The outcome of the "gay science" is pushing philosophy towards the extreme boundaries of what can be thought. The "gay science" leads humankind to engage in a process of acknowledgment through laughter, but the outcomes of such process will be disappointing to the utmost.

Laughter, according to Nietzsche, will lead to discover the inability of rationality (the opposite of the *cogito*), the fictitious nature of the self, the limits of existence, the irrelevance of the individual in the universe, the absence of a final aim (in the "eternal comeback" of time), the will to power as source of any moral idea of 'good' and 'evil'. At the same time, humankind cannot escape the continuous dialectic between good and evil, and its ongoing creative destruction. Ideas of good and evil are constantly changing. Human beings are incoherent by definition and any conception of truth cannot but face such incoherence.

With this respect, we can mention characters as diverse as the *homo œconomicus* (the rational being by essence), Don Quixote, or the narrator in Dostoevskji's *Memories from the Underground*, claiming his right to be irrational. Who of the three does fit better in "the shape of mankind"? Who is the monster? Could the three characters be nothing but different aspects of the personality of a single person, or of any human being?

3 Who is the monster?

Before we can tell who the monster is, we should know the shape of humankind. Before we can tell who the "civil" monster is, we should have a definite knowledge of good and evil. The law knows (presumes to know) the shape of humankind: it can always tell who (or what) the monster is. The trial before a court is the monster-detector device, because it will end with a decision, stating once and forever who did or did not comply with the legal standards that define "humanity."

The comic told us many times that the trial could turn a law-abiding citizen into a monster, or vice versa: it depends on how skillful the defendant's lawyer is. Let me mention just two examples.

In the "Voluntary Witness" episode of Dino Risi's movie *I mostri* (1963) a very skillful and unconcerned lawyer (acted by Vittorio Gassman) convinces the court, by means of a highly rhetorical plea, that a citizen (acted by Ugo Tognazzi), who had voluntarily shown up as a witness in a trial for murder, is completely untrustworthy and a potential criminal. The plea is filled with Latin and legal quotations, which are aimed at diverting from truth. This is the same strategy used by Azzeccagarbugli in his dialogue with Renzo in Manzoni's *The Betrothed*. The lawyer explains to Renzo that, since statutory wordings are very confused, thanks to his skill he will mislead the judges and convince them that apparently applicable statutory provisions do not fit the case.

In the 1992 movie *My cousin Vinny* by Jonathan Lynn, a lawyer (acted by Joe Pesci), though being completely ignorant of legal rules and of any basic court procedures (dress code included), convinces the judge of the innocence of his clients (two young students, charged of robbery and murder). The lawyer's skill consists in a shrewd examination of the documents along with an aggressive and perceptive questioning style, while actual knowledge of the law is not needed.

The three comic examples show that the link between law, trials at courts and justice is fragile, and that charging the law with the task of detecting monsters, or just distinguishing good from evil, may be a dangerous choice. Georges Bataille has taught that the problem with any theory of "nihil" is that, *a contrario*, it implies *something*. Kant's "deluded expectation," which unbinds laughter, is nevertheless an *expectation*: it has an *object*.

Though we know that no Minotaur, or donkey-headed people, mermaids or unicorns do exist, nevertheless, we can *imagine* them and *we did imagine them* to the point that they are part of our cultural history, and even of our legal history, as we have seen above. The imaginary may not be a product of the Understanding, or of the *cogito*, but *it can be thought of*. In a way, therefore, *it does exist*, it has a paramount influence on human behavior, and law cannot escape it (just like any other human creation).

The law may be very funny not only because it is conceited, but also because of its continuous and useless escape from irrationality and, therefore, from reality. By assuming the power to transform reality and to change humankind, the law refuses to acknowledge one of the paramount aspects of humanity: its capability of being irrational, and its need to be irrational, in order to cope with inescapable irrational aspects of life.

Perhaps the most troublesome part of the relationship between law and the comic is *justice*. A commonplace of the comic (mostly of satires) about law is the distance that separates legal rules and their enforcement from justice, or even the very unjust content of some legal rules (though namely aimed at justice). Nietzsche taught that the idea of justice (of 'good') is ever changing: anyway, people have always thought about justice, and it is predictable that they will always do.

If the comic says that "there is no justice in this world," it inevitably implies that there *may be* something called justice. While it may be quite easy to laugh at what is *legal, justice*, generally speaking, is not funny. We all know that there are things that we cannot laugh at, notwithstanding Nietzsche (let us think of the Aristotelean notion of *eutrapelia*). Charlie Hebdo's cartoons about the death of little Aylan Kurdi or the victims of the earthquake of 2016 in central Italy were not funny.

We may suppose that *justice*, though hard to define and ever changing, may be the expressed or implied common ground between the comic and its consumers while the hiatus between law and justice is what makes law and its actors so funny.

The more law is far from justice, the higher the need it feels to protect itself against the comic, by means of rules foreclosing freedom of expression. Comedy and satire have always been weapons of resistance against oppressive regimes. Different rules set on the satire against public figures and institutions from both sides of the Atlantic show different degrees of trust in democratic debate.

4 Life's but a walking monster: *In memoriam* Paolo Villaggio

Let me turn back to the monster and take a couple of hints from Paolo Villaggio's *Fantozzi*:

> Any human conglomeration has its own baleful presence of the organizer of recreational activities. At the corporation where Fantozzi was employed, there was one Filini, of the "Claim and loss department," of course. Fantozzi could never get away from Filini's *monstrous* initiatives; the most dreadful one being the annual football challenge "bachelors vs husbands." The tenzon used to take place in the worst suburban small sports grounds. The players were always "very" reduced in number because of delays, defections, mothers', wives' and medical doctors' restrictions[18]

18 Quotations from the screenplay of the movie *Il secondo tragico Fantozzi* (directed by Luciano Salce, 1976), by Paolo Villaggio, Luciano Salce, Piero De Bernardi and Leonardo Benvenuti. The Italian text reads as follows: "In ogni agglomerato umano c'è sempre la figura funesta dell'organizzatore di manifestazioni ricreative. Nella società di Fantozzi era certo Filini, ovviamente dell'ufficio sinistri. Mai Fantozzi era riuscito a sfuggire alle sue mostruose iniziative, a cominciare dalla più agghiacciante: l'annuale sfida calcistica fra scapoli e ammogliati. Queste tenzoni si svolgono sempre nel più disastrato dei campetti di periferia; le formazioni sono sempre molto ridotte, per ritardi, defezioni, proibizioni di madri, spose e medici curanti."

> To choose the employee, appointed to escort the Mega Director, Clamorous Duke Count Pier Carlo Ing. Semenzara, to gamble in Montecarlo, a godawful raffle was organized in the canteen ... The organizer of the ceremony was accountant Filini of the "Claim and loss department" ... The chance was really *monstruous*: three days in Montecarlo to see Semenzara gamble. If he only had suspected that the chaperon could bring good luck, you got it made for your whole life! [19]

In Villaggio's imaginific language, "monstrous" is something larger than life, too big to fit in any picture, which you cannot escape, be it a calamity, as in the first example, or the chance of your life, as in the second example.

In *Fantozzi* series "monstrous" does not mean unnatural, or exceptional: it is part of our daily life and we all have to cope with it. We can even dream "monstrously forbidden dreams," following the title of a 1982 movie on the reveries of the very unlucky clerk usually acted by Villaggio,[20] or we may build ourselves a "monstrous culture," by means of a careful study of the 1972 pamphlet in which Villaggio satirized the fake and useless erudition of quiz shows.[21]

So what about the law? The law has limited instruments to deal with the ever-changing complexity of life and human nature. The comic's task is to remind us that the law is like Achilles chasing the tortoise in the famous paradox, or the rented tailcoats that Fantozzi and Filini wear in a very famous scene, when they are invited, by chance, to a very exclusive VIP dinner[22]: the sleeves are always too long, and the legs too short.

At the same time, we cannot give up our search for justice (though we suspect, thanks to Nietzsche, that it may be nothing but an elusive ghost), and – apparently – we have no better tools than the law. Law is such stuff as dreams are made on. We laugh at our monstrously forbidden dreams, but we have to keep on dreaming.

---

19 The Italian text reads as follows: "Per la scelta dell'impiegato che doveva accompagnare il Mega Direttore Clamoroso, Duca Conte Pier Carlo Ingegner Semenzara, a giocare a Montecarlo, si tenne in sala mensa un tremendo sorteggione ... Organizzatore della cerimonia: il Ragionier Filini, dell' ufficio Sinistri ... L' occasione era davvero mostruosa: tre giorni a Montecarlo a veder giocare il Semenzara, che se poi avesse sospettato che il suo accompagnatore portava fortuna, era fatta per tutta la vita!" My translation.

20 *Sogni mostruosamente proibiti* (1982), movie directed by Neri Parenti.

21 Paolo Villaggio, *Come farsi una cultura mostruosa* (Milano: Bompiani,1972).

22 Once again, reference goes to the movie *Il secondo tragico Fantozzi*.

5 Laurel & Hardy, *Do Detectives Think?*

He who fights with monsters should look to it that he himself does not become a monster.
Nietzsche, *Beyond Good and Evil*

The comic approach to monstrosity and the law is a cardinal issue also in *Do Detectives Think?*, a short silent movie directed by Fred Guidol in 1927. The main characters are Judge Foozle, acted by James Finlayson, and the two "worst detectives in the whole world" interpreted by Stan Laurel and Oliver Hardy, alias Ferdinand Finkleberry and Sherlock Pinkam. This analysis will attempt to demonstrate how humour can turn a potentially tragic conflict into a comedy and, in so doing, how it can preserve and sustain our ideal of law, namely that 'stuff as dreams are made on'. Indeed, if humour usually subverts the rules, in this movie it subverts the lack of a rule since the real monster is the corruption of the juridical system, the perversion or the degeneracy of the system.

The comic mannerism of the duo Laurel and Hardy, especially when they play Stan and Ollie, is usually based on a number of tit-for-tat exchanges, which they practice in an escalating physical destruction of the place all around them, as it happens in *Big Business* (1929) where, in the presence of a police officer, they foolishly destroy a house and an automobile. In any case, when the playful-aggressive confrontation comes to an end, the opponents are usually reconciled and nobody is ever seriously hurt.

Nonetheless, in *Do Detectives Think?* there is an exception to the rule of analogy and *contrappasso* because Laurel and Hardy play the detectives, that is the law enforcers. But even more, it is significant that they have to protect a Judge. In this particular case, the comic effect is provided by the disproportion between, on the one hand, the weirdness of the two modern anti-heroes and, on the other one, the symbolic value they are supposed to protect and the death threat made by an heinous killer against an unworthy Judge. Even if the storytelling seems to be simple – someone is clumsily up against a difficult situation –, it implies a number of interesting comic inconsistencies.

Right at the beginning of the story, we are in a courtroom and the Justice is reading his judgement of conviction to a defendant who "killed two Chinamen, – both seriously," as we read in a caption. The adverb "seriously" discloses a paradoxical perspective: how can a killing be a frivolous matter? But it also states how the defendant deserves a guilty verdict. We must say that the captions usually show reversal, mockery, punning, that is a subversion of meaning that undermines the cultural system. By putting openly into question our common sense, such discrepancies arouse our sense of humour and, as a consequence, the perception that we have the situation under control. Indeed, following the superiority theory (as formulated by Thomas Hobbes, among others), what is laughable is usually perceived as inferior, and laughter is an expression of the sudden realization of one's own superiority.

There is a second astonishing caption: "This story opens with a lot of people in court – Most of them should be in jail – ." This comment introduces the assumption that justice might not belong to this court, so if we expect the detectives to fail, we should also expect the judge not to properly perform his professional duties. De facto, the statement seems to anticipate a critical or even mockery approach to jurisdiction.

In antithesis to this ambiguous introduction, the law is seen in its *mise en scène* of authority, that is during its liturgy or the fair-hearing. As we know, in order to give anybody access to Justice and to guarantee the legitimacy of the trial, the formalism of the procedure and the rule are essential. By virtue of the importance jurisdiction plays in society, the juridical demands decorum and full respect of its 'sacredness', as we experience whenever we enter a courtroom or in the presence of a judge. In narratological terms, we could state that law occupies a high-mimetic narrative dimension, which makes its storytelling closer to tragedy rather than to comedy. Indeed, being essentially self-ruling, law applies to everybody, but it is not *like* anything else. Moreover, a man serving as a Judge does (or *should*) not embody his own will but the Law itself and, as a consequence, he assumes a power that is actually due to Law.

Against all expectations, in the movie, the attention of the spectator is immediately focused on how the Judge is – seriously and personally – pleased of sending a criminal to jail, as when he says " – And I hope you choke! – ." Or when we are told in another caption "Judge Foozle has charged the jury – He always charged [sic!] everything – ." His snigger and sneer underline his *personal* sense of superiority that enacts a sarcastic dramatization of the relationship between the parties. The etymology of 'sarcasm' means 'tear flesh', in late Greek 'gnash the teeth, speak bitterly', which describes an undeniable aggressiveness. Sarcasm usually conveys a general idea of hostility in the audience, which in a silent movie can only be *visually* communicated. Even if, after Hobbes, the law is primarily mediated by the word, from a semiological point of view the performance over the top, the captions, the low-angle shot that emphasises the ruling role of the character, along with the exasperated state of mind of the Judge unveil a juridical aberration or a monstrous deviation from the legal procedure and the rule. As already stated, any procedure that is incoherent with the Code is the hallway to wrongfulness. Resultantly, the corruption of the juridical rite goes hand in hand with the falling apart of the social function of the law. The Judge's mockery of the murderer destabilizes the audience, who considers his attitude improper, no matter how guilty the felon could be. Actually, we can criticise Foozle, only because we believe in a strong sense of Justice, which makes us feel superior to anyone who challenges its institution.

Nevertheless, we are not yet in the domain of the comic. A deep sense of humour is not yet perceived by the spectator, because there is still a certain empathy shared with the Judge that prevents any kind of amusement: Foozle is not funny, but an uncanny caricature or an exasperated portrait of a Judge, since he does not guarantee the fundamental principle of fair-hearing. On the contrary, he replaces equity and justice with an avenging, merely punishing sentence. According to Baudelaire, the absolute comicality fustigates a universal principle, so that in a caricature we should see the absolute. The spectator cannot laugh at Foozle yet, because he still represents more *himself* than the universal ideal of Justice that he should embody in court. Guidol is still introducing the conflict that Ferdinand Finkleberry and Sherlock Pinkam will be asked to solve in a while.

Convinced that he can tell right from wrong, Judge Foozle – the *alazon* who lays claim to qualities and abilities not rightly his – points at the monster-defendant in order to *do* justice rather than to apply the law. In so doing, he ontologically becomes a monster himself, or “other” than the *persona* of the Judge, namely the mask of Justice that he should wear in court. Nobody is prepared to identify his anomalous figure and, for that reason, he is as frightening as only a monster can be: he is actually dangerous and powerful. He embodies the two sides of the law: good and evil, the rule and the transgression of the rule. Whereas the criminal is clearly what he is, it is impossible to accept the sarcastic mask the judge wears. Foozle turns into a hybrid-monstrous (social) entity who is no longer a symbolic referent or a reference point for the community. While the murderer embodies the meaning of “monster” as a “person of inhuman cruelty or wickedness,” the Judge embodies its meaning of “outrageously wrong.”[23] The latter actualizes the idea of monster suggested by Michel Foucault in his *Abnormal. Lectures at the College de France 1974–1975*, where he writes that “monstrosity requires a transgression of the natural limit, of the law-table, to fall under, or at any rate challenge, an interdiction of civil and religious or divine law.”[24] The Judge is described while he brings

23 See *Online Etymology Dictionary*, http://www.etymonline.com/index.php?Search=monster&searchmode=none (last access June 20, 2018).

24 Michel Foucault, *Abnormal. Lectures at the College de France 1974–1975* [1999], trans. Graham Burchell (London and New York: Verso, 2003), 63. Also available online: https://monoskop.org/images/9/9b/Foucault_Michel_Abnormal_Lectures_at_the_College_de_France_1974_1975_2003.pdf (last access September 5, 2018).

disturbance into the juridical system, namely he does not respect the rights of the prisoner as well as the juridical institution he should enact.[25]

This movie follows the line of complaint that also the visual arts have widely explored in the centuries: from Hogarth's *The Bench* (1758), where the dignity of the Law is merely formal, to Daumiers' *Les gens de justice* (1866), for whom lawyers are presumptuous and Judges uninterested and unconcerned persons, up to Pino Zac's magistrates, who always side with the power, through Francisco Goya, just to mention a few humorous visual memes, the judicial system has been appointed as unfair or unequal because of the men of law. The history of art and literature has often presented frightening figures of judges such as, for instance, the smiling Judge portrayed by Victor Hugo with the caption "regardand mettre une femme à la question",[26] as part of the series *Poème de la sorcière (*1872–1873) including "La Torture," "Pièces du procès. Portraits authentiques de divers diables que la sorcière a eu le tort de fréquenter," and "Gens de la foule qui assistent au supplice." Comic examples of legal aberration include Aristophanes' *The Wasps,* where Philocleon is obsessed by the idea of being part of a jury because in this way even the politicians implore his indulgence; or William S. Gilbert and Arthur Sullivan' light-hearted *Trail by Jury* (1875), in which the chorus of jurymen, shaking their fists, say:

> Monster, dread our damages.
> We're the Jury,
> Dread our fury![27]

In these examples, the role played by the comic approach highlights the social and human need for justice, but the intent to subvert the juridical system hardly ever prevails. Indeed, the natural reaction to monstrosity can be either violence or humour: the first one destroys, the second one aims at a renewed harmony. For instance, Michel Foucault and Victor Hugo have very different polemical and political attitudes.

---

25 See also Jeffrey Jerome Cohen, "Monster Culture (Seven Theses) (Extract)," in *Speaking of Monsters: A Teratological Anthology,* eds. Caroline Joan S. Picart and John Edgar Browning (New York: Palgrave Macmillan, 2012): 17: "the monster threatens to destroy not just individual members of society, but the very cultural apparatus through which individuality is constituted and allowed."

26 Victor Hugo, "Regardand mettre une femme à la question," series "La tortute," pen and brown ink on paper, Maison de Victor Hugo, Inv MVHP-D-930.

27 Arthur Sullivan and William Schwenck Gilbert, *Trial by Jury. A novel and original dramatic cantata* (London: Chappell &Co, 1898), 2, 9, 11. Available at: http://hdl.handle.net/1802/20810 (last access June 20, 2018).

The abnormal power of law in the hands of the wrong man is considered by Michel Foucault in his *Abnormal,* where he reports about a Communard who becomes judge:

> In recent events [that is to say, the Commune; M.F.] these impulsive tendencies found a most favorable opportunity for their realization and free development. The longed-for day finally arrived when he was able to carry out the favorite object of his sinister aspirations: *wielding absolute discretionary power of arrest and requisition and over the life and death of individuals.* He made extensive use of this power; his appetite was violent and he must have had a proportionate satisfaction. *Betrayed by chance, it is said that he had the courage to proclaim his views.* Could this be because he could not do otherwise? As I have already said, R was scarcely twenty-six years old, but his tired, pale, and already lined features bore the imprint of premature old age, his look lacked frankness, due perhaps to severe myopia. In reality, the general and habitual expression of his physiognomy had a certain hardness, *a certain wildness, and an extreme arrogance; his lattened and open nostrils breathed sensuality as did his somewhat thick lips partially covered by a long, bushy, black-and-tawny-tinged beard. His laughter was sarcastic, his words brief and urgent, and his mania for terrorizing led him to inflate the tone of his voice so as to make it resound more terribly.*[28] [My italics]

The statement "Betrayed by chance, it is said that he had the courage to proclaim his views" underlines an unabsolving acerbic wit about the violent attitude of the Judge, while the meticulous physical description of the Communard reminds Guidol's representation of Foozle, sarcasm included. Generally speaking, criminals and judges seem to share the same abnormal, monstrous cruelty.

Anyway, Victor Hugo portrays Judges who become monstrous beings when they apply the law – specifically death penalty – by the book. With this respect, in *The Last Day of a Condemned Man* he writes: "And the judge was not tried for this; nor was the executioner tried for it; and no tribunal inquired into this *monstrous* violation of all law on one of God's creatures!" And also: "What was he doing, this punisher of assassins, while they thus assassinated, in open daylight, his fellow-creature?"[29] Hugo takes position against a magistrate who applies a law that the writer considers highly unfair and inhuman (albeit he forgets the responsibility of the lawmaker!). Nevertheless, he is also against an insensitive society that uncritically accepts a lawful as well as shameful punishment, while

---

28 Jean-Baptiste-Vincent Laborde, *Les Hommes et les Actes de l'insurrection de Paris devant la psychologie morbide (*Paris: 1872), 30–36. Quoted in Michel Foucault, *Abnormal. Lectures at the College de France*, 155–156.

29 Victor Hugo, *The Last Day of a Condemned Man,* trans. by Eugenia de B. (Adelaide: The University of Adelaide, 2014). Available at: https://ebooks.adelaide.edu.au/h/hugo/victor/last_day_of_a_condemned_man/complete.html (last access June 20, 2018).

the condemned (more humanly) implores the writer to let everybody know about his agony. Indeed, as Hugo denounces the popular approval of the mortal *show* taking place in Place de Grève, likewise in *Do Detectives Think?* the spectator is less surprised by the sentence than by an authority that betrays its mandate. This fact will be narratively important in order to understand the comic development of the story: we will be able to laugh at the law or at the Judge because the defendant is really guilty, the sentence is essentially correct and the detectives – for better or for worse – do their job. Hugo and Guidol are telling us that we (absurdly) accept a legal monstrosity such as death penalty, but we cannot renounce the institution of Justice. Actually, it seems that only a critical mind can acknowledge that both monster and law are cultural variables, and *even* the law can have questionable opinions about what right and wrong are.

As an illustrative example, we could consider the *Abu Ghraib Series* realized by Fernando Botero. In these paintings, the famous overblown, buttery, rotund, innocent figures (Boteromorphs) are victims of atrocious tortures, just like the original victims of the photographs taken at Abu Ghraib. Notwithstanding the human horror or monstrosity these conflicting images suggest, the abnormal naked bodies (no matter how humiliated they are) reveal such a mocking challenge to their torturers, that from victims they turn into heroes (see what Gianbattista Vico wrote in his *Vici vindiciae*). We hardly laugh at the pain they represent, but there is an indefinable sense of the grotesque that saves their dignity. The torturer is ideologically subdued and his power is denied, because he does not represent the law or any principle of Justice, even if everything suggests the idea of jurisdiction, such as the prison, the chains, the handcuffs… not least a sentence of the Supreme Court of the United States about torture. The original bodies, which inspired Botero, are definitely tragic, while in the paintings the grotesque allows us to take a conscious control over the monstrous human condition. Still following Baudelaire, humour has taken us back to an absolute principle of Justice.

The law becomes body also in Guidol's movie. By not wearing his robe in trial, which could make his body the simulacrum of his juridical function, Foozle removes the mask of the Judge and lets his face emerge: a monster does not wear any mask. Foozle is not sentencing a murderer, as he is correctly supposed to do, but he is implementing his personal idea of justice, so that he becomes a hybrid *persona*, someone between a man and a man-of-law but still with a crucial juridical responsibility and power. The fall of Foozle-as-man would become the fall of Justice if the context were not comic. The awkward relationship between jurisdiction and justice grounds the comic narrative conflict.

In this dramatic situation, as a reaction, the murderer takes center stage and aggressively shouts his own death sentence against the Judge. The criminal develops into the double of the Magistrate, being him ironically "identical" and "other" at the same time. Surprisingly enough, he reproduces the same snigger and sneer that Foozle previously exhibited, so that the spectator recognizes the physical embodiment of an equal aggressiveness even if the meaning is critically different and the spectator feels as though suspended between forces.[30] The scene becomes a complex system of signification: justice and vengeance overlap. It is as if a renewed ethical professional dimension were needed to restore Justice and order in society.

Media often describe criminals as monsters for their heinousness and inhumanity: as the Bible taught us the "mark of Cain" identifies the criminal as "other" than the norm, and as a consequence it marks the boundary between good and evil. In this specific case, to create the character of the throat-slasher, the film-maker relies on the cultural imaginary mediated by the criminal anthropology of Guillaume-Benjamin Duchenne, as much as on Boris Karloff's monster of *Dr. Frankenstein* (1918), that is a huge, ugly, terrifying, threatening, preternatural creature. Moreover, if we consider the physical mismatch between the judge and the convicted, we may suppose that Guidol might have had in mind also those abnormal phenomena, shocking to the viewers, of the Barnum freak shows, which were very popular in the United States in the twenties.

In such an exasperated and ambiguous context, the defendant is unpredictably as frightening as ridiculous because he evokes and, at the same time, gives a more authoritative (albeit still inappropriate) body to his opposite, that is to say, the original poor little man the judge is. Unaware of his real duties and role in court, Foozle fears for his life and, as a reaction, he jumps on the bench: the fright he wanted to arouse into the throat slasher (his personal victim) is now his own fright. In so doing, he loses his professional decorum and turns from symbol into body. As Bergson observed, "A comic effect is always obtainable by transporting the natural expression of an idea into another key,"[31] and also: "we laugh if our attention is diverted to the physical in a person when it is the moral that is in question"[32] and this seems to be the case. We should acknowledge that a caricature does not punish, but it stigmatizes human baseness, especially through the body. Indeed, from now on, violence and humour will shape the comic narration, and they will find their synthesis in the threatened body of the Law – namely Foozle – and in its defenders, that is the two detectives.

---

30 See also Eric Weitz, *The Cambridge Introduction to Comedy* (Cambridge: Cambridge U.P., 2013), 142.

31 Henri Bergson, *Laughter: An Essay on the Meaning of Comic,* trans. Cloudesley Brereton and Fred Rothwell (London), available at http://www.authorama.com/book/laughter.html (last access June 20, 2018).

32 Bergson, *Laughter: An Essay on the Meaning of Comic.*

As a matter of fact, in court, just for a moment, the observer shares the point of view of the killer. Chaos takes the place of order and all our certainties are turned upside-down. Humour usually creates a plurality of colliding logics, to the point that what is laughable within the comic framework would be unacceptable in real life, but it is the latent, analytical and rational judgement of the observer that triggers the act of laughing. Humour, even when ferocious, does not destroy but it deconstructs in order to show the ideological limits of its target.

When a couple of months later the killer escapes from jail, two detectives are sent to protect the Judge. The comic dimension is now introduced and we start to perceive danger in a very different way. Indeed, since the beginning, the two anti-heroes show their chicken-hearted nature (they are literally scared of their own shadow when they cross the graveyard at night), their incompetence, their ingenuity, but in so doing they circumscribe the comic taste of the movie. The frightened, illogical but intuitive detectives create a comic relief, and their vulnerability makes us face the fear of the throat-slasher. Humour stigmatizes how evil has different degrees of perception and effects, so that the spectator reconsiders what he has just seen and, once again, he feels superior to (all) the characters and the environment, in line with the already mentioned theory of superiority. The title of the movie – *Do Detectives Think?* – eventually illustrates how Finkleberry and Pinkam are unfit and unqualified to serve the law, although their actions are never evil or contemptible. The two detectives lighten the mood and provide a critical comment on a very ambiguous situation. Ironically, the humanity of the heroes minimizes the sense of tragedy, and suggests a moral and realistic perspective of the state of experience. The duo draws our attention to the destructive element,[33] that is to the collision of monsters: on the same stage we have the Judge-monster, the criminal-monster, the enforcer-detectives in an endless chase where the roles are all mixed up, even if we know that the real anomaly is not the existence of evil, but the corruption of the juridical system.

In the meanwhile, we see how Justice Foozle is first deprived of his robe, thereafter he is displaced out of the courtroom to his home,[34] and then, in a turning point of the storytelling, he is seen completely naked in the tub threatened by the killer, who holds a terribly huge knife. Rather than being locked into a tragedy, the sublime of Justice is led, via its representative (the Judge), to

33 See Northrop Frye, *The Anatomy of Criticism* (Princeton and Oxford: Princeton U.P., 2000), 237.

34 At home he is treated with contempt because of his beautiful and young wife. A caption says "The Judge had married for love – Nobody had ever been able to figure out what his wife married for – "

a comic *reductio ad absurdum* as part of a logical process which underlines how the power of the Judge is inappropriate for Foozle.

All this recalls the ballad by George Brassens *Le Gorille*, where the wild beast, which usually performs at local fairs, one day flights from his cage, and decides that it is time to lose its virginity. In order to satisfy its curiosity, between an old woman and a judge, the gorilla chooses the second one:

> ... Mais, par malheur, si le gorille
> Aux jeux de l''mour vaut son prix
> On sait qu'n revanche il ne brille
> Ni par le goût, ni par l'esprit
> Lors, au lieu d'opter pour la vieille
> Comme l'aurait fait n'importe qui
> Il saisit le juge à l'oreille
> Et l'entraîna dans un maquis
> Gare au gorille
>
> La suite serait délectable
> Malheureusement, je ne peux
> Pas la dire, et c'est regrettable
> Ça nous aurait fait rire un peu
> Car le juge, au moment suprême
> Criait: "maman !," pleurait beaucoup
> Comme l'homme auquel, le jour même
> Il avait fait trancher le cou
> Gare au gorille

In this very miserable occasion, the judge cries aloud just like the man he had condemned to death the previous day. Both magistrates are tragic characters because of their unfair behaviour, but, once deprived of their "absolute" power in court, the humour realigns them to the public. The comic interpretation of the juridical institution minimizes the supremacy of the Law and it cancels out the distance between the Law and the people, that is to say, the high-mimetic dimension of it. In the movie, Foozle is made "popular" or accessible by means of his (little) naked body.[35]

---

35 I would like to remember what Victor Hugo says in his *The Last Day of a Condemned Man*: "Happy if, with no other aid than his thoughts, he has mined sufficiently into the subject to make a heart bleed, under the *œs triplex* of a magistrate! Happy if he could render merciful those who consider themselves just! Happy if, penetrating sufficiently deep within the judge, he has sometimes reached the man." The comic relief makes us recognize the man that Foozle is. Victor Hugo, *The Last Day of a Condemned Man* [1829], trans. Eugenia de B. (South Australia: The University of Adelaide Library, 2014), 3. Also available online: https://ebooks.adelaide.edu.au/h/hugo/victor/last_day_of_a_condemned_man/complete.html (last access September 5, 2018).

The synthesis between his being both man and Judge is found in the mask he accidentally wears. It happens that the two detectives create a diversion for the killer, so that Foozle has time to save himself and to put on a sort of Greek *himation*. Anyway, descending the stairs, he falls and a mask slips on the back of his head. Unaware that he looks like a bi-front Giano, Foozle is both a naked little judge made ridiculous by the *himation* and the mask of a severe, but not complacent, supernatural being who evokes reproach instead of vengeance. In this guise, he calls to mind an ancestral collective meaning of justice[36] or the unavoidability of the rule. Perhaps the character of the mask has cancelled its interpreter (Foozle), although only now and unconsciously, the latter embodies (or his body wears) his profession. We can also observe that the mask is much bigger than Foozle's head. In this way, on the one hand it seems to dominate the body and the personality of the Judge, but on the other one it becomes a shelter from the killer. Therefore, for the umpteenth time we assist to the subversion of all certainties: eventually, justice means protection and equity.

As soon as Right is back, the slapstick chase between the killer and the detectives[37] is interrupted. It is the case that when the killer leaves the bathroom, he starts a comic fight with the two detectives, who are actually more preys than hunters. The serious criminal intent of the throat slasher is relieved by a kind of violence made of double takes, paradoxical captions, continuous loss of control of the bodies, a game of mirrors, an awkward use of the police equipment (gun and handcuffs), a crescendo of foolishness that implies a huge knife turning into an even bigger scimitar, unfortunate unexpected events, and so on. In reality, the aggressiveness against the Judge is overcome by the incompetent and disorganized physical engagement of the two detectives. Unlike Foozle, they are professionally committed, and they really try their best, even if fear rules all their actions.

The slapstick chase is taken to an end only when the killer looks at the mask (particularly into the "eyes" of the mask) and he is visibly shaken in fear: the mask works as a wise giant that puts evil at stake. Amusingly enough, even Foozle can look like a virtuous giant! As also Victor Hugo tried to state, notwithstanding the juridical system, it is within ourselves that our aspiration to Justice lies. Positive right cannot but clash with the supernatural presence, but, surprised by the intense and unconventional gaze of the mask, the criminal-monster loses control and he is arrested by Stan Laurel.

---

36 See Simon Dentith, *Bakhtinian Thought. An Introductory Reader* (London and New York: Routledge, 1995), 67.

37 See what Northrop Frye states: "fate, in a tragedy, normally becomes external to the hero only after the tragic process has been set going; Northrop Frye, *Anatomy of Criticism* [1957] (Princeton: Princeton University Press, 2000), 210.

Simultaneously, the body of the Judge puts on, once again, the mask of the ethical dimension of its juridical function, despite the corruption of the system and its institution.

The audience is puzzled and can only laugh about the monsters or the bizarre condition of both Judge and criminal. To the spectator it is obvious that the fear the killer feels for some *papier-mâché* is similar to what the two detectives felt about their shadows when they crossed the graveyard right at the beginning of the movie. As Kant pointed out, laughter arises from the sudden transformation of a strained expectation into nothing.

The aesthetics of humour defined by the two detectives at the beginning of the movie finds a plain completeness at the end. So, from the courtroom as a stage, we have gone through the carnival, that is a process of disguising and a symbolic inversion. The carnivalesque represents the logic of an inverted world, of the identification with the identity of the "other," the suspension of the order and the rules. But the effect of the carnival should lead to the triumph of truth. In the movie Justice is brought back to its real role after its corruption.

We must point out that the audience always leans towards the Judge. The humour prevents the story to become a tragedy. Imagine the Judge to be killed by the throat slasher. In such a hypothesis, the Law would have been described as unable to fulfil its duty, and unreliable for the citizen. Therefore, a positive conclusion of the story is due to laughter. We can laugh because we know we can keep all this legal disorder under control. The spectator gets what he was looking for: the criminal is in jail once again, and the audience feels more intelligent, skilful and wiser than the Judge. In so doing, the appropriate balance between jurisdiction and justice is found. We must admit that a comic change from ignorance to knowledge is not completely accomplished since, in the end, the Judge does not seem to be really conscious of his mistakes. We laugh at Foozle's body and personality, but his abuse of authority and power is not comic at all. We know that at the end of the carnival also utopia comes to the end, but a real restoration of Justice can be achieved only through a new ethical dimension.[38]

I would like to conclude with the words written by Jacques Derrida in an essay called "Prepare yourself to experience the future and welcome the monster":

> Faced with a monster, one may become aware of what the norm is an when this norm has a history – which is the case with discursive norms, philosophical norms, socio-cultural norms, they have a history – any appearance of monstrosity in this domain allows an

---

38 See, Simon Dentith, *Bakhtinian Thought* (London and New York: Routledge, 1995), 76.

analysis of the history of the norms. But to do that, one must conduct not only a theoretical analysis; one must produce what in fact looks like a discursive monster so that the analysis will be a practical effect, so that people will be forced to become aware of the history of normality.[39]

39 Jacques Derrida, "Prepare yourself to experience the future and welcome the monster," *POINTS-INTERVIEWS 1974–1994*, ed. Elisabeth Weber (Stanford: Stanford UP, 1995), 385–387. Available at: http://hydra.humanities.uci.edu/derrida/monster.html (last accesses June 20, 2018).

Fernando Armando Ribeiro

The Monster as a Denial of Difference: A Legal Approach to Kafka's *Metamorphosis*

1 An introductory approach to monstrosity

The study of monstrosity through literature allows some approaches to difficult and critical legal issues. After all, metaphors help us understand things in a more thoughtful and consistent way, surpassing the limits involved in mere abstract concepts. Literature speaks mainly through images, and these images, as Heidegger well said, are imaginings, but never illusions.[1]

Monstrosity is a term often used as a reference to evil in an aesthetic or moral dimension.[2] The construction of the figure of the "monster" often aims to fulfill the political role of maintainer of social norms, an attempt to guarantee the internal cohesion of individuals by the visible demarcation of a field in which behaviors and qualities are naturalized. It gives them an exact measure, as if they were to be "forever so" and "never otherwise," labeling as monstrous everything that tends to exceed that measure.

The monster becomes a compelling and effective way of implementing, through aesthetics, a pattern of profiles, beliefs or behaviors that intend to have significant social acceptance. It is a previously stipulated social sanction that punishes with non-recognition all those who dare to transgress or question the limits of this supposed "normality." We should never underestimate the power of metaphor to the law. After all, as François Ost brilliantly teaches, there is a clear relation and approximation between fantasy (a characteristic of literature) and the reality of the order of things (shown by law).[3]

Aristotle pointed out that deficiency or excess would characterize a prodigy or a monstrosity. That is to say, a two-headed bull or a three-legged horse are rare occurrences and therefore monstrous.[4] Transgression of the pattern is the mother of most so-called monsters. Either because they are seen as defying the order of the gods (*pax deorum*), as in classical antiquity, or as a violation of the natural

1 Martin Heidegger, "Poetically man dwells," in *Poetry, language and thought* [1971] (New York: Harper Perennial Modern Thought, 2013), 226.

2 Julio Jeha, *Monstros e monstrosidades na literatura* (Belo Horizonte: UFMG, 2017).

3 François Ost, *Raconter la loi:aux sources de l'imaginaire juridique* (Paris: Editions Odile Jacob, 2004), 12.

4 Aristotle, *De generatione*, book 1, chapter 4. In Aristotle, *On sophistical refutations* & *On coming-to-be and passing-away* (Cambridge: Harvard University Press, 1955).

https://doi.org/10.1515/9783110654615-011

order, monsters always reveal a difficulty in accepting difference, and personify such exclusion precisely in that nodal point where Lévinas builds his ethics, that is, the face.

2 The face

The novel *The Metamorphosis* begins with the protagonist – Gregor Samsa – metamorphosed into a giant insect. This beginning is already its climax and sets its tone to dive profoundly into a mighty philosophical human conflict which allows us to reflect on the fundamental facets of monstrosity.

After being metamorphosed into an insect, Gregor Samsa is not seen as he is anymore, but as what he appears to be, that is, a monster. However, whilst people see him as a giant insect, he perceives himself as very human inside, capable of asking the same existential questions, of appreciating art, music, and being threatened by the same dreadful obligations. "Am I less sensitive than I used to be then?" questions the protagonist, reflecting about his being.[5]

In that sense, the importance of art is highlighted in two passages of the work where Gregor Samsa is led to change his previous behavior, always so contained and submissive, in order to experience the aesthetic pleasure brought by art. That is to say, in those two passages, he abandons his submissive behavior to be able to gaze at the canvas in his room and also to better listen to the music played by his sister in the dining room.

"The best way to find someone else is not even to look at the color of his eyes."[6] With this statement, Lévinas tries to warn us about the improbability of contact with the face which is unlikely just because he who apprehends the face merely in one's features ends up not apprehending it as such. Thus, if we follow the author's recommendation, we can apprehend the paradox that is inherent to the relation with the face. If, on the one hand, the face is "naked," "defenseless," "threatened," on the other hand it is that very face that leads us to act primarily with love.

The Other, who always comes to me, would be the beginning of any ethical relationship. The Other perceives me as interpellation, exteriority,

---

5 Franz Kafka, *The Metamorphosis*, Kindle edition (n. p.: Ozymandias Press, 2016), 21. Further references in the text, abbreviated as M.

6 Emmanuel Lévinas, *Ethics and Infinity: Conversations with Philippe Nemo* (Pittisburg: Duquesne, 1995), 77.

distance, incomprehension and incompleteness. The Other in me is the unknown. This interpellation would be the "experience *par excellence*," an experiment that leads me to a reflective posture about my own being. That is to say, it challenges me in such a way that the very understanding of myself depends on it, before any possible conceptualization. It remains Other, distant as a possibility of concept, even if close in relation. "The relation between me and the Other that shines in his expression does not end in either the number or the concept. The Other remains infinitely transcendent, infinitely strange."[7]

Thus, infinity "as an inspiration of kindness" is a necessity in my relation to the Other. The Other who, when presenting himself to me as a face, imposes himself in its infinity. The face would be the basis for understanding the ethics in Lévinas. When we recognize that the face of the Other is not reachable and apprehensible by our pre-established categories, it is clear to us why the ethical relation must be placed in new patterns.

> The face of men transcends all possible description, he who thinks he is approaching it by accumulating details – color of eyes, shape of nose and mouth, expressive traits, etc. – would only produce a strange *image to the face* ... The face-to-face relationship should not to be thought of in terms of mutual recognition. The encounter with of the face is a shock that nothing in the context or in explicit words could previously have prepared for. It does not announce itself, it comes. That is what incites Lévinas to describe it as an "epiphany" or as a "revelation," that is to say, as an event that necessarily surprises the subject, or even that takes hold of him and does him harm.[8]

The face as a way of experiencing the Other would be the shock that does not allow the categories of self to apprehend it. The face then becomes an "event" in relation to the self. The self that seeks to absorb the Other from itself is not possible for the structure of the event, which, by itself, when it appears, destabilizes all measures that precede its arrival. The face as the event is an interesting source to understand the same impossibility that his apprehension would be. For the event, infinite in its appearances and possibilities, is already showing the impossibility intrinsic to the face.

---

7 Emmanuel Lévinas, *Totality and infinity: An Essay on Exteriority*, trans. Alphonso Lingis (Norwell/MA: Kluwer Academic Publishers, 1991), 170.

8 Catherine Chalier, *Lévinas: a utopia do humano*, trad. Antônio Hall (Lisboa: Instituto Piaget, 1996), 112–113. *Lévinas: l'utopie de l'humain* (Paris: Editions Albin Michel, 1993). [My translation.]

3 Who is the monster?

The first monstrosity that can be seen in Kafka's narrative is that arising from the painful labor and family obligations that fell upon Gregor Samsa. In fact, his first concern when he perceives himself with the metamorphosed body and unable to get out of bed is that he will miss the 5:00 a.m. train that should take him on a business trip. From then on, all the (inhuman) efforts in which he gets involved are an attempt to meet such obligations and expectations that are cultivated by the family and the company where he works.

Eventually, Kafka lets us realize that Gregor only endured his heavy work routine because of his parents. "Oh God, he thought, what an extraneous career it is that I've chosen! Travelling day in and day out" (M,1). "If I had not held back because of my parents, I would have resigned a long time ago; I would have presented myself to the boss and told him exactly what I thought, from the bottom of my heart. He would have fallen off his desk!" (M, 16).

In that sense, the situation in that home was asymmetrical. While Gregor suffered because of a life of endless journeys and obligations, his father was able to have his breakfast and read newspapers for hours on end. "What a quiet life the family leads" Gregor told himself, and felt, as he stared into the darkness, a great pride that he had succeeded in giving his parents and his sister such a life in such a beautiful house" (M, 14).

The lack of humanity is so great that Gregor fears that the simple fact of missing work for one day due to illness could be viewed with suspicion. And, in fact, his fears will be confirmed the most abruptly. The firm not only sent a manager to Gregor's house to ascertain what was happening, but made several charges against him, putting his job at risk.

After his first appearance to the family, there is a passage that shows Gregor's sensitivity and discomfort with the inhumane way he was treated, especially by his father. In the scene in which the father tries to make his son go back to his room, Kafka describes accurately the astonished and disturbing condition in which Gregor had been before the whistles emitted by the father. "If only there wasn't his father's unbearable whistling. Because of it Gregor totally lost his head" (M,48).

Forbidden to move freely in the house and made a prisoner in his own room, Gregor Samsa feels guilty and ashamed of himself, of his condition, and seeks to find ways to save the family from the discomfort of seeing his miserable condition. That becomes very clear in the passage where, hidden under the couch in his room and feeling very hungry, Gregor Samsa notices his sister approaching. He wonders if she can bring some food that would suit him, but immediately makes the following reflection: "He would rather die of hunger than draw her attention to himself, even though he actually felt an immense desire to leave where he was, under the couch, and throw himself at her sister's feet, begging her to bring him something good to eat." (M, 47)

Gregor Samsa's transformation could be initially seen as liberation from the slavery of his work. Therefore, it could be seen as a radical way of breaking his bonds of servitude to the company and also to the family. Subsequently, however, references to his "incarceration" become frequent in the text and, according to some scholars, may point to the fact that Gregor Samsa did not really want to break the bonds binding him.

That is evidenced by the feeling of guilt and frustration he reveals when he hears the family conversations about the financial situation of the house: "When the conversation came to the need for making money, the first to go through the door was Gregor, and he threw himself on the cool leather couch standing by the door, for he was burning with shame and sorrow" (M, 55).

Gregor Samsa continued with the same good intentions he had always had. He dreamed of being able to send his sister to the conservatory to complete her violin studies, and he felt a deep love for the family. However, his face no longer reflected the expectations that they projected on him. It was now another face, which no longer met the longings for economic support or fulfillment of pre-established social roles. Gregor Samsa was now useless, and his face represented the antithesis of the ideal image built by the family. That expectation, in fact, seems to be something fundamental for Gregor's parents and also for his sister.

Thus, in the first few weeks after the metamorphosis, when the sister became the only person who could enter Gregor's room to bring him food, her parents started viewing her more favourably. Until then, she had been seen as a young, useless girl (M, 58). Such a view will become even more apparent and more poignant at the end of the plot when, sitting on the tram on the way to the city suburb, shortly after Gregor's death, the Samsas share a vision of their daughter overflowing with increasing vitality, and they are overcome with happiness, with the perception that she had blossomed and become a beautiful and exuberant girl. Then,

> as if unconsciously understanding each other only through the eyes, they thought it was time to find her a decent husband. And it seemed to them it was a kind of sign confirming their new dreams and good intentions when, upon arriving at their destination, the daughter was the first to stand up, stretching all her young body. (M, 103)

Such a perception seems to link Gregor's father's subservience to the economic dimension of life. In fact, he does everything to please the tenants of his house, even with the sacrifice of the well-being and privacy of the family. The scene in which the tenants ask Greta to play the violin in the living room for them is paradigmatic. Hearing the request, the father does not even ask his daughter for her consent (M, 85), but immediately gives an affirmative response. And, once in the living room, he and his wife do not even “dare to sit in their own chairs” (M, 85). It is also noteworthy that, after Gregor’s transformation, the father starts wearing a jumpsuit with bank badges.

4 Art is what makes us human

Starving, Gregor could smell the good food being served to the tenants in the living room, as well as hear the noise they made chewing and eating. At one point he says to himself, “How well these tenants eat, while I am here starving to death” (M, 85). However, despite his seemingly brutish animal condition, it will not be these primary instincts of hunger that will make him dare to cross the boundaries that had been imposed upon him. It will be the sound of music coming from the sister’s violin that will encourage him to step freely towards the living room.

Although he was in a poor condition, covered in dust, dirt and leftover food, Gregor could not help but head out to the place where the music was being played by his sister on the violin. At first, the tenants stand very close to the violinist, positioning themselves behind her, as if they wanted to follow the score. In fact, this position may tell us a great deal, as music for them was seen as no more than a set of signs, concretized on the paper sheet, and not in the body of the musician. Soon after, the author tells us that they were not touched by the music, getting up and standing at the window in obvious discomfort.

In a distressed question at the end of the book, Kafka unveils the deeply human facet of Gregor, the one whose recognition had until then been denied, but that is fully embraced by the unconditional hospitality of art: “Was he an animal, knowing that music touched him so much?” (M, 87)

We can perceive art as a revealing element of the human face(s), and also as a space for the recognition of difference. This is especially true if we consider that mere sounds, even when strongly resounding, did not catch Gregor’s attention, which becomes evident in the passage where his mother drops the violin to the floor and, despite the strident sound emitted, Gregor does not even move.

Also noteworthy is Gregor’s perception when returning to his room, when he is surprised by the great distance from the living room to his own room.

Despite his state of weakness, motivated by the music, he had previously overcome it with no difficulty (M, 94).

Therefore, if the sound of music is able to reveal the human behind the supposed "monster", the unmusical and disturbing sound of the sister's hand hitting the table points to the very structure of monstrosity as a refusal to imagine and recognize the face of the Other. In this sense, it is performative that both father and sister always use this gesture before uttering their condemnatory words of Gregor's monstrosity. Let us focus, for example, on this important passage that comes shortly after the scene in which Gregor is seen by the tenants, causing great discomfort in the family:

> "Dear parents," said her sister, and slammed her hand on the table in the form of an introduction, "this situation is unbearable. If you guys may not be able to see it, I see it very well. I do not want to pronounce my brother's name in front of this monster and so I just say this: we have to find a way to get rid of it." (M, 91)

5 Literature and the deconstruction of monstrosity

When Gregor's monstrosity, asserted by Grete, is put in check by the mother, who does not listen to the sister, the gang behavior soon comes to the surface, in a clear manifestation of the Schmittian logic of "friend and foe." In fact, Grete runs to embrace her father, with whom she shares the conviction that the one who now lived among them was not Gregor anymore. Such behavior reachs its peak when the sister abandons "her mother, literally jumping from her chair to the floor, as if she preferred to sacrifice the mother to being close to Gregor, running towards her father" (M, 93).

The radical otherness manifested by Gregor's metamorphosis has much to tell us about the very cut that literature operates in the real, leading us to an encounter with otherness. This phenomenon has explicit importance for law. As Derrida shows us, at every act of calculation there is a need for going beyond calculation, beyond what is calculable. Or, in other words, beyond what is given by order. We must calculate beyond. Thus, the dialog between law and literature is both a challenge and a refounding. It defies the intrinsic violence of legal order and points to a more democratic horizon: that of a democracy to come.

Literature and its intrinsic ability to invent can thus represent the otherness that lurks around the law from outside, offering a possibility of change. And this is an open path to deconstruction. "That the law is deconstructible is not a misfortune. One can even find in it the political chance of all progress."[9]

The encounter between law and literature can represent an act of profanation. As literature touches the legal order, it is negligent with it. From then on, what had been left walled, under surveillance, as if occupying a forbidden place, is brought back to the surface. Barthes's notion of literature as a gesture of "cheating" within language can be very helpful to understand this meaning of literature as an act of profanation to the legal order.[10] For Barthes, as power and language are connected, language's classificatory dimension becomes oppressive, and its use may also mean to subject. That's why literature can be seen as a remedy, or a counterpower. Cheating within language may be the only resource, and it is only possible through literature.

Bringing those contributions to the Law, we can argue that an act of literature towards legal order offers the chance to see what was not yet visible. Literature can be the element that inhibits or undoes the monstrosity that may be established by law. In Kafka's novel we can perceive the consequences resulting from the stratified arrangement of positions, roles, and hierarchies present in the Samsa's house. Beyond its apparent symmetry and order – or perhaps precisely because of them – a monstrous behavior was conceived. That is to say, an order that treats difference as a monster, committing against it monstrous acts, makes room for true monstrosity.

As Agamben has shown, neglecting the frontier is putting oneself beyond it. If literature is the "strange institution that can say anything"[11] it obviously cannot "respect" the frontier and, therefore, when confronting the order, brings a possibility of change, of denouncing the injustices and monstrosities that may be present without being noticed. Therefore, it dynamizes thought, bringing up the discomfort of the question, paving the way for transformation and hospitality.[12] The infinite power of invention, intrinsic to literature, can become a source of hospitality, opening the door for the unexpected other, for difference. Paraphrasing Derrida, an otherness to come.[13]

---

9 Jacques Derrida, *Force of Law: the Metaphysical Foundation of Authority*, trans. Mary Quaitance (New York: Routledge, 1992), 26.

10 Roland Barthes, *A aula*, trad. Leyla Perrone-Moisés (São Paulo: Cultrix, 1988). *Leçon* (Paris: French and European Publications Incorporated, 1989).

11 Jacques Derrida, *This Strange Institution Called Literature*, in *Acts of Literature*, ed. Derek Attridge (London: Routledge, 1992), 33–75.

12 Giorgio Agamben, *Profanations* (Massachusetts: The MIT Press, 2015).

13 Jacques Derrida, *Paixões*, trad. Loris Z. Machado (Campinas: Papirus, 1995), 45–46. *Passions* (Paris: Galillée, 1993).

In Kafka's book, not fitting the family previous patterns (that could easily be compared with legal order) Gregor Samsa was considered a monster. And while the established order was unable to accept him, art was the only resource left for him to assert his humanity.

In some way, here may lie the secret of literature, that 'strange institution' which unveils the other and gives him refuge. Which leads us to an encounter and acceptance of otherness beyond the fears and stratifications in which agonized faces of pseudo-monsters are played out.

Marc Amfreville

"The Sleep of Reason Brings Forth Monsters": Tim O'Brien's *In the Lake of the Woods*

Before even starting my introduction I would like to thank Isabel Capeloa Gil[1] (University of Lisbon), who gave a to-be-published presentation at the Warwick in Venice/Sorbonne seminar in September 2017 entitled "Lex Fugit: on Acts of Legibility" that, starting from the common Latin etymology of words derived from "lex, legis" and "legere," drew inspiring links between law and literature that gave birth to the present interdisciplinary endeavor.

Given the international nature of our symposium, I "naturally" used the English translation of the title of Goya's famous 1799 etching. In our largely Mediterranean context, I would have been better inspired to use the original one, "El sueño de la razón produce monstruos," since it is precisely its double meaning that brought it to my mind in relation to the novel I shall mostly be dealing with today: Tim O'Brien's *In the Lake of the Woods.*[2] It is essential to remember that *sueño* designates both sleep and dream, so that if the title, in typical Enlightened fashion, obviously means that when one lets reason sleep he/she may well be haunted by frightening creatures, it is nonetheless stimulating to envisage that Reason itself projects its own monsters, in a sort of intuition of the Freudian unconscious.

Two details that may not be details at all recommended the choice of Tim O'Brien's too hastily labeled Vietnam-war novel. First, as a leitmotiv the text harps on the missing woman protagonist's dream – once the nightmare of her husband's lost election at the US Senate is forgotten or at least has become less painful a memory after their stay on the Lake in the Wood's shore in Northern Minnesota to go on a romantic trip to... Verona, of all places. As with Goya's etching, the obvious positive association – to love, in this case – is immediately

1 Besides entrusting me with her draft, I would like to thank Isabel Capeloa-Gil for advising me to read the book by Shoshana Felman, *The Juridical Unconscious* and the article by Mieke Bal, "Legal Lust: Literary Litigation," *The Australian Feminist Law Journal* (2015): 1–23, which contributed to my reflections way beyond the quotations that appear in the following pages.
2 Tim O'Brien, *In the Lake of the Woods* (1994) (London: Flamingo, 1995). Further references in the text, abbreviated as ILW.

https://doi.org/10.1515/9783110654615-012

overshadowed by memories of live burial, disaster and death in the actual play by Shakespeare.

The second point was a vivid memory of the last sentence in the book: “Can we believe he was not a monster but a man?” The very final lines of Tim O’Brien’s novel powerfully lead us away from the circumstantial question of the protagonist’s guilt to help us measure the full ethical and philosophical scope of the novel. Indeed, the initial interrogation – “Can we believe?” – goes beyond the condemnation of the protagonist, the American would-be senator caught up in the revelation of the “monstrous” massacre of women and children he took part in during the Vietnam War, some twenty years before his ruined political campaign. The question, couched in what we may challengingly study as “literary,” takes the *inhuman* nature of a (war) crime bordering on a crime *against humanity* for granted the better to ask (us readers, fellow humans) whether we *can believe,* that is, whether we are willing to acknowledge, that monstrosity is part and parcel of our humanity.

One step further, while seeming to claim John Wade’s innocence (etymologically, no evil committed), the novel in fact implies that “human life” itself is the very source of the death drive, and its component, the destruction instinct. However, Tim O’Brien does not stop there: following the revelation of the Vietnam War episode, Wade’s wife has disappeared, and we are taught to distrust the different explanations provided by the text itself until the end. The question raised is ultimately that of all reliability, one that found itself asked at the very origin of American literature.

As this contemporary novel addresses the question of “monstrosity” through the prism of trauma, in its strictest clinical acceptation, it is tempting to bring together *In the Lake of the Woods* and Charles Brockden Brown’s 1798 ground-breaking American Gothic *Wieland; or the Transformation* and 1799 *Edgar Huntly; or Memoirs of a Sleepwalker*. Some two hundred years earlier, a hundred years before the advent of psychoanalysis, the father of American Letters had already perceived and exposed the links between monstrosity, filiation and trauma, and thus drawn the metafictional path of literature’s own questioning. Can monstrosity be anything but fiction?

After a brief part that will endeavor, by recalling Brown’s two main romances, to inscribe O’Brien’s enterprise in the lineage of the most ambitious American Gothic literature, we shall see how his novel may be read in the light of trauma theory, in order to demonstrate finally that the deconstruction of guilt is only one step away from a suspension of judgment, intimately linked to the paradoxical realization of the fictional nature of truth.

1 Filiations

"Before the beginning there is Brown," says Paul Auster's narrator in *Ghosts*. While this innocent pun on the (almost) first American writer and a color synonymous with the original earth may be a way of reestablishing the latter's importance in the New World's fiction, a preliminary word must be said about Shakespeare, undoubtedly an influence for the inventor of the American Gothic, not to mention his innumerable followers – among whom one must count O'Brien. While Iago, Caliban, and Richard III vie for the title of the arch monster in Shakespeare's universe, the crown undoubtedly, naturally, goes to the king. Iago, although seen by Coleridge as the very symbol of the "motive-hunting of motiveless Malignity,"[3] does have reasons – however self-proclaimed – to seek revenge on Othello, just as Caliban, "the deformed slave" and brutish exploited would-be rapist and murderer may well be considered as the icon of a necessary rebellion of the oppressed. Richard III, interestingly enough for us, guilty of infanticide, exactly as Wieland in Brown's novel and US soldiers in O'Brien's, alone stands as the all-assuming monster (the exact opposite of Macbeth, in a way). Some provision is later made, his physical deformity and his having been born with teeth being the possible reflection of a preordained fate, but there remains for the spectator the early Lucifer-like affirmation and vindication of monstrosity: "I am determined to prove a villain" (1.1.39) which obviously has more to do with will than pre-Darwinian determinism.[4]

Brown set out with an altogether different purpose. Wieland, his first novel-scale Gothic villain, kills his wife and children but he does so during a bout of delirium that marks his crossing the threshold of what his century called *mania mutabilis* (bipolar psychosis). As he declares at the bar of his trial – thus inducing some of our future reflections on the intersection of law and literature – he heard the voice of God ordering the quintuple bloody deed, and the monologue provides ample explanations for the reader to understand that he is not "ethically" guilty. To the end, caught up in his religious vision, he will assert that he had to obey God's command, just as Abraham had to sacrifice his only son. Infinitely revealing is the strategic position of Wieland's sister, Clara, who learns to recognize in herself the same murderous streak, that *she*, however, manages to check. The

3 A note by Samuel Taylor Coleridge, "On Shakespeare's plays," *Shakespeare and Renaissance Writers*, available at www.bl.uk/shakespeare (last access November 23, 2018).

4 My special thanks go to Pierre Iselin, Emeritus Professor of Shakespearean studies at the Sorbonne, who generously shared his invaluable knowledge during an inspiring conversation in the preparation of this paper, and to Thomas Pughe, Professor at Orléans University, who kindly proofread the final page.

decisive exculpating factor is the fact that both witnessed, when they were children, the "spontaneous combustion" of their own father, seen by the latter as God's retribution for having failed in his evangelizing mission, by outside onlookers as a scientific phenomenon attested to by medical research at the time, and attributed by reasonable readers (in spite of Clara's highly biased and unreliable account) to a human ordinary and malevolent agent.

Much of the same pattern is at work in Brown's other important novel, *Edgar Huntly; or Memoirs of a Sleepwalker*, in which the narrator's obvious signs of madness (somnambulism was definitely one at the time) and regression from a civilized overly self-confident fool to a blood-thirsty hound capable of various transgressions – among others cannibalism and the unmotivated multiple murder of Indians – are all ascribed to his attending at an early age the slaughter of his parents and sisters by "savages," strangely close to his own representation as *reddened* by the blood of his enemies. Fascinatingly enough, he is totally unaware of his somnambulism until he meets his mirror image in the person of Clithero, whom he found sleepwalking in the wilderness and whose literal roving in the *selva oscura* he will soon imitate, stopping short of falling into his Doppelgänger's incurable murderous dementia.

As I have amply demonstrated,[5] one can consider these two novels as the Ur-examples of trauma fiction in the American novel. Brown radically moved away from the "puerile superstitions and exploded manners, Gothic castles and chimeras" (Preface to *Edgar Huntly*) which he, perhaps schematically, associated with his English predecessors. By resorting to the representation of insanity – the factor common to both novels –, he displays the transgressive excess necessary to secure the interest of his audience. But he also engages in a process of explanation that testifies to an acute intuition of psychological mechanisms that were only to be unveiled some hundred years later, by Freud and Ferenczi, most notably, not to mention his resorting to the representation of the law and the search for trauma-related exculpating circumstances, paving the way for a new vision of guilt that one finds at work in much subsequent criminal fiction, let alone actual trials. As Shoshana Felman announces in the introduction to *The Juridical Unconscious:*

> I will look at the ways in which the law and legal procedures nevertheless seem to be transformed by their interaction with trauma, a transformation that calls for a reformulation and reconceptualization of what it is that the law and trials are about. A dialogue of law and trauma does occur, albeit in nonconventional and nontraditional ways. I analyze this

5 Marc Amfreville, *Charles Brockden Brown: la part du doute* (Paris: Belin, 2000); Marc Amfreville, *Ecrits en souffrance. Figures du trauma dans la littérature nord-américaine* (Paris: Michel Houdiard, 2009).

> dialogue and try to demonstrate and show concretely how the shock of the encounter with the trauma penetrates the trial and impacts the structures of the law in unpredictably reshaping the proceedings and in giving to the trial (to the drama of the law) a new jurisprudential dimension.[6]

Trauma will then be scientifically described by psychoanalysis as originating in a shock, the intensity of which precludes its assimilation by the subject's psyche. But most important for its relevance to literary works, trauma, properly understood and as defined by Freud, implies the deferment of the registration of the said shock. In other words, it takes another traumatic event to bring back the first one to consciousness. More radically expressed, a trauma actually deserves its name when and only when the subject is sent back by one occurrence to a former one, until then buried but active along two possible lines: hypermnesia: that is, the uncontrollable return of the repressed event in the form of fixed haunting images and nightmarish flashes that fail to form a coherent narrative. Or, amnesia: that is, the impossibility to remember what happened in a movement very similar to repression. Both conditions can be accompanied by either anguished nervous states or relative aboulia and depression.

As a final point of theorization that aims at making clear my confronting trauma theory with the findings of literature in the same field (as opposed to an application of the former to the latter), I would add that in the perspective that I have tried to define the very mental operations at work in these two symmetrically opposed reactions to shock concern less the psychology of the involved characters than the signifying mechanisms that *inform* the novels. In other words, while the protagonists' childhood trauma may function as psychological explanations for future inhuman actions, what matters is the way the text itself functions as structured by the defining workings of trauma, i.e. a shock that reveals a former one that in its turn creates the literary possibility – or impossibility – of its own narration. It should also be duly stressed that such a pattern precludes the mechanical assignation of clear-cut causes. Edgar Huntly is capable at various moments of transforming himself into a sanguinary monster, we learn elsewhere what happened when he was a child, but the linear causality is only suggested as *one possible* explanation that the reader may or not supply. It is along this ridge, this demanding path between waking and sleeping, between utter evil and reasons for moral atonement, that O'Brien's novel sleepwalks, or rather tries to glide on the surface of his eponymous lake, whose depths both conceal and reveal former grisly actions.

---

6 Shoshana Felman, *The Juridical Unconscious* (Cambridge Ma: Harvard University Press, 2002), 5.

2 Trauma

In O'Brien's novel, trauma does function, to a certain extent, as an explanatory device, and this of course raises the question of the foundation of the very concept of the perpetrators' trauma. Particularly illuminating in that respect is an article by Saira Mohamed, published in the *Columbia Law Review*, which, I readily admit, has shaken my conviction that our interest in trauma should be limited to victims:

> But whatever comfort or cleanness the distinction between victim and perpetrator might offer, there is value, too, to recognizing the equal humanity of the two categories, and to recognizing the capacity for the project of international criminal law to declare the commonness, the ordinariness, the humanness, of the people who commit these horrific crimes. Acknowledging trauma on the part of perpetrators might convince us that, far from monsters, these are people who make choices – choices that might be not simply stared at but understood.[7]

This leads, however, to an ethical question: should a mass-killing soldier such as the character of John Wade, who takes an active part in the historically notorious massacre of My Lai during the Vietnam war – one that involved the slaughter of about five hundred unarmed villagers, chiefly women, children and old people, suspected of Vietcong allegiance – be the subject of a fictional psychological investigation that seems to atone for his guilt? That there has not been an official recognition of that mass murder of civilians as such, let alone any compensation offered by the United States, makes the whole subject particularly sensitive, and it is indispensable to underscore that the literary work achieved by O'Brien – himself a soldier in Vietnam, and presumably present during this or other military exactions – that unearths hidden springs of action stands, at least in his own view (voiced in a note by the narrator), as remote as possible from a retroactive, obliquely self-serving, form of rehabilitation.[8]

> I arrived in-country a year after John Wade, in 1969, and walked exactly the ground he walked [. . .] I know what happened that day. I know how it happened. I know why. It was

7 Saira Mohamed, "Of Monsters and Men: Perpetrator Trauma and Mass Atrocity," *Columbia Law Review* 115 (2015): 1157–2016, 1167.

8 One must however recall that in one of the chapters entitled "Evidence," decisive lines by Judith Herman are quoted that hierarchize traumas and give pride of place to the perpetrators' condition: "The violation of human condition, and consequently the risk of a post-traumatic stress disorder, is highest when the survivor has been not merely a passive witness but also an active participant in violent death or atrocity." (ILW, 144). See Judith Herman, *Trauma and Recovery* (New York: Basic Books, 1992).

> the sunlight. It was the wickedness that soaks into your blood and slowly heats up and begins to boil. Frustration, partly. Rage partly. The enemy was invisible. They were ghosts. They killed us with land mines and booby traps; they disappeared into the night, or into tunnels, or into the deep misted-over paddies and bamboo and elephant grass. But it went beyond that. Something more mysterious. The smell of incense, maybe. The unknown, the unknowable. The blank faces. The overwhelming otherness. This is not to justify what occurred on March 16, 1968, for in my view such justifications are both futile and outrageous. Rather, it's to bear witness to the mystery of evil. Twenty-five years ago, as a terrified young PFC, I too could taste the sunlight. I could smell the sin. I could feel the butchery sizzling like grease just under my eyeballs. (ILW, 203)

However, can exposing the traumatic roots of an inhumanly violent behavior and describing the ensuing utter psychic destruction of the perpetrator clearly remain totally foreign to a move towards exculpation? The answer to this vexing question may lie in the irresolution of the plot, in the designing of constantly opposing hypotheses that forbids any kind of certainty, and leaves the reader almost as bewildered as the protagonist ("the unknowable"). Before tackling this central "legal" issue, one must try to go back to the strategy of the text.

John Wade, as briefly alluded to in my introduction, has lost the US Senate election and has come to rest in an isolated cottage on the shore of the Lake in the Woods, in northern Minnesota, with his wife Kathy. The core of the plot has to do with Kathy's mysterious disappearance and resembles, to a certain extent, a typical detective story, complete with its good-cop-bad-cop tandem. One morning, she took a motorboat, headed North and never came back. In the form of chapters entitled "Hypotheses," each contradicting the other, the reader learns that she may have eloped with a former lover, may have run away from her husband's madness, may have been killed and drowned by the latter, or may have gone to Canada where he will join her after his own disappearance to start a new life. While no indication whatsoever should lead us to privilege one interpretation over the other, only the one that involves the murder, as clearly trauma-related, will be analyzed in detail.

Studying a different novel by Coetzee, Mieke Bal offers perspectives that one can easily relate to O'Brien's:

> Structurally, narrativity moves into the discussion on a level other than that of the reconstruction of the case *per se*. Narrative knows variegated temporalities, modulated through such figures as analepsis and other "anachronies." Thus narrative is equipped to probe such issues and offer imaginative possibilities for solutions that legal practice cannot quite imitate – analogical reasoning is dangerous – but whose implications it can consider.[9]

9 Bal, "Legal Lust: Literary Litigation," 12.

Only through flashes backward and forward, do we learn little by little why John Wade lost the election. Some material was made public that revealed his active participation in the My Lai massacre, and his subsequent erasing of all evidence concerning his presence there. As the secret is divulged and terminally ruins his political career, the novel, through internal focalization, goes back to the slaughter itself, in terms as vivid as the PTSD flashes that encroach upon Wade's sleepless nights, and adds testimonies of hypothetically "real-life" soldiers, tried in the United States after the end of the war, that confirm the memories of the actual events as described in the third-person extremely crude narration of Wade's experience.

However unbearable this retrospective tale that mimics, through the juxtaposition of various sources and forms, the fragmentation of a profoundly wounded mind, the text does not stop there in its purpose to exhibit the acknowledged mechanisms of trauma. Freud himself established the structural resemblance between the traumas originating in war episodes and those more classically grounded in personal histories of either sexual predation or loss and love deprivation.

> In the traumatic and war neuroses the ego of the individual protects itself from a danger that either threatens it from without or is embodied in a form of the ego itself, in the transference neuroses of peace time the ego regards its own sexual hunger (libido) as a foe, the demands of which appear threatening to it. In both cases the ego fears an injury; in the one case through the sexual hunger (libido) and in the other from outside forces. One might even say that in the case of the war neuroses the thing feared, is after all an inner foe, in distinction from the pure traumatic neuroses and approximating to the transference neuroses. The theoretical difficulties which stand in the way of such a unifying conception do not appear to be insurmountable; one can with full right designate the repression which underlies every neurosis, as a reaction to a trauma, as an elementary traumatic neurosis.[10]

Isn't it tempting then, to envisage that a repressed personal trauma can constitute the first hidden stage of a second one that will fully develop in its pathological consequences? In the case of John Wade, the traumatic chain even resorts to three different episodes. Nearest to the present, Vietnam and more precisely the massacre of women and children. Earlier in his personal history, when he was fourteen, his father's suicide: an inassimilable wound. And earlier even, spontaneously emerging as a flash among others, his father's constantly abusing him as a little boy for his excess weight – a sadistic teasing that the

10 Sigmund Freud, "Introduction to Psychoanalysis and War Neuroses" (1919), Standard Edition of the *Complete Works*. Vol. 17. (London: Hogarth Press, 1955), 210.

boy interpreted as a lack of love and even as an expression of his father's incomprehensible hatred. Only near its ending does the novel finally unite the three moments in an accelerated all-encompassing vision that only makes sense if the reader accepts the logic-defying traumatic line of explanation:

> Yet he could not stop returning. All night long he revisited the village of Thuan Yen, always with a fresh eye, witness to the tumblings and spinnings of those who had reached their fictitious point of no return. Relatively speaking, he decided, these frazzle-eyed citizens were never quite dead, otherwise they would surely stop dying. Same-same for his father. Proof of the loop. The fucker kept hanging himself. Over and over the bastard would offer shitty counsel at the dinner table – "Stop stuffing it in" and then leap out into endless returning, his neck snapped by no point in particular, all points unknown. (ILW, 286)

The last recovered memory, chronologically the first "event," is undoubtedly the most interesting one. While the early suicide of a father may have been used as extenuating circumstances in a trial for subsequent uncontrollable violence, just as the Vietnam ordeal may serve to atone for his wife's (hypothetical) murder, no jury in their right mind would pause to consider such an apparently harmless teasing as possibly justifying any following exactions. This is precisely the point where law and literature diverge. In Mieke Bal's words: "Literature's complexity and, in a sense, lawlessness – its mission to question, not to endorse, the law – has forced its theorists to account for complexity, especially temporal complexity."[11]

Thus, starting from the recognition of a literary "complexity," we can go back to the hypothesis according to which sleepless Wade put water in a kettle and systematically boiled to their destruction every plant in the cabin. It is later clearly stated that this unaccountable violence, as the straw that broke the camel's back after various examples of an absurd behavior and her husband's irrepressible nightly howling, was the cause of Kathy's running away. The association of the destruction of the plants to his Vietnam killings « naturally » bring about the other hypothetical chapter in which he pours down the boiling water into his suddenly awoken wife's face before drowning her body in the lake: a whole page governed by a succession of "maybe(s)":

> Because he loved her? Because he could not help the teakettle from tipping itself forward... There were noises in the night – screechings – his own name, perhaps – but then the steam was in her throat... He remembered thinking how impossible it was. He would remember the heat, the voltage in his arms and wrists. Why? He thought, but he didn't

11 Bal, "Legal Lust: Literary Litigation," 15.

> know. All he knew was fury... Maybe his father. Maybe secrecy. Maybe humiliation and loss. Maybe madness. Maybe evil... He would remember darkness. (ILW, 276)

As readily conceived, the two hypotheses are conflicting and even mutually exclusive. It is the "dark" privilege of literature over law to maintain the two as equipossible, rooted not so much in an incapacity to solve a legal riddle as in the aesthetic will to maintain undecidability.

3 Identification

By means of its narrative strategies, which as we have just seen result in the reader's utter perplexity – and it should be stressed that the two vying hypotheses we have underscored are only two among four – *In the Lake of the Woods* obviously aims at leaving open the question of John Wade's guilt in the disappearance of his wife, but above all at not forcing the logic of trauma into the only possible reading of the plot. Where law, through the conflation of testimonies, needs to establish the truth of events, fiction sets itself the task of opening the realm of possibilities. The two are not necessarily as antagonistic as one may think. As Mieke Bal again suggests:

> The point of a field such as "law and literature," then, resides indeed in the mutual model function that each separate discipline can have for the other. The overlap lies in the methodological care (law) and the relentless imagining possibilities of questioning (literature); in legal and narrative logic respectively; in the need to simultaneously hold up the possibility of truth (law) and the impossibility of determining it (literature). The tensions in each of these interactions are as necessary as they are productive.[12]

The essential part of the critic's reasoning is exemplified in the juxtaposition of the words "possibility" and "impossibility" of determining the truth. Applied to our novel, such congruence between law and literature leads to the realization that the causality of trauma is both affirmed and denied, precisely as the materiality of its ultimate consequence, Kathy's murder is never attested to, or rather, it is, the better to be negated. The text thus invites us to consider the possibility of an action of earlier traumas in the protagonist's life as the trigger of his murderous deeds in Vietnam (they were **ex**actions, something occurring outside himself), but at the same time, the causal chain is fractured by the insertion of the hypothetical chapters and above all by the open ending. It is the

12 Bal, "Legal Lust: Literary Litigation," 22.

main contention of the present paper that by so doing, the writer goes further than merely indicating the somewhat hackneyed tenet according to which we could all be monsters and only place monstrosity at a distance to comfort us in the self-righteous conviction of our normality. As with all clichés, there is truth to this, but for O'Brien, the conditions for the actualization of such virtuality must remain an enigma and thus results in a crisis of truth. As Cathy Caruth has amply demonstrated, trauma has become a way for writers to represent unknowability:

> [. . .] it is this crisis of truth, the historical enigma betrayed by trauma that poses the greatest challenge to psychoanalysis and is being felt more broadly at the center of trauma research today. For the attempt to understand trauma brings one repeatedly to this peculiar paradox: that in trauma the greatest confrontation may also occur as an absolute numbing to it, that immediacy, paradoxically enough, may take the form of belatedness.[13]

O'Brien, fully aware of the poetic potentialities of this paradox, with due respect to the utter individuality of a given character's imagined personal history, however emblematic of a whole generation of young men sent to Vietnam against their will and more or less placed in the condition of becoming the sort of inhuman perpetrators he describes, symbolically resorts to the reality of trauma to represent the utter impossibility of thorough understanding. John Wade has become a stranger to himself. In Rimbaud's famous terms, "I is another," and the initial solecism suffices to describe the total rift in the subject's psyche and forces him/her to face the perhaps more perplexing realization that "Another am I."

The interplay of this "I and Other" is not without recalling the psychoanalytical frame in which the analyst, to a certain extent, identifies with his patient's suffering. As aptly underscored by Louise de Urtubay in her unfortunately untranslated paper on "Freud et l'empathie,"[14] such a process is resolutely different from empathy, even if some American Ego therapy versions of psychoanalysis tend to extol the latter. To summarize her convincing argument, you empathize with what you *consciously* recognize as yours in the other, hence with what he/she already *knows*, whereas identification is a process of approximation (coming closer), to the patient's *unconscious* that the therapist has to recognize, use and control by strict analysis of his countertransferential movements. More severe

---

13 Cathy Caruth, *Trauma. Explorations in Memory* (Baltimore, Maryland: The John Hopkins UP, 1995), 6.

14 Louise De Urtubay, "Freud et l'empathie," *Révue Française de Psychanalyse* 68.3 (2004): 863–875.

than I, Urtubay even indicts empathy as a defense mechanism against what is perceived as the risk of identification, thus depriving the timorous therapist of one of his most efficient tools. O'Brien does not empathize with his character. He identifies with him, and places us in a position to do the same. Just as a psychoanalyst, identifying with John Wade, might impart an interpretation to his fictitious patient ("Don't you think that the old peasant you almost unwittingly killed in a state of rage had to do with the father who repeatedly infuriated you?"), the reader is led to bring together different episodes, such as John's stalking his wife to find traces of her guilt and his drowning her to erase the evidence of his. One step further, identification, as opposed to mere empathy, might help us let resurface a personal buried traumatic event that, in given circumstances, could numb our moral sense and make us transgress the law, be it that of a civil code or more generally the natural law of our kind. The figuration of trauma thus becomes, in typical American Gothic fashion, a way of envisaging a virtuality of evil. "We are sleepwalkers," as Leslie Fiedler,[15] following Brockden Brown's[16] lead, put it. We may not all be monsters, but we may as well *become* monsters, and the hypothesis, both legal and literary, alone deconstructs the alien category the term implies.

To conclude what cannot be concluded since inconclusiveness is one of the lessons of trauma, one is tempted to go back, however improbable that move may appear, to Freud's theory of the Uncanny. His central idea, as well known, is that you are never more scared than by what is most familiar to you, precisely because you have repressed knowledge of the object of your fear. The monster, "a remainder of a familiar and forgotten experience" (Martin-Lavaud, 14, my translation) may well be a case in point. As radically alien as it is presented in the form of a wolf, a murderous (step)mother, an ogre, and the like, the monster has always been close to the child by dint of the fairy tales he repeatedly heard or visualized. Further even, some monsters in children's nightmares do not necessarily spring from known representations: they seem to be self-generated by a need for regression to a state in which good and evil are clearly separated, figured by distinct characters and creatures, that later find "incarnations" in fairytale monsters of all kinds.

Away from the world of childhood, perhaps radically severed from it by his own traumatic experience in Vietnam, O'Brien invents a world where utmost alterity conflates with intimate knowledge, peopled by inhumane humans that

15 Leslie Fiedler, *Love and Death in the American Novel* (New York: Criterion Books, 1960), 161.
16 Charles Brockden Brown, *Wieland; or, the Transformation*. 1798; *Edgar Huntly; or Memoirs of a Sleepwalker. The Novels and Related Works of Charles Brockden Brown*, Bicentennial edition, Sydney Krause ed. (Kent, OH: Kent State UP, 1977).

can only be "maybe-monster," engendered by the sleep *and* the dream of reason. Isn't it infinitely revealing in that respect that in the English translation of Baudelaire's[17] famous address in *The Flowers of Evil* "monster" should be made to rhyme with "brother" and "reader"?

"You know him reader, that refined monster – Hypocritish reader, – my fellow, – my brother!" A poetic conflation that certainly has to do with identification…

17 Charles Baudelaire, *The Flowers of Evil*, trans. W. Aggeler (Fresno, CA: Academy Library Guild, 1954).

Marita Nadal

Southern Gothic: The Monster as Freak in the Fiction of Flannery O'Connor

In *Love and Death in the American Novel,* a founding text in the history of American literary criticism, Leslie Fiedler argues that American fiction is "bewilderingly and embarrassingly, a gothic fiction, nonrealistic and negative, sadist and melodramatic – a literature of darkness and the grotesque in a land of light and affirmation."[1] In the same vein, Teresa Goddu points out the paradox inherent in these characteristics: "America's self-mythologization as a nation of hope and harmony directly contradicts the gothic's most basic impulses." That is why American gothic has come to be mainly analysed as a regional form, placing Southern Gothic at its centre. "By so closely associating the gothic with the South, the American literary tradition neutralizes the gothic's threat to national identity." Identified with violence and doom, "the American South has traditionally served as the nation's 'other,' becoming the repository of everything from which the nation wants to disassociate itself"[2]: racism, classism, irrationality, madness, decay, violence, religious fanaticism, poverty, rural parochialism and sexual deviance. Southern Gothic explores all these subjects, showing a particular fixation with the grotesque – that is, the juxtaposition of contrasting or even incompatible elements – and its aberrant creatures: its freaks.

Significantly, the fiction of Flannery O'Connor epitomizes all these characteristics, foregrounding, in a humorous tone, the grotesque and its peculiar protagonists, which O'Connor herself described as "freaks." Although she explores the darkly comic potential of these grotesque characters with a religious intention, their impact and symbolic role evoke the significance traditionally conveyed by the figure of the monster. As will be discussed below, O'Connor's fiction highlights the disrupting and revelatory power of the freak, despite its apparent marginality; moreover, her narrative portrays the freak in the light of a specific context, exemplifying that monsters in their diverse manifestations embody and reflect the historical, cultural and social features of the country and period in which they appear. As Judith Halberstam argues, [m]onstrosity

1 Leslie Fiedler, *Love and Death in the American Novel* [1960] (Harmondsworth: Penguin, 1984), 29.

2 Teresa Goddu, *Gothic America: Narrative, History, and Nation* (New York: Columbia University Press, 1997), 3–4, 76.

https://doi.org/10.1515/9783110654615-013

(and the fear it gives rise to) is historically conditioned rather than a psychological universal."[3]

The term monster – "perhaps the earliest and most enduring name for the singular body"[4] – derives from the Latin terms *monstrum* and *monere*, which convey a two-fold meaning: not only to show or reveal (*monstrum*), but also to warn and instruct (*monere*). From ancient times, monsters were invested with supernatural meanings: in fact, "they were taken as a showing forth of divine will from antiquity until the hand of God seemingly loosed its grip on the world." Just as the word monster implies otherness and bodily difference, the term freak – whose etymology is not so clear – describes "capricious variegation or sudden, erratic change."[5] It evokes the singular, unusual and abnormal. The phrase "freak of nature," coined in the first decades of the 19th century, came to be applied to abnormal individuals of diverse origins that were exhibited as spectacles of amusement in carnivals and sideshows: albinos, bearded women, Siamese twins, armless and legless wonders, giants, midget triplets, and hermaphrodites, for instance. As Rosemarie G. Thomson argues, freaks exemplify the movement "from a narrative of the marvelous to a narrative of the deviant":

> As modernity develops in Western culture, freak discourse logs the change: the prodigious monster transforms into the pathological terata; what was once sought after as revelation becomes pursued as entertainment; what aroused awe now inspires horror; what was taken as a portent shifts to a site of progress. In brief, wonder becomes error.[6]

In O'Connor's fiction, freaks are no longer prodigious monsters, but peculiar figures that constitute an instrument of revelation rather than a source of entertainment; their freakery has more to do with eccentric behaviour and moral deviance than with corporeal anomaly. In one of her essays, O'Connor discusses the figure of the freak as typical of Southern writing:

> Whenever I'm asked why Southern writers particularly have a penchant for writing about freaks, I say it is because we are still able to recognize one. To be able to recognize a freak, you have to have some conception of the whole man, and in the South the general conception of man is still, in the main, theological.[. . .]. I think it is safe to say that while

3 Judith Halberstam, *Skin Shows: Gothic Horror and the Technology of Monsters* (Durham and London: Duke University Press, 1995), 6.
4 Rosemarie Garland Thomson, "Introduction: From Wonder to Error – A Genealogy of Freak Discourse in Modernity," in *Freakery: Cultural Spectacles of the Extraordinary Body*, ed. R. Garland Thomson (New York and London: New York University Press, 1996), 1–19, 3.
5 Thomson, "Introduction," 3–4.
6 Thomson, "Introduction," 3.

> the South is hardly Christ-centered, it is most certainly Christ-haunted. The Southerner, who isn't convinced of it, is very much afraid that he may have been formed in the image and likeness of God. Ghosts can be very fierce and instructive. They cast strange shadows, particularly in our literature. In any case, it is when the freak can be sensed as a figure for our essential displacement that he attains some depth in literature.[7]

For O'Connor, the literary freak should produce a shocking effect, and above all, convey transcendental values, given her Christian and Catholic concerns. It is significant that her discussion of this figure appears included in an essay titled "Some Aspects of the Grotesque in Southern Fiction." In her analysis of the grotesque, she foregrounds the features of distortion and eccentricity, possibility rather than probability. Distortion should not destroy, but contribute to the final revelation: "Distortion in this case is an instrument; exaggeration has a purpose [. . .]. This is not the kind of distortion that destroys; it is the kind that reveals, or should reveal" (MM, 162).[8] O'Connor describes this kind of fiction as "wild, [. . .] violent and comic, because of the discrepancies that it seeks to combine" (MM, 43). In her letters, O'Connor similarly foregrounds the mixture of humour and terror in the description of her fiction: "everything funny I have written is more terrible than it is funny, or only funny because it is terrible, or only terrible because it is funny."[9]

In O'Connor's fiction, violence is never an end in itself. She makes use of it because, as she argues, "violence is strangely capable of returning my characters to reality and preparing them to accept their moment of grace": "It is the extreme situation that best reveals what we are essentially" (MM, 112–113).

---

7 Flannery O'Connor, *Mystery and Manners* [1969], eds. Sally and Robert Fitzgerald (New York: Farrar, Straus and Giroux, 1970), 44–45. Further references in the text abbreviated as MM.

8 The grotesque is a term "applied to a decorative art in sculpture, painting, and architecture, characterized by fantastic representations of human and animal forms often combined into formal distortions to the point of absurdity, ugliness, or caricature. It was so named after the ancient paintings and decorations found in the underground chambers (*grotte*) of Roman ruins. By extension, *grotesque* is applied to anything having the qualities of *grotesque* art: bizarre, incongruous, ugly, unnatural, fantastic, abnormal." William Harmon, *A Handbook to Literature* [1936] (Upper Saddle River: Prentice Hall, 2006), 244.

Molly Boyd adds that the "crucial element in defining the grotesque, however, is the juxtaposition or fusion of contrasting, paradoxical, and incompatible elements, such as an impossible or horrific event narrated matter-of-factly and with great detail, often provoking a humorous response." Molly Boyd, "The Grotesque," in *The Companion to Southern Literature: Themes, Genres, Places, People, Movements, and Motifs*, eds. Joseph M. Flora and Lucinda H. MacKethan (Baton Rouge: Louisiana University Press, 2002) 321–324, 321.

9 Flannery O'Connor, *The Habit of Being*, ed. Sally Fitzgerald (New York: Farrar, Straus and Giroux, 1979), 105.

O'Connor highlights the juxtaposition of "evil and grace," even if her characters may not be fully conscious of their encounter with the latter. It is remarkable that the freak, sometimes a devilish figure in O'Connor's fiction, becomes the instrument of revelation, the character that provokes the epiphany – the moment of grace. As has been pointed out, this epiphany has a two-fold significance in her fiction: "an appearance or manifestation of a divine being," and "a sudden manifestation or intuitive grasp of the essential nature or meaning of reality through something usually simple and striking." [10] The point is that, frequently, the result of the epiphany is not sufficiently clarified in the text, which generates ambiguity and critical controversy, as many critics have pointed out:

> The wealth of these dualities and paradoxes in O'Connor's fiction – the irony, the symbolic images, narrative displacement, and grotesque epiphanies – amplify the confusion and discomfort of the reader and render her fiction perhaps the most technically complex representation of the modern use of the grotesque.[11]

On the one hand, this ambiguity has to do with O'Connor's preference for "showing" rather than "telling" as a narrative technique, that is, her determination to avoid authorial intrusion: "The writer's moral sense must coincide with his dramatic sense," she remarks (MM, 76). On the other, the confusion is also related to O'Connor's original combination of elements: her intention to evoke mystery and grace through the concrete. She's "looking for one image that will connect or combine or embody two points; one is a point in the concrete, and the other is a point not visible to the naked eye" (MM, 42). Therefore, the fictional qualities of the grotesque characters she envisions "lean away from typical social patterns, toward mystery and the unexpected" (MM, 40). That is how she describes her literary strategies:

> The peculiar problem of the short-story writer is how to make the action he describes reveal as much of the mystery of existence as possible. He has only a short space to do it in and he can't do it by statement. He has to do it by showing, not by saying, and by showing the concrete – so that his problem is really how to make the concrete work double time for him. (MM, 98)

In any case, monsters, by definition, "produce meaning that is beyond any one category of identification."[12] Furthermore, the passing of time has altered

10 Boyd, "The Grotesque," 323.
11 Boyd, "The Grotesque," 324.
12 Marina Levina and Diem-My T. Bui, "Introduction: Toward a Comprehensive Monster Theory in the 21st Century," in *Monster Culture in the 21st Century: A Reader*, eds. Marina Levina and Diem-My T. Bui (New York: Bloomsbury): 1–13, 5.

the perception of O'Connor's work, disclosing its anticipatory power and increasing relevance. Thus, her fiction has become more realistic and less grotesque than it appeared to be in the nineteen fifties. As Harold Bloom argues, in "our new Age of Terror, with trade towers crumbling and anthrax spilling out of letters [. . .] our lives perforce turn more grotesque," while "her fiction is likely to seem even more relevant." [13]

O'Connor's freaks prove to be not only "figures for our essential displacement," as she argues, but also, emblems and reflections of American consciousness. As Scott Poole notes, American monsters "have a history coincident with a national history," that is, they are productive and representative of meanings associated with specific contexts and their historical discourses:

> American monsters are born out of American history. [. . .]. They are living representations of our darkness, simultaneously metaphors and progenitors of the American way of fear and violence. They are creatures of American history, their many permutations in folklore and pop culture impossible to explain without that complex history. American history can best be understood through America's monsters.[14]

Furthermore, O'Connor's freaks are also representatives of contemporary American society and culture because their monstrosity passes unnoticed. As Weinstock argues, "modern monsters are no longer visible to the naked eye"; "they are virtually indistinguishable [. . .] from the rank and file of humanity."[15] Monsters are *us*, O'Connor suggests both in her fiction and in her essays: "The freak in modern fiction is usually disturbing to us because he keeps us from forgetting that we share in his state" (MM, 133).

The tale "A Good Man Is Hard To Find" (1953) is an appropriate point of departure to analyse O'Connor's freaks. In it, a family of six members – which includes a grandmother, two young children, a baby and their parents – leaves Atlanta for a short trip in Florida, but they never reach their destination. On their way they meet the Misfit, a dangerous criminal escaped from the Federal Pen, who kills them one by one. Only the cat, taken by the grandmother without her son's knowledge, and partly responsible for the accident, survives the killing. No doubt, the story – "wild, violent and comic" – foregrounds distortion and depicts all its characters as freaks. Thus, the members of this family

13 Harold Bloom, "Flannery O'Connor," in *Genius: A Mosaic of One Hundred Exemplary Creative Minds* (Fourth Estate: London, 2002): 575–579, 575.

14 W. Scott Poole, *Monsters in America: Our Historical Obsession with the Hideous and the Haunting* (Waco, Texas: Baylor University Press, 2011), 18, 4.

15 Jeffrey Andrew Weinstock, "American Monsters," in *A Companion to American Gothic*, ed. Charles L. Crow (Malden and Oxford: Wiley Blackwell, 2014): 41–55, 45.

have nothing to do with the image of a traditional Southern family; on the contrary, and despite the conservatism associated with the nineteen fifties, they anticipate characteristics of present-day average or even dysfunctional families.

The children's mother, with her face "as a cabbage" and her head-kerchief with "two points on the top like a rabbit's ears,"[16] appears so stupid that is not even fit to stand for the parody of the Southern Belle or lady: in an absurd and comic fashion, she answers "Yes, thank you" (GM, 131) to the Misfit's request to follow her killers and join her dead husband. Most likely, O'Connor parodies here the Southern overemphasis on manners. In turn, Bailey, the children's father, ineffectual and weak, proves incapable of handling his own family, and therefore, even more inadequate to confront the Misfit. His freakishness is emphasised by the ludicrous pattern of his shirt – yellow with bright blue parrots – a pattern that suggests not only a strident style, but also an imitative personality. As for the children, they are not only quarrelsome and impolite, but also perverse. We can now recall their shocking reaction after their car has turned over: " 'We've had an ACCIDENT,' the children screamed in a frenzy of delight. 'But nobody's killed,' June Star said with disappointment" (GM, 125).

The most peculiar characters in the tale are the protagonists: the grandmother and the Misfit. It is the dialogue between them that conveys the coming of grace and the grandmother's epiphany. Ironically, the violent Misfit becomes the disrupting agent of revelation, and the pious and hypocritical grandmother, the recipient of grace. Their conversation – serious and comical at the same time – highlights opposing approaches to life and religion. The grandmother betrays her selfishness, shallow faith, and hypocrisy through her repetitive silly phrases, full of clichés, intended to postpone of even avoid death, such as "You wouldn't shoot a lady, would you?," or "I know you're a good man. You don't look a bit like you have common blood." She even advises the Misfit to pray: "If you would pray, [. . .] Jesus would help you" (GM, 130).

However, the Misfit is too proud to ask for help. His words and behaviour portray him as frank and good-mannered, but also as a sadist and a fundamentalist:

> "Jesus was the only One that ever raised the dead [. . .] and He shouldn't have done it. He thrown everything off balance. If He did what He said, then it's nothing for you to do but throw away everything and follow Him, and if He didn't, then it's nothing for you to do but enjoy the few minutes you got left the best you can by killing somebody or burning down his house or doing some other meanness to him. No pleasure but meanness." (GM, 132)

16 Flannery O'Connor, *The Complete Stories* (London: Faber and Faber, 1990), 117. Further references in the text abbreviated as GM.

All these features depict the Misfit as a tormented quester, as O'Connor intended, but they mainly reflect two elements that are central in contemporary American society: capricious violence and religious fundamentalism. In fact, the Misfit embodies the figure of the serial killer, the most dangerous and prevalent kind of monster in the US today. Accordingly, he also epitomizes the disconnection between appearance and monstrosity. After the shooting of Bailey, the Misfit puts on Bailey's blue parrot shirt, a detail of revealing significance: on the one hand, it suggests the invisibility of monsters – their ordinary and even familiar appearance – and on the other, as O'Connor intended, it evokes the "ties of kinship" (MM, 112) that connect humankind as a whole, contributing to the grandmother's epiphany: "the grandmother's head cleared for an instant. She saw the man's face twisted close to her own as if he were going to cry and she murmured, 'Why you're one of my babies. You're one of my own children!' She reached out and touched him on the shoulder" (GM, 132).

In turn, the Misfit's words at the very end of the tale – "It's no real pleasure in life" – which contrasts with his previous "No pleasure but meanness" (GM, 132, 133), might suggest that he has also experienced his own epiphany, and therefore a change for the better, as O'Connor's comments appear to indicate: "I don't want to equate the Misfit with the devil. I prefer to think that, however unlikely this may seem, the old lady's gesture, like the mustard-seed, will grow to be a great crow-filled tree in the Misfit's heart, and will be enough of a pain to him there to turn him into the prophet he was meant to become" (MM, 112, 113). However, as pointed out above, the epiphanies of O'Connor's fiction are far from transparent, and this tale provides a good example of such ambiguity. In short: the evidence provided by the text tends to highlight brutality, sadism, and finally nihilism, since, as the Misfit concludes, even serial killing has become meaningless: "Shut up, Bobby Lee [. . .] It's no real pleasure in life" (GM, 133).

In "Good Country People" (1955), O'Connor explores nihilism and freakishness in a more clear manner, while violence is more subdued. The story focuses on the female body, especially that of its pretentious and frustrated protagonist, a "bloated, rude, squint-eyed" thirty-two-year-old girl who lives with her divorced mother on a farm.[17] In this case, the character's physical singularity suggests her moral deformity. She has a wooden leg and a Ph.D. in philosophy, is proud of her nihilism and abhors the conventional personality of people like her mother, Mrs. Hopewell, and her employee, Mrs. Freeman. She lives in a

17 Flannery O'Connor, *The Complete Stories* (London: Faber and Faber, 1990), 276. Further references in the text abbreviated as GCP.

state of "constant outrage" (GCP, 273) against the two of them, her surroundings, and the world at large. Although her name is Joy, she has renamed herself with a most horrible one, Hulga, "on the basis of its ugly sound" (GCP, 275).[18] Hulga doesn't like "cats or birds or flowers or nature or young nice men." If it had not been for her serious heart ailment, "she would be far from these red hills and good country people" (GCP, 276).

When a travelling Bible-seller comes to her house – an apparently naive young man, with the phallic name of Manley Pointer – Hulga, sexually inexperienced, decides to seduce him, if only to show her intellectual superiority, taking for granted that he is "just good country people" (GCP, 290). As the dénouement discloses, the Bible seller proves to be a cheat and a fraud, that is, a dangerous freak: after stealing Hulga's glasses and wooden leg, he leaves her stranded in a barn loft – literally disabled – and emotionally raped. And contrary to Hulga's assumptions, his suitcase does not contain bibles, but a flask of whiskey, condoms, and a pack of cards with obscene pictures on their back.

While at the beginning of their fateful date Hulga tries to impress Pointer by boasting about her nihilism with phrases such as: "I don't have illusions. I'm one of those people who see *through* to nothing" (GCP, 287), it is the apparently innocent visitor who conveys the greatest shock – and the final revelation. In reply to Hulga's accusing words "You're a fine Christian," he says:

> "I hope you don't think [...] that I believe in that crap! I may sell Bibles but I know which end is up and I wasn't born yesterday and I know where I'm going! [...]. And I'll tell you another thing, Hulga, [...] you ain't so smart. I been believing in nothing ever since I was born!" (GCP, 290–291)

As in the previous tale, it is through the encounter with the violent and freakish Other that the central character experiences her epiphany, the illumination of grace, and learns that the antagonist is not as different from oneself as she had assumed. But apart from this spiritual message, which O'Connor carefully devised, "Good Country People" conveys a kind of freakishness that the passing of time has made more relevant, both in literature and in real life. Thus, Hulga represents not only the opposite of Southern womanhood or the parody of the traditional Southern Belle (beautiful, religious, submissive, pure, innocent, and feminine), but above all – despite her immature behaviour – she anticipates a

---

18 As Ralph Wood explains, for Hulga's mother, the name evokes "the broad blank hull of a battleship." Yet, "when Flannery O'Connor visited East Texas State College in November 1962, she gave her own version of the name's origin. She said that it came to her in a moment of sheer inspiration, as a hybrid between 'huge' and 'ugly.'" Ralph C. Wood, *Flannery O'Connor and the Christ-Haunted South* (Grand Rapids, Michigan: Eerdmans, 2004), 200.

new type of woman who spread in the nineteen sixties with the emergence of Second-Wave Feminism: atheist, rebellious, intellectual, at odds with conventions and domesticity and eager to escape parental control. The Bible-seller is attracted by her singularity in a way that evokes the freak shows of the past, very popular in the US in the first half of the 20th century: "He was gazing at her with open curiosity, with fascination, like a child watching a new fantastic animal at the zoo" (GCP, 283). Similarly, Mrs. Freeman, a character that foreshadows Manley Pointer, is also fascinated by the abnormal and the bizarre, and in particular by Hulga's grotesque body and artificial leg:

> Mrs. Freeman had a special fondness for the details of secret infections, hidden deformities, assaults upon children. Of diseases, she preferred the lingering or incurable. Hulga had heard Mrs. Hopewell give her the details of the hunting accident, how the leg had been literally blasted off, how she had never lost consciousness. Mrs. Freeman could listen to it any time as if it had happened an hour ago. (GCP, 275)

While Mrs. Freeman is entranced by Hulga's large and peculiar looks, her own appearance is also remarkable, as the narrator observes: Mrs. Freeman's expression is compared to "the advance of a heavy track" and her physical presence to "several grain sacks thrown on top of each other" (GCP, 271). In a similar manner, the description of Mrs. Freeman's daughters, Glynese and Carramae (Glycerin and Caramel in Hulga's version of their names) magnifies the physicality and femininity that Hulga despises. As has been pointed out, "Good Country People" is mainly concerned with "the vicissitudes of being female," "the burdens of fleshly life" and "the physical difficulties of women's lives."[19] No doubt, the images of weight and heaviness associated with these women highlight their bulkiness and physical features, but also underscore their vulnerability. Moreover, the freakishness and humorous tone of the narrative intensify rather than diminish the verisimilitude of the female characters' portrayal as well as that of their surroundings: that is, their belonging to a distinct spatial and temporal context.

On the other hand, the figure of the travelling salesman – a popular type in Southern humour[20] and in this tale the devilish and unexpected agent of grace – prefigures a more sinister kind of monster: the sexual fetishist and psychopath, obsessed with the female body and with collecting women's prosthetic or non-prosthetic parts. In fact, this mysterious stranger, caller and

19 Sarah Gordon, *Flannery O'Connor: The Obedient Imagination* (Athens and London: University of Georgia Press, 2000), 177, 180.

20 Cf. Richard Gray, *Southern Aberrations: Writers of the American South and the Problems of Regionalism* (Baton Rouge: Lousiana State University Press, 2000), 408.

visitor, recurrently found in literature and film, typifies sexual aggression and also the figure of Death, and anticipates characters like Arnold Friend in Joyce Carol Oates's well-known story "Where Are You Going, Where Have You Been" (1966). It is worth pointing out that the psychopath in Oates's text, Arnold Friend, is based on a real one, Charles Schmid, also known as "The Pied Piper of Tucson," charged with the rape and murder of three young women in the mid nineteen sixties.

Last but not least, O'Connor's first novel, *Wise Blood* (1952) – probably "O'Connor's most interesting and challenging text"[21] – deserves analysis, since it brilliantly epitomizes the characteristics of Southern Gothic: violence, religious fundamentalism, the grotesque, and the figure of the freak. As Margaret Earley Whitt remarks, the first reviewers of *Wise Blood* were quick to notice that its characters "were beyond strange." *The New York Times Book Review* said about them: "they seem not to belong to the human race at all." Other journals highlighted the novel's "oddness," its "strange, predatory people," and "its insane world, peopled by monsters and submen."[22]

The novel's plot explores the divergent quest for meaning performed by two young men in a post-war Southern town. The central character, Hazel Motes, recently discharged from service in the Second Word War, returns to the South to meet his family. As he finds no relatives and his home in ruins, he takes a train to the city, where inspired by a street preacher and the memories of his own grandfather – a wandering preacher who had Jesus "hidden in his head like a stinger" [23] – he creates his own church: the Church Without Christ. Most likely, the traumas inflicted by the war have turned his innate religiosity into a monstrous obsession, since, as the narrator remarks in the first chapter, Hazel "knew by the time he was twelve years old that he was going to be a preacher" (WB, 13). This is the furious way Hazel describes his anti-Christian Church:

> "Well, I preach the Church Without Christ. I'm member and preacher to that church where the blind don't see and the lame don't walk and what's dead stays that way. [...]. I'm going to preach there was no Fall because there was nothing to fall from and no Redemption because there was no Fall and no Judgment because there wasn't the first two. Nothing matters but that Jesus was a liar." (WB, 70–71)

21 Marshall Bruce Gentry, *Flannery O'Connor's Religion of the Grotesque* (Jackson: University Press of Mississippi, 1986), 119.

22 Margaret Earley Whitt, *Understanding Flannery O'Connor* (Columbia: University of South Carolina Press, 1995), 15.

23 Flannery O'Connor, *Wise Blood* [1952] (London: Faber and Faber, 1996), 11, further references in the text abbreviated as WB.

His aberrant behaviour reaches its peak when he runs over with his car a man who has been hired to impersonate Hazel and get the money that he has refused to take for his street-preaching. After this murder and the loss of his car, Hazel buys a sack of quicklime, returns to the boarding house, blinds himself, and starts a life of penance.[24] He wraps his body with barbed wire, puts pebbles in his shoes and hardly eats. "I'm not clean, he repeats" (WB, 154). Finally, Hazel abandons the rooming house, in part due to the landlady's marriage proposals; a few days later, a policeman finds him lying unconscious in a ditch and strikes him over the head with his billy club. Hazel dies in the squad car, but the policemen do not notice it and take him back to his lodgings. The landlady talks to him and observes his face, "stern and tranquil" (WB, 159). It is by looking into Hazel's eyes – with her eyes shut – that she experiences the epiphany that closes the novel:

> She had never observed his face more composed and she grabbed his hand and held it to her heart. It was resistless and dry. The outline of a skull was plain under his skin and the deep burned eye sockets seemed to lead into the dark tunnel where he had disappeared. She leaned closer and closer to his face, looking deep into them, trying to see how she had been cheated or what had cheated her, but she couldn't see anything. She shut her eyes and saw the pin point of light but so far away that she could not hold it steady in her mind. She felt as if she were blocked at the entrance of something. She sat staring with her eyes shut, into his eyes, and felt as if she had finally got to the beginning of something she couldn't begin, and she saw him moving farther and farther away, farther and farther into the darkness until he was the pin point of light. (WB, 160)

Undoubtedly, Hazel Motes is one of the most powerful figures in O'Connor's fiction: she described him as "a Christian *malgré lui*," finally unable "to get rid of the ragged figure [Jesus] who moves from tree to tree in the back of his mind."[25] His final asceticism brings to mind the mortification of saints, and especially the life of Saint Paul, also blind for a time and a violent persecutor of Christians before his conversion. In any case, it is clear that Hazel's freakishness embodies the defining features of Southern Gothic: violence and self-inflicted violence,

24 In *Mystery and Manners*, O'Connor emphasises the symbolic role of Hazel's car: "the hero's rat-color automobile is his pulpit and his coffin as well as something he thinks of as a means of escape. He is mistaken in thinking that it is a means of escape, of course, and does not really escape his predicament until the car is destroyed by the patrolman. The car is a kind of death-in-life symbol, as his blindness is a life-in-death symbol. The fact that these meanings are there makes the book significant" (MM, 72). What Hazel arrogantly says about his car is equally significant, especially considering that it is a second-hand, dilapidated vehicle: "Nobody with a good car needs to be justified" (WB, 76).

25 Flannery O'Connor, "Author's Note to the Second Edition," in *Wise Blood* (London: Faber and Faber, 1996), xiii.

murder, bigotry, fanaticism and religious fundamentalism. In a self-reflexive manner, the words of Hazel's landlady to his tenant about his eccentric behaviour encapsulate the freakishness of the novel's plot: "Well, it's not normal. It's like one of them gory stories, it's something that people have quit doing – like boiling in oil or being a saint or walling up cats [...]. There's no reason for it. People have quit doing it" (WB, 154). However, the monstrosity that Hazel represents has not disappeared. On the contrary, it has transcended the boundaries of the American South to suggest the globalization of violence and religious fanaticism, which many times erupt through terrorist attacks. Furthermore, Hazel's freakishness prefigures a variety of contemporary aberrations, such as eating disorders, fornication with minors, and self-mutilation.

In contrast to this character, *Wise Blood* portrays Hazel's foil, an eighteen-year-old boy called Enoch Emery who works in a zoo and becomes obsessed with a "dead shriveled-up part-nigger dwarf" (WB, 120), a mummified figure shown in the city's museum. One day, Enoch steals the mummy and offers it to Hazel as "the new jesus," the idol that the Church Without Christ needs but which Hazel rejects and destroys. After a series of solitary, erratic moves, Enoch stabs a man disguised as Gonga – the "Giant Jungle Monarch" (WB, 121) – to promote a film, steals his gorilla costume, buries his own clothes – not noticing that he was "burying his former self" (WB, 135) – and puts on the stolen costume. As the narrator says: "No gorilla in existence, whether in the jungles of Africa or California, or in New York City in the finest apartments in the world, was happier at that moment than this one, whose god had finally rewarded it" (WB, 136).

In different ways, the narrative portrays Enoch's degradation and his progressive descent into bestiality. Proud of his wise blood, he thinks he's destined for a great mission; he wants "to be THE new man of the future," and "to see a line of people waiting to shake his hand" (WB, 131). In fact, he is just a lonely and alienated youth, "given to stealing," with "a fondness for Supermarkets" (WB, 89), and fascinated by the sensationalism on display at the movie theaters.

As could be expected, the subject-matter of the films on show mirrors the violence and freakishness of the novel's plot: after seeing a poster that shows "a monster stuffing a young woman into an incinerator," Enoch cannot resist watching three pictures in succession. The first is about a scientist named "The Eye" who can mutilate and steal body parts by remote control; the second, about life "at Devil's Island Penitentiary"; the third, "about a baboon named Lonnie who rescued attractive children from a burning orphanage" (WB, 95). Already a thief, Enoch does not become a scientist, but chooses to turn into an ape, trying to imitate the popularity of Gonga and Lonnie. However, rather than attract people's attention and affection, Enoch only causes them to flee in terror at his sight. Mimicking the looks of the mummified figure, he has dwarfed himself into an "it," "hideous and black" (WB, 136).

While Hazel's freakishness moves towards introspection, asceticism and spirituality, Enoch's turns towards materialism, degradation and bestiality.[26] Their pathways become increasingly divergent, but both characters reflect the nihilism, insanity, fragmentation and alienation characteristic of contemporary urban life: in fact, the novel's barren landscape resembles a Southern version of T.S. Eliot's *Waste Land.*[27] Ten years after its publication, O'Connor described *Wise Blood* as a "comic novel" which is "very serious."[28] Now, several decades after, the novel looks darker and more realistic, and the sources of its humour, more disturbing and controversial than ever.

To conclude: O'Connor's freaks, apparently ludicrous and marginal, have a powerful, subversive, and prophetic potential: they are multivalent figures who become recipients of grace and/or instruments of revelation. Their seeming otherness – which mirrors that symbolized by the American South – unveils radical truths, provoking disruption and change. Despite their arrogant, hubristic or even devilish nature, they convey the possibility of grace and the power of mystery. They are freaks of culture, rather than freaks of nature, that is, they absorb meaning out of their historical and social context (the rural and conservative South of the nineteen fifties; the bleak urban landscapes populated by outcasts, hustlers, preachers and crooks) and invest that context with meaning. It is worth noting that despite her Roman Catholicism, O'Connor's epiphanies

---

26 The protagonist's name symbolises vision: in Hebrew, Hazel means "he who sees God"; the shortened name, Haze, suggests difficulty to see clearly. Motes alludes to the passage in the Gospel of Matthew (7:3–5) in which Jesus condemns judging others: "And why seest thou the mote that is in thy brother's eye, but seest not the beam that is in thy own eye?" Ironically, Hazel is unable to see well until he blinds himself. Enoch's name is also biblical, and reflects the character's fragmentation, since it refers to two opposing biblical figures, Enoch, the father of Methuselah, and Enoch, the son of Cain. As Jordan Cofer argues, "Enoch's bifurcation [between the spiritual and the carnal] helps readers to understand Enoch's ultimate choice toward the physical (Enoch, son of Cain), an explanation for his exit from the novel in a gorilla suit." Jordan Cofer, *The Gospel According to Flannery O'Connor: Examining the Role of the Bible in Flannery O'Connor's Fiction* (New York: Bloomsbury, 2014), 44–46.

27 Several critics have pointed out the influence of Eliot's poem on *Wise Blood*. For example, Sally Fitzgerald, O'Connor's editor and friend, argues that although writers such as Sophocles, E.A. Poe, and Nathaniel West were sources of inspiration for this novel, "it was Eliot and his *Waste Land* who provided for [O'Connor] the first impetus to write such a book as *Wise Blood* at all." Sally Fitzgerald, "The Owl and the Nightingale," *Flannery O'Connor Bulletin* 13 (1984): 44–58, 55.

28 O'Connor, "Author's Note," xiii.

are not precipitated by love, but by violence, which associates her fiction with the notion of "regeneration through violence," an element of great mythical significance in the history and culture of the US.[29] She located it in the reactionary, underdeveloped, Christ-haunted South – her homeland – but the violence and monstrosity embodied by O'Connor's freaks have transcended their grotesque patterns and their spatio-temporal boundaries to form part of our daily life – to become the emblem of the human condition in the 21st century.[30]

29 See Richard Slotkin, *Gunfighter Nation: The Myth of the Frontier in Twentieth-Century America* (Norman: University of Oklahoma Press, 1998).

30 The research carried out for the writing of this article is part of a project financed by the Spanish Ministry of Economy, Industry and Competitiveness (MINECO) and the European Regional Development Fund (DGI/ERDF) (code FFI2015-63506P). The author is also grateful for the support of the Government of Aragón and the European Social Fund (code H03_17R).

4 Monstrosity and Migration

Annalisa Ciampi

Kafka's *Trial* and the EU Dublin Asylum System

1 Structure of the essay

This essay examines the complex legal framework put in to place by the European Union (EU) in the implementation of its common asylum policy (the so-called Dublin asylum system) with a view to unveiling the many paradoxes, contradictions and flows – the *monstrosities*, that the system entails.

Paragraph 2 explains the basics of the system, the perverse logic underpinning it and the performance of this set of rules. As it will be shown, the causes lay in the geographical and socio-economic-political context of the EU member states and the wider world. If not immutable, this context is certainly not subject to change in the short term.

The *monstrosities* of the system are further discussed in paragraph 3 through the narrative of Kafka's trial – an enduring trial, where the possibilities of acquittal are always elusive, and a tragic end is always in sight. The defendants are sometimes alternatively, most times simultaneously the EU member states disproportionally affected by the migration phenomenon (Italy in the first place, together with the other Mediterranean countries) and the asylum seekers and other migrants dying in their journey to reach the European soil or *refouled* to their country of origin and/or met with inhuman reception conditions.

The "alternative" possibilities of actual acquittal, apparent acquittal and prolongation of Kafkaesque trial set up under the EU asylum policy, are exposed in paragraph 4.

Paragraph 5 attempts but fails to rewrite the end of the story – with the EU itself as a *monster* and a victim, among many others, of its own policies.

2 The EU legal rules, geography and international context

States are generally free to admit (or not to admit) and expel foreign nationals. This rule, however, is subject to the principle of *non-refoulement*, which underpins both the international regime for the protection of refugees and international human rights law.

https://doi.org/10.1515/9783110654615-014

The origin of *non-refoulement* is in the UN Convention Relating to the Status of Refugees of 1951 – now ratified by 145 states parties. The Convention defines the term "refugee" and outlines the rights of the displaced, and the obligations arising for states in relation thereto.

A refugee is any person who "owing to well-founded fear of being persecuted for reasons of race, religion, nationality, membership of a particular social group or political opinion, is outside the country of his nationality and is unable or, owing to such fear, is unwilling to avail himself of the protection of that country; or who, not having a nationality and being outside the country of his former habitual residence as a result of such events, is unable or, owing to such fear, is unwilling to return to it."

The principle of *non-refoulement* asserts that refugees shall not be returned to a country where they face serious threats to their life or freedom. This obligation is now considered a rule of customary international law, as such binding upon states, international organizations and other international actors, irrespective of ratification of the Refugee Convention or other treaty commitments.

International human rights law has widened the specific refugee protection regime, as it now prohibits for "everyone" – not only persons qualifying for refugee status – the return to situations where there is a real risk of torture or inhuman or degrading treatment or punishments.

The EU is committed to respect these principles. The EU Charter of Fundamental Rights provides for the right to asylum with due respect for the rules of the Geneva Convention of 1951 in Article 18. The prohibition of *refoulement* is enshrined in Article 19.[1] In addition, the EU not only ensures the right of refugees to be granted asylum. It also offers "subsidiary protection" to non-EU nationals or stateless persons who do not qualify as refugees, but in respect of whom there exists a real risk of suffering serious harm because of a death sentence, torture, or, serious and individual threat to life or person by reason of indiscriminate violence in situations of international or internal armed conflict in their country of origin.

1 Under Art. 78 of the Treaty on the Functioning of the EU (TFEU): "1. The Union shall develop a common policy on asylum, subsidiary protection and temporary protection with a view to offering appropriate status to any third-country national requiring international protection and ensuring compliance with the principle of non-refoulement. This policy must be in accordance with the Geneva Convention of 28 July 1951 and the Protocol of 31 January 1967 relating to the status of refugees, and other relevant treaties."

The so-called Common European Asylum System (CEAS) is a set of EU laws, completed in 2005 (at the time of writing under revision),[2] intended to ensure that all EU member states protect the rights of asylum seekers and refugees. Despite its name, however, a true common system has yet to be established.

The existing system consists of minimum standards and procedures for processing and deciding asylum applications, and for the treatment of both asylum seekers and those who are recognized as refugees. Implementation of CEAS, however, varies throughout the EU and a number of member states still do not operate fair, effective systems of asylum decision-making and support, leading to a patchwork of national asylum systems producing uneven results.

These rules apply to most EU member states, but not to the UK and Ireland. Conversely, a particular sub-part of the EU asylum system, the so-called Dublin Regulation,[3] is binding on member states as well as Norway, Iceland, Liechtenstein, and Switzerland as associated non-member states.

The Dublin Regulation is the most infamous piece of legislation, which composes the CEAS.[4] It determines which member state is responsible for examining a given asylum application. The core principle is that the responsibility lies primarily with the member state, which played the greatest part in the applicant's entry or residence in the EU. Unless the person has a family or a visa or residence permit in another member state, the responsible state is the state through which the person first entered the EU, whether the entry was legal or

2 For an updated overview of the legislative framework, see https://ec.europa.eu/home-affairs/what-we-do/policies/asylum_en (last access November 28, 2018). On current efforts aimed at reforming the CEAS, *infra*, note 19 and corresponding text.

3 Regulation (EU) 604/2013 of the European Parliament and of the Council, of June 26, 2013, establishing the criteria and mechanisms for determining the Member State responsible for examining an application for international protection lodged in one of the Member States by a third-country national or a stateless person.

4 The launch of the Schengen area already included the adoption among the then members of the European Communities of common criteria for allocating to one of them (and, by way of principle, to only one of them) the competence to determine the asylum claim and subsequently afford protection to the successful applicant. Such criteria were originally specified in the Convention signed in Dublin on June 15, 1990 by all the Member States and in the Convention implementing the Agreement of Schengen (Articles 28–38), signed in Schengen on June 19, 1990 by some Member States. Those rules were later replaced by EC Regulation No. 343/2003 (the Dublin II Regulation) and, lastly, by EU Regulation No. 604/2013 (the Dublin III Regulation).

not. There the person has an obligation to register and stay until his or her asylum request has been processed – the procedure can take up to two years. Most importantly, if the asylum seeker travels to another member state – which is a concrete possibility particularly within the 22 member states participating in the Schengen area – he or she ought to be transferred back to the state of first entry.

The stated aim of the Dublin system is to prevent positive and (most commonly) negative conflicts of competence regarding the determination of a peculiar personal status, by rapidly identifying a single responsible member state. Because of the routes migrants take, however, it must have been obvious from its very inception that this system was going to put a disproportionate burden on Eastern and Southern countries – in relation to migration flows by land or the Mediterranean Sea, respectively. It was precisely because some member states are more exposed than others that the system was established – so that the "geographical exposure" of some (most notably those in Southern Europe) would not open up the whole territory of the EU (particularly its "geographically protected" Northern countries) to migration flows, thanks to the freedom of movement which lies at the core of the European project.

Geography is not the only factor that determines the migratory flows to certain member states. The geopolitics at the EU borders are another. The Arab spring, the Libyan crisis, the now six-year-old Syrian conflict and the Daesh phenomenon all contributed to the massive increase of migratory flows towards Europe.

Whether the events that occurred between 2013 and 2016 could (or should) have been foreseen or not, they are now well-established historical facts with enduring consequences – a so-called refugee/migration crisis, unprecedented in the relatively recent history of the EU.

The acute crisis in the effectiveness and the shortcomings of the Dublin system have been widely documented in the relevant literature and generally acknowledged. In this international context, it is a very disturbing *monstrosity* that the Dublin system remains in place and continues to add a very substantial legal burden to that already arising from the geographical position of some member states and the geopolitical context of the EU.

3 A Kafkaesque perspective

Why *The Trial* of Kafka? Kafka's *Trial* very well illustrates the absurdity of the situation and decisions (or the failure to decide) under the current EU legal framework.

> "Somebody must have made a false accusation against Josef K., for he was arrested one morning without having done anything wrong."[5]

Who is on trial? Mr. K. is Italy, although Italy is not the only Mr. K. of this story. Other states, most notably Greece, are put to test here. The true victims of the EU asylum policy, however, are the migrants. Moreover, as it will be shown (para. 5), the EU – a monster in itself – is also a victim of its own policies.

One of the EU's singular accomplishments is its open *internal* borders. The treaty that made this possible, known as the Schengen Agreement, went into effect in 1995 and expanded to include 26 countries in and around the EU. It immediately provided a potent symbol of both the ideals and the real benefits of European integration.

The Dublin asylum system openly contradicts this very logic, with its only apparently neutral procedural rules on the criteria for determining the member state responsible for examining an application for international protection – criteria that cannot be derogated from, even in the presence of the arrival of an unusual number of refugees.[6]

One of the consequences is that migrants cannot leave the territory of the state where they entered. Nor can they choose with which state authorities file their application for asylum. Moreover, migrants seeking asylum in a country other than the state of first entry (so-called "secondary migrants"), need to be sent back. The current system, however, is still characterised in practice by differing treatments of asylum seekers and varying recognition rates amongst EU Member States. This divergence is what encourages secondary movements and is partly due to the fact that the current rules grant member states a lot of discretion in how to apply the common EU rules.

In addition to being responsible for processing asylum application, the state of first entry remains responsible, in principle, for the protection ensuing from the status of refugee or person qualifying for subsidiary international

5 This is the opening paragraph of Franz Kafka, *The Trial*, Germany, 1925. This and the subsequent passages quoted in the text are taken from the trans. I. Parry first published in 1994, reissued in Penguin Classics 2015. Further references in the text, abbreviated as TT.

6 The rigidity of these rules has been confirmed by the European Court of Justice (Grand Chamber), judgment of July 26, 2017, *Jafari* (Case C-646/2016), available at http://curia.europa.eu/juris/ (last access November 28, 2018). For a critical comment, see Chiara Di Stasio, "Il sistema 'Dublino' non è derogabile: note a margine della sentenza della Corte di giustizia del 26 luglio 2017, causa C-646/2016, *Jafari*," *Osservatorio sulle fonti* 3 (2017): 1–13, http://www.osservatoriosullefonti.it (last access November 28, 2018).

protection. It also bears the exclusive responsibility for the return of immigrants who do not qualify for international protection, to their country of origin.

It is a paradox and a monstrosity that a legal rule – the default criterion of the state of first entry as the responsible state for examining asylum claims – instead of alleviating an objectively geopolitical disadvantage of some states, was meant and intended to exacerbate it.

Moreover, geography – as we know it – does not change in a reasonable space of time, but in geological eras, i.e. millions of years. The law, as a men-made product, is instead subject to making and remaking, and thus can be changed. It is a further paradox and another monstrosity that while the Dublin Regulation has undergone various revisions, the default criterion has remained unchanged. Even the proposed Dublin IV Regulation under discussion at the time of writing leaves it untouched.[7]

This system also clashes with the principle of solidarity, which informed already the Schumann Declaration of 9 May, 1950, at the origin of the process of European integration, and lies at the essence of the EU.[8] The principle is now enshrined in Article 80 of the Treaty on the Functioning of the EU (TFEU), according to which the policies of the Union on border checks, asylum and migration and their implementation "shall be governed by the principle of solidarity and fair sharing of responsibility, including its financial implications, between the member states." And "whenever necessary," the acts of the Union adopted pursuant to these policies "shall contain appropriate measures to give effect to this principle."[9]

It does not require an international lawyer, let alone an migration expert, to understand that this system would result in an absurdly disproportional and unequal burden on the Southern European states. The European Court of Justice did recognize that it could not "deny that any asylum system, even one without structural weaknesses in terms of reception capacity and capacity to process applications for international protection, would have been seriously disrupted by the unprecedented influx of migrants that occurred in Greece and Italy in 2015."[10] Italy and Greece have found themselves trapped – "arrested," in a way – "without having done anything wrong," indeed.

---

7 *Infra*, para. 4.

8 See the Preamble and Art. 3 of the Treaty on the European Union (TEU).

9 See also Articles 122 and 222 TFEU as well as the Preamble and Title IV ("Solidarity") of the Charter of Fundamental Rights.

10 European Court of Justice (Grand Chamber), Judgment of September 6, 2017, *Slovak Republic and Hungary v. Council of the European* (Joined Cases C-643/15 and C-647/15), available at http://curia.europa.eu/juris/ (last access November 28, 2018).

It would be a hypocrisy, however, to consider migration as a purely inter-state matter and the EU asylum policy as a bundle of issues of equal (or unequal) distribution of burdens of various kinds (financial, economic, social etc.) among member states. Migration is a human and humanitarian phenomenon. Migrants are human beings. They are entitled to refugee protection, when fleeing from persecution for one of the grounds enumerated in the Refugee Convention. Where there exists a real risk of suffering serious harm because of indiscriminate violence in situations of international or internal armed conflict, they qualify for subsidiary protection. Irrespective of international protection, all migrants are entitled to human rights – the right to life and to dignity, in the first place. Far too many migrants die in their journey to reach the European soil or, after making it to Europe, are met with inhuman reception conditions, where not *refouled* to their country of origin.

The defendants that endure the Kafkaesque trial of the EU Dublin system, therefore, are – most times simultaneously to the EU member states disproportionally affected by the migration phenomenon (Italy and the other Mediterranean countries) – the migrants themselves, including asylum seekers.

4 The three possibilities of "acquittal": actual acquittal, apparent acquittal and prolongation

What are the remedies? Is there any possibility to put an end to the Kafkaesque trial set up by the EU under the rules of its common asylum policy? If so, of what kind?

When Mr. K. visits the artist Titorelli, he is famously confronted with these three possible outcomes for his case.

> There are three possibilities; actual acquittal, apparent acquittal, and prolongation. Acquittal is of course best, only I don't have the slightest influence on this kind of verdict. I don't believe there is any person at all who could have an influence on actual acquittal. (TT, 122)

Whatever the evolvement of the political situation in the Northern African states and the improvement of social and economic conditions as a result of aid and development policies by the EU and European and non-European states, migratory flows are not going to disappear.

It is now widely recognized that climate change is one of the root causes of migratory flaws originating in African states (and elsewhere).[11] The warming of temperatures especially in Eastern and the Horn of Africa, moves large masses of people towards the North. This in turn puts a burden on the receiving states already striving to sustain their population in poor living conditions. This phenomenon is generally referred to as economic migration. Economic migrants hardly qualify for refugee or international protection. However, because they reach Europe through the Northern African states (transit states), they are still protected by non-*refoulement* under human rights law.

Whatever the content and success of policies on visas, asylum and migration and of the other "external" policies of the EU (development aid, investment etc.), climate change is an enduring phenomenon and the "migration crisis" will stay with the EU for a while. Paraphrasing Kafka, I do not believe the EU, or any other actors could have an influence on "actual acquittal."

> So he said: "Let's put this actual acquittal to one side then; but you mentioned two other possibilities." "Apparent acquittal and prolongation. Those are the only ones possible," said the painter. [. . .] "the difference in this respect being that apparent acquittal requires concentrated but temporary effort, prolongation a much less intense but lasting one. First then apparent acquittal." (*TT*, 125)

One can certainly ascribe to the category of "apparent acquittal" the insufficient, provisional measures so far adopted by the EU to face the recurring tragic events in the Mediterranean and the unprecedented migratory flows at the EU external borders, since the adoption of the European Agenda on Migration on May 13, 2015.[12] They aim to address an "emergency" created by the Dublin system. Far from correcting it, however, the "remedial" measures so far adopted are based and build upon it.

On September 22, 2015, EU leaders agreed to relocate 120,000 people in dire need of international protection who had arrived or were arriving in Greece

---

11 The United Nations High Commissioner for Refugees estimates that since 2009, one person every second has been displaced by a disaster, with an average of 22.5 million people displaced by climate or weather-related events since 2008. This includes tragedies like the widespread famine in Darfur, monsoons and flooding in Bangladesh and the catastrophic hurricane in Puerto Rico. *Global Report on Internal Displacement* (2018), http://www.internal-displacement.org/global-report/grid2018/downloads/2018-GRID.pdf (last access November 28, 2018).

12 For an overview of the European Agenda on Migration and the measures adopted in implementation thereof, see https://ec.europa.eu/home-affairs/what-we-do/policies/european-agenda-migration/press-material_en (last access November 28, 2018).

and Italy *en route* to other EU states over the next two years. The decision observed that this number corresponded to approximately 43 per cent of the total number of third-country nationals who were in clear need of international protection and who entered Italy and Greece irregularly in July and August 2015; and also, that this plan constituted fair burden sharing between Italy and Greece on the one hand, and the remaining member states on the other, given the overall available figures on irregular border crossings in 2015.[13]

The Decision was intended merely to address an emergency situation, and all the more unsatisfying as adopted by majority voting (with Romania, the Czech Republic, Slovakia and Hungary voting against and Finland abstaining, while Denmark and the United Kingdom are not participating).

Hungary and Slovakia challenged the Decision in annulment proceedings alleging the breach of essential procedural requirements and the proportionality principle. The European Court of Justice dismissed the actions, confirming the validity of the Decision.[14]

In spite of its mandatory character, however, not only Slovakia and Hungary, but also Poland and the Czech Republic (so-called Visegrad Group) have resisted its implementation.[15] In June 2017, the European Commission brought infringement proceedings against these latter three states. The European Court of Justice is likely to find a breach of the obligation to comply with the decision

---

13 Council Decision establishing provisional measures in the area of international protection for the benefit of Italy and Greece, September 22, 2015, http://data.consilium.europa.eu/doc/document/ST-12098-2015-INIT/en/pdf (last access November 28, 2018).

14 The Court confirmed as the proper legal basis for the contested decision, Art. 78(3) TFEU – "In the event of one or more Member States being confronted with an emergency situation characterised by a sudden inflow of nationals of third countries, the Council, on a proposal from the Commission, may adopt provisional measures for the benefit of the member State(s) concerned. It shall act after consulting the European Parliament" – and stated *inter alia* that "the Council, when adopting the contested decision, was in fact required, as is stated in recital 2 of the decision, to give effect to the principle of solidarity and fair sharing of responsibility, including its financial implications, between the Member States, which applies, under Article 80 TFEU, when the EU common policy on asylum is implemented." European Court of Justice (Grand Chamber), Judgment of September 6, 2017, *Slovak Republic and Hungary v. Council of the European*, *supra*, note 10, para. 252).

15 On May 31, 2018, the European Commission reported that 34,689 asylum seekers have been relocated from Italy and Greece to other States participating in the relocation process – thereby participating states have reached 35,30% of commitments enshrined in the Council Decision.. The relocation effort has been uneven between member states – Denmark, Hungary, Poland and the UK have not relocated any asylum seekers. Data published on April 3, 2018, http://www.europeanmigrationlaw.eu/en/articles/datas/relocation-from-italy-and-greece.html (last access November 28, 2018).

by the respondent states. In case of persistent failure to comply, a further action of infringement could in turn result in the imposition of financial penalties. It is very unlikely, however, that the fines will have a deterrent effect on the recalcitrant states, whose refusal to cooperate stems from a radical opposition to the relocation scheme and the principle of shared responsibility at the basis thereof, rather than practical considerations.

In addition, the measures agreed upon relate to asylum seekers only, while the rights of asylum seekers are only a part of the problem to be addressed. The decision leaves it to the affected member states to deal with the enormous mass of economic migrants and their repatriation or resettlement, despite the principles of solidarity and fair sharing of responsibility between the member states, which should govern the whole Union policy on asylum and migration.

Finally, and most importantly, the Dublin system, with the perverse logic underpinning it, remains in place. The temporary and exceptional relocation mechanism over two years from the frontline member states (Italy and Greece) entails only a temporary derogation from the rule according to which these countries would otherwise have been responsible for the examination of an application for international protection. Morevoer, not only was it wholly unsuccessful, but it widened and deepened the divide between some EU countries (the Visegrad group) and the (rest of the) EU.

> "And the proceedings start again?" Asked K. almost incredulously. "Of course," said the painter, "the proceedings start again, but once more there's the possibility, just as there was earlier, of getting an apparent acquittal. You just have to gather all your strength together and never give in." (TT, 127)
> [...]
> "But this second acquittal is again not final," said K. with a dismissive turn of his head. "Of course not," said the painter, "the second acquittal is followed by the third arrest, the third acquittal by the fourth arrest, and so on. That's already contained in the concept of apparent acquittal." K. was silent. "It's obvious you don't think there's any advantage in apparent acquittal," said the painter. "Perhaps prolongation will suit you better. Shall I explain the nature of prolongation to you?" K. nodded. [...] "Prolongation," said the painter; and he stared in front of him for a while as if looking for a really accurate explanation. "Prolongation means the proceedings are kept permanently in the first stages." (TT, 127–128)

Following the publication of many critical studies,[16] the acute crisis in the effectiveness of the CEAS provoked by the events that occurred between 2013 and

16 For a thorough critical appraisal and the proposal of an interesting different "genuine link" approach, see Marcello Di Filippo, "The allocation of competence in asylum procedures under EU law: The need to take the Dublin bull by the horns," *Revista de Derecho Comunitario Europeo* 59 (2018): 41–95.

2016, and the exhortations coming from various actors (including the European Council[17] and the European Parliament[18]), in May 2016, the European Commission put forward a proposal to revise the Dublin III Regulation (the Dublin IV proposal).[19]

The proposal aims to supplement the system with relocation and resettlement mechanisms – but again does not alter the default mechanisms which continues to place the primary responsibility for reception, processing of asylum applications, as well as admission, relocation or return – as the case may be – on the state of first entry.

> The proceedings don't come to a stop, but the defendant is almost as safeguarded against a conviction as he would be if he were free. In comparison with apparent acquittal, prolongation has the advantage that the defendant's future is less uncertain; he is shielded from the shock of sudden arrests and needn't fear he'll have to undertake, perhaps just when his other circumstances are least propitious, the strain and agitation associated with trying to get an apparent acquittal. Mind you, prolongation has certain disadvantages for the defendant which should not be underestimated. I'm not thinking of the fact that it means that the defendant is never free; he's not free in a real sense after apparent acquittal either. There is another disadvantage. The case can't stand still, at least not without adequate reasons. So from outside something must be seen to be going on. From time to time various decrees must be issued, the defendant must be interrogated, examining sessions held, etc. The case has to be kept constantly moving in the small area to which it has been artificially restricted. [. . .] It's all a show. (TT,128–129)

Given the variety of the position of the European institution involved in the legislative procedure (European Commission, Council and European Parliament) and those even more diverse, if not conflicting, of the member states, the

---

17 European Council, Conclusions of 15 October 2015, EUCO 26/15, § 3.

18 European Parliament, Resolution of 12 April 2016 on the situation in the Mediterranean and the need for a holistic EU approach to migration (2015/2095(INI)), A8-0066/2016, 12–4-2016, §§ 33–38.

19 Proposal for a Regulation establishing the criteria and mechanisms for determining the Member State responsible for examining an application for international protection lodged in one of the Member States by a third-country national or a stateless person (recast), COM (2016) 270 final, 4–5-2016, https://eur-lex.europa.eu/legal-content/EN/TXT/?uri=CELEX%3A52016PC0270%2801%29 (last access November 28, 2018). The proposal is part of a legislative package, which includes the recast of *the Dublin Regulation* and of the *Eurodac* Regulation, a proposal for a *Regulation on the establishment of the European Union Agency for Asylum (EUAA)*, a proposal for a Regulation establishing *a common procedure in the EU*, a proposal for a *Qualification Regulation*, the recast of the *Reception Conditions Directive* and a proposal for a Regulation establishing a *Union Resettlement Framework*.

negotiations – at the time of writing still undergoing – do not seem heading towards a rapid or easy conclusion.

In parallel to the ongoing reform of the Dublin Regulation, the EU and its member states have adopted several measures aiming at the so-called "externalization" of the EU migration policy. The EU-Turkey deal of 2016 is the milestone of this strategy.[20] The solutions provided therein are being replicated through the conclusions of memorandums and partnership with Libya, Tunisia etc.[21] An examination of these actions is beyond the scope of the present essay. Suffice here to say that what these efforts have in common is the aim to "contain" the migratory flows beyond the European borders.

Exemplary of efforts currently undertaken are the European Council Conclusions on migration of 28 June 2018, whereby:

> 1. The European Council reconfirms that a precondition for a functioning EU policy relies on a comprehensive approach to migration which combines more effective control of the EU's

20 The main points of the deal are the following: all new irregular migrants crossing from Turkey to the Greek islands as from 20 March 2016 will be returned to Turkey; migrants arriving in the Greek islands will be duly registered and any application for asylum will be processed individually by the Greek authorities in accordance with the Asylum Procedures Directive; migrants not applying for asylum or whose application for asylum has been found to be unfounded or inadmissible will be returned to Turkey; for every Syrian being returned to Turkey from the Greek islands, another Syrian will be resettled from Turkey to the European Union. EU-Turkey Statement, March 18, 2016, Council of the EU, Press Release 144/16, http://www.consilium.europa.eu/en/press/press-releases/2016/03/18/eu-turkey-statement/ (last access November 28, 2018). The General Court of the EU dismissed three similar applications for annulment alleging that the EU-Turkey deal exposed the applicants to risks of *refoulement* to Turkey or "chain *refoulement*" to Pakistan or Afghanistan, thereby obliging them to apply for international protection in Greece, against their will. It found that the EU-Turkey Statement was not an act or international agreement attributable to the European Council, but rather that the real authors were the heads of state or government of the EU member states and their Turkish counterparts. Consequently, the Court declared that it lacked jurisdiction. General Court of the EU, orders of February 28, 2017, *NF, NG and NM v European Council* (Cases T-192/16, T-193/16 and T-257/16), http://curia.europa.eu/juris/document/document.jsf?text=&docid=188483&doclang=EN (last access November 28, 2018).

21 See Kirsten McConnachie, "Refugee Protection and the Art of the Deal," *Journal of Human Rights Practice* 9.2 (2017): 190–196. For a critical appraisal, Cristopher Hein, "Migratory Movements to and from Libya. Italian and European Policy Responses," in *I conflitti in Siria e Libia. Possibili equilibri e le sfide al diritto internazionale*, ed. Natalino Ronzitti e Elena Sciso (Torino: G. Giappichelli, 2018): 265–291; Daria Davitti, Annamaria La Chimia, "A Lesser Evil? The European Agenda on Migration and the Use of Funding for Migration Control," *Irish Yearbook of International Law* 10 (2015): 133–162; Francesca De Vittor, "Responsabilità degli Stati e dell'Unione europea nella conclusione e nell'esecuzione di 'accordi' per il controllo extraterritoriale della migrazione," *Diritti umani e diritto internazionale* 12.1 (2018): 5–27.

external borders, increased external action and the internal aspects, in line with our principles and values. This is a challenge not only for a single member state, but for Europe as a whole. Since 2015 a number of measures have been put in place to achieve the effective control of the EU's external borders. As a result, the number of detected illegal border crossings into the EU has been brought down by 95% from its peak in October 2015, even if flows have been picking up recently on the Eastern and Western Mediterranean routes.

2. The European Council is determined to continue and reinforce this policy to prevent a return to the uncontrolled flows of 2015 and to further stem illegal migration on all existing and emerging routes. [...]

11. Concerning the situation internally in the EU, secondary movements of asylum seekers between member states risk jeopardising the integrity of the Common European Asylum System and the Schengen acquis. Member states should take all necessary internal legislative and administrative measures to counter such movements and to closely cooperate amongst each other to that end.

12. As regards the reform for a new Common European Asylum System, much progress has been achieved thanks to the tireless efforts of the Bulgarian and previous Presidencies. Several files are close to finalisation. A consensus needs to be found on the Dublin Regulation to reform it based on a balance of responsibility and solidarity, taking into account the persons disembarked following Search and Rescue operations. Further examination is also required on the Asylum Procedures proposal. *The European Council underlines the need to find a speedy solution to the whole package and invites the Council to continue work with a view to concluding as soon as possible. There will be a report on progress during the October European Council.* [My italics][22]

> The advocate had an inexhaustible supply of speeches like this. They were repeated at every visit. Always progress made, but the nature of this progress could never be communicated. Work was constantly going on the first plea, but it was not finished [...]. (TT,99)

"You are going already?" asked the painter, who had also got to his feet. "It must be the air in here that's driving you away. I'm very sorry. I've still quite a lot to tell you. I had to condense things a lot. But I hope I made myself understood." "Oh yes," said K., who had a headache from the strain of forcing himself to listen. In spite of this confirmation the painter said everything again in summary form as if he wanted to give K. some consolation to take home with him: "What both methods have in common is that they prevent conviction of the defendant." "But they also prevent actual acquittal," K. said quietly as if he felt ashamed for having realized this. "You have grasped the kernel of the matter," said the painter quickly. (TT,129)

22 European Council conclusions, June 28, 2018, http://www.consilium.europa.eu/en/press/press-releases/2018/06/29/20180628-euco-conclusions-final/ (last access November 28, 2018).

5 The end of the story: a very tragic end?

What is the end of the story?

Kafka's trial has a very tragic end. Unlike Kafka's trial tragic end, the story of the European asylum policy is not written yet.

States are closing off their non-sealable borders: raising walls, refusing entry into their ports, suspending the Schengen Agreement.

Migrants' prospects and conditions deteriorate: "Logic is of course unshakable, but it cannot hold out against a man who wants to live" (TT, 182).

The victims of the current EU Dublin asylum system are simultaneously the Mediterranean states and the migrants, but also the EU – at the same time, a monster with, and a victim of, its own policies.

Yet, the EU is not dead, despite Brexit and its multiple crises of all kinds: not only a migration, but also an economic and financial crisis, a security crisis, and a deep and broad legitimacy crisis. Offshoring its asylum and migration policies primarily aimed to reduce illegal migration and prevent a return to the uncontrolled flows of 2015 will not result in actual acquittal from its responsibilities under international refugee law and human rights – which are also part of EU (primary) law. Perhaps apparent acquittal. At most, prolongation.

> But the hands of the one gentleman were at K.'s throat while the other drove the knife into his heart and turned it there twice. With his failing sight K. could still see the gentleman right in front of his face, cheek pressed against cheek, as they observed the decisive moment. "Like a dog!" he said. It was as if the shame would outlive him. (TT,182)

Matteo Nicolini

Monstrosity "Overseas"? Civilisation, Trade, and Colonial Policy in Conrad's African Tales

> The earth seemed unearthly [...] – there you could look at a thing monstrous and free. It was unearthly, and the men were ... No, they were not inhuman. Well, you know, that was the worst of it – this suspicion of their not being inhuman. It would come slowly to one. They howled and leaped, and spun, and made horrid faces; but what thrilled you was just the thought of their humanity – like yours – the thought of your remote kinship with this wild and passionate uproar.
>
> *Joseph Conrad,* Heart of Darkness, *p. 139.*

1 Civilising black Africa? Trade, progress, and the narrative of *superiority*

"Civilisation follows trade": with this sentence Joseph Conrad introduces the final lines of his renowned African tale *An Outpost of Progress.*[1] Not only does the sentence report the disembarkation of the Manager Director of the 'Great Civilising Company' at a remote trading-station in Congo; but it also makes reference, with irony and sour sarcasm, to the impact of colonisation on the African Continent.

The effects of colonisation need not detain us here: we shall consider them in due course.[2] Suffice it here to brush on up the sentence "Civilisation follows trade." *Per se* it does not convey anything relevant; nor is its meaning groundbreaking. We have got used to equating trade and civilisation within the context of globalised markets, to praise both *global commercial law* and its "aesthetic consequences [...] including [its] sublime effects."[3] Civilisation and trade describe globalisation in accordance with a narrative of *superiority* and

1 Joseph Conrad, "An Outpost of Progress," *Cosmopolis: An International Review* VI (1897): 609–620, and VII (1897): 1–15, rpt. in Joseph Conrad, *Heart of Darkness and Other Tales*, ed. Cedric Watts (Oxford: Oxford University Press, 2008): 1–25, 25. Further references in the text, abbreviated as *OP*.

2 See infra, para 5.

3 Heather Hugues, "Aesthetics of Common Law – Domestic and International Implications," *Louisiana Law Review* 67.3 (2007): 690–749, 696.

https://doi.org/10.1515/9783110654615-015

progress. Global law is indeed the outcome of the "historical process of the worldwide generalization of Western legalism." Embedding the "triumph of civilization," it triggers

> a kind of impending radiant future for humanity, one that is characterized by open markets that ensure (sustainable) development and (environmentally-friendly) prosperity. Commerce would civilize manners; offer everyone the benefits of peace, human rights, representative democracy, and moderate government.[4]

There is something fideistic in such sanctification of the global law. To be honest, there is nothing like *faith* or *sanctity* in globalisation. To the contrary, the narrative of progress hides a *narrative of superiority*: the "radiant future" promised to the human kind covers the "asymmetrical relationship" between the actors of globalisation[5]: on the one hand, there are the international financial actors, whose legitimisation is neither democratic nor representative of the popular will; on the other one, there is no rest for the backward and the "uncivilised." These are indeed excluded from globalisation because of their economic weakness and – in Eurocentric terms – have a limited economic development; but, at the same time, they are treated as inferiors and therefore must bear the costs of financial domination[6]: "the explosion of inequalities, the systematic pillaging of natural resources, environmental catastrophes, [...] the standardization of culture, and endless wars."[7]

Superiority and *progress* also played a crucial role in the last decades of the 19th century, that is, when European powers forged their colonial policies. The aesthetics of globalisation, domination, and colonialism have common features.[8] Firstly, colonialism may be considered as a species of the broader

4 Mikhail Xifaras, "The *Global Turn* in Legal Theory," *Canadian Journal of Law & Jurisprudence* XXIX (2016): 215–243, 216. See also See Gerrit Gong, *The Standard of "Civilization" in International Society* (Oxford: Clarendon Press, 1984); Martti Koskenniemi, *The Gentle Civilizer of Nations: The Rise and Fall of International Law 1870–1960* (Cambridge: Cambridge University Press, 2001), 132 ff.

5 Wolfgang Alschner, "Americanization of the BIT Universe: The Influence of Friendship, Commerce and Navigation (FCN) Treaties on Modern Investment Treaty Law," *Goettingen Journal of International Law* 5.2 (2013): 455–486, 465. "In the twenty-first century, a small handful of global corporations perpetuate the conditions that flourished in the late 1700s.": Bama Athreya, "White Man's 'Burden' and the New Colonialism in West African Cocoa Production," *Race/Ethnicity: Multidisciplinary Global Contexts* 5.1 (2011): 51–59, 52.

6 James Bohman, *Democracy across Borders*. From *Démos* to *Dêmoi* (Cambridge, MA, and London: The MIT Press, 2007), especially Chapter 3.

7 Xifaras, "The *Global Turn*," 219.

8 Sally E. Merry, "From Law and Colonialism to Law and Globalization," *Law & Social Inquiry* 28.2 (2003): 569–590.

concept of domination, which asserts inequality between different groups, and in which one endeavours "to impose its cultural order to the subordinate" ones.[9] Hence, it shares the epistemologies and hierarchies underpinning the processes of domination.[10] Secondly, European powers entrusted their traders and agents with the civilising mission of the backward peoples of Africa. Thirdly, this mission was the main justification European powers used to colonise and exploit Africa, thus disclosing the intrinsic mercantilist attitude of colonialism: the English Empire, for instance, turned into "the English monopoly."[11] Whereas the main object of English colonial policy was political,[12] colonial policies were supported by "British merchants and export industries located in several regions of the Kingdom." This triggered a politico-commercial empire, "a coherent trading area subject in some matters to a relatively uniform system of law."[13] To sum up, the nobly civilising mission upholds Egerton's assumption that "the *raison d'être* of colonies is *to benefit the commerce of the Mother Country*."[14]

2 Civilising Africa and its consequences: or, the policy of monstrosity

Whereas globalisation merely aims to secure the dominance of financial and economic actors, colonial policies also likened trade and civilisation to a specific Continent, that is Africa. Another argument is associated with the narrative

---

9 Sally E. Merry, "Law and Colonialism," *Law & Society Review* 25.4 (1991): 889–992, 890, 894.
10 Mary Gilmartin and Lawrence D. Berg, "Locating postcolonialism," *Area* 39.1 (2007): 120–124, 120.
11 12 Carl. II c. 18. see Nicholas Canny, *The Origins of Empire: An Introduction*, in *The Oxford History of the British Empire*, ed. Nicholas Canny, vol. I, *The Origins of Empire* (Oxford: Oxford University Press, 1998): 1–33, 17.
12 This is apparent in the case of the Navigations Acts: see Hugh Egerton, *A Short History of British Colonial Policy* (London: Methuen & Co., 1897), 2. See also John Reeves, *A History of the Law of Shipping and Navigation* (London: E. and R. Brooke, 1792), 9 ff; Francis L. Holt, *A System of the Shipping and Navigation Laws of Great Britain: And of the Laws Relative to Merchant Ships and Seamen; and Maritime Contracts* (London: J. Butterworth, 1820), 3 ff.; Blair Hoxby, 'The Government of Trade: Commerce, Politics, and the Courtly Art of Restoration,' *ELH* 66.3 (1999): 591–627.
13 See Patrick K. O'Brien, "Inseparable Connections," and Jacob M. Price, "The Imperial Economy, 1700–1776," in *The Oxford History of the British Empire*, ed. P.J. Marshall, vol. II, *The Eighteenth Century* (Oxford: Oxford University Press, 1998): 28–77, 72 and 1–27, 17 respectively.
14 Egerton, *A Short History*, 2 (emphasis added).

of Europe's superiority and domination over Africa. This argument – which I term the *white male superiority* – has been examined with accuracy in feminist studies.[15] It pervades, for example, Rider Haggard's colonial novels, such as *King Solomon*'s *Mines* and *She*.[16] Not only does this narrative entail the superiority of white people over Africans, but it also identifies Africa with the female body: the dark continent is "the testing ground for white male adventure," and allows "androcentric mystique of exploration" to be praised.[17]

Male superiority, domination, and mission delineates the "myth of civilization", which progressively deletes "The many horrors and atrocities which disgrace humanity," thus healing the sufferings of Africa with "the blessings of Christian civilisation."[18] In the 19th century, only masculine physical superiority could bear the difficulties that the penetration of Africa entailed, and therefore face the dangers of the continent. The aesthetics of domination were thus interwoven with the modernist concepts of horror, danger, and monstrosity. These concepts were the main attributes of Africa – the "dark" continent –, as well as of its "backward" societies. A "Decisive action was required to remove [...] barriers to progress," to subdue Africa, and therefore to impose progress over her. This action would thus cleanse Africa from its ancestral horrors.

The imperial adventure was also central in Joseph Conrad's tales, *An Outpost of Progress* and *Heart of Darkness*.[19] Both are percolated by the three main features of European colonial policy: there is the moral obligation of civilisation; imperialism is conceived of as "a sordid saga" of commerce and unjust exploitation of natural resources; European emissaries fight against the atrocities of the

---

15 "[I]mperialist discourse [...], as found in imperialist novels, becomes a man-made discourse, expressing male fantasies, fears, anxieties:" Rebecca Stott, "The Dark Continent: Africa as Female Body in Haggard's Adventure Fiction," *Feminist Review*, 32 (1989): 69–89, 70.

16 Rider H. Haggard, *King Solomon's Mines*, rpt. with illustrations by Walter Paget (London et al.: Cassell and Company Limited, 1898), and *She*, rpt. ed. with illustrations by Maurice Grieffenhagen and Charles H. M Kerr (London: Longmans, Green, and Co., 1890).

17 Stott, "The Dark Continent," 70.

18 The "myth of civiliziation" is in Koskenniemi, *The Gentle Civilizer*, 127. The main quotation is from King Leopold II of Belgium, quoted by Guy Burrows, *The Land of the Pigmies* (London: Pearson, 1898), 287.

19 Joseph Conrad, "Heart of Darkness," *Blackwood's Edinburgh Magazine* (Edinburgh, UK), Vol. 165 (Feb 1899): 164–460; Vol. 165 (Mar 1899): 460–621; Vol. 165 (Apr 1899): 620–781, rpt. in Joseph Conrad, *Heart of Darkness and Other Tales*, ed. Cedric Watts (Oxford: Oxford University Press, 2008): 103–187. See Ian Watt, *Conrad in the Nineteenth Century* (Berkeley and Los Angeles: University of California Press, 1981), 147 ff. On Conrad and Victorian Imperialism see Ian Watt, *Essays on Conrad* (Cambridge: Cambridge University Press, 2000), 4 ff.

continent, thus contributing to a civilising mission which is "depicted as primarily an avidity for commercial profit."[20]

The civilising mission must then confront horror – and the confrontation may have dire consequences:

> The horror at the centre of Africa, the horror that is persistently associated with woman, the horror at the centre threatens to release itself. To lift the veil, to penetrate too deeply into the mysteries of woman into the mysteries of Africa, is to risk releasing something dangerous and potentially deadly.[21]

The risks of the penetration into Africa justified the brutality with which Europeans imposed civilisation over her indigenous population. But this also favoured the exploitation of Africa's resources – among them, ivory, as Conrad constantly reported in both tales.[22] The horrors and atrocities of the European emissaries – which Conrad experienced during his 1890 African journey and that he never forgot[23]– were indeed related both to the imperial discourse and to the white male-centred system of domination, which can be described in accordance with three narratives: *cultural superiority, societal superiority*, and *monstrosity as the outcome of superiority.*

The first narrative is related to the civilising policy, which is ironically depicted in *An Outpost of Progress*. A sardonic sarcasm pervades the whole tale. The two main characters – Kayerts, the short and fat chief; and Carlier, the tall, large-headed assistant (*OP*, 3) – are sarcastically portrayed as "two pioneers of trade and progress" (*OP*, 8). But this contrasts with their real attitudes: "They were two perfectly insignificant and incapable individuals, whose existence is only rendered possible through the high organization of civilized crowds" (*OP*, 5). The same concepts of progress, civilisation, and trade are evoked:

> They also found some old copies of a home paper. [...] It spoke much of the rights and duties of civilization, of the sacredness of the civilizing work [...]
> Carlier and Kayerts read, wondered, and began to think better of themselves.
> Carlier said one evening, waving his hand about, "In a hundred years, there will be perhaps a town here. Quays, and warehouses, and barracks, and ... and ... billiard-rooms. Civilization, my boy, and virtue ... and all. And then, chaps will read that two good fellows,

---

20 Cedric Watts, "Introduction," to Joseph Conrad, *Heart of Darkness and Other Tales*, ed. Cedric Watts (Oxford: Oxford University Press, 2008): xi–xxviii, xii.

21 Stott, "The Dark Continent," 75.

22 *OP*, 14–15; *HD*, 123, 125, 126, 134, 138, 162–163.

23 Frederick K. Karl and Lawrence Davies eds., *The Collected Letters of Joseph Conrad* iii (Cambridge: Cambridge University Press), 1988, 101.

> Kayerts and Carlier, were the first civilized men to live in this very spot!" Kayerts nodded, "Yes, it is a consolation to think of that." (*OP*, 9)

But the same holds true as far as *Heart of Darkness* is concerned. When Marlow, the main character, asks "who is this Mr. Kurtz?", the manager replies: "'The chief of the Inner Station,' [...] He was silent for a while. 'He is a prodigy,' he said at last. 'He is an emissary of pity and science and progress, and devil knows what else." (*HD*, 127). This sharply clashes with the reality of civilisation: Mr. Kurtz is a trading agent, "a species of wandering trader – a pestilential fellow, snapping ivory from the natives," that the manager wants to get hanged in order to "be free from unfair competition" in the sordid and monstrous ivory market (*HD*, 135).

Cultural superiority is then interwoven with the narrative of *societal superiority*. There is indeed praise of the "heavenly mission to civilise" (*HD*, 108) and, at the same time, an extensive use of the word "nigger," which Chinua Achebe wrongly considered as the main evidence for defining Conrad "a bloody racist."[24] Conrad was not a racist, as he regarded the exploitation of Africa as "the vilest scramble for loot that ever disfigured the history of human conscience."[25] He also scornfully criticised European societal superiority when describing the third main character in *An Outpost of Progress*, Henry Price. He is a black from Sierra Leone to whom the natives gave the name of Makola. At the very beginning of the tale, Makola is considered as part of the dangers of Africa: "Then, for a time he dwelt alone with [...] the Evil Spirit that rules the lands under the equator. He got on very well with his god. Perhaps he had propitiated him by a promise of more white men to play with, by and by." (*OP*, 4). God's promise, ironically, overturns Eurocentrism. Makola "spoke English and French with a warbling accent, wrote a beautiful hand, understood book-keeping, and cherished in his innermost heart the worship of evil spirits [...]." To put it differently, his depiction contrasts with the "stupidity and laziness" of Kayerts and Carlier – and "Makola, taciturn and impenetrable, despised the two white men" (*OP*, 3, 4).

The third narrative focuses on the effects of colonial policies, which turned European cultural and societal superiority into *monstrosity*. We have already mentioned *horror* and *atrocity* as the constitutive features of the imperialist discourse. Monstrosity is the effect of the colonial policy, which fostered "man's inhumanity to man."[26] In *Heart of Darkness* such monstrosity is represented by

---

24 Chinua Achebe, "An Image of Africa," *Massachussets Review* 19 (1977): 782–794.
25 Joseph Conrad, "Geography and Some Explorers," *Last Essays* (London: Dent, 1926), 25.
26 Watts, "Introduction," xx.

the *Inferno* of the allegedly white racial superiority: the monstrosity of the civilising mission is patently represented by slave trade – and, as Marlow utters, "after all, I also was a part of the great cause of these high and just proceedings." The description of the black men with "an iron collar on [the] neck, [...] all [...] connected together with a chain whose bights swung between them, rhythmically clinking" is complemented by the inhumanity of the white colonisers: "I've seen the devil of violence, and the devil of greed, and the devil of hot desire; but, by all the stars! these were strong, lusty, red-eyed devils, that swayed and drove men – men, I tell you" (*HD*, 117).

There is an even worse effect of the nobly civilising mission, that is, to make Africans part of the policy of monstrosity. In *An Outpost of Progress*, Makola is the "civilized nigger," who has adopted European habits. Like the European emissaries, he's "very neat in his person;" like the European trading agents, he practises "No regular trade," and sells black men for ivory tusks.

> "I did the best for you and the Company," said Makola, imperturbably. "Why you shout so much? Look at this tusk."
> [...]
> "Slavery is an awful thing," stammered out Kayerts in an unsteady voice.
> "Frightful ... the sufferings," grunted Carlier with conviction.
> [...]
> Kayerts and Carlier then named Makola "you beast!" – a feature, however, they share with him:
> [...]
> As they were going back to the house Kayerts observed with a sigh: "It had to be done." And Carlier said: "It's deplorable, but, the men being Company's men the ivory is Company's ivory. We must look after it." "I will report to the Director, of course," said Kayerts. "Of course; let him decide," approved Carlier (*OP*, 15–17).

3 Subduing the body of monstrosity: colonisation and the "just" sexual harassment

Another metaphor may be borrowed from feminist studies. It equates the Continent with the female body: "The discourses of entering into, penetrating, colonizing, conquering and the dominating of colonized peoples draw upon sexual discourses for the expression of suppressed sexual and imperial anxieties."[27]

---

27 Stott, "The Dark Continent," 70.

It is not just a matter of male sexual superiority, but also one of imperial policy. I contend that the metaphor has to do with a set of complex "relations between sexual and imperialist discourses." The white male is the coloniser; and his civilising mission implies subduing the potentially deadly Continent which is Africa. Exploration and domination thus reaffirm the necessity of exterminating horrors and atrocities, as well as suppressing the worshipping of African evil spirits: as a black body, Africa has a "threatening and primitive sexuality, threatening to consume the virility of the white male."[28]

This is the reason why Africa is depicted as an ominous place. Her penetration is thwarted by her "formless coast [. . .] bordered by dangerous surf, as if Nature herself had tried to ward off intruders [. . . and penetration] was like a weary pilgrimage amongst hints for nightmares" (*HD*, 115). It is haunted by invisible beings:

> A complaining clamour, modulated in savage discords, filled our ears. The sheer unexpectedness of it made my hair stir under my cap. I don't know how it struck the others: to me it seemed as though the mist itself had screamed, so suddenly, and apparently from all sides at one. . . (*HD*, 143)

This also explains the extensive use of noun clauses that remind us of obscurity. Africa is "dark", and her interior is "the heart of darkness:" there you can find "the depths of darkness;" there "a cry, a very loud cry, as of infinite desolation, soared slowly in the opaque air" (*HD*, 143). The continent is then crowed with humans akin to beasts. For his crew, Marlow is endowed with "Fine fellows – cannibals – [. . .] men one could work with." However, during the navigation,

> Their headman [. . .] stood near me [. . .] 'Catch 'im,' he snapped, with a bloodshot widening of his eyes and a flash of sharp teeth – 'catch 'im. Give 'im to us.' 'To you, eh?' I asked; 'what would you do with them?' 'Eat 'im!' [. . .] I would no doubt have been properly horrified, had it not occurred to me that he and his chaps must be very hungry: that they must have been growing increasingly hungry for at least this month past. (*HD*, 144)

In Marlow's opinion, Africa is "so hopeless and so dark, so impenetrable to human thought, so pitiless to human weakness" (*HD*, 92), that only the "sacredness of the civilizing work" might have defeated the hidden evil and the profound darkness of her heart.[29]

---

28 Stott, "The Dark Continent," 81.
29 Thomas Carlyle, *Past and Present* [1843] (London Chapman & Hall, 1858), 302.

The consequences of subduing Africa are twofold. The civilising mission is indeed a *Work for God*: only "religious and believing men who suffer to see the unfortunate blacks held in the ignorance of fetish-worship" could bring light to Africa, allowing faith and commerce to lighten "the dark places of the earth,"[30] make her a kind of Heaven. As King Leopold II, King of the Belgians, asserted in 1876,

> To open to civilisation the sole part of the globe which it has not yet penetrated, to pierce the darkness which envelops the entire population: this, I venture to say, is a crusade worthy of this century of progress.[31]

The second consequence refers to the legal regime suitable for Africa and her backward black population. Africa was situated *beyond the amity lines*, which were first drawn in the *Treaty between France and Spain, concluded at Cateau Cambrésis* (1559). An oral agreement concerning the Indies was attached thereto: The Indies were not formally mentioned in the Treaty, but the oral agreement was made "to the effect that west of the prime meridian and south of the Tropic of Cancer might be made right, and violence done by either party to the other should not be regarded as in contravention to the treaties."[32]

This meant that beyond the amity lines treaties would lose their legal force and ships could be captured and deemed to be a good prize. According to Carl Schmitt, these "global lines" set the scenario for a new international order: it was "European public law, which contributed to limiting European wars." In 16th and 17th centuries, amity lines implied that

> greet areas of freedom were designated as conflict zones in the struggle over the distribution of a new world [...] the designation of a conflict zone at once freed the area on this side of the line – a sphere of peace and order ruled by European public law – from the immediate threat of those events "beyond the line," which would not have been the case had there been no such zone.[33]

30 Carlyle, *Past and Present*, 302 and King Leopold II, quoted in Ruth Slade, *King Leopold's Congo* (Oxford: Oxford University Press, 1962), 75.
31 Quoted in Maurice H. Hennessy's *Congo: A Brief History and Appraisal* (London: Pall Mall Press, 1962), 13.
32 *European treaties bearing on the history of the United States and its dependencies*, ed. Frances G. Davenport, IV vols (Washington, DC: Carnegie Institution of Washington, 1917–1937), 219–220. On the amity lines see Carl Schmitt, *The* Nomos *of the Earth in the International Law of the* Jus Publicum Europaeum, translated and annotated by G. L. Ulmen (New York: Telos Press, 2006), 86 ff.
33 Carl Schmitt, *The* Nomos *of the Earth*, 97.

The lines drew a distinction between justice and injustice. On this side of the lines there was the civilised, Christian world; beyond them, chaos, darkness, unlimited war and freedom of land occupation. This triggered the establishment of separate, new legal regimes for the colonies, which also required tailor-made political structures. This is, for instance, the case of the French *indigénat*, " a regime of exception," an "unspoken and roughly sketched domain of 'non-law', which also defined "the very status of 'native'".[34] These structures, deliberately asymmetrical, reflected the inequality between Europeans and the backward Africans; they were settled in the aftermath of the West African Conference in Berlin (1884–1885): the European powers relinquished their informal empires[35] and laid down the rules for the European partition of the continent, and the exploitation of her natural resources. It is the so-called "scramble for Africa,", which was effectively concluded when the French Protectorate over Morocco was declared in 1912.[36]

Furthermore, partition triggered the creation of "colonial states."[37] The British governance fostered the creation of *Crown Colony governments* – where indirect rule or "government from above" was deed essential "in those lands whose populations are politically and economically backward, and where in

34 Gregory Mann, "What was the 'Indigénat'? The 'Empire of Law' in French West Africa," *The Journal of African History* 50.3 (2009): 331–353, 333, 336.

35 Ronald Robinson, John Gallagher, Alice Denny, *Africa and the Victorians. The official mind of imperialism* (London: MacMillan, 1961); Martin Lynn, 'British Policy, Trade, and Informal Empire in the Mid-Nineteenth Century,' in *The Oxford History of the British Empire*, ed. Andrew Porter, vol III, *The Nineteenth Century* (Oxford: Oxford University Press, 2001): 101–121.

36 Carl Schmitt, *The* Nomos *of the Earth*, 214 ff.; Koskenniemi, *The Gentle Civilizer*, 116 ff. As for Great Britain, "Great Britain and the Partition of Africa, 1870–1914," in *The Oxford History of the British Empire*, ed. Andrew Porter, vol. III, *The Nineteenth Century* (Oxford: Oxford University Press, 2001): 624–650. See also Richard Reid and John Parker, "Introduction. African Stories. Past, Present, and Future," in *The Oxford Handbook of Modern African History*, ed. Richard Reid and John Parker (Oxford: Oxford University Press, 2013): 1–18, 1. On the colonial partition, and on the conventional end-dates for the Scramble of Africa (Italy's invasion of Libya: 1911; the French Protectorate over Morocco: 1912; the Peace of Vereeniging ending the South African war: 1899–1902) see Heather J. Sharkey, 'African Colonial States,' in *The Oxford Handbook of Modern African History*, ed. Richard Reid and John Parker (Oxford: Oxford University Press, 2013): 151–170, 153–154; Jonas F. Gjersø, "The Scramble for East Africa: British Motives Reconsidered, 1884–95," *The Journal of Imperial and Commonwealth History* 43.5 (2015): 831–860; Ieuan Griffiths, "The Scramble for Africa: Inherited Political Boundaries," *The Geographical Journal* 152.2 (1986): 204–216; George N. Sanderson, "The European partition of Africa: Coincidence or conjuncture?," *The Journal of Imperial and Commonwealth History* 3.1 (1974): 1–54.

37 Sharkey, "African Colonial States," 155.

many cases society is organised on a tribal basis."[38] However, the United Kingdom also resorted to *indirect rule*, a method of administration which associated tribal chiefs with colonial governance.[39] Other European colonial powers prompted different colonial policies. Hence, France's *mission civilisatrice* aimed to assimilate African natives, as well as "to propagate the best of French culture along with the rationalist and libertarian values deriving from the Enlightenment and French revolution."[40] As far as French colonial governance is concerned, the revolutionary principles – that is, *Liberté, egalité, fraternité* – may well have been of relevance only at home: "None but Frenchmen should go to the colonies of 'Liberty, Equality, and Fraternity'; for there is Little Liberty, less Equality, and no Fraternity in the French colonies for Whites or Blacks."[41]

Beyond the amity lines, political power turned into a despotic regime,[42] which often reflected the colonial governance and the need to subjugate Africa. This is apparent in the Belgian territory of Congo. King Leopold II of Belgium administered the whole region as the Congo Free State (1885–1908): it was a proprietary estate, and the king governed it "in his private capacity rather than that of a constitutional monarch."[43] The King was probably afflicted by Afromania, a mental disorder that made him a "visionary out of touch with reality" interested only in the pursuit of power at the expenses of the natives.[44] Conrad witnessed the atrocities perpetrated under his rule – and when

38 L. W. White, W. D. Hussey, *Government in Great Britain, the Empire, and the Commonwealth* [1958] (Cambridge: Cambridge University Press, 2015), 194, 226.

39 See Ranger, "The Invention of Tradition in Colonial Africa", 220–221: "there was the acceptance of the idea that *some* Africans could become members of the governing class of colonial Africa, and thence the extension to [them] of training in a neo-traditional context." On *Direct rule* see Frederick D. Lugard's seminal book *The Dual Mandate in British Tropical Africa* (Edinburgh: William Blackwood and Sons, 1922): 192–213; Kristin Mann, Richard Roberts, *Law in Colonial Africa (*Portsmouth (NH)-London: Heinemann-James Currey, 1991), 20. See also J. S. E. Oplot, "The Resilience of the British Colonial Police Legacies in East Africa, Southern Africa, and West Africa", *Police Studies: The International Review of Police Development* 15.2 (1992): 91–92.

40 Sharkey, "African Colonial States," 156.

41 Sir J. Harris, *Dawn in Darkest Africa* (London: Smith, Elder & Co., 1912), 97.

42 Mann, "What was the *Indigénat*?, 333.

43 John S. Galbraith, "Gordon, Mackinnon, and Leopold: The Scramble for Africa, 1876–84," *Victorian Studies* 14.4 (1971): 369–388, 371.

44 Galbraith, "Gordon," 373.

> the news of atrocities in the Congo Free State leaked out, the result was the rise of modern international human rights activism in the form of the Congo Reform Association and, in 1908, the handing of King Leopold's personal fiefdom over to the Belgian state.[45]

In Eurocentric terms, Africa might have triggered the policy of monstrosity, i.e., the release of these primitive impulses in the white colonisers and dominators. The white male discourse described by Haggard might also have contributed to such a policy: beyond the lines, superiority implied the "freedom to act without cultural restraints out in the African bush."[46] Proprietary colonies were not limited to Congo: the same British South Africa Company – a Chartered Company – had "behind it, concentrated in one person, the wealth and capacity of Mr Rhodes."[47]

As they reflect the narrative of property, economy and progress secured by the Berlin Conference, these proprietary colonies represent the "just" title for the acquisition of colonial lands, and therefore the "just" indiscriminate exploitation of Africa – or, as the case may be, of Rhodesia and, in Conrad's tales, of the Congo Free State.[48]

Again, the metaphor of Africa as the female body is compelling. The incorporation of the Company of the King Leopold's self-enfeoffment reminds us of the traditional common-law institute of coverture. Marriage turned the bridegroom into the owner of his wife, who had "to give up her very name as a mark of her becoming his absolute and dependent property."[49] In Blackstone's words:

> By marriage, the husband and wife are one person in law: that is, the very being or legal existence of the woman is suspended during the marriage, or at least is incorporated and consolidated into that of the husband: under whose wing, protection, and cover, she performs every thing; and is therefore called in our law-French a feme-covert.[50]

---

45 Sharkey, "African Colonial States," 157. On such atrocities see Koskenniemi, *The Gentle Civilizer*, 155–156. The harshest critique of Leopold's rule is in Edumnd. D. Morel, *King Leopold's Rule in Africa* (London: W. Heinemann, 1904).
46 Stott, "The Dark Continent," 70.
47 Egerton, *A Short History*, 467.
48 Carl Schmitt, *The* Nomos *of the Earth*, 214 ff. See also Chapter 6 of the General Act on "Rules for future occupation on the coast of the African continent."
49 Samuel Richardson, *Clarissa: Or the History of a Young Lady* (Harmondsworth: Penguin, 1985), 148–149.
50 William Blackstone, *Commentaries on the Laws of England* (Oxford: Printed at the Clarendon Press, 1765–1769), 1.430. See also Norma Basch, "The Legal Fiction of Marital Unity in Nineteenth-Century America," *Feminist Studies* 5.2 (1979): 346–366; J. H. Baker, *An Introduction to English Legal History* (Oxford: Oxford University Press, 2008), 483–484. See *Married Women and the Law: Coverture in England and the Common Law World*, ed. Tim Stretton and Krista J. Kesselring (Montreal and London: McGill-Queen's University Press, 2013).

Such proprietary rights also covered abuses on the wife's body; but, "an abused wife might petition for a court for permission to leave a husband; nothing more."[51] Like coverture, the incorporation of Africa's body in chartered companies and proprietary estates is the "just" title of her occupation, extermination, massacre, and unjust exploitation. It is the "just" title for "just" sexual harassment.

Hence, the horror and fear of being trapped within the depths of Africa's interior are the main justification for land-occupation and the policy of monstrosity – and proprietary harassment is legitimated (i.e., covered) by the narrative of proprietary interests.

4 An alternative narrative: trade as the tread towards monstrosity

The colonial policy upholds an alternative reading of the atrocities and monstrosities European civilisers committed in Africa. This reading is based on Mr Kurtz's description in *Heart of Darkness*. The trading agent has the monopoly of the ivory market. He lives with the natives, in the very depths, in the heart of the dark continent – in the heart of darkness –; and natives have appointed him as their god.

> Everything belonged to him – but that was a trifle. The thing was to know what he belonged to, how many powers of darkness claimed him for their own [...] He had taken a high seat amongst the devils of the land – I mean literally. [...] in the holy terror of scandal and gallows and lunatic asylums – how can you imagine what particular region of the first ages a man's untrammelled feet may take him into by the way of solitude – utter solitude without a policeman – by the way of silence – utter silence, where no warning voice of a kind neighbour can be heard whispering of public opinion? (*HD*, 154)

Like King Leopold, he suffered from an imperialistic megalomania:

> "I had immense plans" he muttered irresolutely [...]
> "I was on the threshold of great things' [...]
> "Your success in Europe is assured in case," I affirmed steadily. (*HD*, 173)

Kurtz is indeed the product of Europe, and is the perfect incarnation of the narratives of progress, superiority, and economic growth which are at the core of colonial policies:

51 Ian Ward, Law and the Brontës (Basingstoke and New York: Palgrave Macmillan, 2012), 46.

> The original Kurtz had been educated partly in England, and – as he was good enough to say himself – his sympathies were in the right place. His mother was half-English, his father was half-French. All Europe contributed to the making of Kurtz; and by and by I learned that, most appropriately, the International Society for the Suppression of Savage Customs had entrusted him with the making of a report, for its future guidance. (*HD*, 154–155)

The expeditions and penetration into the heart of the continent intertwine with the inner journey into this heart of darkness: both journeys – into the darkness of Africa and into man's soul – cannot be disentangled.

What is really relevant here is the journey from Europe to Africa Kurtz (and the civilisers) undertook in order to trade; the root taken by the ships on the Ocean and by the steamers on the Congo river; and the tracks and trails left by the trading agents in the forest. To put it differently: the mere act of trading.

The expressions I have already used in order to define the journey for trading purposes undertaken by the Europeans are all listed in the *Oxford English Dictionary* under the entry "trade." Although the term is a borrowing from the Middle Dutch, its etymology (and that of its cognate Middle Low German word, "trade") is probably the same as of tread, which derives from the Old English "tredan/trædan"(to walk, go, pace).

There is thus an intimate connection between trade and path. Not only did the slave trade cause "Six black men [advance] in a file, toiling up the path." (*HD*, 116), but it also made the population be cleared out:

> Paths, paths, everywhere; a stamped-in network of paths spreading over the empty land, through the long grass, through burnt grass, through thickets, down and up chilly ravines, up and down stony hills ablaze with heat; and a solitude, a solitude, nobody, not a hut. (*HD*, 121)

Hence, trade is a path, a voyage, a journey, an expedition undertaken for trading purposes into the depths of Africa. It also causes the "journey into the unknown regions of the self," where trade (the path) accrues human cupidity.[52] And this therefore turns Africa (the heart of darkness) into the darkness of the heart.

The equation between trade, path, and monstrosity is not unusual in English literature. The epic poem *Beowulf* is, for instance, an expedition undertaken in order to exterminate monsters – Grendel, Grendel's mother, the dragon – that terrify the land of Geats.[53] When Beowulf defeated Grendel for

52 Margareth Atwood, *Survival: A Thematic Guide to Canadian fiction* (Toronto: Anansi, 1972), 113.

53 See John R. R. Tolkien, "*Beowulf*: The Monsters and the Critics," in *Beowulf: A Verse Translation*, ed. Daniel Donoghue (New York and London: Norton, 2002): 103–130.

the first time, the latter returned to its cave, and the path, the trail he trod is covered with blood. In lines 840–845, indeed,

> [. . .] his fatal departure
> Was regretted by no one who witnessed his trail,
> The ignominious marks of his flight
> Where he'd skulked away, exhausted in spirit
> And beaten in battle, bloodying the path,
> Hauling his doom to the demons' mere.[54]

Again, in lines 1345–1356, the monsters trod "beyond the tracks of an exile":

> I have heard it said by my people in hall,
> counsellors who live in the uphand country,
> that they have seen two such creatures
> prowling the moors, huge marauders
> from some other world. One of these things,
> as far as anyone ever can discern,
> looks like a woman; the other, warped
> in the shape of a man, an unnatural birth
> called Grendel by the country people
> in forms days.[55]

Monsters are termed *æglæca*. The term, which is usually referred to monsters, devils, and Satan – is also used to denote human referents, such as in *Beowulf* and *Andreas*. Such a lexical pattern entails the "violent [. . .] deliberate and metaphoric extension of the meaning" of *æglæca* as to encompass human referents.[56]

Such extension is termed the denotation of a name: it "is just the things the name applies to; the things which have these properties which entitle them to be called by the name."[57] Human referents may also be *æglæcan* – i.e., may have monstrous qualities – because the community may probably have already encountered *æglæcan*-human beings in the whole body of their past experience. Monstrosity refers both to the path and to the journey, as well as to the act of trading. This causes a metaphorical transaction between the purpose of

---

54 *Beowulf: A Verse Translation*, 22–23.

55 *Beowulf: A Verse Translation*, 36–37.

56 Doreen M.E. Gillam, "The Use of the Term '*Æglæca*' in *Beowulf* at Lines 893 and 2592," *Studia Germanica Gandensia* III (1961): 145–169, 148. See also Leonard J. Peters, 'The Relationship of the Old English Andreas to Beowulf," *PMLA* 66.5 (1951): 844–863.

57 Ivor A. Richards, *Interpetation in Teaching* (London: Routledge & Kegan Paul; New York: Harcourt, Brace, 1938), 372–373.

the trade (the monster) and the trade itself: the innermost regions of the human being.[58]

In *Beowulf*, the use of *æglæca* thus designates the warrior with superhuman strength that fights against the monsters: to this extent, Beowulf is the "monster" amongst men: "*æglæca* meets *æglæcan*."[59] Like Beowulf, the emissaries of the nobly civilising mission fight against Africa's monstrosity; and, like Beowulf, Europeans are almost inhuman themselves. It is evident that Beowulf's inhumanity is not sinister nor inexcusable. The metaphorical transaction is a real path: "Beowulf knows himself. He accepts his lot, believing that it is his duty to face the monster alone."[60]

5 "The mind of man is capable of anything": turning the path into trade, and trade into monstrosity

By contrast, in Conrad's tales – but the assumption holds true as far as the whole African colonial saga is concerned – the metaphorical transaction underpinning the *colonial policy of monstrosity* aims to hide the real commitments of the journey undertaken for trading purposes. The path towards the innermost regions of the self is thus full of all the pejorative connotations that are usually listed under the term *æglæca*. Africa's wealth and resources whet men's cupidity, competition, lust, covetousness, unscrupulousness; and the imperialistic adventure accepts neither limitations nor constraints stemming from the human rights discourse which should underpin the civilising mission. The emotion attached to such bestial characteristics discloses that emissaries of civilisation "are outside the range of human understanding": but the path leads to the discovery that the policy of monstrosity is hostile to men.[61] As for the backward Africans this is evident:

> It was unearthly, and the men were – No, they were not inhuman. Well, you know, that was the worst of it – this suspicion of their not being inhuman. It would come slowly to one. They howled and leaped, and spun, and made horrid faces; but what thrilled you

58 Ivor A. Richards, *The Philosophy of Rhetoric* (Oxford: Oxford University Press, 1939), 94; Gillam, "The Use," 162.
59 Gillam, "The Use," 169.
60 Gillam, "The Use," 168.
61 Gillam, "The Use," 168.

> was just the thought of their humanity – like yours – the thought of your remote kinship with this wild and passionate uproar. (*HD*, 139)

Pondering the atrocities committed by King Leopold, Conrad thinks that "The mind of man is capable of anything" – even to hide the policy of monstrosity by turning the path (the journey) into pure trade. Firstly, the policy of monstrosity was incorporated under commercial law. Chartered companies were thus endowed with the *mission civilisatrice*: their "main business [. . .] is trade and [..] they become rulers only in consequence of trade"– and the same Congo Free State was termed as "The King Incorporated."[62] Trading Companies are at the very heart of both *Heart of Darkness* and *An Outpost of Progress* –in the latter, there is indeed the Great Trading Company. Secondly, market competitiveness – the manager's big concern in *Heart of Darkness* – was secured by the General Act of the Berlin Conference on West Africa, signed on the 26th day of February, 1885. As Art. 1 of the Act solemnly stated, "The trade of all nations shall enjoy complete freedom: [. . .] 1. In all the regions forming the basin of the Congo and its outlets."[63] Thirdly, free trade was intended to suppress slavery and slave trade, in accordance with Art. 6 of the General Act.[64] But such provisions contrast with the reality of colonialism, and the widespread of forced labour in colonial Africa,[65] as Conrad reports.

> They were dying slowly – it was very clear. They were not enemies, they were not criminals, they were nothing earthly now – nothing but black shadows of disease and starvation, lying confusedly in the greenish gloom. Brought from all the recesses of the coast in all the legality of time contracts, lost in uncongenial surroundings, fed on unfamiliar food, they sickened, became inefficient, and were then allowed to crawl away and rest. These moribund shapes were free as air – and nearly as thin (*HD*, 118).

However, trade is not common-law coverture. And the law cannot definitively incorporate the policy of monstrosity nor totally inhibit the brutal cupidity that lies in man's innermost self. Nor can the mask of progress and civilisation prevent the ultimate purpose of trading from being solemnly declared:

---

62 Egerton, *A Short History*, 466; Neal Ascherson, *The King Incorporated* (London: George Allen & Unwin, 1963).

63 Matthew Craven, "Between law and history: The Berlin Conference of 1884–1885 and the logic of free trade," *London Review of International Law* 3.1 (2015): 31–59.

64 See Article 6 of the General Act: "All the Powers exercising sovereign rights or influence in the aforesaid territories bind themselves to watch over the preservation of the native tribes, and to care for the improvement of the conditions of their moral and material well-being, and to help in suppressing slavery, and especially the slave trade."

65 Albert Nzula et al., *Forced Labour in Colonial Africa* (London: Zed Press, 1979).

> The word "ivory" rang in the air, was whispered, was sighed. You would think they were praying to it. A taint of imbecile rapacity blew through it all, like a whiff from some corpse. By Jove! I've never seen anything so unreal in my life. And outside, the silent wilderness surrounding this cleared speck on the earth struck me as something great and invincible, like evil or truth, waiting patiently for the passing away of this fantastic invasion. (*HD*, 125)

Again, Conrad discloses what lies beneath trade, civilisation, and progress. These concepts look like a magic formula, an empty box to be filled by colonial powers:

> Society, not from any tenderness, but because of its strange needs, had taken care of those two men, forbidding them all independent thought, all initiative, all departure from routine; and forbidding it under pain of death. They could only live on condition of being machines. (*OP*, 6)

And the *void to be filled*, of which progress consists is apparent in the final lines of *An Outpost of Progress*. At the beginning of the essay, I made reference to them when reporting the disembarkation of the Manager Director of the 'Great Civilising Company' at the trading-station. Hence, we have just one little thing to close the loop. Kaynerts and Carlier realised they are but slave-dealers, and that "There's nothing but slave-dealers in this cursed country [. . .] There's nothing here: there's nothing but you and I." (*OP*, 21) They began to quarrel and, fearing that Carlier would make him his slave, Kayerts shot Carlier.

Coverture has failed – and trade revealed its own unhuman, monstrous character. The steamer approaches; and the policy of monstrosity turns into trade and civilisation – and as the latter follows trade – into progress.

> Progress was calling to Kayerts from the river. Progress and civilization and all the virtues. Society was calling to its accomplished child to come, to be taken care of, to be instructed, to be judged, to be condemned; it called him to return to that rubbish heap from which he had wandered away, so that justice could be done. (*HD*, 25)

"Kayerts heard and understood." He understood that progress and trade are mere shapes, beneath which there is the void of cupidity. Like global law, colonial law only hides over the monstrosity of human domination over other human beings. It is like death; it is, in Milton's words,

> The other shape,
> If shape it might be called that shape had none
> Distinguishable in member, joint, or limb;
> Or substance might be called that shadow seemed,
> For each seemed either, black it stood as night,
> Fierce as ten furies, terrible as Hell,

And shook a dreadful dart: what seemed his head
The likeness of a kingly crown had on.[66]

The Managing Director of the Great Civilizing Company finally disembarks, and appreciates the effects of colonial progress and civilisation. Kayerts has understood that, like death, progress's "shape [...] shape had none" – and swung himself off. There is nothing to do; nothing to say. Nothing, but death. The white man had tried to subdue Africa with little outcome. There is nothing to do. Like Kayerts, who "irreverently, [...] was putting out a swollen tongue at his Managing Director," we should only take it with humour.

66 John Milton, *Paradise Lost*, ed. Stephen Orgel and Jonathan Goldberg (Oxford: Oxford University Press, 2008), II, 666–673. See Edmund Burke, *A Philosophical Enquiry into the Origin of Our Ideas of the Sublime and Beautiful* (London, 1757), 44.

Roberta Zanoni

Harry Potter and Monstrous Diversity: The Brexit Case

1 Reality and fiction

"One apprehends reality only through representations of reality, through texts, discourses, images."[1] In the contemporary mass media saturated scenario people's perception of reality is often constructed and negotiated, it can be said that mass media have become a lens through which people perceive the world and the reality which surrounds them. The media give audiences a language which inevitably shapes their thoughts "More broadly than simple consent, language, as something particularly human, shapes how we see the world in general [...] while we do not always realise it, language acts as a determinate factor in the formation of our perceptions of the world."[2]

Although this process may seem elitist and is often hegemonic, contemporary culture at its core, whilst mediated, comes from people's reality. Culture absorbs the main trends of the reality it is immersed in, and records people's tastes and desires, and re-presents them to the audience in a new mediatised light.

> Culture is a living, active process: it can be developed only from within, it cannot be imposed from without or above. [...] Popular culture is made by the people, not produced by the culture industry. All the culture industries can do is produce a repertoire of texts or cultural resources for the various formations of people to use or to reject in the ongoing process of producing their popular culture.[3]

In the cultural representation of reality all the latter's components will be reproduced to a greater or lesser extent: also some minute details, practices, and beliefs will be incorporated in this type of representation, and, at times – as in the Harry Potter books – they will only surface on a second or more accurate scrutiny. The Harry Potter series can be said to be deeply engrained in British popular culture in particular, and, nowadays – after the global success of the books and films – in international culture in general. For what concerns British

1 Richard Dyer, "Introduction," in *The Matter of Images* (London: Routledge, 2002), 3.
2 John Collins, Ross Glover "Introduction," in *Collateral Language*, eds. John Collins Ross Glover (New York: New York University Press, 2002): 1–15, 4.
3 John Fiske, *Understanding Popular Culture* (London: Routledge, 1989), 23, 24.

https://doi.org/10.1515/9783110654615-016

popular culture, the books perfectly represent the feeling of nostalgia for a mythical past typical of the numerous cultural representations of "old" Great Britain. While the books are set in contemporary Britain, indeed, the magical world's dresses, buildings, and social and school systems recall an unspecified past. Furthermore, the setting of the books in well-known British places has fostered the identification of the audience and the connexion of the events to reality. The use of magic realism, suggesting that the magical world exists within the real one and sometimes interacts with it, has made readers believe they could almost come into contact with the fictional enchanted world in their everyday life: the train which brings wizards and witches to Hogwarts School of Magic departs from platform 9 and ¾ in Kings Cross Station in London, at which people access in the space between platforms 9 and 10 of the real station; Diagon Ally, the place where the main wizarding shops are, is accessed through the Leaky Cauldron, a pub in Charing Cross Road[4]; Harry and Mr. Weasley access the Ministry of Magic through a phone box in a street in London; and St. Mungo's Hospital for Magical Maladies and Injuries is hidden in a "large, old-fashioned, red-brick department store called Purge & Dowse Ltd,"[5] "in the very heart of London."[6]

The transposition of the books to cinema, in addition, has contributed to the worldwide diffusion of J. K. Rowling's stories. The books and films, moreover, have accompanied the lives of generations, becoming part of popular culture and entering real life.

The Harry Potter saga, indeed, demonstrates the power of fiction not only to draw inspiration from reality but also to influence it. Interestingly enough, on September the 1st, 2017, the day portrayed in the last chapter of the Harry Potter saga "Nineteen years later" – the day in which Harry's son Albus goes to Hogwarts, catching the train at Kings Cross station in London – people actually gathered in Kings Cross station in order to participate in that fictional moment. The event, happened ten years after the last book had been written, does not only show the enduring influence of Harry Potter on his readers' lives, and consequently its contemporary resonance, but it is also emblematic of the remarkable encounter of fiction and reality and of their mutual relationship.

A real-life Quidditch association was born in 2005, and in nine years it led to the establishment of the international Quidditch championship involving teams from all over the world:

4 J. K. Rowling, *Harry Potter and the Half-Blood Prince* (London: Bloomsbury, 2005), 107.
5 Rowling, *Harry Potter and the Order of the Phoenix*, (London: Bloomsbury, 2003), 426, 427.
6 Rowling, *Harry Potter and the Order of the Phoenix*, 426.

> Quidditch is the world's only mixed-gender, full-contact sport, and is played everywhere from Turkey to Canada to Uganda to Australia to Hong Kong. It is truly a worldwide sport, and is enjoyed by athletes of all ages and athletic backgrounds.
> [...]
> Real-life quidditch was created on a sunny Sunday afternoon in 2005 by Xander Manshel and Alex Benepe, students at Middlebury College in Vermont, USA. Their idle Sunday pastime laid the foundations for the full contact and gender inclusive sport played today. They began playing regular intramural games, and in 2007 played the first intercollegiate match. [...]
> As quidditch grew, more international governance was needed outside of the USA. A new, truly international IQA was born in 2014 when the IQA split from US Quidditch. Since then, the IQA has worked to ensure equitable representation and development in all corners of the globe.[7]

People from all over the world are bringing socks to Dobby's statue at the Harry Potter Exhibition in the Warner Bros Studio in London to replicate a scene from the book.[8] Some of the books Harry and his friends read during the saga, such as *Fantastic Beasts and Where to Find Them*,[9] *Quidditch Through the Ages*,[10] have actually been published.

It can thus be said that the Harry Potter saga has come to be part of British popular culture, a symbol of British identity both nationally recognised and exported abroad which has also been capable of influencing real-life events.

These observations tend to demonstrate that the fictional world can sometimes hold in itself the seeds of real-life manifestations, and that fiction can sometimes predict what will happen in the everyday world due to its capacity to profoundly scrutinise human passions and inclinations. In particular, the analysis of the ascent of Lord Voldemort and his condemnation of Muggle-borns to acquire power makes it possible to draw a parallel with the climate of fear and of xenophobia induced by the Brexit Leave campaign following the victory in the referendum on June 23rd, 2016. My reflection will thus follow the idea of the construction of identity and of otherness inside popular culture, demonstrating in which way the latter has revealed a trend which later has

---

7 International Quidditch Association website, available at: http://www.iqasport.com/about/history (last access July 25, 2018).

8 Jess Denham, "Harry Potter fans are trying to free Dobby by leaving socks on the Warner Bros Studio Tour," *Independent*, October 1, 2015, available at: https://www.independent.co.uk/arts-entertainment/films/news/harry-potter-fans-are-trying-to-free-dobby-by-leaving-socks-on-the-warner-bros-studio-tour-a6674936.html (last access August 4, 2018).

9 J. K. Rowling, *Fantastic Beasts and Where to Find Them* (London: Bloomsbury, 2017).

10 J.K. Rowling, *Quidditch Through the Ages* by Kennilworthy Whisp (London: Bloomsbury, 2001).

been detected in real life. Furthermore, I will elucidate the parallels between the books and the real-life situation in order to demonstrate that the former have succeeded in representing a typically British society tenaciously divided in terms of identarian and class distinctions, the same society from which Brexit originated.

2 Different perspectives on diversity

Furthermore, I will elucidate the way in which the fictional rhetoric often works as the real-life one, speaking through commonplaces or through general concepts universally shareable and appealing to the largest possible audience. It is in this context that the concepts of "the monster" and of "monstrosity" become so appealing. When representing reality, fiction inevitably alters it, it mitigates it or brings it to its extremes: in the imaginary rhetoric difference becomes monstrosity. The monster represents people's fears, their negative or hidden feelings. The figure of Lord Voldemort in Harry Potter epitomises and gives voice to contemporary fears and represents evil on the fictional level.

> The monster is the limit, [...] the monster combines the impossible and the forbidden. [...] although it is a breach of the law [...] the monster is, so to speak, the spontaneous, brutal, but consequently natural form of the unnatural. It is the magnifying model, the form of every possible little irregularity exhibited by the games of nature. In this sense [...] the monster is the major model of every little deviation. It is the principle of intelligibility of all the forms that circulate as the small change of abnormality. The recurring problem of the nineteenth century is that of discovering the core of monstrosity hidden behind little abnormalities, deviances, and irregularities. [...] The characteristic feature of the monster is to express itself as, precisely, monstrous, to be the explanation to every little deviation that may derive from it.[11]

Voldemort is the Dark Lord, "He Who Must Not Be Named"; he unscrupulously uses the powerful whereas highly dangerous and destructive Dark Arts, an evil magic employed in order to make others suffer and in order to achieve personal and malevolent goals. At the same time, also Harry, the positive hero of the story, is sometimes attracted by this type of magic, and, in some occasions, contemplates the option of making use of it. Voldemort's and Harry's lives are connected, both symbolically and physically: Harry's and Voldemort's wands are made of two feathers of the same bird, the phoenix; and in Harry resides a

11 Michel Foucault, *Abnormal: Lectures at the Collège de France* 1974–1975, trans. Graham Burchell (London: Verso, 2003), 56, 57.

part of Voldemort's soul. However, they are also linked on a more profound level, they are the same person *in potentia*: their characters are very similar, they were both outcasts, orphans raised by Muggles; they felt different because they did not understand their magical powers when they were young; they both spoke Parseltongue, the snakes language; they were both accepted to Hogwarts, and gained Dumbledore's protection; they both had great courage and often disrespected the rules. They represent the possible development of the same person's life: their paths part when Harry decides to do good and Voldemort to be evil. In both lives, however, shades and traces of the other are present, and Harry's leanings and interest for his own dark hues demonstrate the allure of evil and transgression also in a righteous life. The monster is thus both the stranger, the complete evil, the *unheimlich,*[12] something people want to avoid, and at the same time it represents one of the innermost parts of all human-beings, connected to the fascination with the unknown, with what is prohibited, or what is beyond people's reach. It is the lure of that part of our personality which we feel hidden within ourselves and we fear to let emerge. Indeed, since Voldemort is He Who Must Not Be Named, people in the magical world try to erase him from their language in order to erase him from their consciences. This practice, however, gains the opposite effect, because it engenders curiosity and beguilement for what is foreign, new, or mysterious.

Indeed, not only does the monster stand for what is fearful, but also for what is hidden, in this sense representing both the outcasts of society and people's most repressed and obscure feelings and instincts. The monster, in this acceptation, is sneaking, creeping, perfectly embodied by the snake Nagini, the alter ego of Lord Voldemort. He Who Must Not Be Named represents the "different": at the beginning of the story he is the "other," excluded and rejected from society and compelled to hide in order to escape the power of law.

In *Harry Potter and the Philosopher's Stone* he is believed to be hiding somewhere in Albania, while he is concealed on the back of Professor Quirrel's head. In this case, he represents the monster as a parasite, as secreted and secluded from society, capable of existing and of participating in social life only at the expenses of others:

> Harry would have screamed, but he couldn't make a sound. Where there should have been a back to Quirrell's head, there was a face, the most terrible face Harry had ever seen. It was chalk white with glaring red eyes and slits for nostrils, like a snake. "Harry Potter..." it whispered. Harry tried to take a step backward but his legs wouldn't move. "See what I have become?" the face said. "Mere shadow and vapor ... I have form only

12 Sigmund Freud, *The Uncanny*, trans. David McLintock (London: Penguin, 2003).

> when I can share another's body… but there have always been those willing to let me into their hearts and minds…."[13]

In *Harry Potter and the Chamber of Secrets* Voldemort comes back in the shape of a diary in which his young self is incarnated and from which he takes power by alluring a student into giving him/her vital energy and in performing acts on his behalf. He is still weak, but the episode shows his growing appeal and the power of fear which transforms an insubstantial menace into something real and dangerous.

In *Harry Potter and the Prisoner of Azkaban* Voldemort's servant Wormtail is freed and runs to him: this key event will mark the return of the Dark Lord, as Professor Trelawney, the divination teacher, had predicted:

> *It will happen tonight. The Dark Lord lies alone and friendless, abandoned by his followers. His servant has been chained these twelve years. Tonight, before midnight… the servant will break free and set out to rejoin his master. The Dark Lord will rise again with his servant's aid, greater and more terrible than ever he was. Tonight… before midnight… the servant… will set out… to rejoin… his master…*[14]

In these books the appearances of Voldemort are very few and his power is extremely limited but his name or the definitions attached to him are pervasive: most of the time he is made present by the others' discourses. People, in this sense, are creating their own fears through their cogitations.

Voldemort finally makes his return in *Harry Potter and the Goblet of Fire* and demonstrates he has gathered more supporters when the Death Eaters join him in the graveyard where he has managed to take a human shape again.[15]

In *Harry Potter and the Order of the Phoenix* the Minister of Magic, Cornelius Fudge, hides the signs of Voldemort's reappearance, at first because he does not believe in it but also to keep the appearances of order and normality in society and in order not to lose credibility thus being removed from his office. Fudge tries to find excuses to explain the anomalous events taking place because he subconsciously does not accept the return of Voldemort.

> In *Harry Potter and the Goblet of Fire*, Fudge refuses to believe in Voldemort's return and continues to ignore rather than accept the truth, all to avoid alarming the wizarding world. In *Harry Potter and the Order of the Phoenix* he uses the press to cast a negative

---

13 J. K. Rowling, *Harry Potter and the Philosopher's Stone* (London: Bloomsbury, 1998), 236.
14 J. K. Rowling, *Harry Potter and the Prisoner of Azkaban* (London: Bloomsbury, 1999), 324 [Italics in the text].
15 See chapter 33 of J. K. Rowling, *Harry Potter and the Goblet of Fire* (London: Bloomsbury, 2000):559–571, titled precisely "The Death Eaters."

> light on wise Dumbledore (Hogwarts School's Headmaster) and Harry, exposing the latter as a liar. He also tries to control the local magical world's "education centre," i.e. Hogwarts, placing his Undersecretary, Dolores Umbridge [...], first as a teacher and then as Headmaster in the same school.[16]

The monster, in this case, is what is removed, He Who Must Not be Named, the unsaid of society, whose menace grows stronger and stronger also because he is not openly fought and confronted. Voldemort, however, has started raising an army; therefore, the Order of the Phoenix – an army of good wizards and witches – is re-established to fight him. In this chapter of the saga the Ministry uses the press to discredit Dumbledore for political reasons, and Harry because he is the one who witnessed the return of Lord Voldemort:

> Characters who previously belonged to the ranks of "good people," like public servants or Fudge, now completely change their stance, acting in the same way as the worst dictators, gradually taking possession of the press, the political organisation, the Ministry of education, and, above all, the judicial system.
>
> The protagonist's trial becomes, in fact, only the first one of the important signals that the war is approaching. The government, ignoring the warnings to the point of foolishness, becomes thereby, with no holds barred, an accomplice of all the terrible events that will be described later.[17]

In *Harry Potter and the Half-Blood Prince* Voldemort starts threatening both the magical and the non-magical world, in which he starts killing Muggles, thus demonstrating that his power has grown and that he does not need to hide anymore. He represents darkness approaching, which is capable of both scaring and at the same time tempting many wizards and witches.

In *Harry Potter and the Deadly Hallows* Voldemort manages to enter society, taking control of its central bodies: the ministry of magic, the press, and Hogwarts school. He thus creates his own society, reversing the conception of the "others": the outcasts are now the people he wants to exclude because they are not conforming to his idea of identity – i.e. Muggles and Muggle-borns. In Voldemort's rhetoric they become monstrous.

The bad-good, dark-light oppositions found in the books[18] give an overly simplistic representation of reality which, although mitigated, can underline

---

16 Giovanna Ligugnana, "An Invented Executive: The Ministry of Magic in *Harry Potter*," in *Fables of the Law*, eds. Daniela Carpi, Marett Leiboff (Berlin: de Gruyter, 2016): 419–435, 424.

17 Daniela Carpi, *Fairy Tales in the Postmodern World* (Memmingen: Winter, 2016), 155.

18 As previously stated dark hues and inclinations can be found also in the positive characters and, in particular, in Harry. However, his allegiance to the good side is always clear to the reader.

the major developments in the contemporary political scenario. Voldemort's power is very weak in the first books, his popularity is restricted to few conservative characters part of the nobility and belonging to the pure-blood lineage who keep their allegiance concealed in case of his return: some of them even deny their past loyalty in order to be able to live in the society which had once cast out the Dark Lord. His power, however, increases more and more throughout the books, and in the last one, *Harry Potter and the Deathly Hallows*, he manages to gather a whole army.

Similarly, in the Brexit scenario, the far-right, pro-Leave Ukip party did not enjoy a wide favour in the early years but managed to have a strong influence on the public opinion in the referendum. It relied on the need for identity some people felt very strongly and on the racial hatred and fear silently influencing people's actions. The Leave propaganda spoke as the fictional one and was as effective.

The discourses on "the other" of the Leave Campaign were based on general notions of identity and nationality, mostly stereotypes stemming from popular culture. The "British Identity" promoted during the campaign corresponded to vague acceptations of Britishness mostly related to race and citizenship but highly general and adapted by every individual to his/her own system of values.

> [Identity] [...] is represented as the function of some pre-political, socio-biological or bio-cultural feature, something genetic – like 'race,' blood and kinship – that sanctions especially harsh varieties of deterministic or absolutist thinking about identity. In these circumstances, identity chases to be an on-going process of self-making and social interaction. It becomes instead a *thing* – an entity or an object – to be possessed and displayed.[19]

Similarly, in Harry Potter identity is strongly factual, it has racial connotations, people are defined by their alleged blood purity: Muggles "nonmagic folk,"[20] born in the non-magical world; Muggle-borns, wizards and witches born from Muggle parents; Half-bloods, wizards and witches with one Muggle parent; Mudbloods, a derogatory and offensive term referring to the two latter ones:

> Mudblood's a really foul name for someone who is Muggle-born – you know, non-magic parents. There are some wizards – like Malfoy's family – who think they're better than everyone else because they're what people call pure-blood [...] I mean, the rest of us

19 Paul Gilroy, "Diaspora and the Detours of Identity," in *Identity and Difference*, ed. Kathryn Woodward (London: Sage, 1997), 307.

20 J. K. Rowling, *Harry Potter and the Philosopher's Stone* (London: Bloomsbury, 1997), 40.

> know it doesn't make any difference at all. Look at Neville Longbottom – he's pure-blood and he can hardly stand a cauldron the right way up."[21]

Squibs are non-magical beings born in a wizarding family, and Pure-bloods are wizards and witches coming from a wizarding ancestry. One of the very interesting aspects of the books is that also the positive characters, such as Harry, Ron and Hermione have internalised this type of rhetoric and express themselves through these terms. They use all terms except the derogatory and offensive "mud-blood." They obviously do not share the exclusive and discriminatory ideas of Lord Voldemort, but their way of speaking demonstrates the deep entrenching of these distinctions in their culture – a fictional culture which inexorably reflects the real-life it stemmed from.

The Harry Potter books and Brexit propaganda demonstrate the power of language to artfully conceive discourses and images apt to shape the public opinion. Voldermort's discourses on the supremacy of wizards on Muggles and of the latter suffering for the sake of a "Greater Good" are based on a generic concept of Good – possibly universally shareable because all people allegedly want to do and to pursue Good – but adopted, in this case, to sustain a totalitarian practice. Remarkably, also Dumbledore had shared these beliefs in his young age:

> wizard dominance being FOR THE MUGGLES' OWN GOOD – this, I think, is the crucial point. Yes we have been given power and, yes, that power gives us the right to rule, but it also gives us responsibilities over the ruled. We must stress this point, it will be the foundation stone upon which we build. Where we are opposed, as we surely will be, this must be the basis of our counter-arguments. We seize control FOR THE GREATER GOOD.[22]

This kind of generalised discourses and oversimplified rhetoric is very similar to that adopted by the Leave Campaign, which promoted concepts such as "security at home" and "taking back control": "Political language has to consist largely of euphemism, question-begging and sheer cloudy vagueness."[23]

The political strategy adopted by Lord Voldemort was based on hatred and condemnation of all Muggle-born wizards and Muggles. The discourses on immigrants, based on general notions of identity and nationality – mostly stereotypes of "Britishness" or "Englishness" coming from popular culture – can be

---

21 J. K. Rowling, *Harry Potter and the Chamber of Secrets* (London: Bloomsbury, 1998), 74.
22 J. K. Rowling, *Harry Potter and the Deathly Hallows* (London: Bloomsbury, 2007), 291. [Emphasis in the original]
23 George Orwell, "Politics and the English Language", in *The Orwell Reader* (Harcourt: Brace and Company, 1956), 363, 364.

compared to the ideological definition of Muggles in the books which derive from indisputable, and at the same time meaningless, categorisations, such as those based on blood. Identity becomes phenomenological rather than ontological: it is something a person possesses and not what someone is, his/her character and actions, defining his/her inclusion within a particular group. Dumbledore himself stigmatises this conviction: "You place too much importance, and you always have done, on the so-called purity of blood! You fail to recognise that it matters not what someone is born, but what they grow to be!"[24]

The apparent impossibility of Voldemort's ascent and the unexpected fast spreading of his power and convictions fictionally represent the same evolution as the Brexit Leave campaign. At first perceived as farcical and inconclusive, then gaining more and more power, and finally winning, the Leave Campaign lead to episodes of racism and hatred towards immigrants after the Brexit Referendum. Voldemort's discourses on the supremacy of the wizards and the loathing for the "other" and the "different," which have inspired his and other figures in the books, were probably registering a sentiment of insecurity and of xenophobia which was silently creeping into British Popular Culture when the books were written. The same feelings emerged and were given prominence when the EU question was raised.

The Leave Campaign was based on many points trying to foster British national identity on its own and, at the same time, as opposed to others. The ideas of "taking back control of the borders," of "wanting the country back," and the insinuations on the possibility of Turkey joining the EU, with a consequent allegedly unrestrained migration flow, all played a strong role in drawing the attention of people towards the defence of their identity as opposed to an unspecified and vague 'other': "defining a nation and its identity is in part about inclusion and exclusion. Who is to be included as British? Who is to be excluded as non-British, as different? The answers to such questions are historically specific – and often politically explosive."[25] The campaign failed to acknowledge that "nationality is not natural but contingent: it changes with historical circumstance."[26]

In this sense, once more, reality proves to influence fictional works which then seem to be forecasting some real-life events because of their capacity to register beforehand the popular trends and inclinations. Popular culture

24 Rowling, *Harry Potter and the Goblet of Fire*, 708.

25 Jeremy Paxman, "Preface," in *The English. Portrait of a People* (London: Michael Joseph, 1998), iii.

26 Paxman, "Preface," iii.

generalises and exploits the feelings of the multitude, in this way depicting real life. The cultural background which has given life to the books, thus, is the same which has brought to the Brexit Referendum. It is in this sense that literature demonstrates its capacity, through the author's fantasy, to register even the slightest particulars of reality and, sometimes, to presage what will happen in the future. Furthermore, the Brexit Leave Campaign made use of the same generalised notions and stereotypes which nourished the Harry Potter series.

Additionally, while Great Britain has often been considered a welcoming and multicultural country, the victory of the Leave Campaign has demonstrated that the feelings of hatred for the immigrants and the consequent defence of the "pure" origin of the British have never died. The same feelings of hatred for those who are different, and the same classist and divided society portrayed in the books have surfaced after the victory of the Leave Campaign, which has in some way legitimised the loathing for the other – a reaction which highly distanced itself from the actual purpose and meaning of the referendum. Furthermore, the Manichean rhetoric used by the Ukip party presents some similarities with the rhetoric used by Voldemort in the Harry Potter books.

3 Harry Potter and Brexit

The parallels between the books and real-life events are multiple: Cornelius Fudge, the Minister of Magic, is compelled to resign because he did not believe in the return of Lord Voldemort. He undervalued and apparently unwittingly covered Voldemort's return. The figure of Cornelius Fudge can be compared to that of David Cameron, the one proposing the Brexit referendum in the first place because he was sure of the Remain victory, while then resigning after the defeat. The fictional and the real Minister are similar in their undervaluing people's inclinations and popular beliefs, which costed them their position.

The feeling produced in some people by the victory of the Leave Campaign matches the feeling of despair depicted in the books when the Ministry is subdued by Lord Voldemort who also changes the statue in the Atrium – previously depicting "a noble-looking wizard [...] a beautiful witch, a centaur, a goblin and a house-elf"[27] – with one titled "Magic is Might" portraying Muggles crushed by the weight of a stone on which two wizards are standing. The hate for the Muggles has been, therefore, institutionalised. Muggle-borns are

27 Rowling, *Harry Potter and the Order of the Phoenix*, 117.

interrogated on their origins by the Ministry representatives questioning their belonging to the magical world and threatening their lives:

> Recent research undertaken by the Department of Mysteries reveals that magic can only be passed from person to person when wizards reproduce. Where no proven wizarding ancestry exists, therefore, the so-called Muggle-born is likely to have obtained magical power by theft or force.[28]

The totalitarian strategy of Lord Voldemort concerns also the mass media. In Harry Potter's magical world, the main newspaper is the *Daily Prophet* – a sort of mixture between newspaper and television because of the nature of wizarding photographs as moving images. The *Daily Prophet* is the voice of the establishment and conveys the views of the government; the only discordant voice is that of *The Quibbler,* a paper edited by Xenophilius Lovegood who often publishes invented or peculiar news but who gives voice to Harry and stands on his side (until his daughter is taken and he decides to support Voldemort's propaganda in order to save her). When Voldemort takes possession of the *Daily Prophet* the facts start to be altered: Dumbledore, the most famous and beloved wizard in the previous books, is disparaged and discredited, and Harry Potter becomes the "Undesirable n°1." The reversal and loss of certainties creates a general sense of insecurity. It also demonstrates that a totalitarian power needs to take over the mass media in order to guide public opinion, giving pre-eminence to artfully constructed messages, devised to support its authority.

In a similar fashion, the Leave Campaign made wide use of newspapers in order to reach the largest possible audience. The front cover of *Metro* on June the 20th featured the Vote Leave catchphrase "take back control."[29] The front covers of *The Sun* on June the 14th and that of the *Daily Mail* on June the 22nd openly favoured the Leave Campaign. The former displayed the words "Be-LEAVE in Britain, Vote to quit EU," and the latter "If you Believe in Britain vote Leave." Obviously also the Remain Campaign made use of mass media in general and newspapers in particular. However, the catchy slogans and the well-devised images conceived by the Leave propaganda profited of the resonance given them by the newspapers and managed to reach and have an impact on a very high number of people with simple, easily understandable, and approachable concepts.

Voldemort's ascent from a very low status to a large consensus can be compared with the fast escalation of the Ukip party's popularity: once considered

---

28 Rowling, *Harry Potter and the Deathly Hallows*, 172.
29 *Metro*, London: Associated Newspapers, June 20, 2016.

as a minor party at first losing in the polls and believed to be weak, it only gained a position in the political debate in the year before the Referendum. Its influence and power raised "following the tragic death of Labour MP Jo Cox and a controversial Ukip migration poster"[30] in the last weeks before the referendum.

The migration poster displayed a considerably large group of mainly dark-skinned migrants and refugees in a lengthy queue in a field. The caption to the picture was constituted by the red words "BREAKING POINT"[31] in capital letters, the subtitle to this caption was: "The EU has failed us all," "we must break free of the EU and take back control of our borders" written in white and in a smaller font. The implications of the image are stunning: it suggests that there was a hoard of people pushing at the borders of the UK and that the EU wanted them to enter, it also played on the possibility for Turkey of entering the EU, thus allegedly opening the doors of the UK to even more migrants. The image, however, was utterly misleading: it did not portray the UK border at the time of the referendum but a queue of migrants and refugees at the Croatia-Slovenia border in October 2015. The time of release and the power it had on public opinion, nonetheless, strongly influenced the outcome of the vote. The poster was also criticized by Johnson and by other supporters of the Leave Campaign, but the effect it had on the public is an example of the profound resonance this kind of images can have in the consciences of the multitude. As elaborate "works of fiction" they have often a stronger impact than real news.

The killing of MP Jo Cox, on the other hand, represents a controversial episode which gives an impression of the tense situation in the period right before and after the Referendum. The murder was perpetrated by a Nazi fanatic who allegedly shouted "Britain first" while murdering the woman.[32] The victim was a labour MP who had campaigned on international human rights, on the Syrian civil war, on Gaza, and who was a Remain supporter. While her killing could be seen as demonstrating the reasons of the Remain Campaign, it actually intensified the climate of fear and insecurity perceived by the population, and, in an unexpected way, it further emphasised the

---

30 Daniel Dunford, Ashley Kirk, "How right or wrong were the polls about the EU referendum?," *The Telegraph*, June 27, 2016.

31 Available at: https://politicaladvertising.co.uk/2016/06/20/breaking-point/ (last access July 25, 2018), [capital letters in the original].

32 Peter Walker, "Jo Cox murder trial: 'Thomas Mair repeatedly shouted 'Britain First' before shooting and stabbing MP,'" *Independent*, November 14, 2016, available at: https://www.independent.co.uk/news/uk/home-news/jo-cox-murder-trial-tommy-mair-britain-first-thomas-mp-killer-court-latest-a7416021.html (last access July 29, 2018).

need for "security at home," highlighted by the Leave Campaign. Moreover, it demonstrated how entrenched in culture the propaganda pro Britain had become in its opposition to an unspecified "other": a monstrous entity menacing British people both from the outside and from the inside, threatening their identity and their safety. However, there was – and there still is – no shared conception of British identity, everyone could possibly provide his/her own definition of such an intricate concept, which is often reduced to being born in Great Britain and being of British descent. This definition, however, does not take into consideration those second or third generation immigrant citizens who, from this viewpoint, are not considered British because of their race.

> Being English used to be so easy. They were one of the most easily identified peoples on earth, recognised by their language, their manners, their clothes and the fact that they drank tea by the bucketload. It is all so much more complicated now. When, occasionally, we come across someone whose stiff upper lip, sensible shoes or tweedy manner identifies them as English, we react in amusement: the conventions that defined the English are dead and the country's ambassadors are more likely to be singers than diplomats or politicians.[33]

Analogously, in the Harry Potter books old-fashioned and racist definitions divide the society and an emblematic killing precedes the ascent of Lord Voldemort. Professor Charity Burbage, the Muggle-Studies teacher, is killed by Voldemort because:

> [She] taught the children of witches and wizards all about Muggles. . .how they are not so different from [wizards] [. . .] Not content with corrupting and polluting the minds of wizarding children, last week Professor Burbage wrote an impassioned defence of Mudbloods in the *Daily Prophet*. Wizards, she says, must accept these thieves of their knowledge and magic. The dwindling of the pure-bloods is, [she] says [. . .], a most desirable circumstance . . . she would have us all mate with Muggles.[34]

Her killing also demonstrates the need of erasing the "other," in this case, from Voldemort's perspective, the Muggles, from the consciences of the younger people. The interference in education is part of the seizure of power of every totalitarian system. The debate on the other is expunged: if education is subdued – as it initially happens in *Harry Potter and the Deathly Hallows* – also the future will be under control.

---

33 Paxman, "Preface," iii.
34 Rowling, *Harry Potter and the Deathly Hallows*, 17, 18.

4 The aftermath of Brexit

The use of the deceiving poster previously mentioned demonstrates the utmost simplification and manipulation of the EU-question at the hand of the Leave propaganda: "To pretend that migration to the UK is only about people who are not white is to peddle the racism that has no place in a modern, caring society. That's why Unison has complained about this blatant attempt to incite racial hatred and breach UK race laws."[35] This type of propaganda, indeed, failed to acknowledge that migration to the UK from Europe concerns also white people; that the exit from the EU will not ultimately stop the migration flow to the UK; and that the foreign people already living in UK as citizens are not touched by the exit from the EU. The racial hatred directed to the preservation of British identity, thus, testified to the generalisation and oversimplification of the various purposes of the Brexit Referendum.

Both real life and fictional episodes demonstrate the presence of a sneaking feeling of hatred and fear characterising British culture – which can ultimately be registered in the international scenario as well – and which finally emerged after the victory of the Leave Campaign. After the Brexit vote, indeed, a series of episodes of racism and hatred were registered in the UK. These episodes were curiously often directed towards the Muslim and the Polish communities already living in the UK – and thus possibly immune from the referendum's outcome – they were pressed to "go home," or were menaced to be killed. Writings on walls and flags read as follows: "EU rats go home now,"[36] "no more Polish vermin,"[37] "Kill all Muslims,"[38] "Brits only, no foreigners," "Born in England, Live in England, Die in England."[39]

---

35 Dave Prentis' claim reported by Heather Stewart and Rowena Mason, "Nigel Farage's anti-migrant poster reported to police" in *The Guardian*, June 16, 2016.

36 Available at: https://europe.liveuamap.com/en/2016/5-july-torquay-united-kingdom-eu-rats-go-home (last access July 25, 2018)

37 "Huntingdon 'Polish vermin' cards case remains a mystery," *BBC website*, November 27, 2016, available at: https://www.bbc.com/news/uk-england-cambridgeshire-38107645 (last access July 25, 2018)

38 "The British Brexit Referendum Has Spurred Increased Racism" in *The Islamic Post*, June 26, 2018, available at: https://www.islamicpostonline.com/featured/2018/06/26/the-british-brexit-referendum-has-spurred-increased-racism-report/ (last access July 25, 2018).

39 Available at: https://www.google.it/search?q=born+in+england+live+in+england+die+in+england&source=lnms&tbm=isch&sa=X&ved=0ahUKEwjx1rS6u7rcAhUtzIUKHZ98ATsQ_AUICigB&biw=1366&bih=651#imgdii=EgMhuX5W9eW5CM:&imgrc=lRrKqKdrrqJXeM: (last access July 25, 2018).

These episodes demonstrate that the EU question was not thoroughly understood in its economic and political terms but that it had been interpreted by some as only concerning immigration and, more broadly, the defence of identity against difference. In this case, moreover, the erroneous interpretation led some people to believe that the fight against immigration could touch also people already living and working in the UK. The EU question was highly misinterpreted and produced an intensification of British or English Nationalism. The use of the term English in some of the allegations of the supporters of the Leave Campaign demonstrates little comprehension of the reasons of Brexit. This outcome has probably depended largely on some faults in the Remain propaganda and on the very resolute and very effective, although often misleading, Leave propaganda.[40]

After the victory of the Leave campaign many Europeans living and working in the United Kingdom felt abandoned, unwanted by a nation which had previously encouraged and welcomed multiculturalism, a country often seen as a place where individuals could work, study and develop their individuality inside British culture. Thus, a feeling of incredulity was engendered by the result of the referendum and by the subsequent episodes of racism observed all around the country and directed also against immigrants coming from non-EU countries. The aftermath of the referendum testified to the use made by the Leave campaign of abstract and general concepts, often based on national identity as opposed to "the Others," "where the special magic of identity has been invoked in manipulative, deliberately over-simple ways"[41] completely incoherent with the EU question.

---

40 On this matter see, among the many others, the articles appearing after the results of the referendum and the consequent surge of hate and fear: Patrick Butler, "Politicians fuelled rise in hate crimes after Brexit vote, says UN body. UN committee says politicians should share blame for surge in racist crimes during and after EU referendum campaign," *The Guardian*, August 26, 2016, available at: https://www.theguardian.com/politics/2016/aug/26/politicians-rise-hate-crimes-brexit-vote-un-committee (last access July 28, 2018); May Bulman, "Brexit vote sees highest spike in religious and racial hate crimes ever recorded. Race and faith attacks reported across UK increase by highest rate on record since the referendum," *Independent*, July 7, 2017, available at: https://www.independent.co.uk/news/uk/home-news/racist-hate-crimes-surge-to-record-high-after-brexit-vote-new-figures-reveal-a7829551.html (last access July 28, 2018); Satnam Virdee, Brendan McGeever, "Racism, Crisis, Brexit," *Ethnic and Racial Studies* 41.10 (2018): 1802–1819; David Brown, "UK 'more racist after Brexit,' Rising xenophobia and hate crime since EU vote," *The Times*, May 12, 2018, available at: https://www.thetimes.co.uk/article/uk-more-racist-after-brexit-qb7hd7xl7 (last access July 25, 2018).

41 Gilroy, "Diaspora and the Detours of Identity," 304.

The same feeling of disbelief is observable in Harry Potter: Hermione, the most intelligent and prepared pupil at Hogwarts and one of the heroes of the story, is, indeed, a Muggle-born – as Harry's mother was. Her ability and intelligence are prized and encouraged by Hogwarts' teachers and by most of her fellow-students but, in the last book, the episodes of racism towards the Muggles make her feel unsafe to the point that she makes her parents forget about her through a spell. She thus metaphorically disavows her origins in order to try and save her parents. She unwillingly erases her identity in order to survive:

> To live with difference is viewed as living in jeopardy, for difference is a threat that corrupts and compromises identity. In these circumstances, the safety of sameness [. . .] can only be recovered by either of two options that have regularly appeared at this point in this dismal logic: separation or slaughter.[42]

Analogously, also other characters in the story must hide their identity, their "difference," even before the ascent of Voldemort. In the books, indeed, the theme of difference and of racial prejudice is often displayed, also because of the presence of magical creatures of various natures. Many characters, for instance, share the prejudiced idea that werewolves and giants are harmful and dangerous creatures – while the book demonstrates that their aggressive behaviour has depended on the hostile treatment they have been reserved by wizards, and that, as in all communities, the acts of some individuals can negatively mark the reputation of a whole group. Remus Lupin, one of Harry's teachers and friends and a member of the Order of the Phoenix, is a werewolf and has to hide his nature in order to avoid criticism from other people. He eventually loses his job because his presence in the school would create apprehension in the pupil's parents due to their narrowminded consideration of werewolves as dangerous creatures mostly derived from popular culture and hearsay. Lupin is the first to denounce acknowledge the consideration he is reserved by society: "You have only ever seen me amongst the Order, or under Dumbledore's protection at Hogwarts! You don't know how most of the wizarding world sees creatures like me! When they know of my affliction, they can barely talk to me!"[43]

People in these stories, indeed, often misjudge creatures of a "half" nature as divergent from the norm, and, thus, as dangerous. The other striking case is that of Hagrid, Harry's first friend in the magical world and one of the gentlest characters in the book. When people discover he is half-giant

42 Gilroy, "Diaspora and the Detours of Identity," 310.
43 Rowling, *Harry Potter and the Deathly Hallows*, 175.

his nature becomes a target of derision and causes mistrust in his capacities. Moreover, Hagrid himself keeps his origin secret in order to avoid being discriminated and rejected. Even in peace-times many people define the "others" as monsters, because, according to an ill-informed and unfounded logic, they are less than human, and they consequently deserve to be segregated or put in a condition of servitude. The werewolves are considered aggressive and untameable creatures and even Ron shares the widespread opinion on the giants: "Harry, they're just vicious, giants. It's like Hagrid said, it's in their natures, they're like trolls... they just like killing, everyone knows that."[44]

Similarly, centaurs, according to the malevolent and authoritarian Professor Umbridge and many others, are "*Filthy half-breeds! Beasts! Uncontrolled animals!*"[45] The house-elves, in particular, are considered as lower creatures by everybody except Hermione. When she creates the Society for the Promotion of Elfish Welfare, Harry does not want to be involved – even if he had liberated Dobby, the Malfoys house-elf – and Ron thinks house-elves enjoy their condition. Even these positive characters – who will eventually change their minds in the end – at this point of the story do not seem to see the inequal treatment of these creatures, which are considered as less-human, and, thus, less eligible to equal rights with humans.

> [Hermione:] "I've been researching it thoroughly in the library. Elf enslavement goes back centuries. I can't believe no one's done anything about it before now."
>
> "Hermione – open your ears," said Ron loudly. "They. Like. It. They *like* being enslaved!"[46]

Harry's society is thus highly classist, divided into groups which, according to the popular belief, are not supposed to intermingle. When, however, a mixture takes place this seems to put in danger the pre-constituted order of society and is thus labelled as something monstrous. In this sense, the logic of social distinction is substantially entrenched in the fictional culture as it is in the real one. British society, indeed, is highly partitioned and class mobility is rather infrequent:

> there are still very clear strata in our society, each with different levels of social, cultural and economic capital. Considering factors like education, salary, professions, and household ownership, the BBC's own Great British Class Survey discovered seven distinct

44 Rowling, *Harry Potter and the Goblet of Fire*, 374.
45 Rowling, *Harry Potter and the Order of the Phoenix*, 665.
46 Hp and the Goblet of Fire, (London: Bloomsbury, 2000), 198.

> classes in total, with an elite (representing roughly 6% of the population) residing above a wide spectrum of working and middle classes.[47]

It is therefore plausible that J. K. Rowling's fictional world was highly influenced by the society she lived in, by the logic of power and by the social dynamics of Great Britain at the time she wrote the books.

Nonetheless, a remarkably striking parallel often highlighted by critics when analysing Voldemort's "blood purity" rhetoric, is, understandably, that with the Nazi propaganda and the promotion of racial purity. The author, J.K. Rowling, however, claims she did not use Nazism as a source of inspiration for the negative aspects of the books:

> Ms Rowling said she had invented the idea that some wizards were not considered to be "pure," and realised the similarities with the Nazis' beliefs only afterwards when she visited a museum dedicated to the Holocaust, in which six million Jewish people died. [...] Ms Rowling then explained how she had discovered that this fictional prejudice held by some wizards against non-magical people [muggles] bore a strong resemblance to the way the Nazis thought. "If you think this is far-fetched, look at some of the real charts the Nazis used to show what constituted 'Aryan' or 'Jewish' blood," she said. "I saw one in the Holocaust Museum in Washington when I had already devised the 'pure-blood', 'half-blood' and 'muggle-born' definitions and was chilled to see that the Nazis used precisely the same warped logic as the Death Eaters. "A single Jewish grandparent 'polluted' the blood, according to their propaganda."[48]

Undeniably, however, many aspects of the books bear a significant resemblance with the rhetoric of the Nazi regime and propaganda:

> [After Voldemort has occupied it] [b]esides the appearance of the place, the Ministry actually recalls the darkest shadows of the European early twentieth-century totalitarian regimes: not only the complete control of the civil servants' lives and activities, but also the dreadful aspects of hate, racism and segregation, that led then (and, regrettably, sometimes still do) to the most despicable crimes against humanity. Here, the author replicates somehow that pattern, with the Government (the Ministry) opposing the pure-bloods to the so-called Muggle-borns (i.e. those possessing magical powers but whose parents are ordinary "human" beings), trying to expel (if not, to eliminate) these latter from the system. The best example is given by the "Muggle-Born Registration Commission" that

---

47 David Robson, "How important is social class in Britain today?," *BBC Future*, April 7, 2016, available at: http://www.bbc.com/future/story/20160406-how-much-does-social-class-matter-in-britain-today (last access July 25, 2018). On this subject see also: David Cannadine, *Class in Britain* (London: Penguin, 2000).

48 Ian Johnston, "Author 'chilled' to learn Harry's half-blood status has Nazi parallels," *The Scotsman*, July 28, 2004, available at: http://www.scotsman.com/news/uk/author-chilled-to-learn-harry-s-half-blood-status-has-nazi-parallels-1-540890) (last access July 25, 2018).

> appears in *DH*, Chapter 13, but that the author already mentioned in Ch. 11, where, in the pages of the main newspaper, the *Daily Prophet*, Harry and friends discover that the Ministry is inviting Muggle-borns to present themselves for interview, in order to discover the way they came to possess magical power.[49]

Also some other characteristics of Nazism seem to find a parallel in the Harry Potter books: from the similarity between Voldemort's and Hitler's figures and discourses, to the Arian appearance of the pure-bloods Malfoy family all characterised by light hair, skin, and eyes, to the use of a sort of police-force, the Death Eaters, only responding to Voldemort.

The claim that the author was not aware of these issues might, however, still be true. Indeed, Nazism and its propaganda have durably affected people's life and culture so severely that they have come to be part of a shared cultural baggage which, even if not plainly referred to, often emerges in narrations concerning difference and racial hatred. Nazism had such a critical role in world history that it is impossible to claim not to have been inspired by it when referring to discourses on the purity of blood. On the other hand, these discourses have become so entrenched in contemporary communication that the process of reproduction might have taken place unawares. What the author was portraying, thus, was possibly not Nazism but the British Culture of the ages in which she was writing, which was inevitably influenced by Nazism as all Western-world cultures of the second half of the 20th century.

Thus, her inspiration might come from a sentiment of fear, of British identity being threatened by multiculturalism, silently creeping (or sneaking as the figure of Voldemort's serpent Nagini skilfully symbolises) over the years and finally emerging through the Leave campaign. The definition of national identity comes, indeed, from a sense of loss, from a need of belonging to a particular group, which inevitably will define itself through the exclusion of others:

> To share an identity is apparently to be bonded on the most fundamental levels: national, 'racial,' ethnic, regional, local. And yet, identity is always particular, as much about difference as about shared belonging. It marks out the division and sub-sets in our social lives and helps to define the boundaries around our uneven, local attempts to make sense of the world.[50]

British identity before Brexit seemed to be a matter of popular culture, of a series of practices linked to nostalgia and stereotypes which characterised the

49 Ligugnana, "An Invented Executive: The Ministry of Magic in *Harry Potter*," 430.
50 Gilroy, "Diaspora and the Detours of Identity," 301.

people of the nation both at home and abroad.[51] The acts of hatred and racism following the referendum, however, demonstrate the presence of an underlying discontent, which was present also before the Referendum, and which is well depicted in the books: "How social groups are treated in cultural representation is part and parcel of how they are treated in life."[52] The Referendum had the effect of liberating this dormant force which has been creeping in British popular culture through the ages. It is in this sense that the fictional representation of the books has foretold the subsequent course of events.

5 Conclusion

Popular culture undoubtedly represents reality in a stereotypical and generalised way, but, at the same time, it draws on everyday life for inspiration. Therefore, fiction is often able, through the use of popular culture, to predict real-life events. The *Harry Potter*'s books prove to be part of this process. Firstly, because they belong to British Popular Culture and, secondly, because they offer the opportunity of drawing a parallel with ensuing real-life events.

Furthermore, when reality and fiction intertwine the difference feared in real-life becomes monstrous: the monster becomes "a manifestation of that which disturbs the social 'norm,' or troubles an existing understanding of what is acceptably human."[53]

The analysis of the ascent of Lord Voldemort and his condemnation of Muggle-borns to acquire power has allowed me to draw a parallel with the climate of fear and of xenophobia induced by the Brexit Leave campaign and the following victory in the referendum on June 23rd, 2016. My reflection has followed the idea of the construction of identity and of otherness inside popular culture, arguing that the latter has described a trend which, afterwards, has been witnessed in real life.

The same climate of acrimony, moreover, has lately been experienced on the international scenario. In Europe where the Italian newly elected government's debated treatment of the migrant landings is bringing the migration question to the fore of the political debate; and in America with the latest episodes of racism and segregation derived from Trump's policy, such as the

---

51 Paxman, "Preface."

52 Dyer, "Introduction," 1.

53 Alexa Wright, *Monstrosity: The Human Monster in Visual Culture* (London, New York: I.B. Tauris, 2013), 2.

project of the construction of a wall between USA and Mexico, and the separation of young children from their families at the borders. Conceivably, thus, the Harry Potter books have been able to register an historical sentiment of fear of the "other" which has recently been observed not only in the British scenario after Brexit but which is characterising our world on an global scale:

> The reality in which we live is less and less a univocal reality with well-defined limits, it has become a more and more complex and articulated net consisting of the intertwining of different worlds, among which, most important and real in their own way, are those created by works of *fiction* (from literature to cinema, to comics to TV series). For this reason, it is impossible to know reality, neither to think one's own time, if people still believe [...] that the real world is something other, and independent, from the net of worlds created by the works of *fiction*.[54]

54 Simone Regazzoni, *Harry Potter e la filosofia* (Il Melangolo: Genova, 2008), 9 [My translation].

Appendix

François Ost

From Me, Martin, the Five-Pawed Bear, A Letter to My Judges

This is addressed to you, Father Bertrand d'Ossau, Abbot of the Priory of Sarrance, on this April 11 in the year of our Lord 1548.

Tomorrow I will be executed – hung by the hind paws, on the gallows erected before the Church of the Sainte Famille in Pau. Before that, I will be whipped in the square, and Pierre de Molières, the Deacon of the Parish, will have solemnly read the bans of excommunication that have been pronounced against me. The whole population will be gathered; it will be Sunday, as people are coming out of High Mass: the peasants and the Count's court, the children and the elderly, the clerics and the bourgeois – even the animals will be rounded up so that they will not miss any of the show and will also be persuaded of the defeat of the forces of Satan before the power of our Holy Church. At least I will be spared the human mask and costume that were inflicted on a homicidal sow in 1386 at Falaise, in the Duchy of Normandy. I am trying to calm my mind by thinking that Paco, the Spanish executioner who came to see me in my cell in accordance with the tradition, showed me more humanity than my judges: he promised me that he would stun me during the night to shorten my suffering.

I am entrusting this letter to Lahure, my jailer, who has become my friend, and who is from Sarrance like you. I am addressing you, Bertrand d'Ossau, because I know you will be able to listen to me. Indeed, I have been told that you refused to extend to my judges the hospitality of your chapter hall because you disapprove of them putting me on trial. I do not know you, but I am grateful to you for that action. And then I am also thinking of the statue of Our Lady from the River Gave that you honour in your priory: the statue before which the bull knelt down to pray. I think that you must understand how much closer we animals are to the things above than are the humans who censure us.

Do I fear the death that awaits me tomorrow? No, not really: death is natural, and we animals encounter it every day. However, an immense sadness

Note: Although it is purely fictional, the text that follows is based on a set of real historical events: civil and religious proceedings, arguments and pleadings are amply documented in the court records of some 230 trials of animals in Europe between 1120 and 1846. (That is the number of trials for which the archives have been preserved. It can be presumed that the real number was much higher.) The sources are vast, but I have based my account mainly on two works: Jean Réal, *Bêtes et juges* (Paris: Buchet-Chastel, 2006) and Jean Vartier, *Les procès d'animaux* (Paris: Hachette, 1970).

https://doi.org/10.1515/9783110654615-017

knots in my throat when I think of my dear Forest of Issaux and its delicious young plants, the little Lake of Ansabère where I sometimes caroused, the Lescun hollow and nights under the stars… I am wondering whether, if there is a heaven for bears, I will meet Lady Pierrette, my faithful companion, again?

Lahure, with whom I have been conversing throughout my eighteen weeks in incarceration, is doing me the favour of holding the quill. You will have understood that, although I can speak, naturally, no one has ever taught me to write. Lahure, who has a little education, is therefore doing me this service, and I give him my sincere thanks. Today, thus, I have decided to speak. During my trial, I walled myself up in silence. First of all, it was a question of dignity – how could I respond to the collection of absurd accusations with which I was burdened? And then, as you can imagine, if I had begun speaking in the midst of the trial, that would have been sufficient for them to accuse me of devilry. I was nonetheless thinking, and I engraved in my memory all the contradictions in that interminable trial, the procedural tactics, the prosecutors' quibbles, the way my judges circumvented issues.

It was I, Martin the bear, who was in question, and yet no one ever cared what I thought; no one ever tried to see things from my point of view. It was the trial of the "Bear" in general, an abstract bear that does not exist anywhere, a bear that is a product of men's imaginings, the bear the Church needed at this point in time – so the one that was found guilty did not have much to do with me. In the end, I wonder whether the human mask on the sow in Falaise was not an expression of the truth: the beast that is excommunicated and put to death is nothing other than a projection onto us of the darkness of men's hearts.

Yes, it is true: I was born with a fifth paw. Nature made me that way. Although it makes my walk slightly ungainly, it has never prevented me from running over hill and vale. My peers have never rejected me, and Lady Pierrette gave me three fine litters. I cannot say that humans have shown me as much humanity. When I was captured on that sad day last November, not far from Bedous, and I was shown in the streets of the village, children threw stones at me, calling me *lou pedescaou* (barefoot). Their elders were no better, for they burned the pads of my front paws, forcing me to walk upright, thereby exhibiting that scandalous fifth paw. Their pastors were worse, for they quickly saw that involuntary appendage as a sign of the Devil, obvious proof of my moral disorder.

I thus became the first bear to be put on trial for dealing with the Devil. With all due respect to my judges, I have come to wonder where they could have found any precedent. There was indeed that rooster, burned alive in Bale in 1474 for having laid an egg, which was seen as a "crime against nature." However, the link was weak and my judges undecided. That is why they undertook to fortify the case against me. Was I not involved in some way in the many disappearances of sheep, of which the shepherds of Escot and Accous have complained? And the damage caused as far away as in the stables of the Valley of Barétous – were there not deep scratches on the victims' flesh? There were whispers in the cottages that on certain nights the shadow of a bear had been seen near the scenes of crimes, ... and then also – shame – people began to hint about "the crime of which we cannot speak." Some remembered the public burning at the stake the previous February of the widow Catherine, native of Urdos, not far from the place where I was captured. That poor woman, forced by widowhood to do her late husband's work as a shepherd, was accused of witchcraft and – now it is remembered – relations with a bear. Obviously, that was me, the abettor, the guilty one – it could be only me, who had been scouring the Valley of Aspe for so long, shamelessly exhibiting my scandalous nature and repeatedly performing devilish actions. Thus, justice would be done, a perfect perpetrator had been found – worthy of the emotion arousing the population – and peace would return to our gentle valleys.

I thus found myself accused of Satanic monstrosity, of a series of assassinations of sheep and other domestic animals, and, to top it all off, of the "crime of which we cannot speak."

While the charges against me were serious enough for my fate to no longer be in doubt, the authorities still faced complications. A sensitive procedural problem remained: the ordinary crimes were under the jurisdiction of the seigneurial courts, but the monstrosity and "crime of which we cannot speak" required the intervention of the ecclesiastical courts. The Bailiff of Pau, seized with many complaints from shepherds, fully intended to exercise his right to bring me to justice. However, the Bishop of Bayonne, to whose ears echoes of the scandal had come, argued for the need for spiritual intervention in such an obvious case of abomination. He immediately charged Hugues de Manerville, a Dominican whose formidable polemical talent had done marvels in Inquisition proceedings, to take my case on immediately.

Although the subtleties of these clashes in jurisdiction largely escaped me, I knew enough to understand that it was entirely in my interest to fall into the hands of the provost rather than to be judged by the clerics of the Inquisition. Occasionally, magistrates can show clemency, and it was said in the corridors of my prison (Lahure, always thoughtful, reported this encouraging fact to me) that Jacques Boivin, the Bailiff of Pau, had even recently acquitted a colony of weevils, charged with having harmed the vines of the Abbey of Luc-de-Béarn, going so far as to give them exclusive enjoyment of a piece of municipal land as "sufficient pasture" in consideration of their "natural right to sustenance." A contract for the piece of land was drawn up "in due form and for perpetuity," although not without granting the villagers a right of way.

I beg you to pardon me for this abundance of details, but you must admit that, in the state into which I was plunged, no point was to be overlooked and all was to be used to support my legitimate hope to escape this nightmare.

As we could have expected, alas, the Church's point of view had to prevail, for I was soon visited in my cell by the ecclesiastical judge to subject me to the official reading of the charges brought against me. It was not that I was expected to understand anything, even less that I would put up any resistance – but the formalities had to be respected. Found guilty, most certainly, but in due form: that is how the Holy secular justice of the Church works. However, there was one piece of good news: the cleric announced to me that I had been assigned legal counsel, my own defence attorney, a certain Bruno Vallençon, whom Lahure soon told me was an honest man, not discouraged by lost causes.

. . . I am returning to my dictation again, after an interruption. Lahure was offering me freedom: night has fallen, it is raining outside, my flight would go unnoticed, he says! However, I firmly decline that generous offer, which would expose him to risk and force me, from now on, to lead the life of a fugitive from justice, a lamentable escapee, tracked by dogs and followed by men's insults. That is not my idea of the life of a free bear. I have a better way to spend my last hours, thanks to your help, dear Bertrand d'Ossau. I will lay down in writing the record of my trial so that posterity will have testimony of it, and, perhaps, the fault will be recognized.

The attorney I had been promised did not delay in coming to visit me to prepare my defence. It was not that he was seeking to speak with me, but he needed, it seemed, to "gauge the beast" – was I really the monster that had been described to him? I sensed that he was indeed an honest man, although I could not feel he had any empathy for me; his defence would be distant and professional, and I would never know whether he truly believed, personally, the insane allegations of devilry and monstrosity. Lahure nonetheless encouraged me, telling me of Vallençon's successes in the cases of "scores of calamities": clouds of grasshoppers, invasions of rats and mice, colonies of weevils that, like the plagues of Egypt, sometimes descend upon the harvests. He was especially famous for his procedural skill in the case of the mice in the Valley of Aran. A summons to appear had been addressed to them, vainly, on the square before the Abbey church, and Bruno Vallençon had argued, not unreasonably, that since the rodents were scattered across the valley, they were unable to take cognizance of it. That was admitted, and it was ordered that the summons would be read the following Sunday in all the parishes, with a time limit of three weeks. Once again, it was in vain. In no way discouraged, my attorney then pointed out the long distances that had to be covered by animals as tiny as his clients, and also the perils of the road, with the danger of cats at every turn. The argument did indeed seem reasonable, and a new extension was granted... so that, in the end, on the day scheduled for the trial, winter had come and the accused had found it wiser to move away to milder climes.

I was quickly persuaded of my attorney's talent for evasion during the first session of my trial (which was held in the Inquisition chambers in Pau, since you refused to let them use your chapter hall). After reading the charges against me, he immediately raised an objection that the court had no jurisdiction, claiming that I should be transferred to the civil jurisdiction of the Bailiff: his argument was that the jurisprudence had established that the earliest offences – the theft of animals – determined the jurisdiction, no matter what the nature of later crimes. This was a thorny problem, and the ecclesiastical judge was discomposed; the hearing was suspended. However, when the debates began again, Hugues de Manerville had found a strategy: raising the tone and frowning his brow, he exhumed a record showing that one of the crimes had been perpetrated on a Friday – a Friday! – eating meat on a Friday: the sin was abominable, the sacrilege established. Moreover, the attorney felt the need to recall the death sentence handed down to the pig of sinister memory who had eaten the consecrated host in a sacristy, and the impious mule that, mistaking a font for a drinking trough, had quenched its thirst in a church.

It was thus agreed that my trial would follow its course in the ecclesiastical court. I could no longer expect anything from the clemency of men: my monstrosity would from then on be decided by combat between divine and demonic powers.

Often, over the course of these last weeks, I discussed with Lahure the reasons for the Church's persecution of we animals – calamitous clouds of grasshoppers, pigs and female donkeys guilty of sundry thefts, and now me, a five-pawed bear. Lahure thinks that by taking the side of peasants lamenting the ruin of their harvests and shepherds driven to desperation by raids on their herds, the Church displays very necessary compassion, and reassures them by giving them the feeling that the required measures are being taken – measures that are all the more welcome when the phenomenon seems inexplicable, as in the cases of invasions by insects and rodents. What better intercessors, in such cases, than the specialists of the supernatural? Indeed, that is probably one of the reasons, although there is competition in that field. Who has never dealt with one of those magicians or healers who always has a recipe at hand: one who can provide a spell to keep cockroaches away, another a potion to protect grape vines? When there was a profusion of leeches in the lakes of the Encantats, there was even one who recommended that a virgin "in her moons" circumnavigate them barefoot at night... Lahure and I agreed it was a question of controlling the realm of the supernatural during such periods of collective anxiety.

I would like to add, if I may, dear Bertrand d'Ossau, hoping that I will not grieve you as a man of the Church, that these moments of doubt are also opportunities for restoring solid control over the faithful, so attracted to impious ways, so inclined to vice, so ungrateful to our Holy Mother the Church. At each of these episodes, the preachers climb up to their pulpits, hurling reproaches down upon their flocks, encouraging them to do penance and to pay tithes immediately. Solemn processions are organized, extended fasting scheduled, spontaneous collections set up – a whole people, persuaded of its guilt in such events, waits anxiously for the order of the world to be restored, in the hope that, in the end, God will remember to be merciful to it. If I may, it is a win-win situation, for if, by chance, the animals go away spontaneously, the Church will have triumphed, but if, on the contrary, the evil persists despite all the effort, it will be because the repentance was not sincere enough, the tithing inadequate... and the Church still wins.

It remains that the merits of the case, as I was soon to see, lay in the obsession with the presence of evil, by which minds are haunted, and which the Church itself cultivates, under the pretext of fighting it. The wolves that occasionally devour a sheep, the weevils that breed in the millions and travel in clouds, the ewes that comfort shepherds on certain lonely nights, the cats that have only one black sin, namely, the colour of their fur, and now me, encumbered by my fifth paw – we are all considered outlaws, banished from Salvation, objects of sacred terror, excluded from humanity, and soon deprived of Communion. Different and thus dangerous, strange and therefore guilty, frightening and thus necessarily evil-minded, soon agents of the Devil – What do you think of this, dear Bertrand d'Ossau, you who seem to be dubious of the proceedings that are brought against us? Does your heart not go out to that bull, kneeling down before the statue of the Virgin that you revere in your oratory? Are you not more on the side of Saint Hubert and the hart in the Ardennes Forest, or St. Francis of Assisi and the fearsome wolf of Gubbio? Why is it that my humble jailer, who is faithfully writing down these thoughts, and also Paco, who will execute me tomorrow, understand these things spontaneously, unlike their pastors and lords? It is probably because they know us better, since they live together with us on farms, and share, like shepherds, our life outdoors, under the stars...

However, time is passing and the poor candle lighting my cell is burning low. I must tell you about the next part of my trial. On January 25, the date set for the hearing on the merits, the ecclesiastical judge (have I told you his name? Bernard Hautesoie – another one who, I hope, will be tortured by remorse for the rest of his days), gave the floor to Hugues de Manerville for the reading of his petitions. The prosecutor did not spend much time on the disappearances of livestock or on the damage in the stables; aside from the concerns about Friday, which have already been mentioned, it seemed that he was not really interested in trivial affairs, such as food, which is moreover normally under the jurisdiction of civil courts, but was engaged in a permanent personal fight against Satan. He had more than enough grounds for the two other charges. He began by casting suspicion on me by recalling the recent case of poor Catherine, convicted of sorcery and burned in the public square – had she not acknowledged having had carnal relations with the Beast? As everyone knows, the Beast is a master of disguise, taking on various appearances – such as, in our lands, that hirsute animal, the size of a man, displaying its shameless sex. Or, even worse, a creature that exhibits, like the monster here, a supernatural appendage, the least disputable sign of its moral abomination – and the prosecutor drew all eyes to me with a sweep of his arm, me, the accused, whom, in accordance with his express recommendations, had been carefully bound upright to a post so that none of my infirmity could be hidden. Encouraged by the strong impression that he had just produced, the incorruptible Dominican immediately continued with the punishment required in the case of such crimes: death by hanging, naturally, and by the back paws, to prolong the lesson for those assembled. However, once again, what was essential was not the banal physical killing; what was important was re-establishing the order of the spiritual world. The ritual affirmation of the triumph of the forces of Good over sacrilegious provocations: only excommunication would be fitting. I would thus be solemnly informed of my present and eternal exclusion from Divine mercy.

A sacred silence had invaded the hearing room, and when the judge gave the floor to my attorney with a strangled voice, I wondered what words could possibly come out of his throat. Highly experienced and the true professional that he was, Bruno de Valençon calmly returned to each of the complaints made against me, one by one, suggesting in passing that the large number could even be a sign of the lack of merits. He led with an argument with which he had been successful in other cases: brandishing the Bible open to Genesis, he reminded the Court that animals had been created by the Almighty on the sixth day, that is, a day before man. The irrefutable legal conclusion: animals have a right to sustenance, a prior, ancestral right, which it would be unjust – even sacrilegious – to challenge. Those creatures were desired by God himself, who ensures their survival by guaranteeing their right to sustain themselves – was it not written at *Genesis* 1:31: "And God saw everything that He had made, and, behold, it was very good."

Spurred on by that first success, my attorney drove the point home by referring to the flood: "When God decided to drown the entire Earth to erase all sinful humanity, except for Noah and his family, did he not have a pair of each species of animal brought into the Ark – yes, the entire animal kingdom, Monseignor Judge, including bears, like Martin here." Are we to be less tolerant than God himself?

The way being now clear on the Biblical level, my attorney returned to more legal considerations. How could his client be accused of theft and murder when Saint Thomas himself acknowledged in his *Summa Theologica* that to commit a crime one must be capable of reason and free action? Yet, "animals are governed only by instinct, such that they cannot be constrained by anything but the natural law", as the famous attorney Rambaud had argued, with success, in a similar case.

Those were certainly strong reasons, but everyone could feel that the principal accusation of devilry had not been neutralized; we still remained on the ordinary level of civil "petty theft", if I may say so, familiar ground for my protector. When he broached the question of bestiality and my claimed monstrosity, it was clear he was less at ease, as if he too were impressed by the seriousness of the stakes. He indeed tried to worm his way around the accusation by arguing that no exhibit in the case established the truth, or even the likelihood, of my encounter with the widow Catherine – pointing out in passing the terror that the appearance of a five-pawed bear would have created. That was a remark that, I have to admit, pained me at the time. Taking yet another step forward, my attorney insinuated that, while Catherine had of course admitted that guilty business, her testimony had to be treated cautiously since it had been obtained under torture – "torn out", he dared to suggest. That point was significant, but decidedly too daring: already, Hugues de Manerville was standing, white with anger: "Do you dare to cast doubt on the full authority of a decision rendered by the most Holy Church?" – and the ecclesiastical judge sharply put my attorney in his place: "Learned counsel, please, stick to the facts."

The problem was that, with respect to my monstrosity, there was no "fact" – only an immense misunderstanding, ancestral fear and a mountain of prejudice. How could it be explained to them that the inconvenient appendage was only a natural accident, and no stranger, in the end, that the hump that Jesus had removed from an unfortunate whom he had met on the road? Unable to find the words he needed to open hearts, if not minds, my attorney simply concluded rapidly by contesting the application of excommunication to my case. The Fathers of the Church were very clear, he argued, about the fact that such severe punishment applied logically only to beings who had already entered the Church by Holy Communion, which was clearly not the case of his client. Would not excommunicating a bear therefore be just as sacrilegious as claiming to baptize a stone or a dog?

Once again, Valençon scored a point, but, I dare say, the final word had already been spoken: his victories were sterile, for the Court had already judged me. After a few minutes recess to give the appearance of deliberations, the judge read the sentence. It would thus be death by hanging, preceded by whipping and excommunication for "abominable and atrocious crimes." The judgment further specified that the sentence would be carried out on Wednesday, April 11, the week preceding the very Holy celebration of Easter. No one, not even my attorney, deigned to look me in the eye. I would disappear into the order of Creation, and soon the evidence of my case would be burned, as would, tomorrow, the gloves of the executioner, so that no trace would remain of the stain I represented.

... It is I, Lahure, who is writing now. It is three in the morning, and Martin, succumbing to fatigue, has gone to sleep. I do not have the heart to wake him. I therefore plan, Eminent Reverend, to give you this letter the next time I pass through Sarrance.

... Martin has finally woken up, and he wants to add something – I will return to recording his words.

Yes, I dropped off. In my sleep, I dreamt of the donkey and the cow in the manger, of the sheep nearby, of the camels of the three wise men – more numerous around the Creator than the people, who counted only a few shepherds, a carpenter, a very young woman and three visionaries from the East. I caught myself dreaming of a god for animals, of a church, in which beasts would be the ministers. Can you understand that, Bernard d'Ossau? Will you have a big enough heart, like François or Hubert, not to burn these papers immediately? Will you have the courage to give testimony to denounce these iniquitous proceedings brought against us?

In my somnolence, I dreamt of a reign of simple folk, where there would be no witches, stakes or "crime of which we cannot speak" – only creatures of God who go along their way, and sometimes perform humane actions – or should I say "beastly"? – such as that of Paco, who will stun me to shorten my suffering.

Tomorrow, when I will be displayed in the square before the Church of the Sainte Famille, I will not do anything spectacular to make my mark in history. I have to admit that I considered doing so for a moment – I can imagine the judge's face if I suddenly proclaimed "and yet I am innocent!" or "glory to God, I beseech His Grace!" or something like that. No, I will maintain the dignified, silent aspect that has never left me, and, casting my eyes one last time towards the south, I will dream of the rays of the Sun rising over the summits of Gavarnie, with the morning dew and the first humming of the bees.

Filippo Sgubbi

Monsters and Criminal Law

Within our culture, aesthetics and ethics are intertwined with each other: external harmony is regarded as a sign of moral good. Similarly, the word "monster" - departing from the etymological origin of the term - suggests that which is horrifying, not only physically but also morally and socially: thus evil, cruelty and horror. Monstrosity is thus a core concept within criminal law and has always been so.

These notes will be divided into three sections:

- Monsters punished by the criminal law
- Monsters created by the criminal law (and the media)
- Monsters within the criminal law.

1 Monsters punished by the criminal law

Within this perspective, criminal law punishes human actions that have already been carried out. The moral and social monster is punished for the acts committed by him or her. A distinction must be drawn between imaginary and real monstrosity. On the one side, imaginary monstrosity is the product of popular anxiety and collective superstition, although is at the same time exploited by politics in order to achieve objectives related to order, control and social discipline. Power produces monsters: the misdeeds of monsters legitimise social hegemony and often act as justification for wars, invasions (consider the Iraq War and the fake news concerning Saddam's weapons of mass destruction) or torture. This may go as far as to identify state power with a monster. On the other hand, "real" monstrosity manifests itself through offences that generally involve bloodshed and are committed repeatedly and/or particularly brutal.

1.1 On imaginary monsters and monstrosity

Looking back into even not too distant history, monsters had to be punished also for acts that were considered to constitute a danger to social order, even though they had never been committed and only existed in the fantasies of the community and of the inquisitors. Thousands of witches were burned at the stake for various misdeeds against people and animals, for having engaged in

https://doi.org/10.1515/9783110654615-018

sexual relations with the devil, for having caused natural disasters and for other monstrous acts. Normally a person became branded as a monster following the dissemination within a community of defamatory gossip and slander. This phenomenon is characteristic of social groups organised into tribes, which tend to be closed, inward-looking and superstitious: here the need is felt to seek out and identify a scapegoat to whom all of the evils afflicting the group could be ascribed. Even though the monstrous acts were non-existent, they were confirmed by witnesses and those accused often confessed under torture, following which they were liable to draconian punishment under the criminal law, including even death. The monster shoulders the burden of social sins and evils, which he or she is forced to expiate.

1.2 On real monsters and monstrosity

At present the definition – and classification under the criminal law – of a monster is reserved to the crimes of murder where committed serially and/or with particular savagery, and to acts of terrorism. However, history is unfortunately also rich with examples. The Holocaust was characterised by monsters and by monstrosity, as have been the numerous instances of genocide, crimes against humanity and war crimes committed also in recent years. Starting from the Nuremberg and Tokyo trials, followed by the International Criminal Court in The Hague and the Criminal Tribunal for the Former Yugoslavia, a large number of monsters and acts of monstrosity have been brought to justice. It should however be noted that the concept is rapidly expanding, also as a result of the sensationalism typical of the media, with the term monster frequently being used also in relation to the perpetrators of sexual violence, also where this does not result in death.

2 Monsters created by interaction between the criminal law and the media

This is a recent phenomenon. The desire to land a scoop results in the monster's face being "plastered over the front pages."

Whether or not the monster of the week actually committed the crime, or was completely innocent, is of secondary importance. Within the mass media, and perhaps even more so on social media, the unfortunate individual is branded as the perpetrator, even on the basis of merely preliminary investigations, or even exclusively on the basis of popular opinion. This entails a singular return to the past. Such outcomes are unfortunately often brought about by investigators themselves: when confronted with murders with a major social resonance that arouse particular emotion amongst the general public, police and prosecutors often take rushed decisions and, overcome by the characteristic panic generated by media pressure, identify the presumed guilty persons, who are then thrown to a public hungry for monsters.

We may recall for example the murder of Meredith Kercher some years ago in Perugia. The Italian Supreme Court itself levelled some particularly sharp criticisms against the conduct of investigations in that case. According to the Court, the "media clamour [...] certainly did not assist in the search for the truth" in relation to the murder and the "international repercussions" of the case resulted in a "sudden acceleration" of investigations "in the spasmodic search" for the guilty, "who could be presented as such before international public opinion."

3 Monsters and legal monstrosity within the criminal law

Unfortunately, the dream of reason also generates "legal" monsters, perhaps less conspicuous than those depicted in Goya's etching, yet still expressive of human misery and also very tangibly immediate in their everyday existence. Italy (as is the case in many countries) is permeated by strong irrational tendencies.

Populism and demagogy: a direct relationship is established without institutional mediation between the politician and the masses.

Vindictive justice: public opinion calls for rapid and summary justice, especially in relation to the suspected crimes of socio-political elites.

These tendencies can be catalysed precisely by the law and by criminal justice. The body politic offers a frustrated and dissatisfied public constant increases in punishment and the creation of new offences, in an attempt to satisfy its primordial instincts fuelled by emotions. It is in this way that the expansion of the law and of criminal justice becomes irresistible.

However, we have also witnessed a profound transformation of procedural dynamics. The burden of proof is in some cases reversed: there is no equality of arms between the parties to proceedings (prosecution and defence), and it falls to the accused to demonstrate his or her innocence, thereby undermining one of the core foundations of the culture of criminal law.

This is not all. Preventive measures are becoming more widespread, in spite of warnings from the European Court of Human Rights. These entail restrictions on freedom rights along with the confiscation of the assets of individuals who have never been convicted of any offence, but who are only suspected of having done so. This is seriously detrimental to the most elementary guarantees of a fair trial as provided for also under international conventions.

These – along with others, which I shall not cite in this presentation – are the genuine legal monstrosities within the legal order.

Contributors

Marc Amfreville is Professor of American Literature at the Sorbonne. He has written numerous articles on 19th-century authors, most notably on C. B. Brown, Irving, Hawthorne, Bierce and Melville. Some publications also concern 20th-century authors (T. Williams, F. O'Connor, P. Everett, E. Evenson, J.A. Phillips…). He has written three book-length essays on Brown, Melville, Wharton, and one on trauma and literature, entitled *Ecrits en souffrance* (2009) and edited several collections of articles, most recently one on the representation of trauma (sillages critiques, Revues.org). He is also a psychoanalyst, has run writing workshops in a psychiatric day-care hospital for teenagers and has started publishing papers in that field. He is the translator of about fifty American contemporary novels and has participated in the edition and translation of Melville, Fitzgerald and London's complete works for the Gallimard "Pléiade" collection.

Heinz Antor is Professor of English Literatures and Head of the Department of English at the University of Cologne. He is editor of the journal *Anglistik: International Journal of English Studies*. He has published widely on anglophone literature from the sixteenth to the twenty-first century, postcolonial, inter- and transcultural studies, Canadian and Australian literature.

Paola Carbone is Associate Professor of English Literature at the IULM University, Milan. Her fields of research include narrative theory, contemporary British culture and the novel, and the relationship between literature and new communication technologies. She has published several works on postmodern, postcolonial and digital literature.

Daniela Carpi is Honorary Professor of English Literature at the University of Verona. Her fields of research are: Renaissance theatre, critical theory, postmodernism, law and literature, literature and science, literature and visual arts. She is the author of four monographs, 29 edited volumes and journals, more than 100 articles. She is the managing editor of *Polemos, a Journal of Law, Literature and Culture*; a member of Academia Europaea; the founder and president of AIDEL (Associazione Italiana di Diritto e Letteratura); a member of the Advisory Board of the series "Edinburgh Critical Studies in Law" and of the Centre for Cultural Studies in Graz. She is adjunct Professor at Southern Cross University, Australia. Among her latest publications: the monograph *Fairy Tales in the Postmodern World. No Tales for Children* (Winter, 2016) and the volume *As You Law It. Negotiating Shakespeare* (edited with François Ost, De Gruyter, 2018).

Annalisa Ciampi is Professor of International Law at the University of Verona and a Visiting Professor of European Human Rights Law at Monash University. She served in various capacities, including as member of the European Committee of Social Rights, expert to the Committee of Legal Advisers on Public International Law of the Council of Europe, ad hoc judge of the European Court of Human Rights, legal adviser to the Italian Ministry for Foreign Affairs, visiting professional with the Legal and Advisory Section of the Office of the Prosecutor of the International Criminal Court and most recently as UN Special Rapporteur on the rights to freedom of peaceful assembly and of association. She has published extensively in the fields of public international law, international criminal law and human rights.

https://doi.org/10.1515/9783110654615-019

Cristina Costantini is Associate Professor of Private Comparative Law at the University of Perugia. Her fields of research are Comparative Law, Law and Literature, Law and Philosophy, Law and Politics, Legal Theory, Law and Theology, Legal History. She is member of Selden Society (London). Among her publications: *La Legge e il Tempio: Storia comparata della giustizia inglese* (Carocci, 2007). Her latest monograph is: *Nomos e rappresentazione. Ripensare metodi e funzioni del diritto comparato* (Mimesis, 2017).

Jean-Michel Ganteau is Professor of British Literature at the University Paul-Valéry Montpellier 3, where he is Vice Chancelor for Research. He is the editor of the journal *Études britanniques contemporaines*. He is the author of two monographs: *David Lodge: le choix de l'éloquence* (PUB 2001) and *Peter Ackroyd et la musique du passé* (Houdiard 2008). He has co-edited several volumes of essays with Christine Reynier: *Impersonality and Emotion in Twentieth-Century British Literature* (PULM, 2005), *Impersonality and Emotion in Twentieth-Century British Arts* (PULM, 2007), *Autonomy and Commitment in Twentieth-Century British Literature* (PULM, 2010), *Autonomy and Commitment in Twentieth-Century British Arts* (PULM, 2012), and *The Humble in 19th to 21st-Century Literature and Arts* (PULM, 2017). He has also co-edited various volumes of essays with Susana Onega: *The Ethical Component in Experimental British Fiction since the 1960s* (CSP, 2007), *Trauma and Ethics in Contemporary British Literature* (Rodopi, 2011), *Trauma and Romance in Contemporary British Literature* (Routledge, 2012), *Contemporary Trauma Narratives: Liminality and the Ethics of Form* (Routledge, 2014). He has published many articles on contemporary British fiction, with a special interest in the ethics of affects in France and abroad. His study entitled *The Ethics and Aesthetics of Vulnerability in Contemporary British Fiction* was published in the Routledge Contemporary Literature series in 2015.

Svend Erik Larsen is Professor Emeritus of Comparative Literature at the University of Aarhus. He has been a member of Academia Europaea since 2004 and was chair of its Section for Literary and Theatrical Studies from 2010 to 2014, now class chair of humanities and member of the board. He is co-editor of the international journal for comparative literature *Orbis Litterarum*. Author/co-author of 10 books and more than 400 articles and editor of a series of national and international anthologies and special issues. Latest book: *Literature and the Experience of Globalization* (Bloomsbury, 2017). He has been a Visiting professor and lecturer across the world and organizer of national and international conferences. He is Yangtse River Visiting Professor, Sichuan University, for the years 2016-2019.

Marita Nadal is Professor of American Literature at the University of Zaragoza. Her main fields of research are Gothic fiction, and modern and contemporary US literature. She has edited *Trauma in Contemporary Literature: Narrative and Representation* with Dr. Mónica Calvo (Routledge, 2014) and is the author of several articles on Henry James, Edgar Allan Poe, Joyce Carol Oates and Flannery O'Connor. She has been a member of Professor Susana Onega's Research Group since 1995.

Matteo Nicolini, Ph.D in European and Italian Constitution Law (University of Verona) is Associate Professor of Public Comparative Law in the Department of Law at the University of Verona. His fields of research include comparative methods, Italian and European constitutional law, federalism and regionalism, judicial review of legislation, law and literature, African law, legal geography, and legal linguistics. He is the author of monographs, essays, and articles in Italian, Spanish, and English. His most recent monograph is *L'altra Law of the Land. La famiglia giuridica "mista" dell'Africa australe* (BUP, 2016). He is also the editor of several collections and author of several law-and-literature papers.

Susana Onega is Professor of English Literature at the University of Zaragoza: She is the Head of a competitive research team working on contemporary narratives in English, and a member of Academia Europaea since 2008. She has written numerous articles and book chapters on contemporary British literature and narrative theory. She is the author of five books monographs, including *Form and Meaning in the Novels of John Fowles* (UMI Research Press 1989), *Metafiction and Myth in the Novels of Peter Ackroyd* (Camden House, 1999), *Jeanette Winterson* (Manchester UP 2006) and she has edited or co-edited several books, among which *Narratology. An Introduction* (Longman, 1996: Routledge 2014), with José Angel García Landa, *The Ethical Component in Experimental British Fiction since the 1960s* (Cambridge Scholars Publishing, 2007), *Ethics and Trauma in Contemporary Narrative in English* (Rodopi, 2011), *Contemporary Trauma Narratives: Liminality and the Ethics of Form* (Routledge, 2014), and *Victimhood and Vulnerability in 21st-Century Fiction* (Routledge, 2017), all with Jean-Michel Ganteau, and *Traumatic Memory and the Ethical, Political and Transhistorical Functions of Literature* with Constanza del Río and Maite Escudero-Alías (Palgrave 2017).

François Ost is Professor Emeritus at the University Saint-Louis, Brussels. He is the president of the group FNRS Law and Literature. His publications include *Raconter la loi. Aux sources de l'imaginaire juridique* (Odile Jacob, 2004), *Sade et la loi* (Odile Jacob, 2005), *Shakespeare. La Comédie de la Loi* (Michalon, 2012); *Le droit, objet de passions?* (Académie Royale de Belgique, 2018). Since 2004 he has been a member of the Académie Royale des Sciences, des Lettres et des Beaux Arts de Belgique.

Carlo Pelloso is Associate Professor of Roman Law at the Department of Law of the University of Verona; he lectures in Ancient Greek Legal Systems at the University of Padua. Among his recent publications: "Protecting the Community: Public Actions and Forms of Punishment in Ancient Athens," in *Oxford Handbook of Ancient Greek Law*, eds. E. Harris, M. Canevaro (Oxford, 2015), and "Ephesis eis to dikasterion: Remarks and Speculations on the Legal Nature of the Solonian Reform," in *Symposion. Conferências sobre a História do Direito grego e helenístico* (Coimbra, 2016).

Fernando Armando Ribeiro is Professor of Law at the Catholic University of Minas Gerais, Brazil. His fields of research are: Law and Literature, Philosophy of Law and Hermeneutics. He is also a Judge in the State of Minas Gerais, and Member of the Academy of Letters and Sciences of Minas Gerais. He is in the scientific board of the journal of Brazilian Judges Association, and was awarded with a Fullbright scholarship as Senior Researcher at the University of California at Berkeley (USA).

Giuseppe Rossi is Associate Professor of Comparative Private Law at the IULM University, Milan. His main research interests are in the fields of antitrust, media and telecommunications law, intellectual property and consumer protection.

Filippo Sgubbi is Professor Emeritus of Criminal Law at the University of Bologna. His research interests are mainly in the fields of corporate criminal law and financial criminal law. Among his publications: *Il reato come rischio sociale – Ricerche sulle scelte di allocazione dell'illegalità penale* (Bologna: Il Mulino, 1991); "Il mercato della legge penale", IUS17 (2008): 27–28; "L'exemple en droit italien en matère boursière et de la protection de l'épargne," *Les Petites Affiches, La Loi 396*.134 (2007): 36–39.

Anna Enrichetta Soccio is Professor of English Literature at the University "G. D'Annunzio" (Chieti-Pescara). She is currently a member of the C.U.S.V.E. (Centro Universitario di Studi Vittoriani ed Edoardiani) and part of the editorial board of *RSV, Rivista di Studi Vittoriani* and *Merope*. She is also a member of some literary associations (A.I.A., ESSE, The Gaskell Society, The Philip Larkin Society, A.N.D.A., A.I.D.E.L.). Her interests are mainly focused on Victorian literature and culture and on the trends of British poetry from the Second World War to the present. She has participated in many conferences and seminars as a speaker and convenor, both in Italy and abroad.

Roberta Zanoni obtained a PhD in Foreign Languages, Literatures and Cultures at the University of Verona. Her main research interests are Literature and Mass Media, and Literary Transpositions and Translations. She has recently co-edited the volume *Bestiarium. Human and Animal Representations* (Mimesis International, 2018) and published the essays: "*Snowpiercer*, il cibo nella realtà distopica," in *Cibo come cultura. Dialoghi Interdisciplinari*, eds. Chiara Battisti and Sidia Fiorato (2018), "La trasposizione cinematografica dell'opera di Shakespeare," in *Shakespeare e la Modernità, Atti delle Rencontres de l'Archet, Morgex* (2018).

Index

https://doi.org/10.1515/9783110654615-020